Hands On
Visual InterDev™ 6

Send Us Your Comments:

To comment on this book or any other PRIMA TECH title, visit Prima's reader response page on the Web at **www.primapublishing.com/comments**.

How to Order:

For information on quantity discounts, contact the publisher: Prima Publishing, P.O. Box 1260BK, Rocklin, CA 95677-1260; (916) 632-4400. On your letterhead, include information concerning the intended use of the books and the number of books you wish to purchase. For individual orders, turn to the back of this book for more information, or visit Prima's Web site at **www.prima-tech.com**.

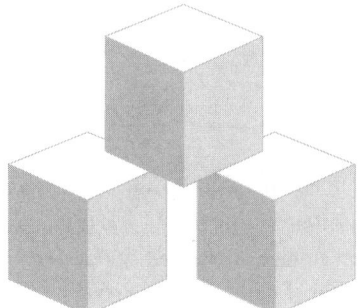

Hands On
Visual InterDev™ 6

Sharon J. Podlin

Microsoft Certified Instructor

PRIMA TECH

A Division of Prima Publishing

© 1998 by Sharon J. Podlin. All rights reserved. No part of this book may be reproduced or transmitted in any form or by any means, electronic or mechanical, including photocopying, recording, or by any information storage or retrieval system without written permission from Prima Publishing, except for the inclusion of brief quotations in a review.

A Division of Prima Publishing

Prima Publishing and colophon are registered trademarks of Prima Communications, Inc., Rocklin, California 95677.

Publisher: Matthew H. Carleson
Managing Editor: Dan J. Foster
Senior Acquisitions Editor: Deborah F. Abshier
Project Editor: Kevin W. Ferns
Technical Reviewer: Brady Merkel
Copy Editor: Robert Campbell
Interior Layout: Marian Hartsough
Indexer: Sharon Hilgenberg
Cover Designer: Prima Design Team

Microsoft, Windows, Windows NT, Internet Explorer, Visual Basic, Visual InterDev, FoxPro, Visual Studio, and FrontPage are trademarks or registered trademarks of Microsoft Corporation.

Important: If you experience problems running Visual InterDev 6, go to Microsoft's Web site at **www.microsoft.com**, or check the online help for technical support information. Prima Publishing cannot provide software support.

Prima Publishing and the author have attempted throughout this book to distinguish proprietary trademarks from descriptive terms by following the capitalization style used by the manufacturer.

Information contained in this book has been obtained by Prima Publishing from sources believed to be reliable. However, because of the possibility of human or mechanical error by our sources, Prima Publishing, or others, the Publisher does not guarantee the accuracy, adequacy, or completeness of any information and is not responsible for any errors or omissions or the results obtained from the use of such information. Readers should be particularly aware of the fact that the Internet is an ever-changing entity. Some facts may have changed since this book went to press.

ISBN: 0-7615-1678-6
Library of Congress Catalog Card Number: 98-66443
Printed in the United States of America

98 99 00 01 02 DD 10 9 8 7 6 5 4 3 2 1

*This book is dedicated to my husband, Mark,
who supports me in everything I do,
and my son, Hunter,
who is the joy of my life.*

—SJP

Acknowledgments

I would like to thank Debbie Abshier for giving me the chance to write this book. It was an opportunity that I had been looking forward to for a long time.

—SJP

About the Author

SHARON J. PODLIN is a graduate of the University of Texas and is president of PTSI, a consulting firm that specializes in the development and presentation of computer training courses. Sharon has more than 16 years' experience in the industry and has worked primarily with Fortune 100 companies, including JCPenney, Hyatt International Hotels, and United Airlines. She actively participates in the Microsoft Certified Professional program and is a Microsoft Certified Trainer for a wide range of products, including Microsoft SQL Server, Excel, Visual Basic for Applications, and Windows NT. She can be reached via e-mail at **podlin@compuserve.com**.

Contents at a Glance

	Introduction xxiii	
Chapter 1	Features of Visual InterDev 6.0	1
Chapter 2	The Visual InterDev Environment	15

HANDS ON PROJECT 1
THE TRAVEL SITE 41

	Project Overview 42
Chapter 3	What Is the Travel Site? 43
Chapter 4	Gathering Content for the Travel Site . . . 51
Chapter 5	Designing the Travel Site 59
Chapter 6	Building the Turtle Island Solution 79
Chapter 7	Testing the Travel Site 117
	Project 1 Summary 125

HANDS ON PROJECT 2
THE DATABASE WEB PROJECT 127

	Project Overview 128
Chapter 8	What Is the Database Web Project? . . . 129
Chapter 9	Gathering Information for the Database Web Project 135
Chapter 10	Designing the System 145

CONTENTS AT A GLANCE

Chapter 11	Building the Database Web Project	167
Chapter 12	Testing the System	201
	Project 2 Summary	217

HANDS ON PROJECT 3
THE CORPORATE WEB SITE 219

	Project Overview	220
Chapter 13	What Is the Corporate Web Site?	221
Chapter 14	Gathering Information for the Corporate Web Site	225
Chapter 15	Working in the Corporate Web Development Environment	231
Chapter 16	Building the Corporate Web Site	249
Chapter 17	Testing the Corporate Web Site	287
	Project 3 Summary	299
Chapter 18	Creating Your Own Visual InterDev Templates and Themes	301
Chapter 19	Working with Cascading Style Sheets	307
Appendix A	Recommended Naming and Programming Conventions	331
Appendix B	Tables Relationships	337
Appendix C	The Timelines Design-Time Control	341
Appendix D	What's On the CD-ROM	347
	Glossary	351
	Index	367

Contents

Introduction xxiii

Chapter 1 Features of Visual InterDev 6.0 1

Features of the Visual InterDev Interface. 2
    The Toolbox 2
    The Integrated WYSIWYG Page Editor 5
    The Site Designer 7
    The CSS Editor 8
Visual InterDev Database Tools 8
    Local Working Mode 9
    Debugging Tools 10
    IntelliSense Support 11
    Wizards 11
Understanding Visual InterDev Capabilities 12
    Multiple Scripting Language Support 12
    Active Server Pages 12
    The Scripting Object Model (SOM) 12
    Dynamic HTML Support 13
    Database Support 13
Summary 14

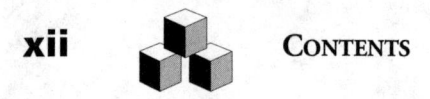

Chapter 2 The Visual InterDev Environment 15

Starting Visual InterDev. 16
Parts of the Visual InterDev Environment. 21
Customizing the Windows in the Visual
    InterDev Environment 22
Visual InterDev Programmer Tools 24
The Visual InterDev Window. 25
    Menus. 25
    Toolbars. 26
    The Toolbox 31
    The View Window. 32
    The Properties Window 33
    Project Explorer. 34
    The Object Browser. 34
    The Visual Component Manager 34
    The Task List Window. 35
    The Watch Window. 36
    The Online Help System 36
Basic Steps for Developing a Web Solution
    Using Visual InterDev 36
    Step 1: Determining the Purpose of Your Site 37
    Step 2: Determining the Point of View of the Site 37
    Step 3: Write a Mission Statement for the Site. 38
    Step 4: List the Requirements for the Site 38
    Step 5: Identify Your Content. 38
    Step 6: Design Your Pages and Identify the Browser. 39
    Step 7: Decide on the "Mood" of Your Site 39
    Step 8: Determine If You Want to Provide
        Links from Your Site to Others 39
    Step 9: Build the Site 40
    Step 10: Test and Debug Your Site 40
    Step 11: Deploy Your Site. 40
Summary. 40

CONTENTS

HANDS ON PROJECT 1
THE TRAVEL SITE 41

Project Overview 42

Chapter 3 What Is the Travel Site? 43
Design Objectives for the Travel Site. 43
Learning Objectives for the Home Page Project. 45
   Starting a New Web Project 45
   Applying a Theme to Your Home Page 45
   Adding Navigation to Your Pages 46
   Working in Different Modes. 46
   Using an Editor 47
   Testing the Web Solution 48
Summary. 49

Chapter 4 Gathering Content for the Travel Site 51
Choosing a Format for Your Home Page. 52
Determining the Text for Your Home Page 53
Selecting the Graphics for Your Home Page. 54
Selecting Other Elements for Your Home Page 55
Putting It All Together 56
Summary. 56

Chapter 5 Designing the Travel Site 59
Starting a New Web Project 60
Creating a Home Page 63
   Adding Text to Your Home Page 65
   Using the Quick View Tab 66
   Formatting Text 67
      Changing the Font of Text 67
      Changing Other Text Settings 68

Contents

- Using Paragraph Formats 69
- Adding a Graphic to Your Home Page 69
- Saving a Page 71
- Previewing a Page in a Browser 72
- Changing the Look and Feel of Your Home Page 73
  - Working with Themes 73
    - Changing the Theme of a Project 74
    - Removing a Theme from a Project 74
  - Adding Navigation to Your Pages 76
- Working Locally 77
- Working Offline 78
- Exiting Visual InterDev 78
- Summary 78

Chapter 6 Building the Turtle Island Solution 79

- Understanding Visual InterDev's Modes 79
  - Local and Master Modes 80
    - Working in Local Mode 81
    - Making Copies of Master Files 82
    - Setting Your Project to Local Mode 83
    - Working in Master Mode 84
  - Synchronizing Master and Local Files 84
    - Updating the Master Application 85
    - Discarding Changes Made to a Local Copy 86
    - Updating the Local Web Application 86
    - Refreshing the Project Explorer 86
  - Working Offline 87
- Expanding the Project 88
  - Adding Files to the Project 88

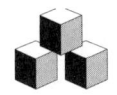

    Working with Themes at the Page Level 90
    Working with the Global Navigation Bar 91
Using an Editor. 97
    Using Design View. 98
    Using Quick View 98
    Using Source View. 99
    Working with HTML 100
    Changing Your Default View 108
Adding Links from Your Page. 109
    Viewing Links for an Item 110
    Changing the Layout of the Link View Diagram 112
    Using the Broken Links Report. 114
    Repairing the Broken Links 115
Summary. 116

Chapter 7   Testing the Travel Site. 117

How Do You Test a Web Page?. 117
Deploying Your Solution 118
    The Preparation Stage. 119
    Actual Deployment to the Web Server. 120
        Deploying with FrontPage Server Extensions 121
        Deploying without FrontPage Server Extensions. . . . 122
        Deploying Manually. 122
    Verification of the Production Server Content 122
Common Error Messages 123
Summary. 124

Project 1 Summary 125

HANDS ON PROJECT 2
THE DATABASE WEB PROJECT 127

Project Overview 128

Chapter 8 What Is the Database Web Project? 129

Requirements for the Database Web Project 130
Goals of the Database Web Project 131
    Creating a Database Project 131
    Connecting to a Database. 132
    Using Visual Database Tools and
        the Data View Window 132
    Querying and Displaying Database Information
        for Your Web Page 133
    Using FormManager. 133
    Debugging Your System 133
Summary. 134

Chapter 9 Gathering Information
for the Database Web Project 135

Understanding Visual InterDev's Data Environment 136
Selecting the Database for Your Site 140
    How Much Data Will Be Stored? 140
    How Many Users Will Use the System?. 142
    What Type of Support Is Available? 143
    What Existing Systems Are in Place? 143
    The Choice for Your Application 144
Summary. 144

Chapter 10 Designing the System 145

Creating a Project with a Database Connection 146
Using the Data View Window 148

Viewing the Contents of a Table. 152
Querying Your Data. 153
    What Is a Query?. 153
    Accessing the Query Designer. 154
    Saving the Query 159
Viewing the Records from Your Home Page 159
    Adding a Recordset Control 159
    Adding Databound Controls to Your Page. 161
    Adding Record Navigation 163
    The Professional Edition versus
      the Enterprise Edition. 165
Summary. 166

Chapter 11 Building the Database Web Project 167

Using Visual InterDev with Access 168
    Connecting to an Access Database 168
    Displaying the Results of an Access Query. 172
Using Scripts 174
    Working with Objects, Properties, and Methods 175
      What Is an Object?. 175
      What Is a Method?. 175
      What Is a Property? 176
    Understanding What Happens When You
      Open a Page. 176
    Viewing Data Using a Script. 176
Working with Other Design-Time Controls 180
    An Overview of Other Data-Bound
      Design-Time Controls 180
    Using the Grid Control 181
    Using a Check Box. 186
Using the FormManager. 186
Summary. 200

Chapter 12 Testing the System 201

    The Debugging Process 202
    Types of Errors 203
    Using Breakpoints to Test Your Web Solution 203
    Using Just-in-Time Debugging 207
    Using Watches 209
    Stepping through Lines in a Script 211
    Debugging Server Script 312
    Understanding the Colors in Source View 214
    Summary 216

Project 2 Summary 217

HANDS ON PROJECT 3
THE CORPORATE WEB SITE 219

    Project Overview 220

Chapter 13 What Is the Corporate Web Site? 221

    Requirements of the Corporate Web Site 221
        Using Visual SourceSafe 222
        Adding Multimedia to Your Site 222
        Setting Up Security 223
        Utilizing Visual InterDev's Programming Features 223
        Working with Active Server Pages (ASPs) 223
        Understanding the Difference between
            Client and Server Scripts 223
        Using the Immediate Window 224
        Error Handling 224
    Summary 224

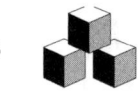

Chapter 14 Gathering Information for the Corporate Web Site........225

Using Visual SourceSafe............................226
Writing VBScript Code.............................227
Security...229
Summary..230

Chapter 15 Working in the Corporate Web Development Environment........231

Setting Up Visual SourceSafe........................232
Installing Visual SourceSafe on the Master Web Server.....232
Adding Source Control to Your Project.................239
Working with Source Control........................240
    Checking Files Out.............................240
    Adding Files to a Source Control-Enabled
        Web Application.............................242
    Getting the Master Version of a File................242
    Checking Files In..............................243
    Discarding Changes to a File......................244
    Enabling Multiple Checkouts......................244
Disabling Source Control...........................245
Summary..247

Chapter 16 Building the Corporate Web Site........249

Building on an Existing Page.........................249
Adding Multimedia to Your Site......................250
    Adding a Background Sound......................250
    Adding a Video File to Your Application.............251
Using Visual InterDev's Programming Features...........251
Working with Active Server Pages (ASPs)...............252
Creating an Active Server Page.......................253
Setting Your Page Language.........................255

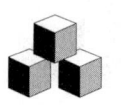

Understanding the Difference between
   Client and Server Scripts. 255
The Scripting Object Model. 256
   Understanding Objects. 256
   Enabling the Scripting Object Model 258
   Visual InterDev Objects. 258
   Working with Properties. 262
   Using Methods and Functions 262
   Setting Your Client Script Language 263
   Using the Script Outline. 264
Building Your VBScript Knowledge 265
   Understanding Variables. 265
      Declaring Variables. 266
   Assigning a Value to a Variable 267
      Constants. 267
   Scope. 268
Using Message Boxes and Input Boxes
   to Receive User Input. 268
Using Conditional Logic 273
   Using Conditional Operators 274
Using the If Statement to Validate User Input 276
   Record Navigation Using Script 280
Summary. 286

Chapter 17 Testing the Corporate Web Site 287

Debugging Scripts 288
Using the Immediate Window 289
   Printing Values in the Immediate Window 289
   Using the Print Method in the Immediate Window. . . . 289
Error Handing. 291
A Testing List. 292
Setting Up Security 292
   Security Locations 293

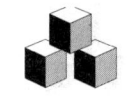

Operating System-Level Security................294
Web Server-Level Security.......................294
Database-Level Security........................295
Using Source Control Security...................295
Web Application-Level Security.................295
Using Global.asa File Processing for Security........296
Adding Security Pages..........................296
Setting a Web Application's Permissions............297
Summary..298

Project 3 Summary................299

Chapter 18 Creating Your Own Visual InterDev Templates and Themes 301

Creating Themes......................................302
Designing Templates..................................303
Summary..306

Chapter 19 Working with Cascading Style Sheets................307

What Are Cascading Style Sheets?.....................308
Using the CSS Editor.................................309
Editing a Cascading Style Sheet......................310
    The Font Tab....................................311
    The Background Tab..............................314
    The Borders Tab.................................317
    The Layout Tab..................................320
    The Preview Tab.................................323
    The Lists Tab...................................324
    The Advanced Tab................................325
    The Source Tab..................................328
Summary..329

**Appendix A Recommended Naming and
            Programming Conventions** 331

Appendix B Tables Relationships 337

Appendix C The Timelines Design-Time Control 341

Appendix D What's On the CD-ROM 347

Glossary 351

Index 367

Introduction

At the end of the nineteen-eighties, a major event took place whose ramifications we are still experiencing: the creation of the World Wide Web. The World Wide Web has simplified our means of obtaining large amounts of information. It affects our education, entertainment, and business. The Web has moved from a simple, accessible vehicle for data to a feature-rich, multimedia environment. It is no longer the domain of educators and serious computer geeks! Everyone from Mom and Pop stores to Fortune 100 companies are racing to the Web. And this race has created a need for sophisticated Web application development tools. Web users and developers require and demand the same features they are used to having when developing desktop applications, including database access, the ability to include business logic, and debugging tools. Visual InterDev 6.0 is designed to meet these needs.

Most of the books on the market today about Visual InterDev take the approach of a reference manual. Reference manuals have a serious limitation—they are designed only to be referred to. They are not necessarily designed to teach you anything other than commands. This book breaks that mold, in that it is designed to teach you not only how to use Visual InterDev, but how to develop Web applications using Visual InterDev.

Goals of This Book

This book is designed to provide you with the skills you need to build working Web sites with Visual InterDev, with emphasis on the database capabilities essential to today's business and commercial sites.

The key concepts of using Visual InterDev are organized into three projects. The first project is an introduction to Web solution development using Visual InterDev. The second project focuses on using the database capabilities of Visual InterDev. During this project, you will get hands-on experience using Visual InterDev to access data from Microsoft SQL Server and a Microsoft Access database. The final project introduces you to using Visual InterDev in a multideveloper environment and gives you experience creating scripts for use with your application.

How to Use This Book

This book is broken into five main parts. The first part provides concise background information so that you may quickly begin to learn and use Visual InterDev.

The next three parts are projects. By completing these projects, you'll get a sense of how to design and create Web applications using Visual InterDev. You will learn how to analyze requirements, build the interface, create the code needed to add functionality to the application, and test and debug your applications.

The first project provides an overview of Visual InterDev. In this project, you'll create a simple home page and add text and graphics to it.

The second project builds on the knowledge that you gain from the previous project so that you can expand the capabilities of your Web site. In this project, you'll add database capabilities to your home page and learn to connect to a database, query data, and display the results.

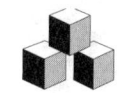

The final project demonstrates how to use Visual InterDev in a corporate environment. You'll be introduced to Visual SourceSafe, which is a tool designed to aid development in a multiuser environment. You'll see the benefits of using the Site Designer, and you'll add some multimedia capabilities to your Web site. Finally, you'll learn about Visual InterDev's programming features.

Chapter 18, "Creating Your Own Visual InterDev Templates and Themes," provides some additional exercises you may find useful. The appendixes and glossary at the end also provide some helpful definitions, programming conventions, and tables relationships you may need.

This book allows you to experience creating Web solutions from start to finish using the Visual InterDev environment. You'll learn Visual InterDev, not merely as a student, but as a developer, through hands-on interaction.

Conventions Used in This Book

To make it easier for you to use this book, Prima uses some conventions for consistently presenting different kinds of information. You should review these conventions before moving on in this book:

- **Menu names, commands, and dialog box options.** In virtually all Windows programs, each menu name, command name, and dialog box option name contains an underlined letter called a *selection letter*. You use the selection letter to make that particular selection via the keyboard, usually in conjunction with the Ctrl or Alt key. This book indicates selection letters as underlined letters, as in View.

- **Code and items that appear onscreen.** Any VB code discussed in this book is presented in a special typeface to make it easy to distinguish from the rest of the text. When reference is made to an error message or other information that appears onscreen, it is also printed in the special typeface.

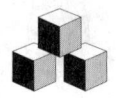

- **Text you type.** When you need to type some text to complete a procedure, or when I provide an example of text you can enter, the text you need to type appears in bold.

Special Elements

At times, you may require information that supplements the discussion at hand. This special information is set off in easy-to-identify sidebars, so you can review or skip these extras as you see fit. You'll find the following types of special elements in this book:

Buzzwords are used to provide definitions of new terms.

Tips provide shortcuts to make your job easier, or better ways to accomplish certain tasks.

Notes provide supplemental information that might be of interest to you but is not essential to performing the task at hand.

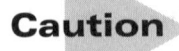

Cautions alert you to potential pitfalls or warn you when a particular operation is risky and might cause you to lose some of your work.

ON THE CD

This icon is used to refer you to items found on the CD that accompanies this book.

Necessary Software

For most of the projects in this book, the only additional software you need is Microsoft Access 97. You will also need either Microsoft Internet Explorer 4.0 (or later) or a browser that's IE-compatible, such as CompuServe's CIS 3.0, to complete most of the exercises. When you install Visual InterDev, it checks your system for Internet Explorer 4.x and will upgrade or install Internet Explorer if necessary.

In addition to this list of software, I recommend that you use Windows NT if you are running the Web server (such as Personal Web Server) on the same machine. You will also need Windows NT if you want to run SQL Server on the same machine.

This book also assumes that you are running at least the Professional Edition of Visual InterDev; nevertheless, a few of the chapters are geared toward the Enterprise edition. Visual Studio, Professional Edition, includes the following development tools:

- Visual Basic 6.0
- Visual C++ 6.0
- Visual FoxPro 6.0
- Visual InterDev 6.0
- Visual J++ 6.0

This book was developed using Visual Studio, Enterprise Edition, which has all the tools found in the Professional Edition plus several additional tools geared toward enterprise solution development. The following is a list of the tools found in the Enterprise Edition that can be used in conjunction with Visual InterDev for Web solution development:

- **Database Designer**. This tool graphically represents tables and their relationships. It can be used to create and modify database objects.

Introduction

- **Deployment**. This tool assists you with the distribution and debugging of Web application components.
- **Internet Information Server 4.0**. This is a complete FTP, Gopher, and World Wide Web information service. It requires Windows NT as its operating system.
- **Transaction Server 2.0**. Transaction Server is a component-based transaction processing system for developing, deploying, and managing enterprise, Internet, and intranet server applications.
- **Query Designer**. This is a great tool for creating SQL statements. It allows you to create SQL statements using a simple graphical interface.
- **SQL Debugging**. This is used to debug SQL Server-stored procedures and triggers.
- **SQL Server 6.5**. SQL Server is a relational database management system used for the storage and administration of enterprise data.
- **Visual Database Tools**. Using the Visual Database Tools, you can create tables; create views; select a table view; modify a table's size; copy tables; add columns to tables; create and manipulate stored procedures; and create, open, copy, and delete triggers.
- **Visual Component Manager.** Use this tool to work with components so that you can publish, find, and reuse them.
- **Visual SourceSafe 6.0.** Visual SourceSafe is a source control tool that you use to manage your projects, regardless of the file type.

> **Note:** The Enterprise Edition has more tools in it than this list shows. These are just the tools that apply to development using Visual InterDev.

Necessary Hardware

The following is a list of hardware required to run the client and server components of the Visual InterDev development environment:

- A PC with a 90 MHz or higher processor; a Pentium or higher processor is recommended (I designed the projects for this book using a 200 MHz Pentium system and wished I had a faster one.)
- Microsoft Windows 95 or later operating system or Windows NT Workstation operating system version 4.0 or later
- 16MB of RAM for Windows 95; 24MB for Windows NT Workstation 4.0 (I seriously recommend at least 32MB for either of these platforms.)
- At least this much hard-disk space (depending on components selected):
    - For Visual InterDev: 81 to 98MB
    - MSDN Library: 57 to 493MB (optional)
    - Internet Explorer 4.0 or later: 43 to 59MB
    - Windows NT Option Pack: 20 to 200MB (optional, needed if you plan to run Personal Web Server)
    - Microsoft SNA Server 4.0: 50 to 100MB or more (optional, needed if you are running certain server components)
    - Microsoft SQL Server 6.5: 80 to 95 MB (optional)
- A CD-ROM drive
- A sound card and speakers
- A VGA or higher-resolution monitor (I recommend Super VGA.)
- A mouse or compatible pointing device

Chapter 1

Features of Visual InterDev 6.0

The Web, the Internet, intranets, extranets—it seems these days this is all you hear about. And because of this, more and more people are getting involved with Web application development. Some developers are new to the entire development arena, but Web developers are migrating from other development environments such as Visual C++ or Visual Basic. I even hesitate to use the term "migrate," because it implies that they are leaving those environments, which is hardly the case. They are actually extending their reach into the vast world of the Internet.

Programmers today are not content to keep their applications on their desktops. And the new breed of developer has very specific expectations and requirements of a development tool.

With this in mind, Microsoft created Visual InterDev. Visual InterDev is a rapid application development environment used to create data-driven Web applications. The first version of Visual InterDev was a good start to providing the environment that Web developers needed. In designing this version, the Visual InterDev team had five goals to meet, which are documented in the Visual InterDev reviewer's guide. They needed to provide:

- Rapid application development for professional Web developers
- Integrated development tools
- An improved Web application programming model
- Team-based development
- Enterprise application development

Features of the Visual InterDev Interface

The Visual InterDev interface, also referred to as the IDE (integrated development environment), is designed to be similar to the IDE found in Microsoft Visual Basic and Microsoft FrontPage. When you first start Visual InterDev, you will notice that its interface is partitioned into several windows, as shown in Figure 1.1.

The Toolbox

The Toolbox, shown in Figure 1.2, is a palette of tools that allows the drag-and-drop design of applications. The Toolbox consists of reusable visual components and is customizable. You may have noticed that the Toolbox has tabs which are represented as buttons at the top and bottom of the Toolbox window. The tools that you will find yourself using the most, at least at first, are the HTML tools.

CHAPTER 1 • FEATURES OF VISUAL INTERDEV 6.0   3

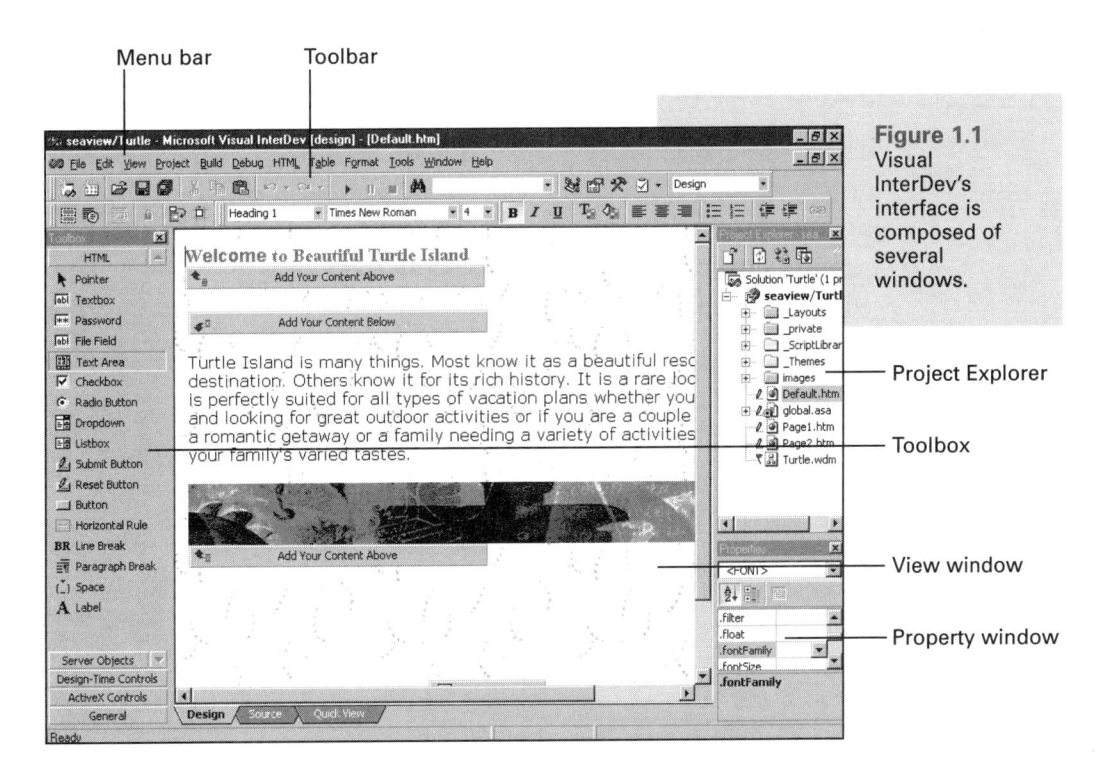

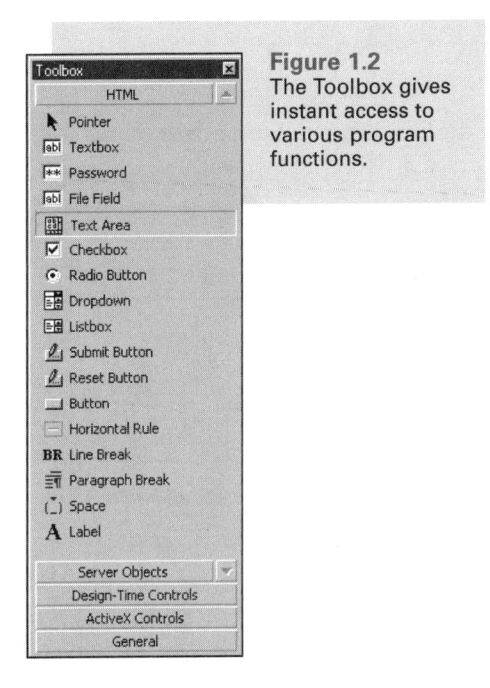

Figure 1.1
Visual InterDev's interface is composed of several windows.

- Menu bar
- Toolbar
- Project Explorer
- Toolbox
- View window
- Property window

Figure 1.2
The Toolbox gives instant access to various program functions.

Each tool has a purpose. The following list gives you an overview of what each HTML Toolbox object is used for:

- **Text box**. If you want to provide areas in which the user types information, use a text box, which holds text that the user either entered or changed.

- **Password**. This creates a text box that displays typed characters as bullets instead of the characters actually typed.

- **File field**. This is a file upload element that looks like a text box with a Browse button next to it. When the Browse button is selected, a Choose File dialog box displays.

- **Text area**. This creates a multiline text input control.

- **Check box**. A check box control is used to denote a toggle selection. Check boxes are typically used in and/or situations. For example, I can choose to print a catalog using one or more of the following options (each option represented by a check box): border, large font, and pictures.

- **Radio button**. Use radio buttons to display multiple choices for an item. Radio buttons only allow a user to select one available option.

- **Drop-down**. The drop-down control is used to display a list of items from which the user can choose. It can be used to replace option buttons. A general rule of thumb as to when to use drop-down controls and when to use list boxes is this: If you need more than three option buttons, convert them to a list box. A drop-down control appears as a single line box with a selection button to the right of the box. When the selection button is clicked, a list of several items displays. Functionally, drop-down controls are identical to list box controls. The main difference is that drop-down controls take less "screen real estate."

- **List box**. This is a cousin to the drop-down control. The list box is also used to display a list of items. It differs in that instead of inviting you to click on the selection button to display several available items, as you do with a drop-down control, it appears as a long rectangle that always displays several items.

CHAPTER 1 • FEATURES OF VISUAL INTERDEV 6.0

- **Submit button**. This creates a button that has the text "Submit" on it. When this button is clicked, the form is submitted. In other words, the data on the form is sent to the server to be processed.

- **Reset button.** This creates a button that has the text "Reset" on it. When this button is clicked, the form resets the form's controls to their specified initial values.

- **Button**. Buttons are a frequent control used to prompt a user to select an action. For example, you may have a page with the following buttons on it: Yes, No, and Cancel. A user clicks on the desired button, and the associated action is initiated.

- **Horizontal rule**. This adds a horizontal line (rule) across your page.

- **Line break**. This inserts a line break.

- **Paragraph break**. This inserts a paragraph break.

- **Space**. This inserts a nonbreaking space.

- **Label**. One way to create static areas of text on your pages is to create label controls. You won't find yourself using labels often, as you can type text directly on the page rather than add a label control.

The Integrated WYSIWYG Page Editor

You'll do your basic document and spreadsheet creation in a WYSIWYG (What You See Is What You Get) environment. You surf the Net in a WYSIWYG environment, so why not develop in a WYSIWYG environment? The New Page Editor has a Design view (see Figure 1.3) that allows you to edit and create content for your Web application in a WYSIWYG workspace. You are not restricted to using the Design view to create your pages; you can also use the Source view (see Figure 1.4), which allows you to write HTML and scripts directly.

6   Hands On Visual InterDev 6

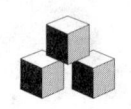

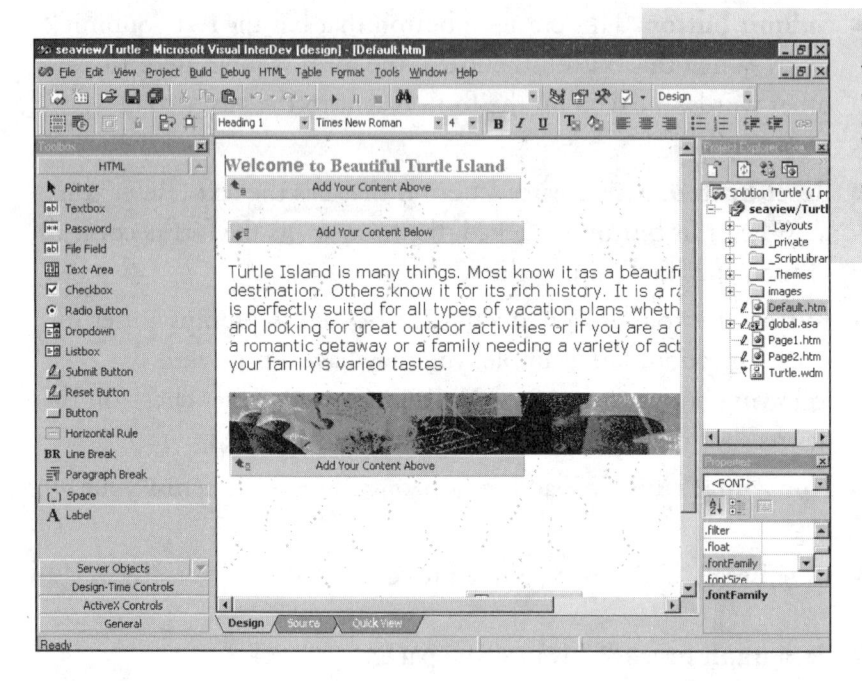

Figure 1.3
The Design view lets you create your Web page using a WYSIWYG interface.

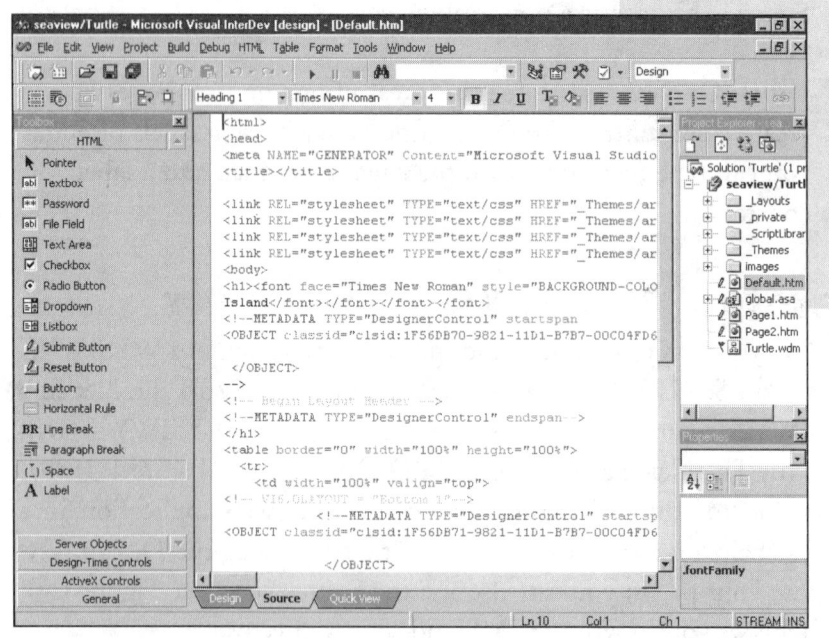

Figure 1.4
The Source view allows you to view and edit the HTML and other scripts for your page. This is the source for the page you see in Figure 1.3.

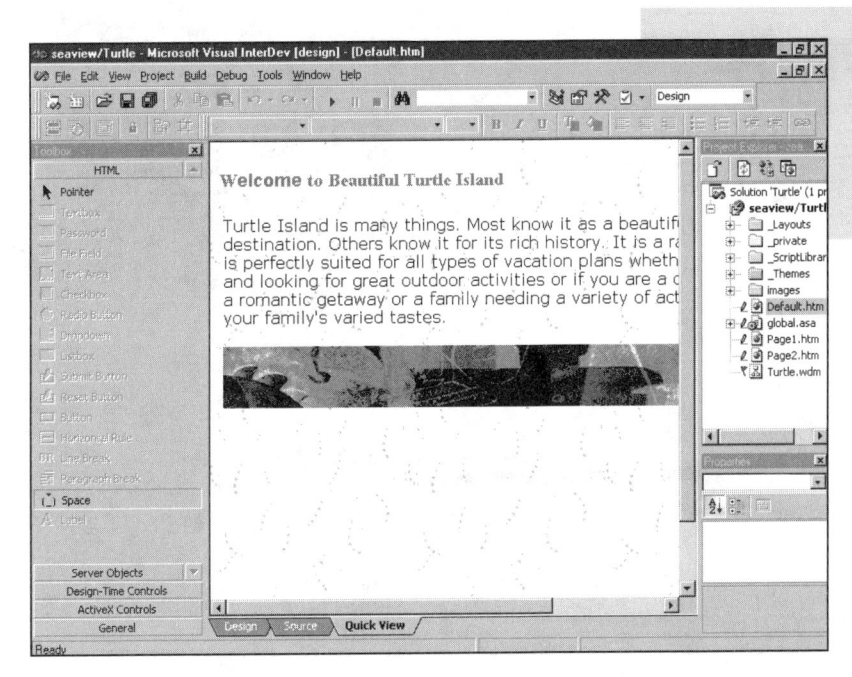

Figure 1.5
This is the same page as seen in Figure 1.3, this time shown in Quick view.

The Design view and the Source view are integrated so that a change made in either view is reflected in both views. To see how the page will look in a browser, select Quick view, as shown in Figure 1.5.

The Site Designer

Constructing the structure and dependencies of a Web site is not the most fun thing in the world, but it is definitely an important task. Haven't you been to a Web site that takes you along a merry path to a brick wall, leaving you to wonder, "Where am I?"

Visual InterDev provides you with a great tool called the Site Designer, used for constructing Web site structure and dependencies. The Site Designer, shown in Figure 1.6, allows you to perform this task visually as it creates the actual file structure and navigation bars based on a customizable theme.

Figure 1.6
The Site Designer allows you to set and view the site navigation structure.

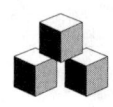

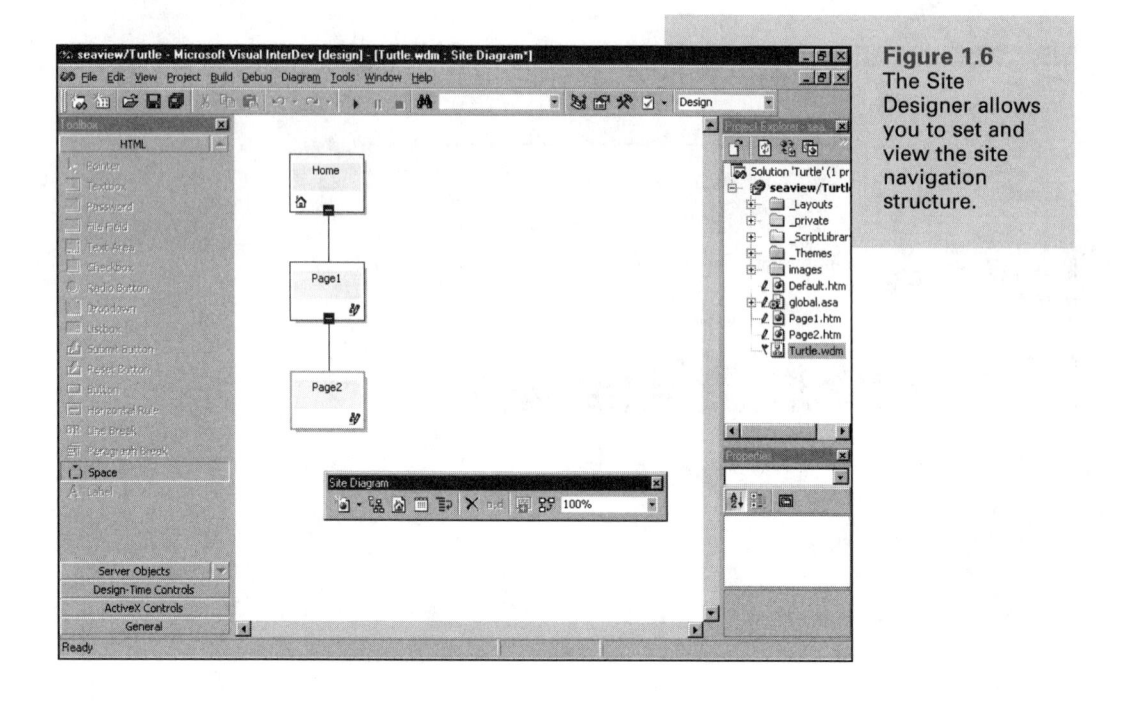

The CSS Editor

The CSS (cascading style sheets) Editor (see Figure 1.7) allows you to create and edit style sheets. Style sheets define the attributes of HTML-formatted information, and all HTML documents that reference the style sheet will look and feel the same.

Visual InterDev Database Tools

Using Visual InterDev's database tools, you can perform a variety of database management tasks using a graphical interface. These tasks include browsing data in tables and creating queries. (Chapters 10 and 11 have more detailed information on database tools.) These tools include the following:

- **The Data Connection wizard.** This tool helps you set up a data connection from your Visual InterDev project. Connecting to a database from a Visual InterDev project allows you complete control over your database.

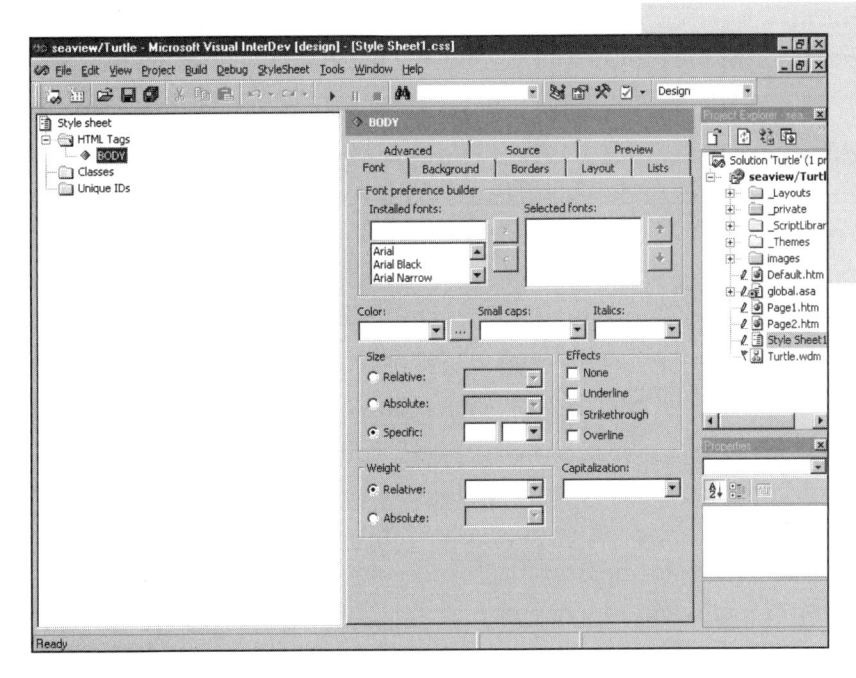

Figure 1.7
The CSS Editor allows you to set the attributes used by your project's cascading style sheet.

- **The Data View window**. The Data View window provides a live view of the data to which your database or Web project is currently connected. The Data View window provides a graphical interface for creating, viewing, and editing the database objects to which you are connected.
- **Query Designer**. The Query Designer is a graphical interface used to create SQL statements.
- **Data-bound Design-Time Controls**. Data-bound DTCs (Design-Time Controls) are used to create pages that display from and write data to a database. Examples of data-bound DTCs include labels and text boxes.

Local and Master Working Mode

Visual InterDev allows you to work in either Local or Master mode. Local mode allows you to work independently of the master files. In Local mode, you do your development, testing, and debugging. Once you are happy with any changes you have made, you deploy (that is, copy) them to the master server. This doesn't mean that you can't work directly on the master copy of the project, but it is usually preferable to work on the local copy so that you do not impact the users of your Web site.

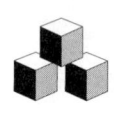

Local mode's benefits really come into play in the multideveloper environment. Here, each developer can make a copy of the project on his or her own local system. The developer can then make any needed changes, test the changes, and debug them without impacting the other developers or the master application. Once they are through, developers can deploy their changes back to the master server. This feature is discussed in detail in Chapter 6.

If you don't want to work in Local mode, you have the option of working in Master mode. Master mode allows you to work directly with the files on your Web server so that any of the changes you make to the application are immediately reflected to your users. Master mode is discussed in more detail in Chapter 6.

Debugging Tools

As I have noted, Visual InterDev was developed with the programmer in mind. And what do programmers expect in a development environment? They expect debugging tools! (These tools are discussed in detail in Chapter 12.) Debugging tools include:

- **Breakpoints.** Breakpoints stop your script execution at a designated point. When you stop a procedure, its source is displayed and you can test it.
- **Watches.** Watches are expressions that you want to track in your code.
- **Stepping through a procedure.** You can execute your code line-by-line and watch the effect each line has on your application.

IntelliSense Support

Many users of Visual InterDev have also developed in other Microsoft languages such as Visual C, Visual Basic, or Visual Basic for Applications. One of the features that programmers like in these development environments is IntelliSense statement completion, which is also available in Visual InterDev.

When you start typing the name of an object, IntelliSense displays a list of methods and properties available for that object. Once you select a method or property, IntelliSense displays parameters needed by that method or property. This saves a lot of trips to Help!

Wizards

Visual InterDev provides wizards such as the Scriptlets wizard for assisting with many formerly complex tasks. Some of the available wizards include:

- **Sample Application wizard**. This wizard is used to install the Visual InterDev Gallery sample application. It can also be used to install third-party Web applications. In addition to these functions, you can use the Sample Application to install your own custom Web applications.
- **Web Project wizard**. When you select File, New Project and choose New Web Project, the Web Project wizard starts. This wizard walks you through project creation by asking you to select a server, layout, and theme for your project.
- **Data Connection**. Even though Microsoft's documentation doesn't refer to this as a wizard, I do, because it walks you through the steps needed to add a data connection to your project.
- **Create a New Data Source wizard**. This wizard, accessible when adding a data connection to your project, makes creating a new data source easy, by prompting you for the required file and other database information.

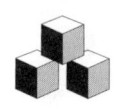

Understanding Visual InterDev Capabilities

Visual InterDev supports a variety of scripting languages and database access methods. This means that you can develop Web solutions with high-end features and capabilities.

Multiple Scripting Language Support

You can write scripts in any scripting language that you are comfortable with. The two most common scripting languages used when developing Web applications in Visual InterDev are Microsoft Visual Basic, Scripting Edition (VBScript) and ECMAScript, a standard scripting language (either the Microsoft JScript or JavaScript implementations). This book focuses on VBScript, which is discussed in Chapters 12 and 16.

Active Server Pages

Visual InterDev has extensive support for Active Server Pages. Active Server Pages (ASP) is an open compile-free environment that allows you to combine HTML, scripts, and ActiveX server components to create dynamic Web-based solutions. Active Server Pages are discussed in more detail in Chapter 16.

The Scripting Object Model (SOM)

As far as languages are concerned, you aren't hip if you don't do objects! Since Visual InterDev is obviously hip, its scripting languages use objects. Its implementation is called the *scripting object model (SOM)*. The scripting object model introduces the familiar object-oriented programming model to HTML and script programming. The scripting object model defines a set of objects with events, properties, and methods that you can use to create and script your application. The scripting object model allows you to create Web applications in much the same way you create applications in environments such as Visual Basic and Microsoft Excel. The scripting object model is discussed further in Chapter 16.

Dynamic HTML Support

The Visual InterDev editor supports DHTML through statement completion options and by displaying the document object model hierarchy in Source view. Visual InterDev 6.0 supports DHTML in Microsoft Internet Explorer 4.0.

> **Tip:** DHTML (dynamic HTML) is a set of additions to HTML that allows page authors and developers to dynamically change the style and attributes of elements on an HTML page at the client side, as well as insert, delete, or modify elements and their text after a page has been loaded.

Database Support

When creating your data-driven Web applications, you can use any ODBC or OLE DB data source. The process of connecting to a data source is discussed in Chapters 10 and 11. The data sources that you can connect to from your Visual InterDev project include:

- Microsoft SQL Server
- Microsoft Access
- Microsoft Visual FoxPro
- Oracle
- Informix
- Sybase
- DB/2
- dBase
- Paradox
- Text files
- Microsoft Excel
- Other ODBC-accessible databases

Summary

This chapter presented an overview of Visual InterDev's capabilities and features. This should give you an awareness of some ways that you can use Visual InterDev as a Web development tool. The next chapter lays the real groundwork for developing Web solutions with Visual InterDev. It provides background information about the elements that make up the Visual InterDev environment, and it gives you an understanding of the entire application development process.

CHAPTER 2

The Visual InterDev Environment

This chapter gives you the foundation you need to work with Visual InterDev. As a developer of Internet sites, you need to be aware of the Visual InterDev environment as well as understand the development process used in creating a Web site with Visual InterDev.

Visual InterDev is a visual development environment (VDE) that provides you with a quick, graphical interface for site development. This interface has several advantages over traditional development tools. The first advantage you'll notice is in interface design. You actually interact with the interface as you go. This not only allows for quick development, but it allows you to create a prototype for your clients to review.

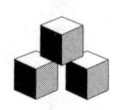

Another advantage of Visual InterDev is that it provides quick site development. In other development languages, such as Visual Basic, this feature is commonly known as *rapid application development (RAD)*. The development cycle of Visual InterDev occupies a fraction of the time required in a more traditional language. And since you can create the interface visually rather than develop code for its creation, you are released from having to learn an entire set of statements. This doesn't mean that you can't transfer your existing knowledge of Web site design to Visual InterDev. If you want to work with HTML instead of the visual interface, for example, you are free to do so.

Visual InterDev's interface is designed to be familiar in look and feel to a Windows 95, Windows 98, or Windows NT developer. If you have used any of the other elements of the Visual Studio suite of products, you will find that many of the elements of Visual InterDev are similar to those found in Visual Basic. It has been my experience that about half of the people who decide to use Visual InterDev are new to Internet solution development. You may or may not have ever created a Web page before. In this chapter, I'll start with the basics and quickly build from there.

Starting Visual InterDev

Start Visual InterDev as you would start any other application: Simply double-click on its icon or select it from the Start menu. Visual InterDev prompts you as to whether you want to start a new project or open an existing one. A *project* consists of the files that combine to create the application you are developing. So in Visual InterDev terms, you are working on a project when you are creating a site. The New Project dialog box has three tabs:

- **New**. Use this option to create a new project.
- **Existing**. To access an existing project, select this tab.
- **Recent**. If you want to do a project that you have been working with recently, go to this tab.

CHAPTER 2 • THE VISUAL INTERDEV ENVIRONMENT   17

> **Note**
>
> Before starting Visual InterDev, you'll need to connect to your Web server. This Web server may be one you access via the Internet, or it may be one local to your system or intranet, such as a Personal Web Server. You'll need to determine what Web server you are using and connect to it before beginning this exercise. You'll also need to know the name of your server. I am using a Personal Web Server on my local system.

To start Visual InterDev and begin a new project, do the following:

1. From your Windows desktop, select Start. Select Programs, Microsoft Visual Studio 6.0. Choose Microsoft Visual InterDev 6.0. Visual InterDev starts, and the New Project dialog box displays (see Figure 2.1).

2. Select New Web Project.

3. Type **First** for the Name and click on Open. In a few moments, the Web Project Wizard starts, as shown in Figure 2.2.

4. Select the server you want to use. The server may or may not be listed in the What server do you want to use? drop-down list box, so you may need to type it in.

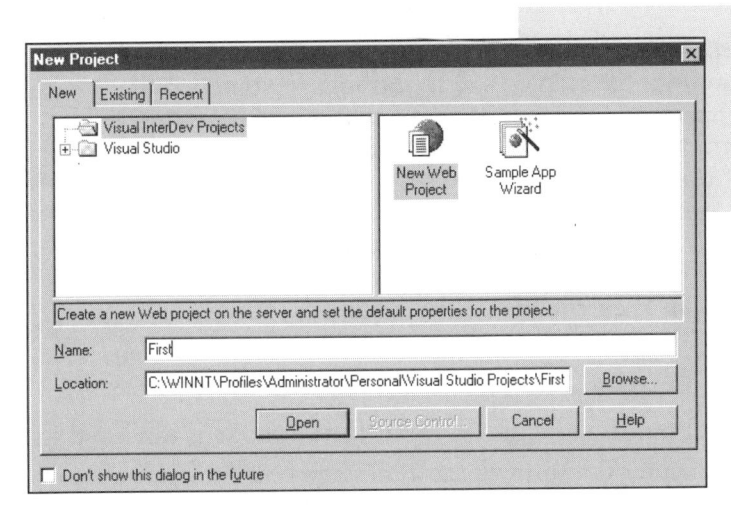

Figure 2-1
The New Project dialog box allows you to start a new project or open an existing one.

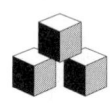

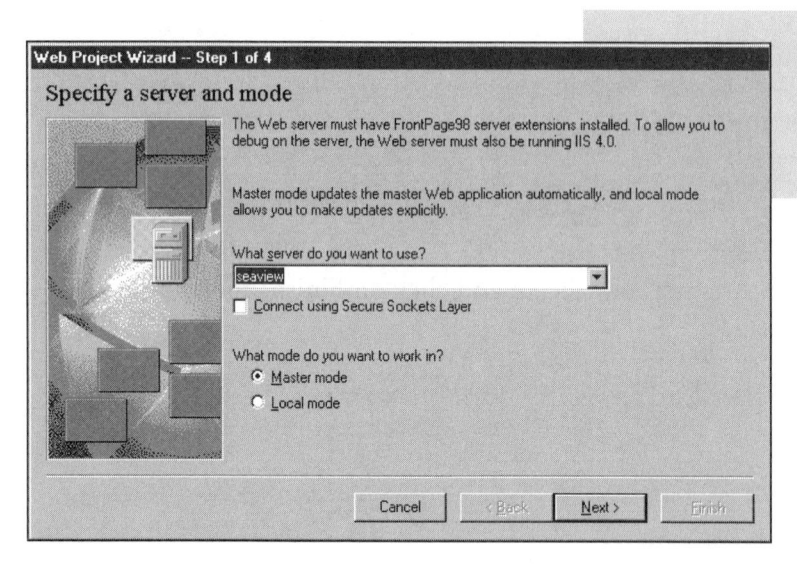

Figure 2.2
The Web Project Wizard starts by prompting you to select your server.

> **Note**
>
> Visual InterDev is a (to put it politely) memory-intensive application. I started writing this book using a system with only 16MB of RAM, but quickly upgraded it to 32MB, realizing significant performance gains. If you have only 16MB of RAM, it may take a while to load the Web Project Wizard and create the project itself.

> **Tip**
>
> Visual InterDev's system requirements state that you can run the program under Windows 95. If you talk to someone at Microsoft, however, he will highly recommend that you install it on a Windows NT machine. One of the problems you may encounter when running Visual InterDev on a Windows 95 machine is that it will be unable to see Personal Web Server (if that is the server you are using). To resolve this problem, log onto the Internet and then create a new project. You can then connect to Personal Web Server.

5. Select Local mode and click on Next. (Local mode is discussed in detail in Chapter 6.) You will see a message box letting you know that Visual InterDev is contacting the Web server. This may take

CHAPTER 2 • THE VISUAL INTERDEV ENVIRONMENT

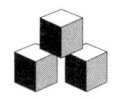

a few moments. When the server is contacted and a connection is made, Step 2 of the Web Project Wizard displays (see Figure 2.3).

6. For now, keep the name First. Click on Next. Step 3 displays, as shown in Figure 2.4.

7. Select Bottom 1 and click on Next. The wizard's Step 4 displays (see Figure 2.5).

8. Select Arcs for your theme and click on Finish. You will see a

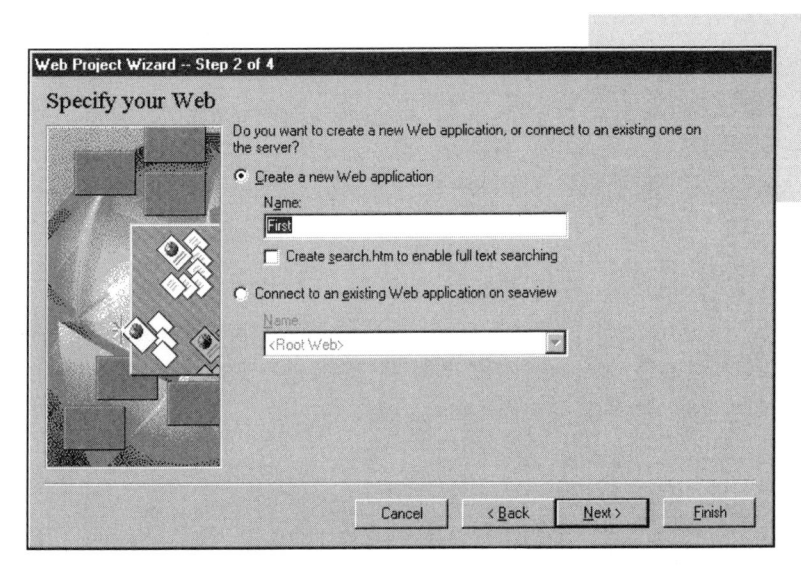

Figure 2.3
The next thing you need to do is name your Web application.

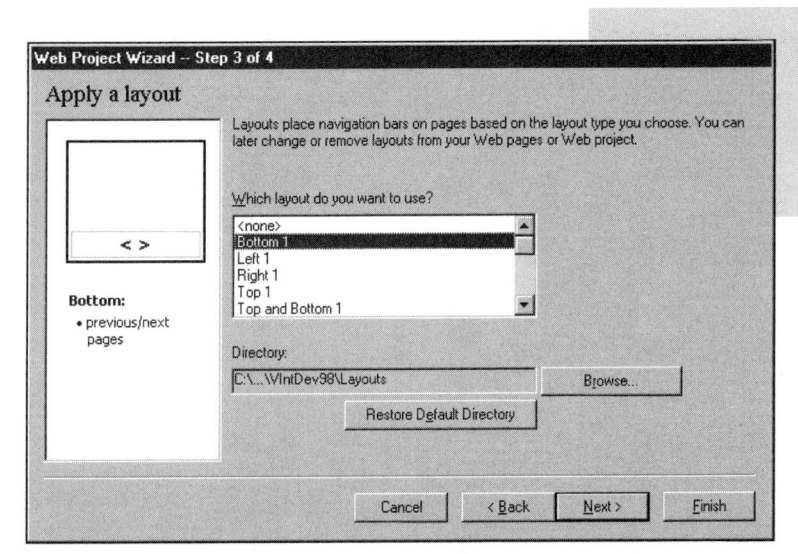

Figure 2.4
The layout you select determines placement of navigation bars on your pages.

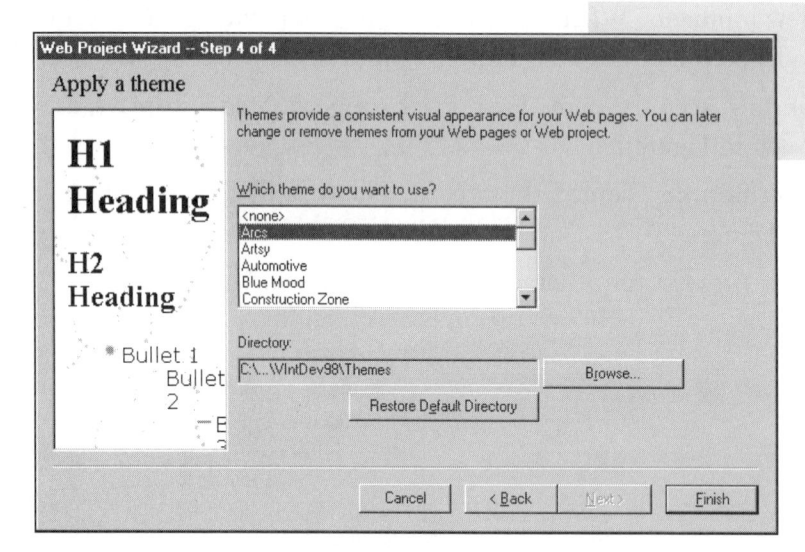

Figure 2.5
A theme controls the appearance of your Web pages.

message telling you that Visual InterDev is creating your project file. This process, depending on your system, can take a few minutes. When it is done, the Visual InterDev development environment displays (see Figure 2.6).

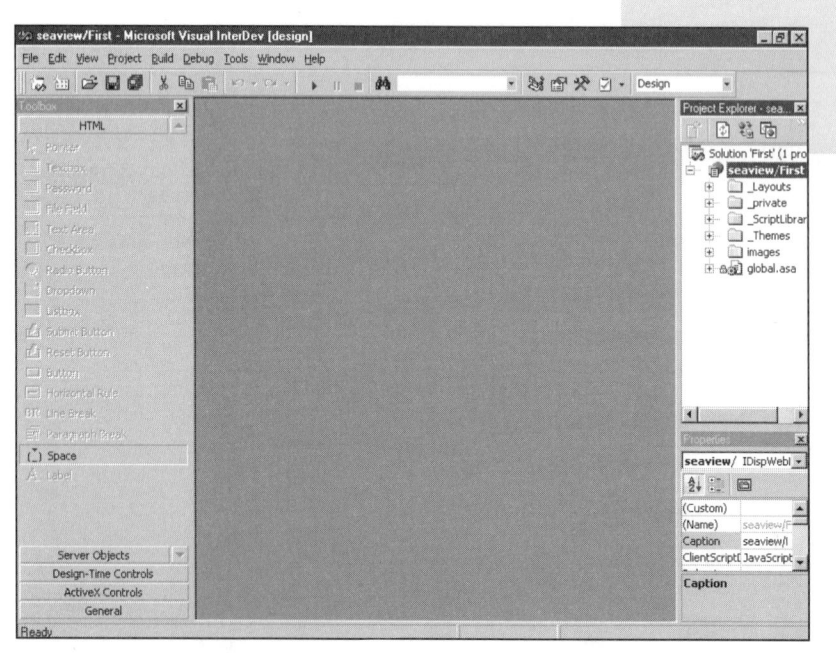

Figure 2.6
You are now ready to create a Web solution!

CHAPTER 2 • THE VISUAL INTERDEV ENVIRONMENT

Parts of the Visual InterDev Environment

The Visual InterDev development environment provides you with several tools to aid you in creating your solution. Figure 2.7 illustrates the windows that open by default when you start a Visual InterDev project.

You can have several windows open in the Visual InterDev environment at one time. Each of these windows can be resized, moved, and docked. This capability allows you to customize the appearance of your work environment to best suit your needs.

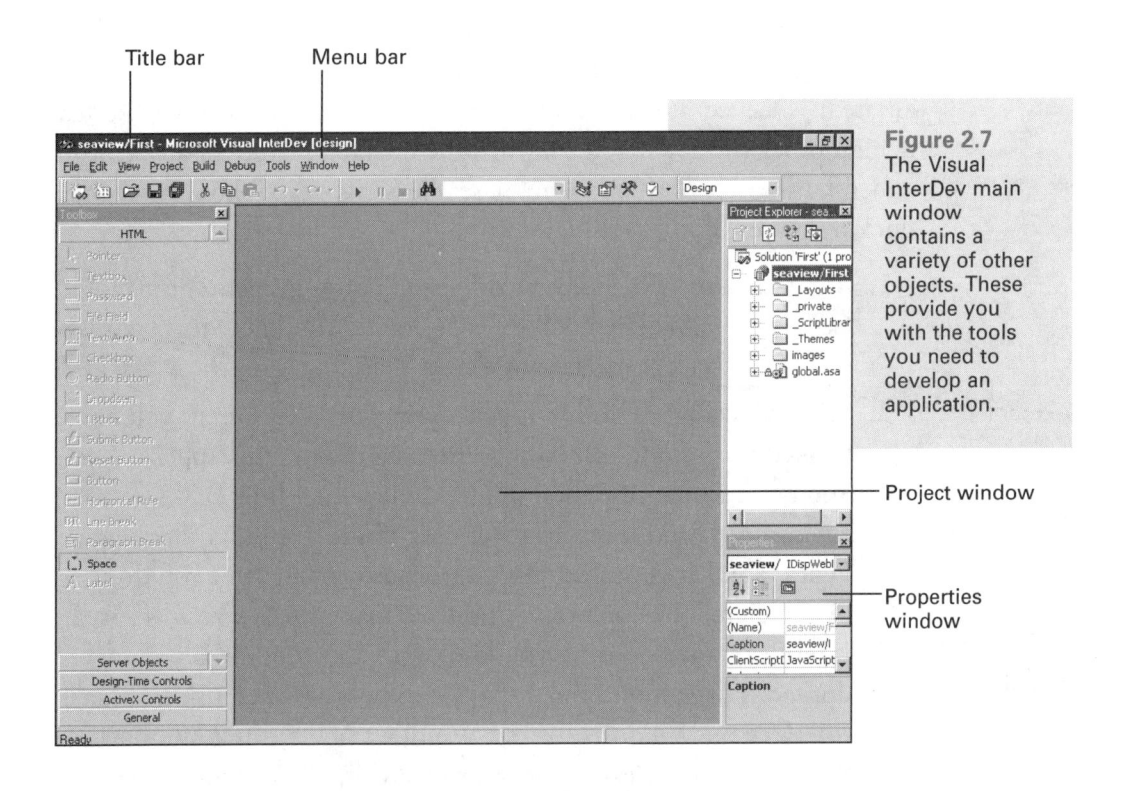

Figure 2.7
The Visual InterDev main window contains a variety of other objects. These provide you with the tools you need to develop an application.

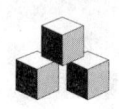

Customizing the Windows in the Visual InterDev Environment

Sometimes you may want a particular window to take up more or less space on your screen. Resize a window in Visual InterDev as you would anywhere in the Windows environment: Drag one of the borders until the window is the desired size.

Similarly, move a window, toolbox, or toolbar as you would in any standard Windows application: Click on its title bar and drag it to its new location.

Visual InterDev allows you to dock windows, toolboxes, and toolbars. This anchors the item to another dockable item. If an item is dockable, when you move the item, it snaps to the location. If an item is not dockable, you can move it anywhere on the screen and leave it there. It won't snap to a location. Docking an item provides an advantage over moving an item. Docked items always remain visible; they can't be hidden behind other windows. You can turn the docking feature of an item on and off using its pop-up menu. Use the steps that follow to change docking options:

1. Right-click on the Toolbox's title bar. A pop-up menu displays (see Figure 2.8). The Toolbox is dockable. You know this because there is a check mark next to Dockable.

2. Select Dockable. This is a toggle option. By selecting it, you have toggled this option off. Now something unsettling happens. The Toolbox becomes the focal point of the Visual InterDev environment and takes up the center of the screen, as shown in Figure 2.9. I had you do this on purpose in case later you do it by accident. The Toolbox's window is maximized, which is Visual InterDev's way of letting you know that the window is no longer docked. I have found this behavior to be true when using Visual InterDev on Windows 95 and Windows NT but not Windows 98. If you do not experience this behavior, you can go to step 4.

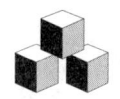

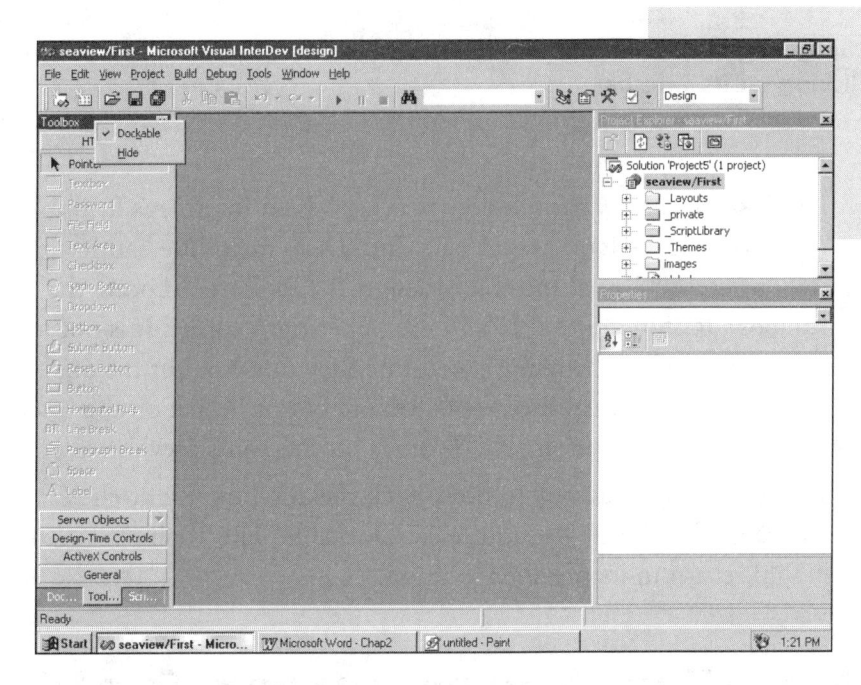

Figure 2.8
As you can see, most of the dockable items have their dock feature turned on.

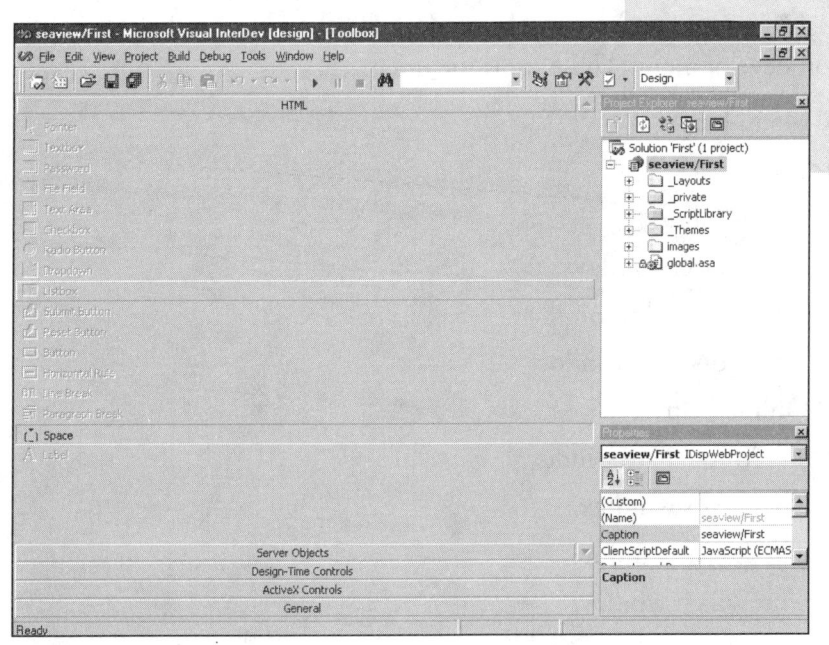

Figure 2.9
Undocking a window may have startling results!

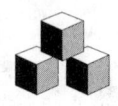

> **Tip:** You can quickly dock and undock a window by double-clicking on its title bar.

3. The Toolbox is now the window that has Visual InterDev's focus. You know this by looking at Visual InterDev's main title bar. It says "Microsoft Visual InterDev [design] – [Toolbox]." Locate the Toolbox's Restore button. It is in the upper-right corner. It is not the one located in the main Visual InterDev title bar, but the one located beneath Visual InterDev's Restore button. Click on the Toolbox's Restore button. The Toolbox returns to its previous size.

4. The next thing you need to do is dock the Toolbox. Right-click on the Toolbox's title bar and select Doc_k_able. The Toolbox should return to its previous location.

Visual InterDev Programmer Tools

Visual InterDev provides a rich set of tools you can use to help in application development. These tools include:

- Menu bars
- Toolbars
- The Toolbox
- The Project window
- Property Explorer
- The Properties window
- Online help
- The Immediate window
- The Autos window
- The Locals window
- The Watch window

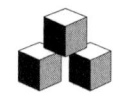

- The Threads window
- The Call Stack window
- The Running Documents window
- The Task list
- The Visual Component Manager
- The Object Browser
- The Document Outline
- The Data view
- The Script Outline

The Visual InterDev Window

The Visual InterDev window is available to you once you have started Visual InterDev and elected either to create a new Web project or to open an existing one. This section will introduce you to some of the tools just listed.

Menus

Menus provide an easy way to access the commands available to you through Visual InterDev. Two kinds of menus are supported: the menu bar and pop-up menus.

The menu bar is an interface element that should be familiar to you from working with Windows applications. It gives you access to most of the commands that you use to control Visual InterDev's environment. Menus you have probably used in other applications include the File, Edit, and Help menus. Visual InterDev's menu bar is illustrated in Figure 2.10.

Visual InterDev provides context-sensitive menus that display in a pop-up format, as shown in Figure 2.11. To access a pop-up menu for an object, right-click on that object.

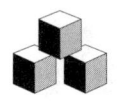

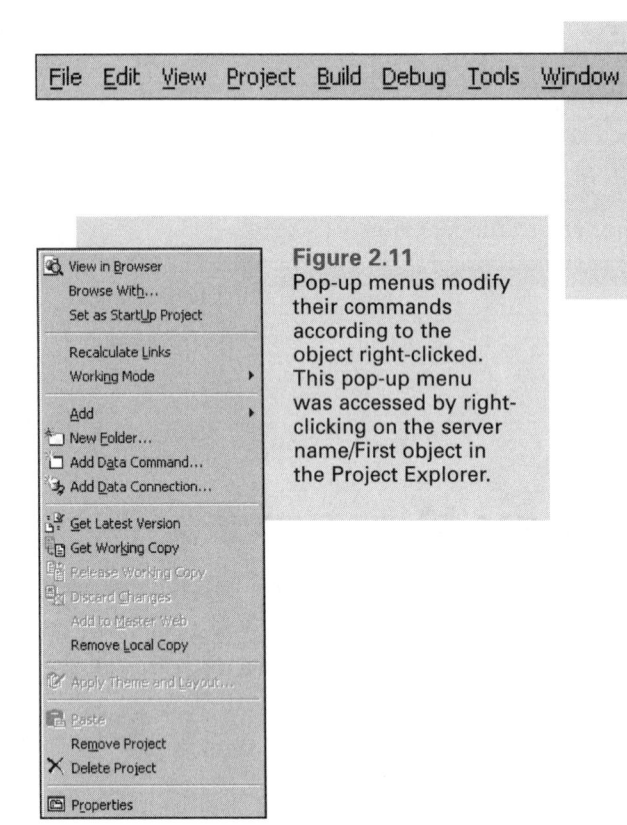

Figure 2.10
Visual InterDev's menu bar has menus that are common to most Windows applications. These menus can be accessed either by using your mouse or keyboard.

Figure 2.11
Pop-up menus modify their commands according to the object right-clicked. This pop-up menu was accessed by right-clicking on the server name/First object in the Project Explorer.

Toolbars

Below the menu bar is the toolbar. The toolbar provides you with an alternative to the menu bar for executing commonly used commands. Visual InterDev has several available toolbars. You can easily access these via the View menu. When you first start Visual InterDev, three toolbars are displayed:

- **Standard**. The Standard toolbar is the default toolbar for Visual InterDev. Its toolbar buttons represent the most commonly used Visual InterDev commands (see Figure 2.12).
- **Design**. The Design toolbar (shown in Figure 2.13) is for use in Design mode. Its tools allow you to control your document display in Design view and absolute positioning for objects in your document.

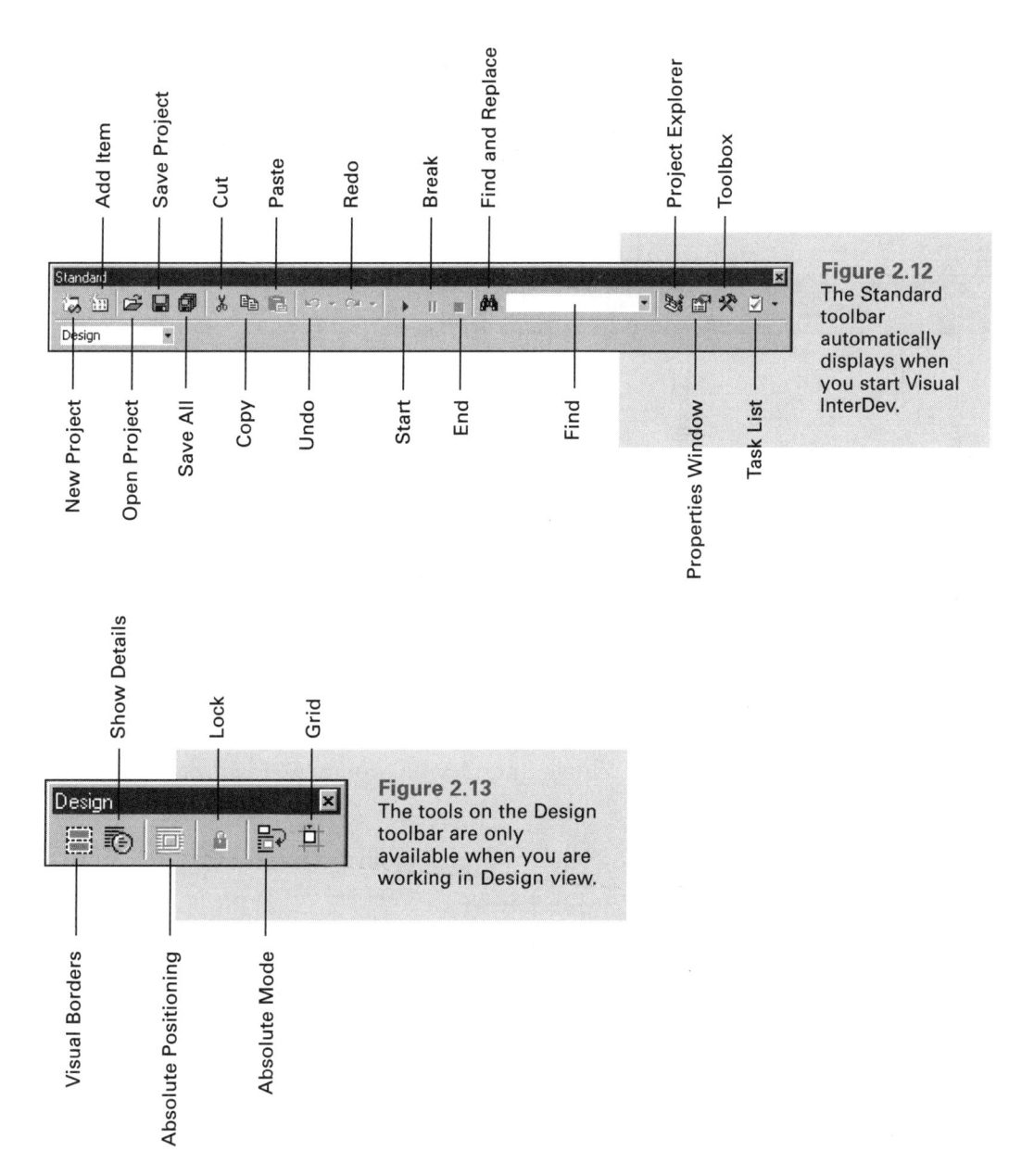

Chapter 2 • The Visual InterDev Environment

Figure 2.12
The Standard toolbar automatically displays when you start Visual InterDev.

Labels (top): Add Item, Save Project, Cut, Paste, Redo, Break, Find and Replace, Project Explorer, Toolbox

Labels (bottom): New Project, Open Project, Save All, Copy, Undo, Start, End, Find, Properties Window, Task List

Figure 2.13
The tools on the Design toolbar are only available when you are working in Design view.

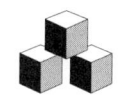

Labels (top): Show Details, Lock, Grid

Labels (bottom): Visual Borders, Absolute Positioning, Absolute Mode

- **HTML.** Use the tools on the HTML toolbar (see Figure 2.14) to do such things as change the font of a text element, change the background color, and change the indention of text.

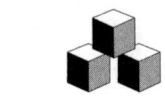

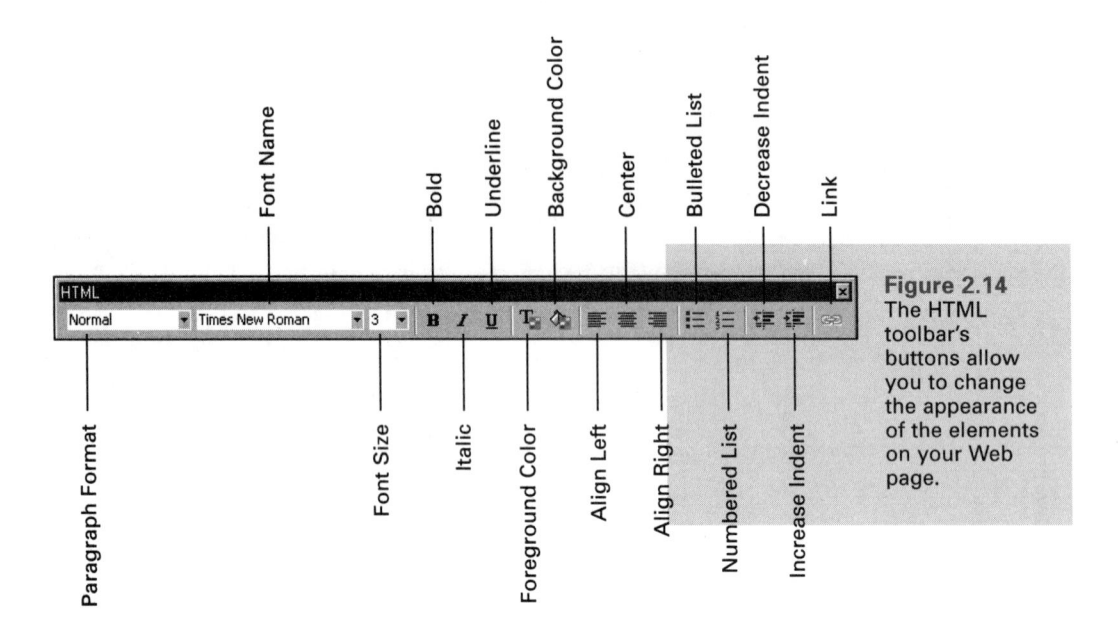

Figure 2.14
The HTML toolbar's buttons allow you to change the appearance of the elements on your Web page.

Visual InterDev does not limit you to the toolbars it comes with. You can add or remove buttons from any of the existing toolbars, and you can create a new toolbar from scratch. This capability allows you to further customize the Visual InterDev environment to meet your needs and preferences.

Adding and removing buttons from a toolbar is easy to do. To remove a toolbar button, follow these steps:

1. Right-click on a toolbar to display the toolbar shortcut menu.
2. Select Customize to display the Customize dialog box, as shown in Figure 2.15.
3. There are two ways to remove a button from a toolbar. The quickest way is to simply drag the unwanted button off the toolbar. This option works only when the Customize dialog box is displayed. The other way to remove a toolbar button is to right-click on the unwanted button to display its shortcut menu. This shortcut menu is available only when the Customize dialog box is displayed. Select Delete to remove the toolbar button. For this example, I won't delete any buttons.

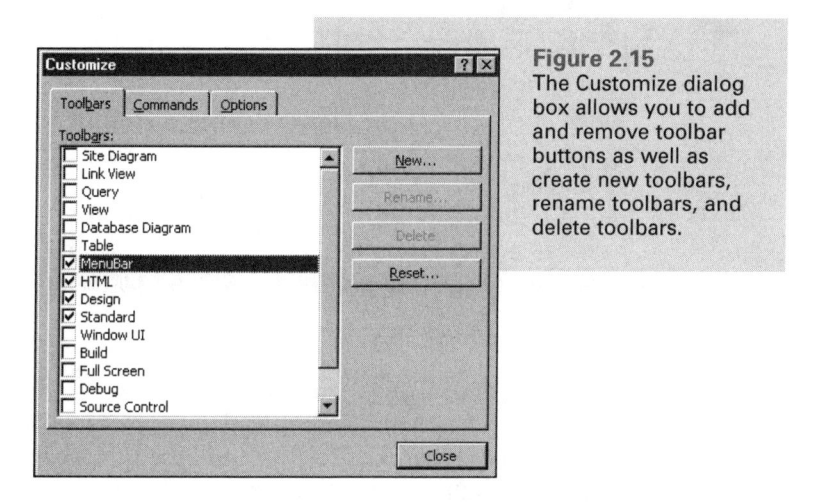

CHAPTER 2 • THE VISUAL INTERDEV ENVIRONMENT   29

Figure 2.15
The Customize dialog box allows you to add and remove toolbar buttons as well as create new toolbars, rename toolbars, and delete toolbars.

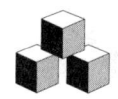

4. Click on Close to close the Customize dialog box.

Adding a toolbar button to a toolbar is done through the Commands tab of the Customize dialog box. On this tab, toolbar buttons are organized into groups that match Visual InterDev's menu system. Use the following steps to add a button to a toolbar:

1. Right-click on a toolbar to display the toolbar shortcut menu.
2. Select Customize to display the Customize dialog box.
3. Select the Commands tab to display the available toolbar buttons, as shown in Figure 2.16.

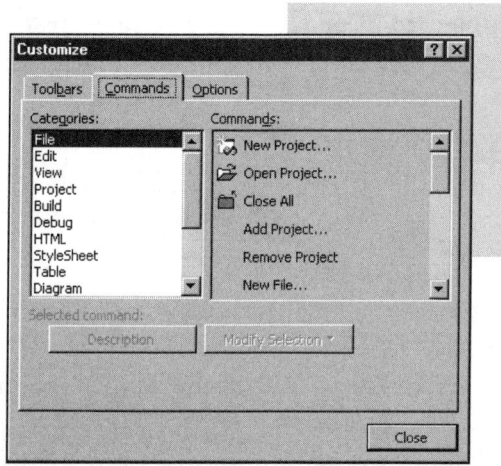

Figure 2.16
The Commands tab of the Customize dialog box contains the commands that you can add as toolbar buttons to your toolbars.

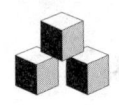

4. Select the menu category you want from the Categories list box.
5. Select the desired command you want from the Commands list box. The icons to the left of the listed commands represent the toolbar button's image.
6. Drag the command onto a toolbar. A vertical bar appears on the toolbar, representing the location of the toolbar button. After you move the icon to the desired location, drop the command. This adds the toolbar button.

> **Tip:** If you add and remove toolbar buttons and then want to return to the default toolbar buttons for that toolbar, select the toolbar's name from the Toolbars tab of the Customize dialog box. Click on Reset to return the toolbar to the way it was at the point of installation. This only applies to the built-in toolbars.

Rather than modifying the built-in toolbars, you may want to create one from scratch. As with adding and removing toolbar buttons, you use the Customize dialog box to create new toolbars. To create a new toolbar, follow these steps:

1. Right-click on a toolbar to display the toolbar shortcut menu.
2. Select Customize to display the Customize dialog box.
3. Select the Toolbars tab.
4. Click on New to display the New Toolbar dialog box (see Figure 2.17).

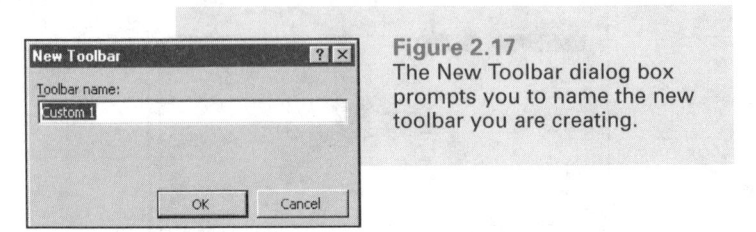

Figure 2.17
The New Toolbar dialog box prompts you to name the new toolbar you are creating.

5. Type a name for the toolbar in the Toolbar Name text box. The name can contain spaces.

6. Click on OK to save the name. The new toolbar is a small gray square, as illustrated in Figure 2.18.

Figure 2.18
When you first create a new toolbar, it is merely an empty container waiting to receive toolbar buttons.

7. Add the desired commands to the new toolbar using the steps discussed earlier in this section.

> **Tip**
>
> To delete a toolbar, select the toolbar's name from the Tool<u>b</u>ars tab of the Customize dialog box and click on <u>D</u>elete.

The Toolbox

In traditional development environments, your tool set was limited to the keyboard. This is not true in Visual InterDev, where your tool set has been extended to include a whole palette of tools found in the Toolbox (see Figure 2.19). Using the controls found in the Toolbox, you create your interface. By using Toolbox controls, you can add these and other elements to the user interface (Chapter 1 has a description of the HTML controls available through the Toolbox):

- Labels
- Command buttons
- Check boxes and option buttons
- List and combo boxes
- Animation
- Calendars
- Status bars

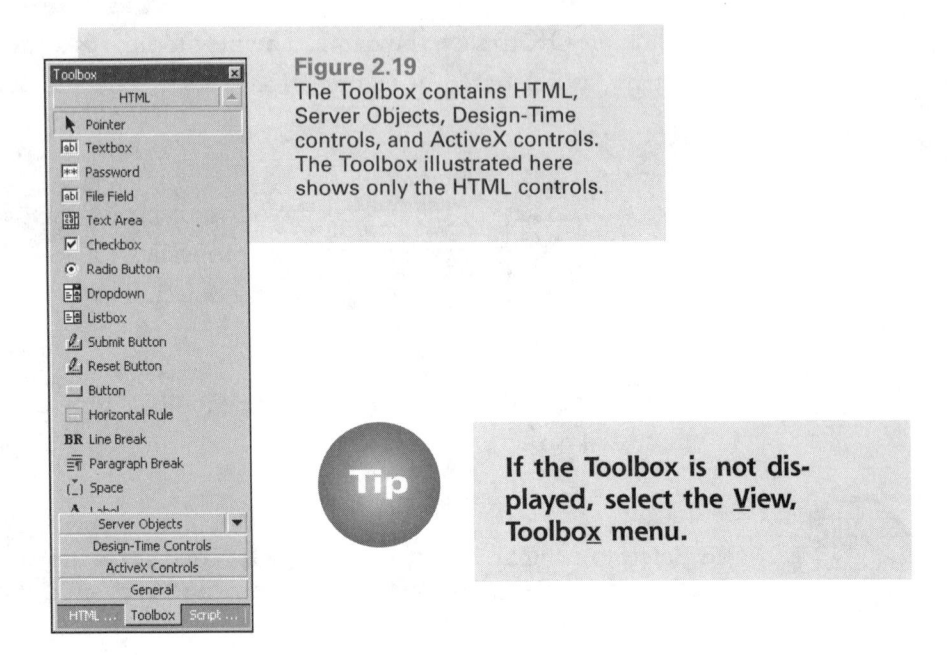

Figure 2.19
The Toolbox contains HTML, Server Objects, Design-Time controls, and ActiveX controls. The Toolbox illustrated here shows only the HTML controls.

Tip: If the Toolbox is not displayed, select the View, Toolbox menu.

The View Window

The View window (see Figure 2.20), located at the center of the Visual InterDev parent window, allows you to design your project, view the source code being generated by your actions, and see a preview of the page you are working on.

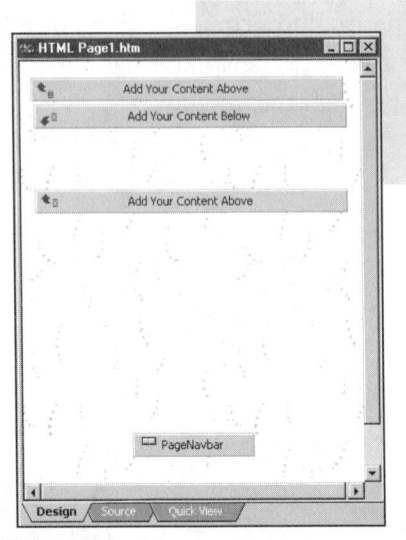

Figure 2.20
The View window, as the name implies, provides a variety of views into your project.

The Properties Window

You will often want to change the look and behavior of pages and objects. This is done with *properties*. When you design your interface, you'll use the Properties window (see Figure 2.21) to change the characteristics (properties) of the objects in your project. Examples of properties are the .FontSize and .textAlign properties. These properties control the font size and alignment of a text object. The Properties window has these parts:

- The main part of the Properties window is its list box. This list box displays the properties available at design time for the currently selected control.

- At the top of the Properties window is a drop-down list box, which displays the name of the currently selected object.

- Beneath the Name drop-down list box are two buttons. The first one, named Alphabetic, alphabetizes the current list of properties. The second one, named Categorized, arranges the properties by categories when selected.

- At the bottom of the Properties window is a pane that displays a short description of the selected property.

> **Tip**
> You can quickly dock and undock the Properties window by double-clicking on its title bar.

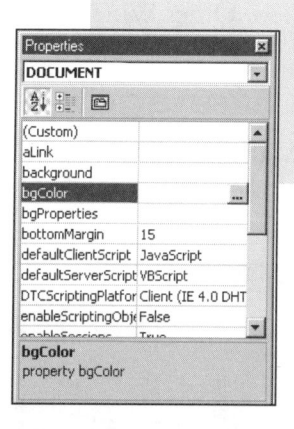

Figure 2.21
The Properties window allows you to change characteristics of an object without using code.

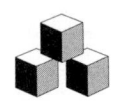

Project Explorer

Earlier in this chapter, a project was defined as a collection of files that are required for the creation of your solution. The Project Explorer window gives you a quick way to navigate back and forth between these files. Figure 2.22 shows the Project Explorer window.

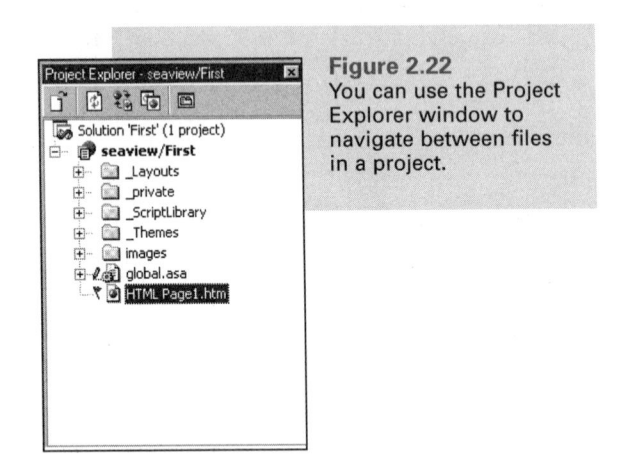

Figure 2.22
You can use the Project Explorer window to navigate between files in a project.

The Object Browser

You may have used an Object Browser if you have worked with a Microsoft development language such as Visual Basic. The Object Browser (see Figure 2.23) displays classes, properties, methods, events, and constants available from object libraries and the procedures in your project. It is useful for finding objects available for you to use in your scripts. It is also useful as a way to access online Help. The Object Browser can be displayed by selecting View, Other Windows, Object Browser.

The Visual Component Manager

With the Visual Component Manager (shown in Figure 2.24), you can organize, locate, and add components in your Visual InterDev project. The Visual Component Manager is displayed by selecting View, Other Windows, Visual Component Manager.

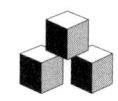

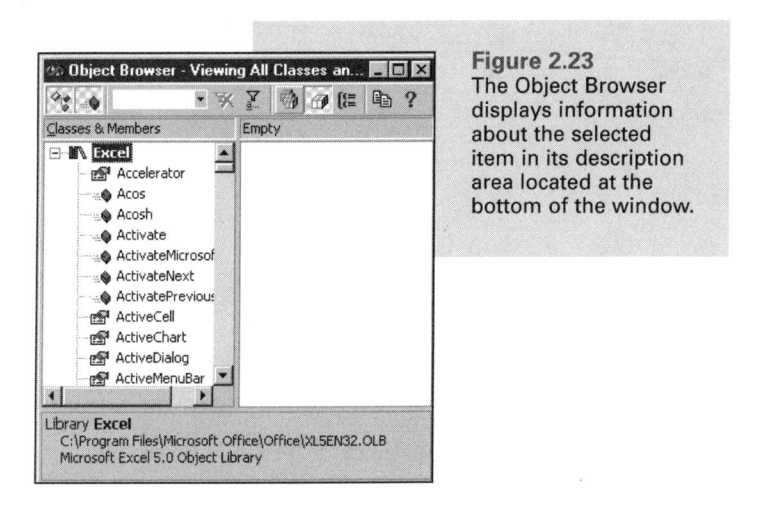

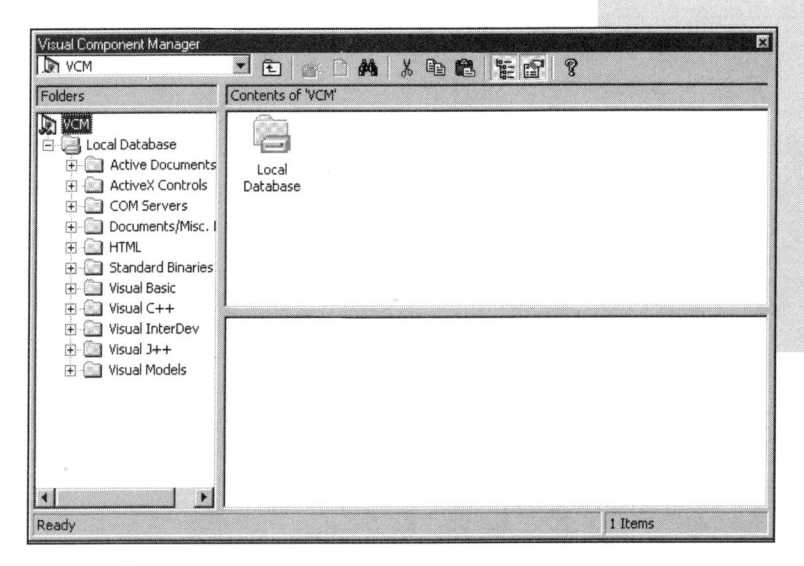

Figure 2.23
The Object Browser displays information about the selected item in its description area located at the bottom of the window.

Figure 2.24
The Visual Component Manager manages not just your Visual InterDev components but components created by other Visual Studio tools that may be located on your system.

The Task List Window

The Task List window is a great tool for those who have to write stuff down (or type it in) or they forget it. It allows you to enter tasks, categorize them, and prioritize them. Think of it as a mini project manager. The Task List window can be displayed by selecting View, Other Windows, Task List.

> A *task* is an item of work. It is a "to-do" item that relates to the project.

The Watch Window

One of the tools you have available to assist you in the debugging process is watch expressions. A *watch expression* is a variable or expression whose value you wish to monitor as your application progresses. Select View, Debug Windows, Watch, to display the Watch window.

The Online Help System

Visual InterDev offers outstanding online help. Help ranges from tutorial-style information to a language reference. You can get context-sensitive help by pressing F1.

If you have access to the Internet, you can access the Microsoft on the Web option through the Help menu. Then you can connect to one of the Microsoft-provided Visual InterDev Web sites listed on the submenu.

I could go on and on about the twenty-odd windows available in Visual InterDev, but I think you get the idea that Visual InterDev is definitely a feature-rich environment. It's time to get down to the bare bones of solution development.

Developing a Web Solution Using Visual InterDev

When starting a new Web project, you may feel a temptation to jump in with both feet and start creating. Before a single key is pressed, or mouse clicked, however, you need to design your solution. The more time you spend designing your system, the easier your life will be once you start working with that system on a daily basis.

As I said in the introduction to this book, I have been a Visual Basic developer for many years. I have taken the development steps that I've used in that environment and modified them for the Visual InterDev development process. (Hey, if it works, stick with it!) This list illustrates these steps:

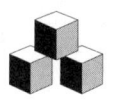

- Determine the purpose of your site.
- Determine the point of view of the site.
- Write a mission statement for the site.
- List the requirements for the site.
- Identify your content.
- Design your pages and identify the browser.
- Decide on the "mood" of your site.
- Determine if you want to provide links from your site to others.
- Build the site.
- Test and debug your site.
- Deploy your site.

Step 1: Determine the Purpose of Your Site

The first step in designing your site is to analyze what you wish to communicate. In other words, identify the goal of the site. Is it to present information about your business? Is it to be used for taking orders? You need to know why you are creating this system.

Step 2: Determine the Point of View of the Site

Once you have identified the goal of the site, determine the point of view of the site. Who is this site being created for? An example of a site that needs a definite point of view is an informational Web site about a place. If I am a tourist, my point of view of the system would consist of wanting to find out what I can about vacation options for this location, such as which hotels I could stay at and what could I do in the way of entertainment. If the Web site is geared at luring businesses to relocate to this place, I would want totally different information, such as tax rates, school information, and housing prices. The tone of the text would be different as well. A Web site that would be used by a vacation planner would have a lighter, fun feeling to its text, whereas one geared at the business owner would have a more professional tone to it.

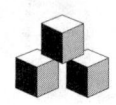

Step 3: Write a Mission Statement for the Site

Once you know the goal and point of view of the site, write it as a mission statement. This doesn't have to be done in incredible detail. It may be a single sentence. An example of a mission statement is "This site will allow vacation planners to access information about our location." Though it is tempting to skip this step, you'll find that by doing it you'll be more focused during the other steps in the site creation process.

Step 4: List the Requirements for the Site

Once you have the mission statement, determine and list the requirements for the site. This requirements document assists you in creating the site layout and determining business requirements. Refer to this list at various points of your design and make sure that you have not strayed from the intent of the site. When you have completed the site, use this document as a checklist to verify that the initial system requirements have been met.

Step 5: Identify Your Content

After determining what the system needs to do, identify the content needed to accomplish it. This content may simply be text. Using the example of a site for vacation planning, you may pull the information directly from a brochure that you got from the local tourist agency. Some of this content may be simple text, and other parts may be in a table form. More often than not, a Web developer is provided with text for the Web site from a variety of sources.

Or you may want to include data that is actually located in a database, since Visual InterDev allows you to incorporate database information into your site. For example, you may want to provide a listing of hotels in the area; a database would be a good way to store this listing because you could modify it without having to modify your Web site. That way if you needed to add or delete a hotel, or change a hotel's rate, you could change it in the database, and the change would be reflected on your Web site.

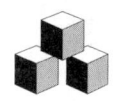

And don't forget that visitors like multimedia features. You'll need to gather graphics, photos, video clips, and sound clips to include on your site.

Step 6: Design Your Pages and Identify the Browser

Once you know what you want to include on your Web site, you can begin to organize it. You'll probably find that the text, data, tables, and such naturally fall into separate topics. Use these topics to break the content into pages for your site.

The capabilities of the browser or browsers you plan to support will also shape the design of your pages. For example, are you planning to use Active Server Pages (ASP)? You need to make these kinds of decisions because not all browsers support all features. You'll probably want to design for the browser you think most of your audience will use, or else you may want to design your pages so that you'll have the largest possible audience. In the latter case, you'll need to design your pages with fewer advanced features so that more and older browsers can view it.

Step 7: Decide on the "Mood" of Your Site

The colors used by your site, the background selected, the font used, and so on all impact the mood of your site. You can either select each of these elements separately, or you can apply a theme to do some of the work for you.

Step 8: Determine If You Want to Provide Links from Your Site to Others

A common courtesy in the Web world is to provide links from your page to other pages that the user may find useful or interesting. If you wish to provide this functionality, you'll need to determine the sites you wish to link to from your site.

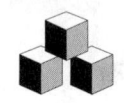

Step 9: Build the Site

Up to this point, you've planned and documented. Now you are ready to create. You'll add Web items to your project, perhaps add a database connection, and develop scripts. When you are through, you'll have a prototype of your site to show to your client. Then you'll go back and make any client-requested changes and other modifications.

Step 10: Test and Debug Your Site

You'll want to thoroughly test your site, making sure that there aren't any broken links or scripts that perform incorrectly. You'll probably find some errors that you'll have to use Visual InterDev's rich set of debugging tools to resolve.

Step 11: Deploy Your Site

When your Web site is beautiful and bug-free, it's time to deploy it so that it is available to your users. Once you put your site on the production Web server, it is a good idea to test it one more time to locate any possible link and script issues.

Summary

Congratulations! Now you're ready to start your first Visual InterDev project. This chapter covered the following topics:

- Creating a new Visual InterDev project
- Familiarizing yourself with parts of the Visual InterDev environment
- Customizing the windows in the Visual InterDev environment
- Using Visual InterDev programming tools
- Understanding the basic steps for developing a Web solution using Visual InterDev

You will use the information discussed here as a foundation for learning to use Visual InterDev. In Chapter 3, you will be taken through the process of creating a basic Web site so that you'll have the hands-on experience you need to create your own sites.

Hands On Project 1

The Travel Site

- Starting a new project
- Choosing a theme and layout for your project
- Creating a home page
- Adding text to a page
- Using the Quick View tab
- Formatting text
- Previewing a page in a browser
- Working locally
- Working offline
- Working in Master mode
- Adding files to the project
- Working with the global navigation bar
- Working with HTML
- Adding links from your page
- Overview

Project Overview

Your first project is a Web site for a fictitious resort location named Turtle Island. The goal of the site is to provide basic information for tourists wishing to learn about the vacation opportunities in the area. When you complete this project, you will know how to start a project from scratch. You'll have the opportunity to add pages, text, and graphics to the project.

Once the project is completely built, you will learn and apply testing techniques. You also will learn to deploy your solution.

CHAPTER 3

What Is the Travel Site?

Up to this point, you've gained familiarity with the Visual InterDev environment. Now it's time to get specific and start your first project. This chapter begins the process by describing the project you're going to create and by giving you an overview of the key topics presented in the remaining chapters in this section.

Design Objectives for the Travel Site

Your first project is a Web site for a fictitious resort location named Turtle Island. The goal of the site is to provide basic information for tourists wishing to learn about the vacation opportunities in the area. You can see one of the completed pages for the site in Figure 3.1. This site needs to include:

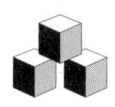

- Descriptions of the various tourist sites
- Pictures of some of these sites
- A look and feel that invokes the "special magic" of the area (to use a marketing phrase!)

This list covers the basic system requirements of the application, but you should consider some other user requirements before you begin developing the application:

- A menu system that affords quick access to various areas of the site
- Links to other sites that the user may find helpful
- The ability to e-mail questions to a representative at the site

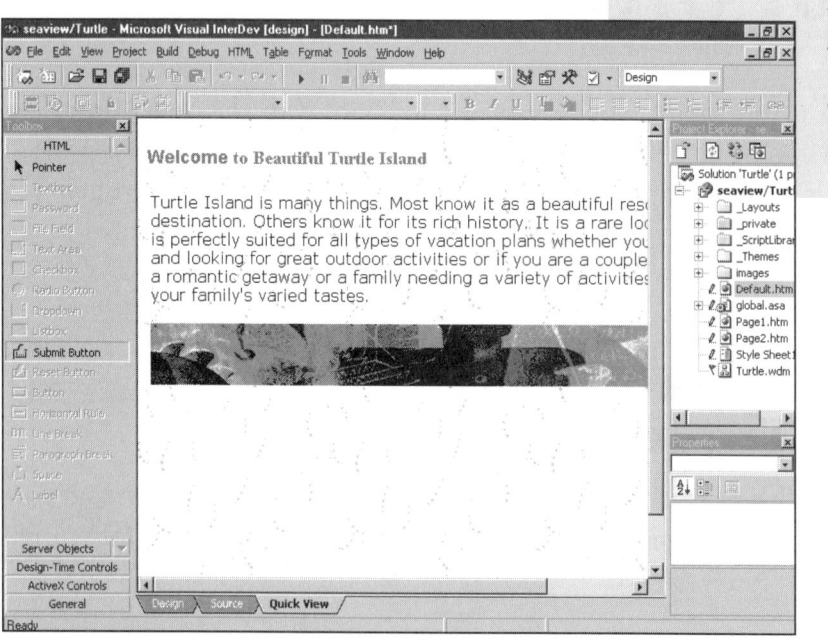

Figure 3.1
The completed home page captures the magic of Turtle Island.

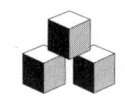

Learning Objectives for the Home Page Project

What should you hope to accomplish in terms of learning Visual InterDev while creating the home page? This project is designed to get you started as a Visual InterDev developer and therefore introduces some key concepts. The following sections describe these key concepts.

Starting a New Web Project

This project offers you the foundation you need to build your Web solution. As a matter of fact, you'll learn how Visual InterDev defines a solution and how to create a Web site and add files to it. You'll also learn how to build your Web project into a Web application.

> As Visual InterDev defines it, a *solution* is a collection of Web projects and dependent projects that organizes a Web application.

Applying a Theme to Your Home Page

To me, one of the most fun parts of working with Visual InterDev is using its themes (see Figure 3.2). *Themes* allow you to quickly give your Web sites a professional look. Themes consist of a set of graphics and a cascading style sheet that controls styles, font, and other elements. They allow you to add a lot of visual appeal and consistency to your project without a lot of work! In Chapters 5 and 6, you'll learn how to:

- Apply a theme to an entire project
- Preview a theme
- Apply a theme to a single file
- Remove a theme

> *Cascading style sheets (CSS)* are used to enforce a standard look and feel throughout your Web site.

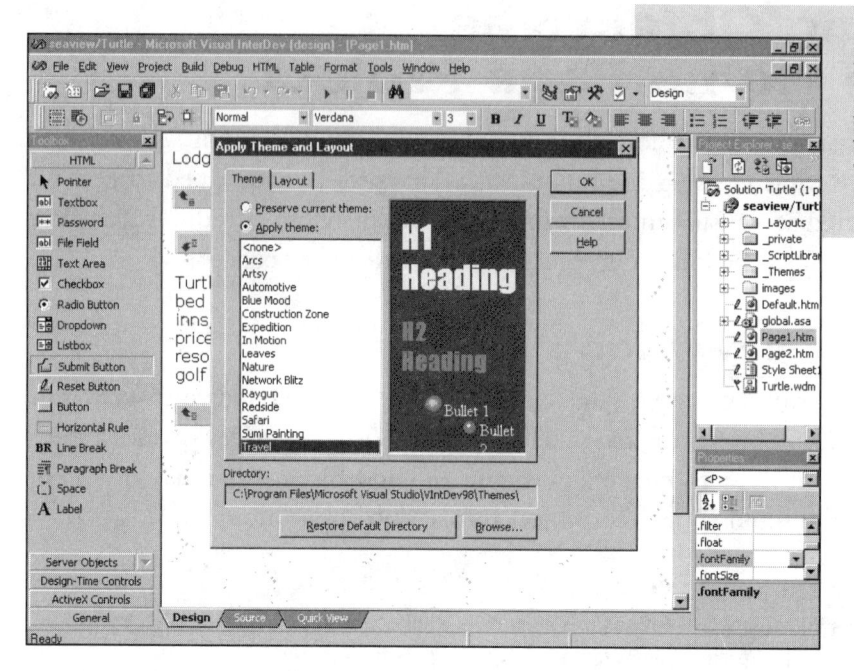

Figure 3.2
Visual InterDev provides you with several themes to use with your projects.

Adding Navigation to Your Pages

You'll learn to add navigation to your pages. *Navigation* allows your Web solution's users to move quickly and efficiently around the different areas of your site. Figure 3.3 is an example of a page that has a navigation bar that allows you to return to the previous page and go to the next page in the site. In Chapter 6, you'll learn how to apply a layout to add navigation as well as use the PageNavbar control to add navigation bars to your project.

> A *layout* is a template for the way that information, navigation bars, and graphics are positioned on a page.

Working in Different Modes

Visual InterDev allows you to work both online and offline. When you are working online, you have two options: You can work directly with the

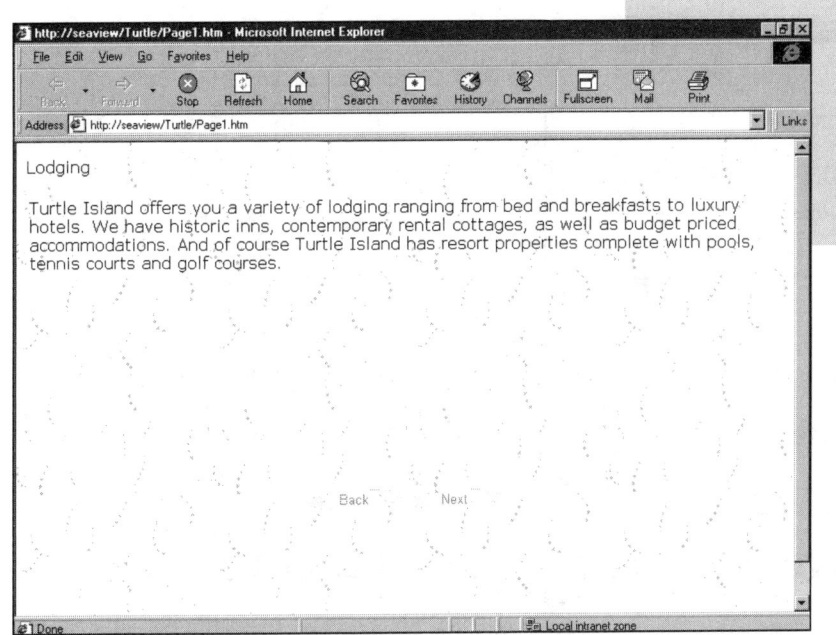

Figure 3.3
By clicking on navigation buttons, your users can access the different pages in your site.

master Web files in master mode, or you can develop your own working model of the Web application or its parts in local mode. This part of the project, covered in Chapter 6, introduces you to working locally.

You'll also get an opportunity to work offline. This means you'll work without a connection to the master Web server.

Using an Editor

Once you've created the files in your project, you may want to work with them using an editor. Visual InterDev allows you to choose from a variety of editors, including the HTML editor, the style sheet editor, a text editor, Microsoft FrontPage, or an external editor of your choice. In Chapters 5 and 6, you'll work with files in the HTML editor's different views (see Figure 3.4). Using these views, you will edit the layout of your Web page and create scripts.

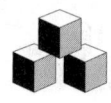

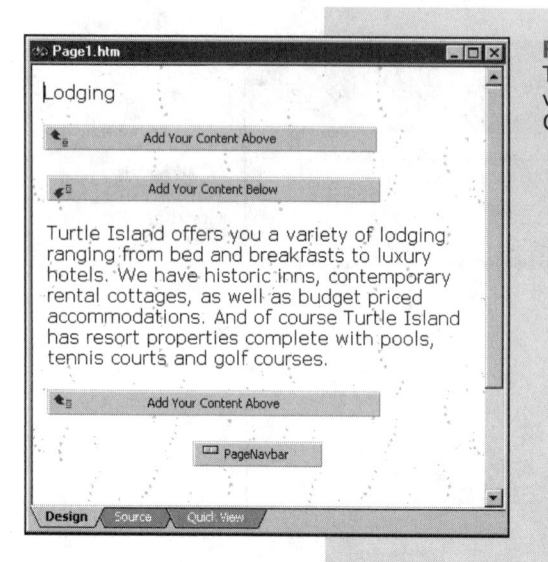

Figure 3.4
The HTML editor has three views: Design, Source, and Quick Preview.

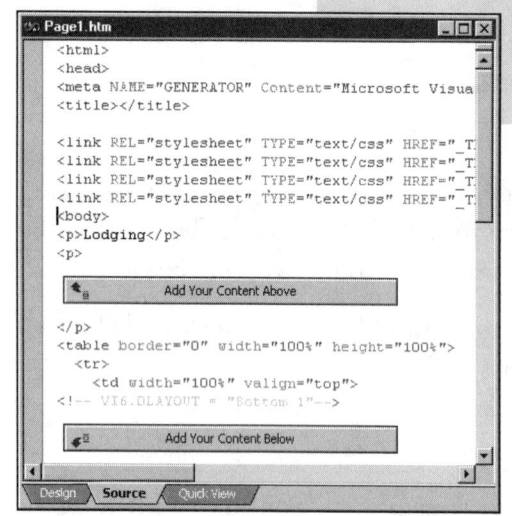

Testing the Web Solution

Once you are ready to test your Web application, you will view its files in the Web browser. In Chapter 7, you'll learn how to preview your local Web application so that you can test its functionality and links before releasing it to the master server.

Summary

Now it's time to start your project. The next chapter takes you through the up-front design considerations. The remaining chapters associated with this project take you from start to finish through a simple Web project. Upon completion of the project, you'll have the skills you need to design and build a multiple page project, incorporate navigation into your sites, understand Visual InterDev's modes, and test your Web site.

Even if you've had some experience using Visual InterDev, you should benefit from the solution-development approach of this project. Remember that the best way to learn Visual InterDev is to use Visual InterDev. Reading an introductory book on Visual InterDev may have given you a good foundation, but you won't fully appreciate that knowledge until you use it.

CHAPTER 4

Gathering Content for the Travel Site

In the previous chapter, you got an overview of what will become your first Web site using Visual InterDev. With this information, you are going to analyze the project's needs for text, pictures, content, and general organization.

The first thing you'll do in this chapter is list the elements you need to get from the client for whom you are developing the Web site. These elements may come to you as pieces of paper with typed or handwritten text, or they may take the form of files.

The second major task of this chapter is to organize the information determined in the first section. This process breaks the information into groups. These groups aid you in determining the pages needed by the solution.

Due to the graphical nature of Visual InterDev, in developing a solution, you should first think about the user interface. Before you can design the interface, you should know what type of elements you need to get from your client. Then you can plan how to present the information and application to the user.

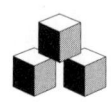

There are two common approaches to designing the user interface. Some developers, for instance, prefer to sketch the needed pages before creating them. The main advantage to this approach is that it helps them organize the solution before they commit to the actual creation of the solution. This approach may also succeed when several developers are working on the same project. By sketching the pages before implementing them, the team can agree on standards for a consistent interface.

The second approach is to simply start creating the interface immediately using Visual InterDev. Quite honestly, this is the more common approach. The developer starts placing elements on pages and creates the interface as he or she goes.

No matter which approach you use, you need to analyze the elements you need from your client, whether that client is someone you're working with or that client is you! After determining the design elements, you can decide how to break them up into pages. This leads you through the process of designing the Web site.

Choosing a Format for Your Home Page

The format of your Web site consists of two things: layout and theme. As you may recall from the preceding chapter, a *layout* is a template for the way that information, navigation bars, and graphics are positioned on a page. A *theme* is a set of graphics, fonts, and other page elements that impart a consistent visual appearance to a page. When you conceived a new project, you were asked to select a layout and a theme. When you start adding pages to your project, you'll see the impact of the selected layout and theme.

Determining the Text for Your Home Page

In the previous chapter, you determined that the goal of the home page is to provide basic information for tourists wishing to learn about the vacation opportunities on Turtle Island. Here is some of the text you'll need:

- **Introduction.** This will welcome visitors to the site and entice them to explore further.
- **Outdoor recreation.** Many vacationers look for a variety of outdoor activities when planning a vacation. Turtle Island has a large assortment of these, including golf, tennis, and fishing. You'll need to get a paragraph or two describing each of these offerings.
- **Other activities.** Since this is an island, beaches are an obvious attraction. You'll also want to discuss things like activities for kids, tours for the ecology-minded, and shopping.
- **Hotels and restaurants.** Part of planning a vacation is deciding where to stay and where to eat. You need to include this information as well.

> **Note**
> I have a friend who, without a doubt, would have included copious amounts of text just on the golfing opportunities. Another person who saw my proposed site said she would have included tide information, since spending time on a warm, sunny beach is important to her. The bottom line is that each person will bring his or her own experiences and preferences to the design process. What would you add to the preceding list?

Where are you going to get this text? With any luck, your client will provide it so that you don't have to write it yourself. You'll probably be presented with an assortment of pieces of paper, brochures, and books. You'll pull the text you want to use from these items. The text for this project is presented in the next chapter.

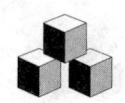

Selecting the Graphics for Your Home Page

To lure someone to your island, you'll need pictures. You'll want to include pictures that work with the text on your site, so you'll probably include photos of such things as beaches, golf courses, and tennis courts, along with other things vacationers love.

In addition to photos, you may want to include some other graphic elements, such as these:

- If your tourist bureau has an official logo for the area, you may want to use it on the introductory page or on all pages as a common element.
- You may want to select a graphic to be used as a button. For example, you may want to use a turtle as a button.
- If the site is sponsored by one or more groups, you may want to include their logos on one or more pages.
- You may want to include the logos of the main resort destinations in the area, such as golf courses and hotels.

Again, the question is, where will I get this stuff? Depending on your client, you'll be given photographs, brochures, and books from which you'll be expected to scan pictures, or you'll be given actual files to work with. What kind of ideas did you have when you started thinking about the graphics needed for this site? I imagine that you could come up with quite a list without even trying.

One thing you may want to do when trying to find graphics for your sites is to go to www.yahoo.com/Computers_and_Internet/Graphics/Clip_Art/. At this location (see Figure 4.1) on the Web, you'll find an extensive list of other sites that offer graphics, many of which are public domain or copyright free. I'm sure that you will get lots of ideas just from cruising these sites. And by the way, don't go overboard with graphics. Nobody cares how beautiful a site is if it takes forever to load!

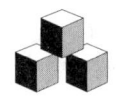

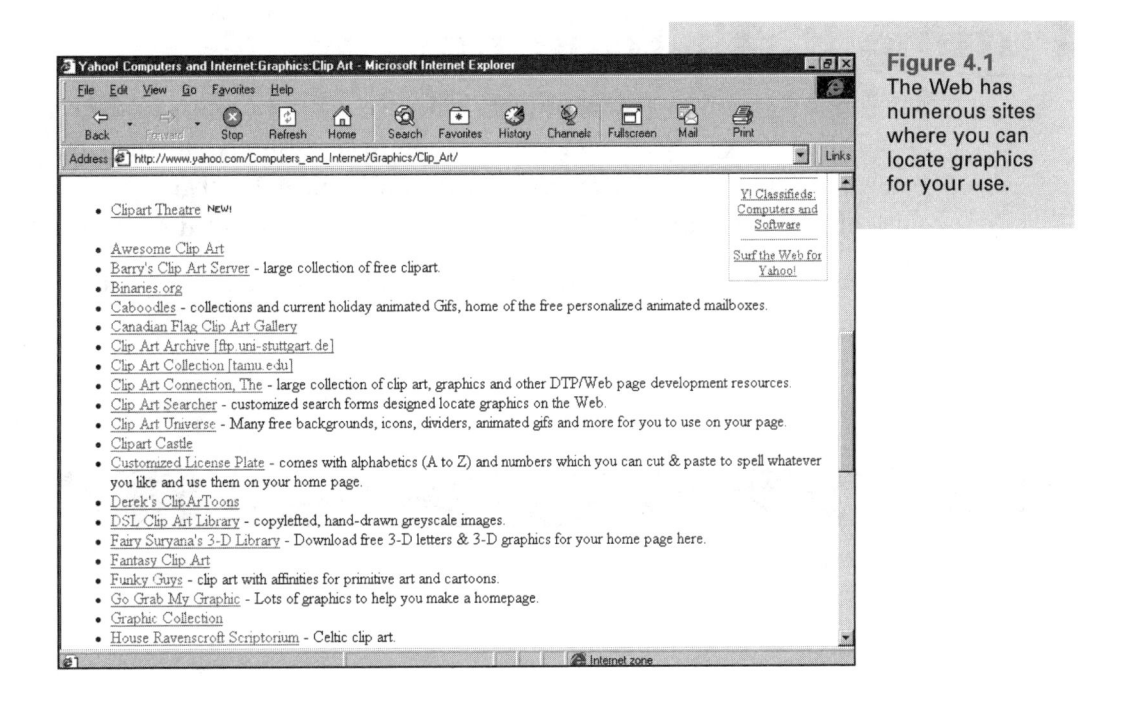

Figure 4.1
The Web has numerous sites where you can locate graphics for your use.

Selecting Other Elements for Your Home Page

Graphics and text are not the only things that you can include on your Web site. For example, you may want to include sounds. Wouldn't it be nice if the visitor could hear the sound of waves as the page loaded? Video is another option. You may want to include a short clip of the waves on the beach or of a golfer swinging a club on the site. Remember to be frugal with these types of elements. You don't want a Web site that is so busy (so much going on at one time) and intensive that it is visually unappealing and takes what seems an eternity to load.

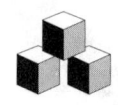

Putting It All Together

As you can see, even a small project can have many elements to track. For this project, you should create a spreadsheet similar to the one shown in Table 4.1 to track your information. Table 4.2 will give you an idea of how your spreadsheet might look after you have filled it in.

This spreadsheet is included on the CD and is named Track VI Project.XLS. It is a Microsoft Excel file.

Table 4.1 Site Tracking Worksheet

Project Name:
Layout Selected:
Theme Selected:

Text

Description	Page Location	Received From	Format	File Name

Graphics

Description	Page Location	Received From	Format	File Name

Other Elements

Description	Page Location	Received From	Format	File Name

Table 4.2 Sample Project Tracking Worksheet

Project Name: Turtle Island
Layout Selected: Bottom 1
Theme Selected: Arcs

Text

Description	Page Location	Received From	Format	File Name
Introduction	Intro Page	Client	Word file	Intro
Outdoor Activities	Outdoor	Client	Word file	Outdoor
Other Activities	Other	Client	Word file	Other
Facilities	Facilities	Client	Word file	Facilities

Graphics

Description	Page Location	Received From	Format	File Name
Turtle Island Logo	Intro Page	Client	Graphic file	Turtle
Golf Course	Outdoor	Client	Graphic file	Golf
Tennis Courts	Outdoor	Client	Graphic file	Tennis
Hotel/Resort	Facilities	Client	Graphic file	Hotel
Historical Ruin	Intro Page	Client	Graphic file	Ruin
Village Shops	Other	Client	Graphic file	Shop
Farmers Market	Other	Client	Graphic file	Market
Marsh	Outdoor	Client	Graphic file	Marsh
Pier Scene	Intro Page	Client	Graphic file	Pier
Beach at sunrise	Other	Client	Graphic file	Beach

Other Elements

Description	Page Location	Received From	Format	File Name
Video Clip of Waves	Other	Client	Video file	Waves

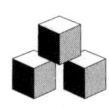

Using a spreadsheet like this one allows you to track your elements and forces you to organize them into pages. In later chapters, you will build on the elements in this spreadsheet, but this spreadsheet is sufficient for this phase of your project.

Summary

Chapter 3 began the Web development process by describing the project that you are going to create. It also gave you an overview of the key topics presented in the remaining chapters in this section.

This chapter divided this analysis stage of your project into four tasks: choosing the format of your project, choosing the text for the project, choosing the graphics needed by the project, and selecting other elements for your home page.

With the analysis stage complete, you are ready to start designing the pages for this solution. The next chapter focuses on giving you the skills you need to complete this step in the Visual InterDev development process.

CHAPTER 5

Designing the Travel Site

In this chapter, you are going to take the basic steps to build your project. The skills and techniques presented in this chapter have two goals. The first goal is for the newer Visual InterDev developer. If you have not worked with Visual InterDev much up to this point, you will learn a variety of basic skills in a short period of time. If you are a more experienced Visual InterDev developer, this chapter will give you a quick review of project development techniques and familiarize you with the Visual InterDev interface.

Starting a New Web Project

In Chapter 2, you created a simple Web project just so that you could view the parts of the Visual InterDev development environment. The files within a Web application can consist of several different file formats that you modify during the design phase of your project. These file formats include:

- HTML pages
- Active Server Pages (ASPs)
- Style sheets
- Site diagrams
- Image files
- Layouts
- Themes

You build a Visual InterDev Web project into a Web application. Web project files are stored in two places, the server and the local machine. In Visual InterDev, you manage working files locally and maintain master files on a server. Before editing files, you retrieve files from the server. This means that working copies of the files are placed into your local Web application.

A project is also part of a larger container, the solution. A *solution* is a collection of Web projects and dependent projects that organizes a Web application.

When you create a new project, the Web Project Wizard takes you through the steps for project creation. It has you select a server and a mode. To create this home page, do the following steps. You do not need to save any of the files created in the first project:

1. If you haven't started Visual InterDev, start it now. Select File, New Project. The New Project dialog box displays.
2. Verify that Visual InterDev Projects is selected in the first pane and select New Web Project in the second pane.

3. Type **Turtle** for the Name and click on Open. In a few moments, the Web Project Wizard starts.

4. Select the server you want to use. The server may or may not be listed in the What Server Do You Want to Use? drop-down list, so you may need to type it in.

5. Select Local mode and click on Next. Local mode will be discussed in detail in Chapter 6. You will see a message box letting you know that Visual InterDev is contacting the Web server. This may take a few moments. When the server is contacted and a connection is made, the Step 2 dialog box of the Web Project Wizard displays.

6. You are going to keep the name Turtle, so click on Next. Step 3 displays. You can preview the appearance of a layout by selecting it. The placement of navigation bars (according to the selected layout) is displayed in the preview pane located on the left side of the Web Project Wizard window, as shown in Figure 5.1.

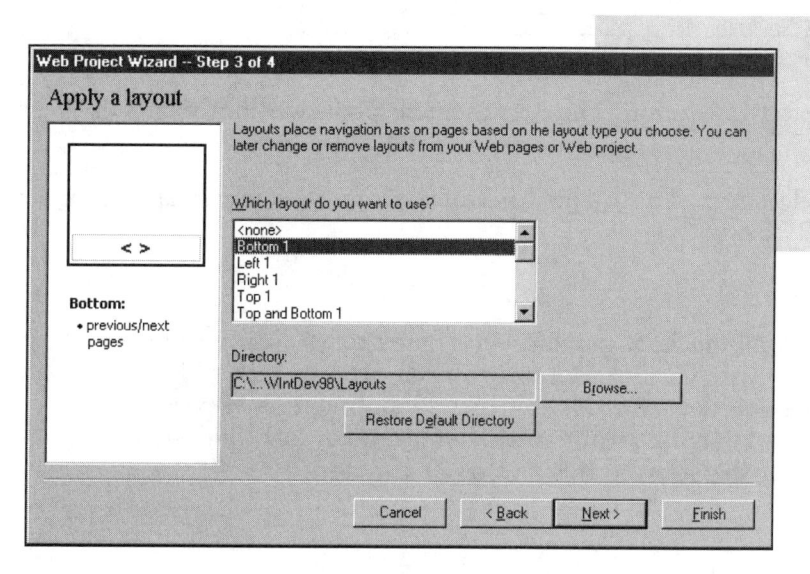

Figure 5.1
Navigation bars will be placed on the pages in your project according to the layout you select.

Hands On Project 1 • The Travel Site

7. Select Top and Bottom 1. Notice the look of the layout in the preview pane.
8. Select Bottom 1. This is the layout you are going to use for this project.
9. Click on Next. Step 4 displays. Just as with layouts, you can preview the themes that are available, as shown in Figure 5.2.

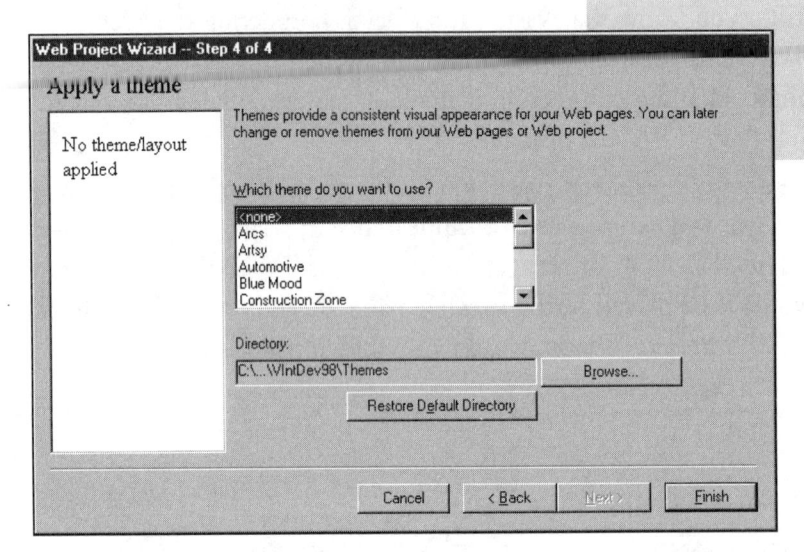

Figure 5.2
Themes provide the visual character of a project.

10. Select In Motion. The Arcs theme is previewed in the preview pane.
11. Select Arcs. This theme has a nice, clean, uncluttered appearance.

> **Note**
> I know all this cool graphical stuff may tempt you to pick a theme other than In Motion. You can actually pick any theme you want for this exercise, though you must pick Bottom 1 for the layout so that you can correctly follow some of the steps in this and other chapters.

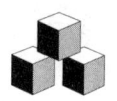

12. Click on Finish. You will see a message telling you that Visual InterDev is creating your project file. This process, depending on your system, can take a few minutes. When it is done, the Visual InterDev development environment displays.

Creating a Home Page

A home page typically has links to other pages. These pages can be both within and outside the site. The other pages in your Web site will typically have a link back to the home page. Most developers set up their Web sites so that the home page is the first page that a user sees. This is not a requirement, however.

You can easily add a home page to your Web application using a *site diagram*. A site diagram provides you with a graphical representation of the navigation structure of a Web site. It uses a tree diagram to show what pages you have in your project and how they relate. To create a new home page:

1. Select Project, Add Item. The Add Item dialog box displays, as shown in Figure 5.3.

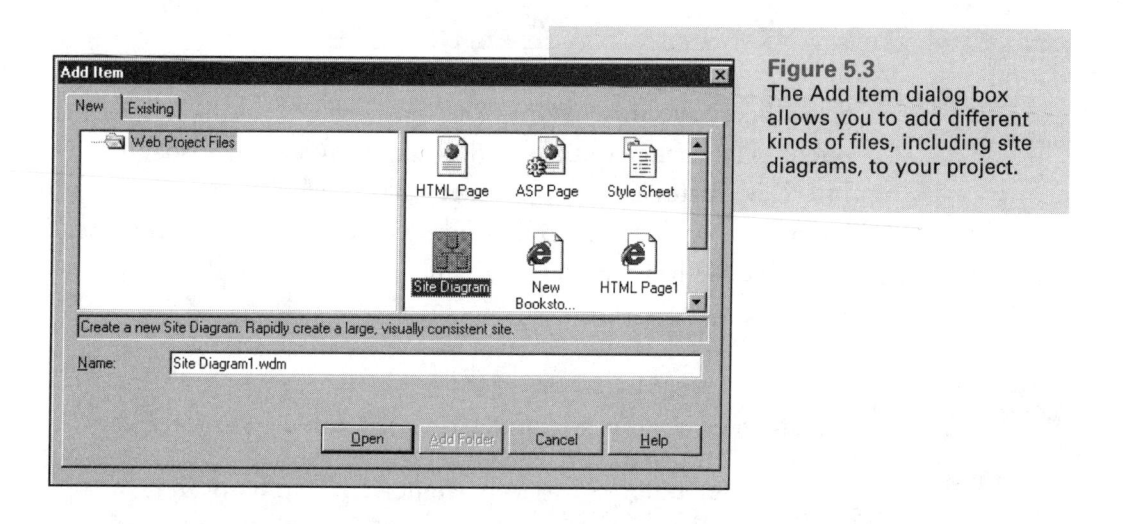

Figure 5.3
The Add Item dialog box allows you to add different kinds of files, including site diagrams, to your project.

HANDS ON PROJECT 1 • THE TRAVEL SITE

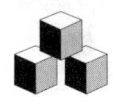

2. Select Site Diagram from the Web Project Files folder.
3. Type Turtle for the Name and click on Open. The Site Diagram is added to the project, and the Site Diagram displays, as shown in Figure 5.4. A page graphic displays in the site diagram with the name "Home."

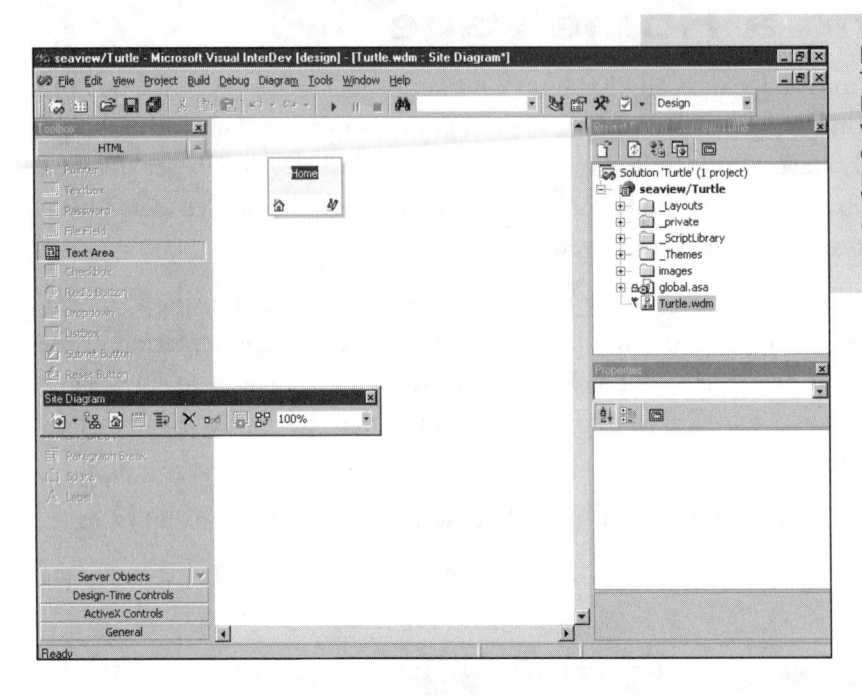

Figure 5.4
The Site Diagram is your work area to create the pages for your Web site and decide how to link them.

4. Select File, Save Turtle.wdm. You know the old rule, "Save often!" The change to the site diagram is saved, and Visual InterDev creates a new home page called Default.htm, index.htm, or Default.asp depending on the Web server you use. Once the file has been saved, it will be listed in the Project Explorer.

Note Microsoft Internet Information Server uses default.asp for a home page, and Microsoft Personal Web Server uses default.htm for a home page on Windows NT systems and index.htm on Windows 98 systems. The examples in this book were built using Personal Web Server.

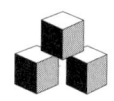

5. Click on the page graphic located in the Site Diagram to select it.
6. Select <u>V</u>iew, <u>O</u>pen. The page is opened in Design view, as shown in Figure 5.5.

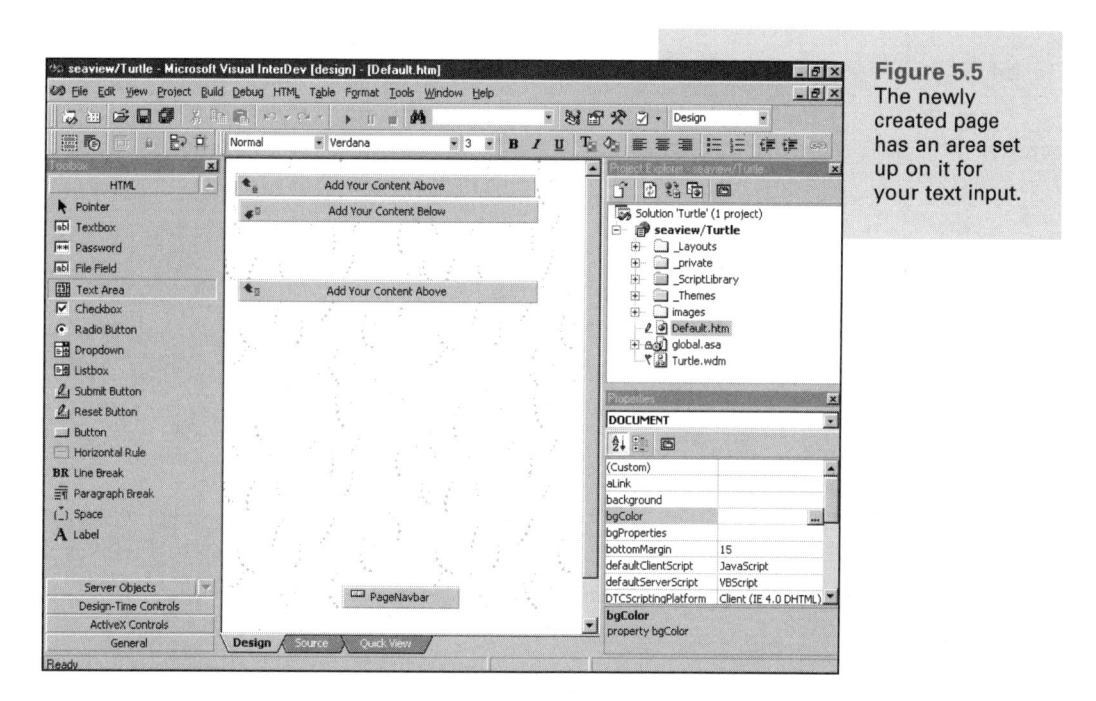

Figure 5.5
The newly created page has an area set up on it for your text input.

Adding Text to Your Home Page

As you can see, your home page is set up with predefined text areas. You are ready to start typing. In this chapter, you are going to keep the text short; you will build on it in the next chapter. To add text to this page, follow these steps:

1. Click before the gray bar that says "Add Your Content Above."
2. Press Enter to insert a blank line.
3. Type **Welcome to Beautiful Turtle Island**.
4. Click on the blank line under the gray bar that says "Add Your Content Below."
5. Type **Turtle Island is many things. Most know it as a beautiful resort destination. Others know it for its rich history. It is a rare location that is perfectly suited for all types of vacation plans,**

whether you are single and looking for great outdoor activities, a couple looking for a romantic getaway, or a family needing a variety of activities to meet your family's varied tastes.

Using the Quick View Tab

Visual InterDev has a great feature called Quick View. This allows you to preview the page without leaving the editor. When you use Quick View, you see how the page would look in Microsoft Internet Explorer 4.0. To Quick View your work, follow these steps:

1. Click on the Quick View tab located at the bottom of the Design window. The page displays as it would if it were being displayed by Internet Explorer (see Figure 5.6). It isn't very exciting at this point, but at least you get the idea.

2. Click on the Design tab to return to Design view.

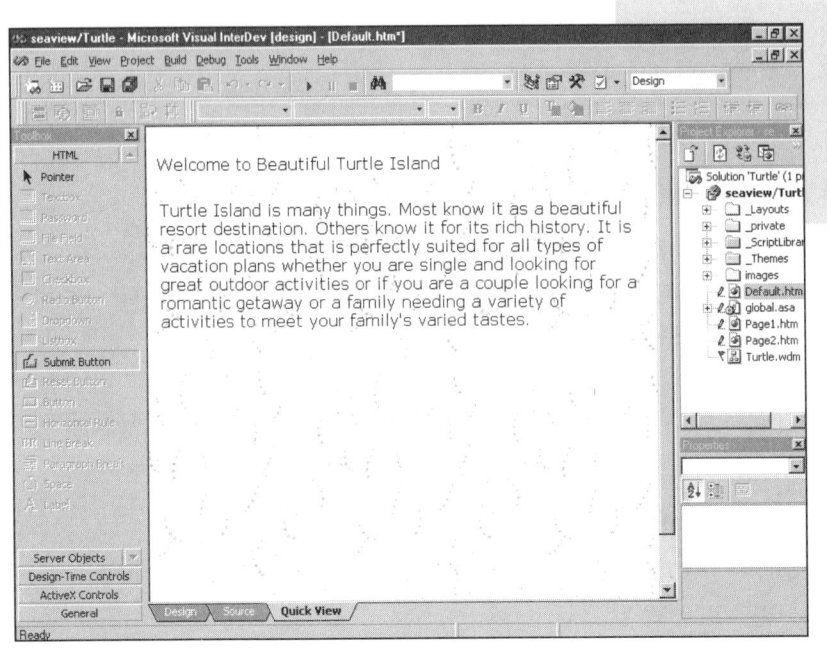

Figure 5.6 One of Visual InterDev's nicest features is its ability to quickly preview your work.

Formatting Text

If you are used to working with Microsoft Word, you should feel comfortable formatting text in Visual InterDev. If you aren't used to working with Microsoft Word, don't worry about it. Formatting text in Visual InterDev is really easy using the toolbar buttons available on the HTML toolbar (see Figure 5.7).

Figure 5.7
The HTML toolbar provides the tools you need to format the text on your page.

Changing the Font of Text

If you've worked with any Windows word processor, you know that to change the font of text, you highlight it and select a new font. To change the font, complete these steps:

1. Highlight Welcome to Beautiful Turtle Island.
2. Select Times New Roman from the Font Name drop-down toolbar element. The text reflects the change.
3. Position your cursor anywhere within the word Welcome.
4. Select Arial from the Font Name drop-down toolbar element. The entire word "Welcome" has its font set to Arial. If the insertion point, or cursor, is located within a word when you select a new font, Visual InterDev changes the font for that whole word.
5. Highlight just the W in Welcome.
6. Select Times New Roman from the Font Name drop-down toolbar element. Just the W reflects the change.

Note Don't worry about the text looking less than attractive at this point. You'll clean it up later.

Changing Other Text Settings

You can change a variety of things about your text. You can change its size, make it bold or italic, or underline it. You can also change its color and alignment. To experiment with these features, follow these steps:

1. Highlight Welcome to Beautiful Turtle Island.
2. Select 4 from the Font Size drop-down toolbar element. The text reflects the change.
3. Click on the Bold toolbar button. The text becomes bold.
4. Click on the Italic toolbar button. The text becomes italic.
5. Click on the Bold and Italic toolbar buttons again to remove these attributes.
6. Click on the Foreground Color toolbar button. The Color Picker dialog box displays (see Figure 5.8).

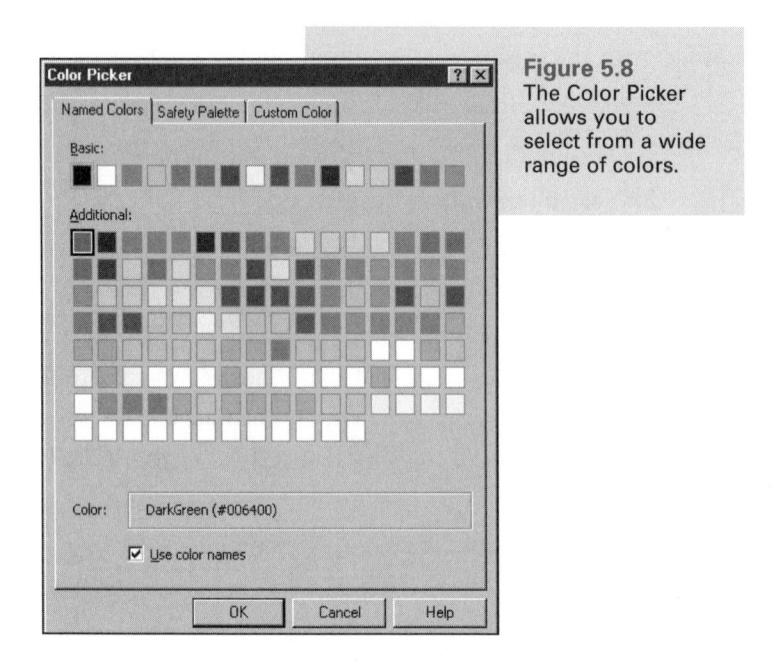

Figure 5.8
The Color Picker allows you to select from a wide range of colors.

7. Select a darker shade of green and click on OK. The text reflects the change.
8. Click on the Center toolbar button to center the text on the page.

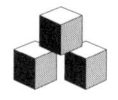

Using Paragraph Formats

As you saw in the previous section, Visual InterDev gives you a lot of flexibility when it comes to formatting text. But what if you don't want to do that much work? Visual InterDev addresses that need by providing you with HTML's paragraph formats. HTML Paragraph formats are named entities that allow you to quickly apply text attributes. To apply a paragraph format, follow these steps:

1. Position your insertion point anywhere within the text, "Welcome to Beautiful Turtle Island." Styles apply to a paragraph, so you don't have to highlight the whole paragraph.
2. Select Heading 1 from the Paragraph Format drop-down toolbar element. The selected paragraph has a new font, font size, and color.
3. Click on the Quick View tab. It looks a little better than it did before.
4. Click on the Design tab to return to Design view.

Adding a Graphic to Your Home Page

Adding multimedia, such as .GIF, .WAV, or .AVI files, to a Web page helps enliven the overall appearance and presentation of a page. You can easily add graphics and other HTML elements to your home page using the WYSIWYG approach of Design view in the HTML editor. To include a graphic on your home page:

1. Add a blank line after the second paragraph on this page.
2. Right-click on the images folder in Project Explorer. A pop-up menu displays.
3. Select Add, Add Item. The Add Item dialog box displays.
4. Select the Existing tab.
5. Select Image Files from the Files of Type drop-down list box.
6. Locate C:\Program Files\Microsoft Visual Studio\VintDev98\Samples\Gallery\content\themes\travel\TRABANNA.GIF and click on Open. The file is added to the project.
7. Select HTML, Image. The Insert Image dialog box displays, as shown in Figure 15.9.

Figure 5.9
The Insert Image dialog box allows you to insert available graphics into your current page.

8. Click on Browse. The Create URL dialog box displays, as shown in Figure 5.10.

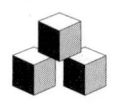

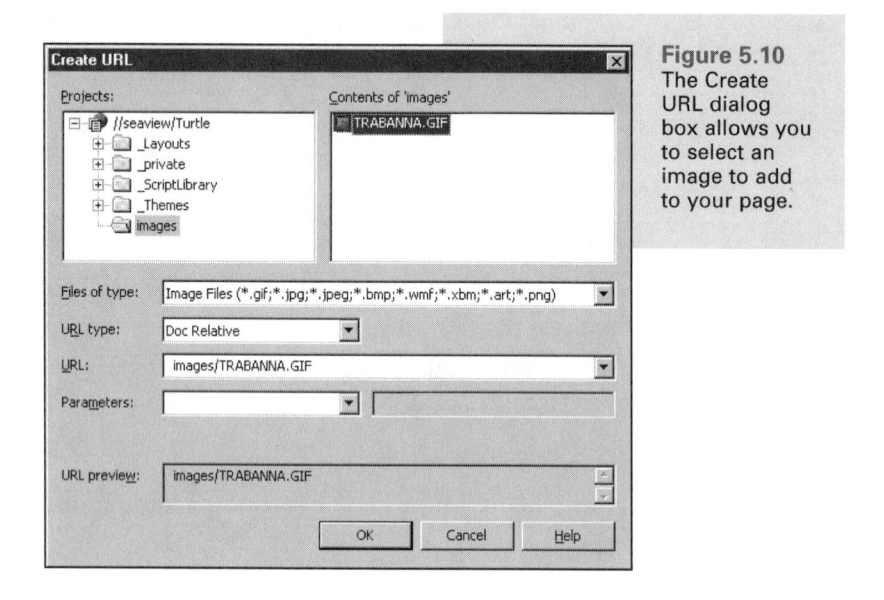

Figure 5.10
The Create URL dialog box allows you to select an image to add to your page.

9. Double-click on the folder icon for images to open it.
10. Select TRABANNA.GIF and click on OK. The file's name is placed in the Picture Source box.
11. Type Travel Banner in the Alternate Text box. This is the information you want visitors to see if the image doesn't display.
12. Click on OK.
13. Click on the Quick View tab. The page is really starting to shape up now, as seen in Figure 5.11.

CHAPTER 5 • DESIGNING THE TRAVEL SITE

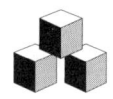

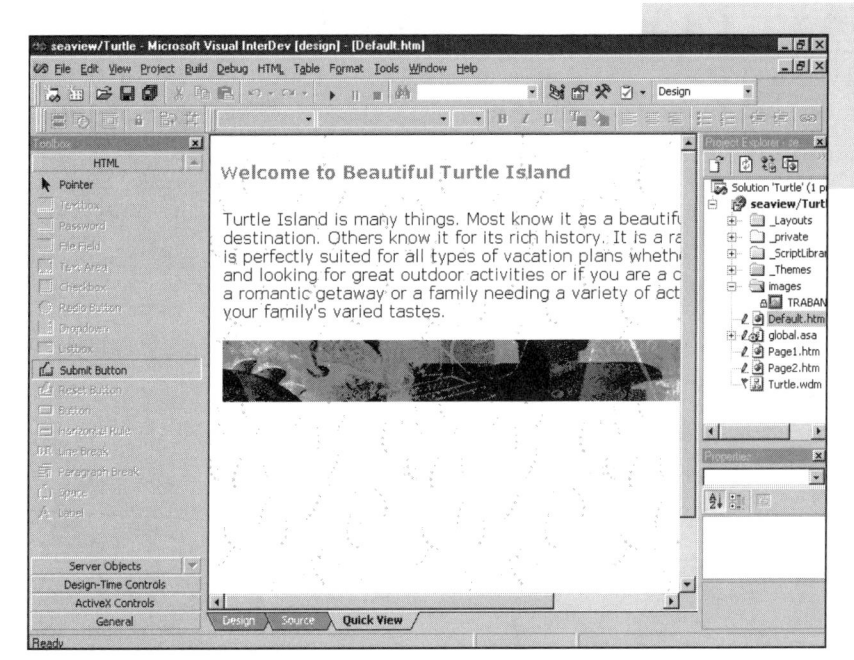

Figure 5.11
With very little work, your page shows improvement.

14. Click on the Design tab to return to Design view.

Saving a Page

As with any of your work, you should save frequently. Saving a file in Visual InterDev is like saving a file in another Windows application. Complete these steps:

1. Click on your home page to make sure it has Visual InterDev's focus.

> When an object is said to have the *focus*, it has the application's attention.

2. Select <u>F</u>ile, <u>S</u>ave (you will see the name of your home page listed as part of the menu name). The file is saved to your local machine.

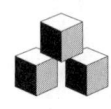

Previewing a Page in a Browser

You'll also want to look at your solution periodically in an actual browser. When you install Visual InterDev, the default browser is Microsoft Internet Explorer.

You can launch the default browser from Visual InterDev. To preview a page in a browser:

1. Select Default (the extension may be .HTM or .ASP, depending on the server you are using) or Index.htm from Project Explorer.
2. Right-click on Default and select View in Browser. The page displays in Internet Explorer (the automatically installed browser), as shown in Figure 5.12.

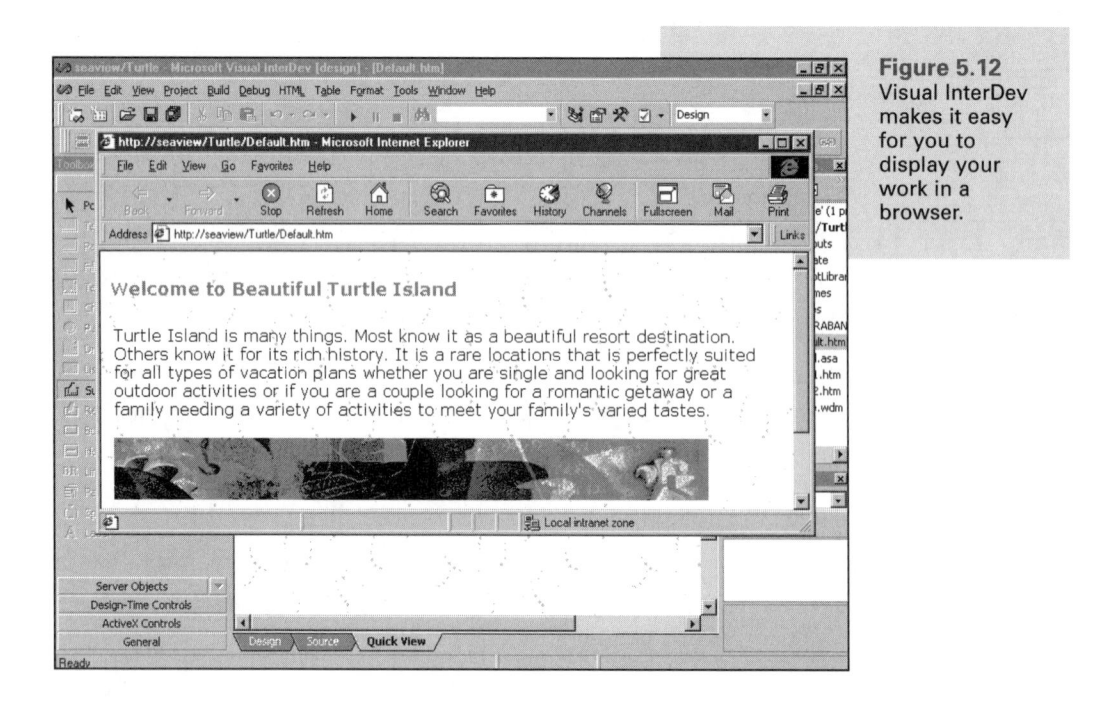

Figure 5.12
Visual InterDev makes it easy for you to display your work in a browser.

3. Close Internet Explorer. You return to Visual InterDev.

Changing the Look and Feel of Your Home Page

When you created your project, you selected a theme and a layout for it. You can select a different theme and a different layout any time you want to. This is a great feature because it allows you to experiment and prototype the look of your solution while developing the content of the solution.

Working with Themes

When you created your project, you selected a theme. As you have seen in this project, themes provide the visual appeal of a Web site. Some of the visual settings provided by themes are:

- Background images
- Bullet styles
- Fonts
- Font sizes
- Font colors
- Paragraph formats

The goal of a theme is not only to make your Web solution visually appealing, but also to make it visually consistent. Each page in your solution will have a similar look and feel because of its theme.

> **Note:** Even though themes are typically applied to a project, you can also apply a theme to a single page in a project.

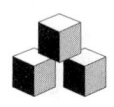

Changing the Theme of a Project

You can select a different theme after you have created your project. Follow these steps to apply a different theme to your project:

1. Select the project name from Project Explorer, which is default/Turtle.
2. Right-click on the project name and select Properties. The Project Properties dialog box displays (see Figure 5.13).

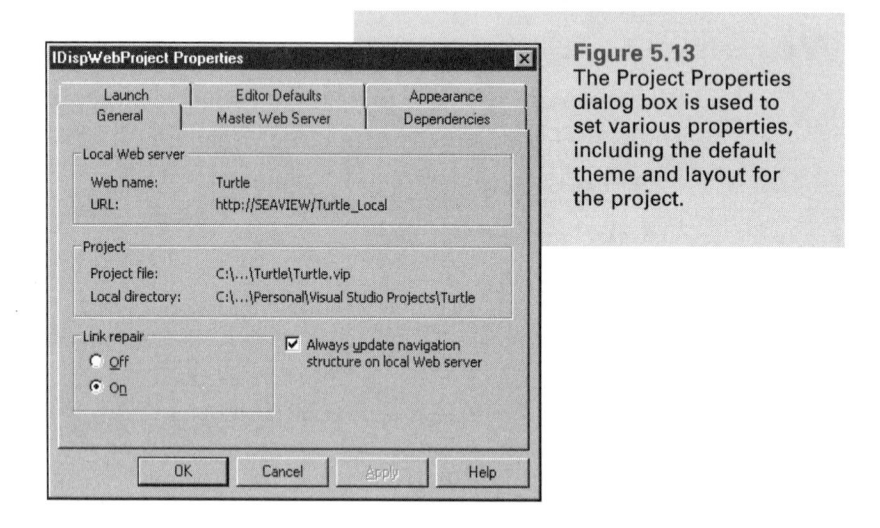

Figure 5.13
The Project Properties dialog box is used to set various properties, including the default theme and layout for the project.

3. Select the Appearance tab.
4. Click on Change. The Apply Theme and Layout dialog box displays (see Figure 5.14).
5. Select Apply Theme.
6. Select a theme from the list. It displays in the preview pane.
7. Click on OK. The new theme is applied to the project.
8. Click on OK to close the Project Properties dialog box.

Removing a Theme from a Project

You are never stuck with a theme. As a matter of fact, you don't have to use a theme at all if you don't want to. You can select to have no theme

Figure 5.14
The current theme is displayed in the Apply Theme and Layout dialog box.

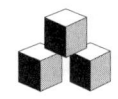

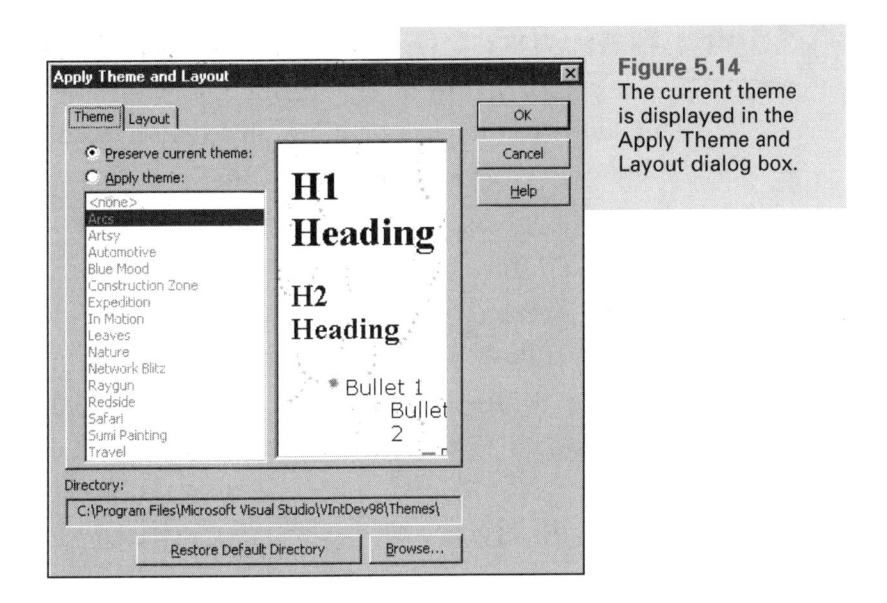

applied to your project. Since this project already has a theme, you'll need to remove it. To remove a theme from a project:

1. Select the project name, which is default/Turtle, from Project Explorer.
2. Right-click on the project name and select Properties. The Project Properties dialog box displays.
3. Select the Appearance tab.
4. Click on Change. The Apply Theme and Layout dialog box displays.
5. Select Apply Theme.
6. Select <none> from the top of the list.
7. Click on OK. The change is applied to the project.
8. Click on OK to close the Project Properties dialog box.

The theme is no longer applied to the project, but the theme files still exist in the project. You can verify this by looking for the theme files in Project Explorer. If you want to remove the files from the project, select the theme you no longer want from the Themes folder in Project Explorer. Right-click on the unwanted theme and select Delete.

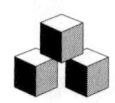

Adding Navigation to Your Pages

Layouts allow you to quickly define navigation bars for your project. This allows you to click on a button to move to another page in your Web site. To select a different layout for your project, follow these steps:

1. Select the project name from Project Explorer, which is default/Turtle.
2. Right-click on the project name and select Properties. The Project Properties dialog box displays.
3. Select the Appearance tab.
4. Click on Change. The Apply Theme and Layout dialog box displays.
5. Select the Layout tab (see Figure 5.15).

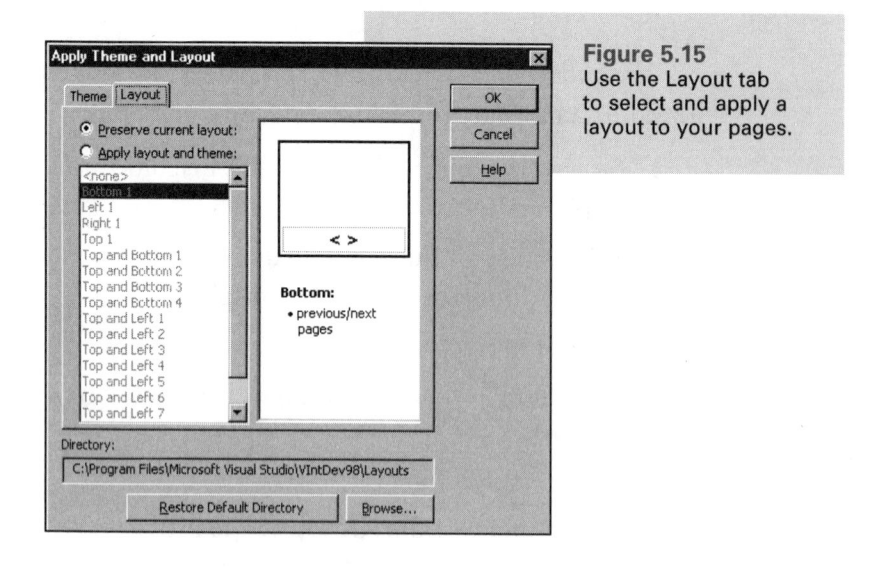

Figure 5.15
Use the Layout tab to select and apply a layout to your pages.

6. Select Apply Layout and Theme.
7. Select Top 1 from the list. It displays in the preview pane.
8. Click on OK. The new layout is applied to the project.
9. Click on OK to close the Project Properties dialog box.

Just as you could with themes, you can remove a layout. To remove a layout, repeat these steps, but select <none> as the layout. For this project, you want to have a layout, so don't remove the layout. As a matter of fact, return the project to its previous state:

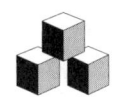

1. Select Edit, Apply Theme and Layout. The Apply Theme and Layout dialog box displays.
2. Select the Theme tab. The Theme page displays.
3. Select Apply Theme.
4. Select Arcs from the list. It displays in the preview pane.
5. Select the Layout tab. The Layout page displays.
6. Select Apply Layout and Theme.
7. Select Bottom 1. It displays in the preview pane.
8. Click on OK. The new theme and layout are applied to the project. A message box displays, prompting you to save your work.
9. Click on Yes. The changes are reflected in the view.

Working Locally

Visual InterDev provides two options for working online. In this chapter, you worked in Local mode.

In *Local mode*, you make changes to a working copy of the Web application without affecting the master Web application, because you are working with local copies of the Web project files that reside on your workstation. This means two things to you as a developer. One is that if you are working with others on the same project, you can make changes without interfering with the other developers on your team. But Local mode doesn't just provide benefits in the multideveloper environment. Even if you are the only developer on a project, you may want to develop in Local mode. By working in Local mode, you can prototype new versions of a project without affecting the original. This gives you a lot of flexibility to experiment with your Web pages without fear of ruining the current running version of the Web project. Once you are happy with the changes you have made, you will have to update the master Web application.

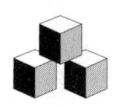

The other option is to work in *Master mode*. When you are working in Master mode, changes to the project and its files are saved to both the local workstation and the master files on the Web server. Local mode and Master mode are discussed in detail in Chapter 6.

Working Offline

If for some reason you need to work without a connection to the master Web server, you can choose to work offline. For example, you can place a local copy of your Web application on a laptop and work on the files offline. To enable offline mode, you would select Project, Web Project, Working Mode, Work Offline.

Exiting Visual InterDev

You're off to a great start, and you're ready to take a break. To exit Visual InterDev, follow these steps:

1. Select File, Exit. You'll be prompted to save changes.
2. Answer Yes to any file save prompts. Visual InterDev closes.

Summary

Good job! You've created your first Web solution. Hopefully you are thinking to yourself, "That was easy!" That's the point of Visual InterDev, to make it easy to do Web development. You've created your first project, added content in the form of text and graphics, and viewed it in your browser.

The next chapter is going to build on what you've done here. You are going to start adding pages to your project and learn how to link these pages together. You are also going to start looking at and working with the code that is being created for you behind the scenes by Visual InterDev.

CHAPTER 6

Building the Turtle Island Solution

In the last chapter, I basically had you jump in and create a simple Web application. You learned about themes and layouts as well as how to add text and graphics to a page. That chapter was designed to be an exercise in the basic functions of Visual InterDev. Now you are going to take a step back and discuss some of the concepts and theories behind what you did as you created a Web solution.

Understanding Visual InterDev's Modes

First, you will look at the project architecture of Visual InterDev. After completing Chapter 5, you now know that Visual InterDev is designed to enable you to focus on the content and appearance of your Web application. Visual InterDev shields you from the issues of file and source management by handling them for you. The first project you created added a graphic to your Web page. You might need clarification on two terms that I've been using— *Web application* and *Web project*. A Web application contains the files that hold your Web content and functionality for your Web site. These files include .htm, .asp, and image files. A Web project is not part of the Web application file set, but is a file used by Visual InterDev to point to the files associated with your Web application. You use the Web project to identify and manipulate your Web application files. The project file is the road map that the Web application consults to traverse the files the application uses.

When you start a project, a project file is created. This project file remains on your local computer. When the Web application is deployed, the project file does not get copied with it. The only files that are copied as part of the deployed Web application are those that contain your content (such as .htm files) and those that contain functionality (such as .asp files).

The files that the project file points to are listed in the Project Explorer. Use the Project Explorer to select the file you wish to work with. You can also perform tasks on files in the project by right-clicking on a file and using the pop-up menu.

Local and Master Modes

The other thing that you may not realize is that when you create a project, you are actually working with two separate Web applications. One set resides on the master Web server. These files are available to other developers or to your end users.

The other set of files resides on your local computer. When you make changes to the files in your project, the changes are made to the local set of files. This means that the changes you make to the project are not reflected in the master copy and do not affect the end users that use your Web solution.

This approach allows you to work independently of the master files. When you work on the local copy of the project, you are working in Local mode. You do your development, testing, and debugging in Local mode. Once you are happy with any changes you have made, you deploy them on the master server. Nothing here prevents you from working directly on the master copy of the project, but it is usually preferable to work on the local copy so that you do not impact visitors to your Web site.

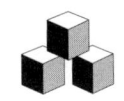

In a multideveloper environment, each developer can make a copy of the project on his own local system. He then makes any changes, tests the changes, and debugs them without impacting the other developers or the master application. Once he is finished, he can deploy his changes back to the master server.

Working in Local Mode

When you create a new project, you are prompted to choose to work in either Local mode or Master mode. As I've already said, if you choose to work in Local mode, the changes that you make are saved only to your local version of the files. The master Web application will only be updated with your changes when you choose to do so.

You may or may not have noticed what happened on your local system when you created your new project. First, a new folder was created to hold the local copy of your Web application. Within this folder, a subfolder was created. The Web server uses this subfolder when you preview or debug the pages of your project.

Files created include a series of Web project definition files. These files have the following extensions:

- .vip (Visual InterDev project file)
- .sln (solution definition file)
- .vic (Visual InterDev Cache file)

Other files and folders are also created on the basis of the layout and theme that you selected for the file. Other files and objects that may be a part of your Web application are listed here:

- You will probably have several files containing HTML code (.htm).
- You may also have some server scripts (.asp).
- The visual design of your application is created using templates, themes, layouts, images, and multimedia files.

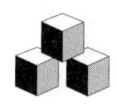

- Additional functionality can be added to your application using design-time controls.
- Record sets allow you to do data publishing as part of your application.
- If you wish to design interactive pages, you'll use ActiveX controls.

When you work in Local mode, the changes you make are applied to the local Web application. The local Web application mirrors the structure of the master Web application, though it may not mirror the content of the application. Think of the local copy as an editable snapshot of the master Web application.

Making Copies of Master Files

One of the requirements of working in Local mode is that you need to have copies of the master Web application files on your local system. Visual InterDev lets you get either write-enabled copies or read-only copies. Write-enabled copies are editable and are used to update the master Web application. To get a write-enabled copy of a file, follow these steps:

> **Note:** If you don't have Visual InterDev running, start it now. Select Turtle from the Recent tab when prompted.

1. In the Project Explorer, select TRABANNA.GIF.
2. Select Project, Web Files, Get Working Copy.

Often when you are testing your application, you'll find that a page has other files linked to it, such as graphics files. To be able to test these links while in Local mode, you'll need copies of these related files. To get related files, complete these steps:

1. In the Project Explorer, select your home page (Default.htm or Index.htm).
2. Select Project, Web Files, Get Latest Version.

Chapter 6 • Building the Turtle Island Solution

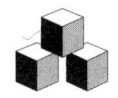

Instead of copying several single files and then getting its related files, you may find it easier to get a local copy of the entire Web application. To copy the entire Web application to your local system, follow these steps:

> **Caution:** Depending on the size of the Web application, this process may take quite a bit of time and space on your local system.

1. Select Project, Web Project, Refresh Project View.
2. Select Project, Web Files, Get Latest Version.

> **Note:** If you have any write-enabled copies on your local system when you perform this procedure (and the master version is newer), you will be prompted to merge, replace, or skip those copies.

Setting Your Project to Local Mode

It's easy to work locally. As a matter of fact, you created the project in the last chapter while working locally. To work locally, you'll need to open or create a project. Then you'll select local as your project mode. To work in Local mode, you'll need to have local copies of the files you want to work on. As long as you have those files, you can open them, edit them, and save your changes. Don't forget that the changes you make are saved only to the local copy and do not affect the master copy. You'll want to preview and test your changes at this point. When all is well, you'll update the master Web application.

To set the working mode of your project to Local mode, select Project, Web Project, Working Mode, Local.

> **Note:** You may have been in Local mode already. In this case, follow through on switching to it as an exercise.

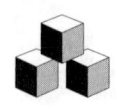

Working in Master Mode

If you decide to work in Master mode, the changes that you make to your local versions of the files are saved to the local and master versions simultaneously. When you start a new project and choose to work in Master mode, Visual InterDev still creates the save folders and files on your local system that it created when you selected to work in Local mode. In addition to those files and folders, it creates files and folders on the master Web server. Some of the files and folders are listed here:

- A folder referred to as the master Web application folder is created. This folder holds the master copies of the Web application. This folder is usually created as a subfolder of the Web server's root and has the same name as the Web application.

- An empty startup page named Global.asa may be created. Global.asa acts as a controlling hub for your application and is executed when a visitor opens a page of the application.

- If you chose to use the search functionality in your application, Search.htm will be created.

To place your project in Master mode, select Project, Web Project, Working Mode, Master. A message box displays, as shown in Figure 6.1. Click on Yes.

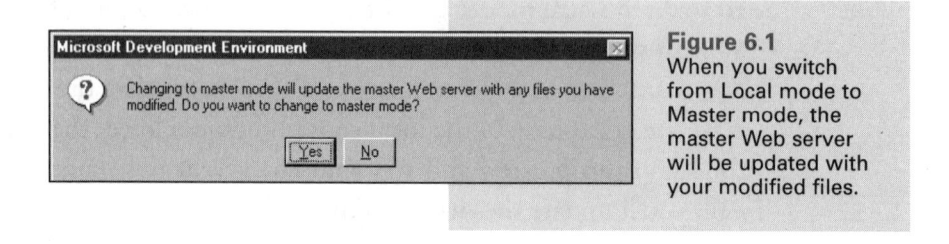

Figure 6.1
When you switch from Local mode to Master mode, the master Web server will be updated with your modified files.

Synchronizing Master and Local Files

Now that you know about the local and master copies of your work, you may be wondering, "How do I deal with applying changes to the two copies?" This is where *synchronization* comes into play. Synchronization is the process of updating either the local or master copies of your files. Because there are two copies of your Web application, you have several potential reasons for synchronizing your files. The first and possibly most obvious is that you want to apply the changes you have made to the local copy to the master copy. Another reason is that you are working in a multideveloper environment and want to get the latest version of the master application onto your local system. You may also want to refresh your Project Explorer file list. The Project Explorer file list lists the files found in the master and local applications. You may not want all the files found in the master application on your local system, but you may want to know about them.

> *Local files* that have not been copied to the master directory are called *personal files*. *Master files* are those that exist on the master server and are not in your local directory.

Updating the Master Application

Let's say that you've been working in Local mode and are ready to add your changes to the master Web application. The process of updating your master Web application with your local files is called *releasing* your files. To update the master Web application, follow these steps:

1. In the Project Explorer, select the files you want to save to the master Web application.
2. Select Project, Web Files, Release Working Copy. Your local files are copied to the master Web server.

Note If another developer has made changes to the master version since you got the copy you changed, the Merge dialog box displays. This dialog box allows you to review the differences and accept or reject the changes.

Discarding Changes Made to a Local Copy

Have you ever made a bunch of changes to a file and afterward decided you didn't like them? Visual InterDev lets you discard your changes and replace your local copy with a copy of the same file from the master Web application. Use these steps to discard changes to a local copy:

1. In the Project Explorer, select the files you do not want to save to the master Web application.
2. Select Project, Web Files, Discard Changes. Your local copy of each selected file is replaced by the master version of the file, and therefore changes to the local copy are discarded.

Updating the Local Web Application

Here's the next scenario: You've been out of the office for a few days, and you decide that you'd like to get the changes to the master Web application copied to your local system. You do this by updating, otherwise known as synchronizing, your local application with the master application using these steps:

1. In the Project Explorer, select the project with the files you want to get.
2. Select Project, Web Project, Synchronize Files. Any master files that have been changed are copied to your local application.

Refreshing the Project Explorer

Earlier I said that you might want to update the list of local and master files shown in the Project Explorer. This is called *refreshing your project view*. Any files that have been added, deleted, renamed, or moved in the master Web application are reflected in your Project Explorer.

To refresh the Project Explorer, select Project, Web Project, Refresh Project View. A message box may display letting you know the files are being refreshed. If you are prompted, answer Yes to All to reload files.

Working Offline

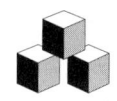

Maybe you need to demonstrate your Web application at a location that doesn't have a server connection. Or maybe the server is down. Fear not, you can work offline.

If you are working offline, any command that requires a connection to a server is not available. When working offline, you can open a project, edit local copies of files, and preview your work. All this can be done without a connection to a Web server.

To work offline, you open or create a project. Just as with Local mode, you'll need to have a local copy of the files you want to work on. Then you set the working mode of your project to work offline. You're now ready to work offline. You can open files, edit them, and save your changes.

> **Note** You must be online to rename files in the project, move files, or modify the site structure.

As you can see, working offline is similar to working in Local mode. Preview and test your changes. When you are ready, apply your changes to the master Web application, set your project working mode to work online, and update the master Web server.

Use these steps to set your project to offline:

1. In the Project Explorer, select the Web project you want to take offline. Make sure you have local copies of the files you want to work on and related files you need for testing in your local Web application.

2. Select Project, Web Project, Working Mode, Work Offline. You are now set to work offline. Answer Yes to All if you are prompted about reloading files. Now go through the process of returning the project to online mode. Work Offline is actually a toggle menu selection, so you are going to use the same steps to return to online mode.

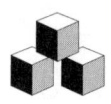

3. Select Project, Web Project, Working Mode, Work Offline. You are now set to work online. Answer Yes if you are prompted about reloading files.

When you work with your project in offline mode, you work with the project in basically the same way that you would in Local mode. There are a few commands that you can't perform in offline mode, including the following:

- Update the master Web application.
- Release working copies of files.
- Get the latest versions of your project from the master Web server.
- Move files in the project.

Expanding the Project

A couple of years ago, a single-page Web site was common. This is no longer true. Most Web sites have multiple pages. At this point, you are ready to add pages to your project. To do this, you'll use a *site diagram*. A site diagram is a graphical representation of the pages in your Web project. Lines between the pages in the site diagram represent the navigation structure of your project.

Adding Files to the Project

Adding pages to your application is really easy to do. All you do is add a page to your project and then determine how you want to incorporate the page into your navigation scheme. You add the page in the site diagram, and it becomes part of the project. To add pages to your application, use these steps:

1. Double-click on Turtle.wdm from the Project Explorer to open it.
2. Select Project, Add Item. The Add Item dialog box, shown in Figure 6.2, displays.

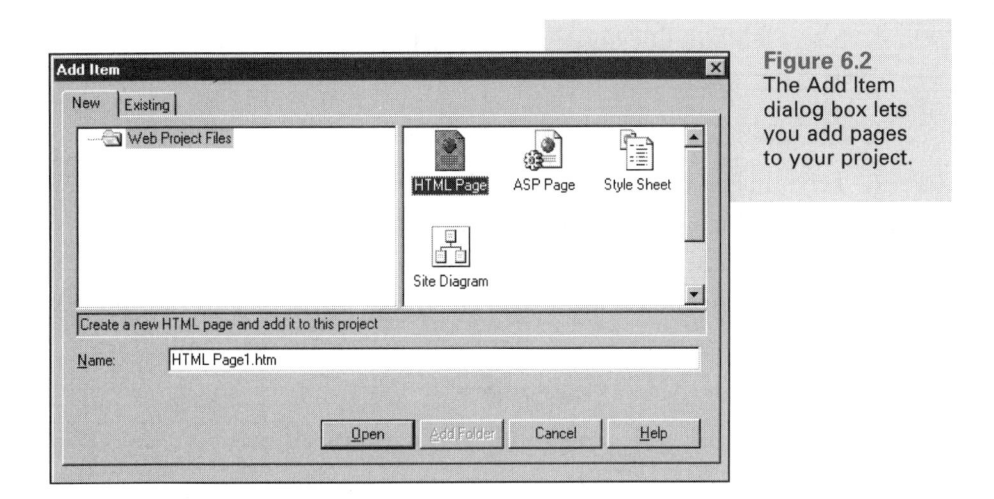

CHAPTER 6 • BUILDING THE TURTLE ISLAND SOLUTION   89

Figure 6.2
The Add Item dialog box lets you add pages to your project.

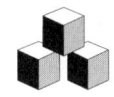

3. Select HTML Page and click on Open. In a few moments, the newly created page opens (see Figure 6.3).

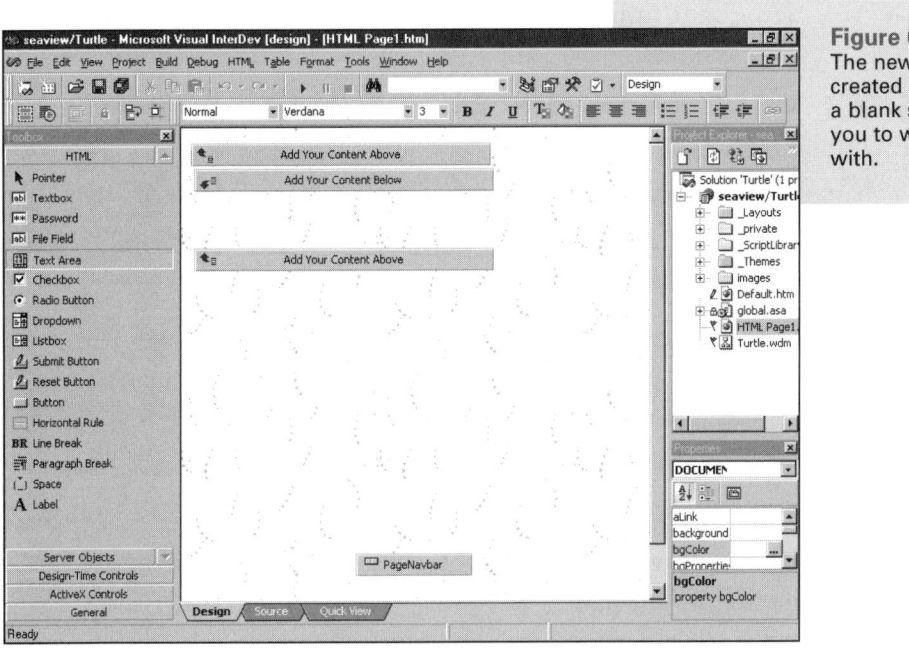

Figure 6.3
The newly created page is a blank slate for you to work with.

4. Insert a blank line above Add Your Content Above.
5. Type Lodging.
6. Click in the area below Add Your Content Below.
7. Type this text: **Turtle Island offers you a variety of lodging ranging from bed and breakfasts to luxury hotels. We have historic inns, contemporary rental cottages, as well as budget-priced accommodations. And of course Turtle Island has resort properties complete with pools, tennis courts, and golf courses.**
8. Add another page to the project.
9. Insert a blank line above Add Your Content Above.
10. Type **Shopping**.
11. Click in the area below Add Your Content Below.
12. Type this text: **Turtle Island is a shopper's paradise! After all, you can only spend so many hours a day outside before longing for the cool indoors and some stimulating bargain hunting!**
13. Save Page1.htm, Page2.htm, and Turtle.wdm.

Working with Themes at the Page Level

Establish a consistent visual appearance for your pages to give your Web site a professionally designed look. You can use a Microsoft theme to give your home page visual consistency. To create a consistent visual look:

1. In the Project Explorer, select your Page 1.
2. Select Edit, Apply Theme and Layout. The Apply Theme and Layout dialog box displays.
3. Select the Theme tab.
4. Select the Apply theme button.
5. Choose Travel from the list box. A graphic of the theme appears in the preview pane.
6. Click on OK. The Theme is applied to this page.
7. Select File, Save. The changes are saved.

Working with the Global Navigation Bar

When designing a site with multiple pages, you'll need a way for your user to navigate your site. Visual InterDev lets you do this using a *global navigation bar*. A global navigation bar has links to the most used or useful links for your site. Using the Diagram menu from the site diagram, you can add pages to the global navigation menu. You can also use the Add/Remove Global Navigation Bar toggle button found on the Site Diagram toolbar. To add a page to your global navigation bar, follow these steps:

1. Select Window, Turtle.wdm to open the site diagram.
2. Drag Page 1 from the Project Explorer into the site diagram.
3. Drag Page 2 from the Project Explorer into the site diagram.
4. Select Page 1 from the site diagram.
5. Select Diagram, Add to Global Navigation Bar. The page is added to the global navigation bar, which is denoted by the same page icon that appears on the page in the site diagram.
6. Select Page 2 from the site diagram.
7. Click on the Add Global Navigation Bar toolbar button found on the Site Diagram toolbar. The page is added to the global navigation bar, which is denoted by the same page icon that appears on the page in the site diagram.

Once you've added pages to the global navigation bar, there is very little to do in the way of maintaining it. As a matter of fact, unless you plan to remove a page from the global navigation bar, you'll only need to change the order of the pages with this feature. You can move a page either up or down. To reorder pages, follow these steps:

1. Select Diagram, Reorder Global Navigation Bar. The Reorder Global Navigation Bar dialog box displays, as shown in Figure 6.4.
2. Select Page 2 and click on Move Up to make it the first item in page order.
3. Select Page 2 and click on Move Down to make it the last item in page order.

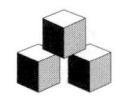

Figure 6.4
You can change the order of the pages in the global navigation bar using this dialog box.

4. Click on OK to close the dialog box.
5. Select the Home page.
6. Select <u>V</u>iew, View in <u>B</u>rowser. If you are prompted to save changes, answer <u>Y</u>es. Your application is displayed in Internet Explorer, as shown in Figure 6.5.

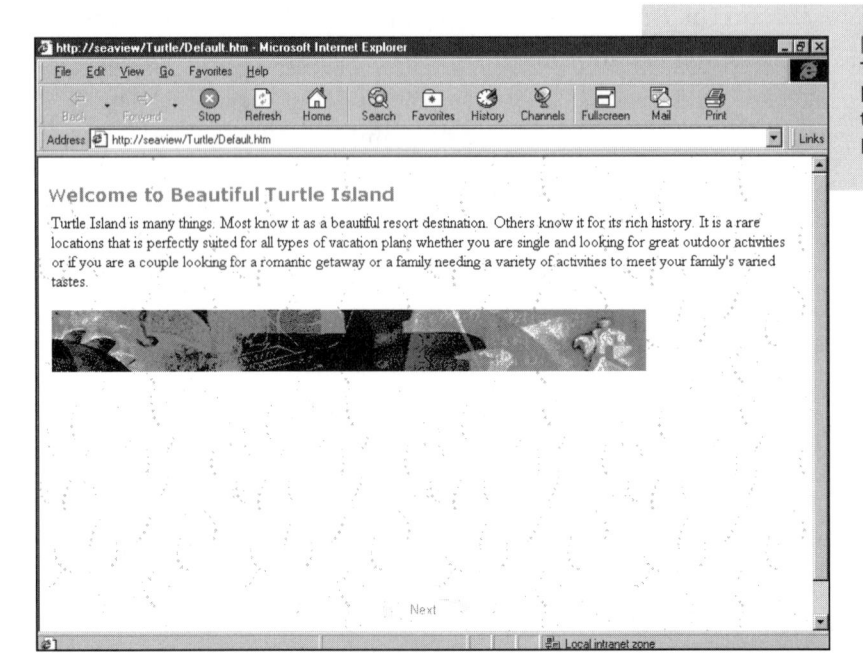

Figure 6.5
The navigation bar allows you to move from page to page.

CHAPTER 6 • BUILDING THE TURTLE ISLAND SOLUTION   93

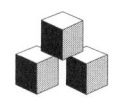

> **Note**
>
> This exercise relies on the PageNavBar control on your home page. To use the PageNavBar control (which should have been added to your page when you selected a layout), you must have the Microsoft FrontPage 98 Server Extensions installed on your system. These are typically part of the Visual InterDev installation.

7. Click on the Next button. Page 1 displays.
8. Click on the Next button. Page 2 displays.
9. Click on the Back button. Page 2 displays.
10. Close Internet Explorer. You are returned to Visual InterDev.
11. Open Page 1 in Design view.

The PageNavbar control (see Figure 6.6) on your page automatically generates navigation bar links based on the navigation structure you created in your site diagram.

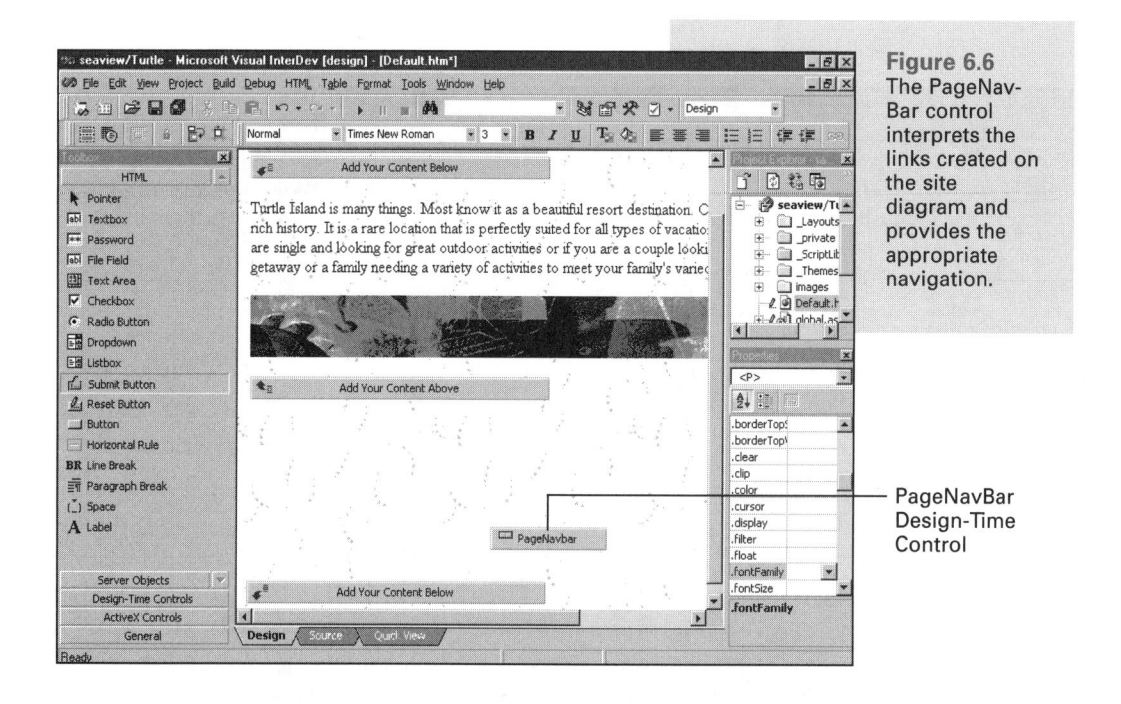

Figure 6.6
The PageNav-Bar control interprets the links created on the site diagram and provides the appropriate navigation.

PageNavBar Design-Time Control

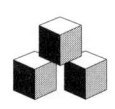

You haven't had a chance to work much with properties yet. Properties allow you to set attributes for objects on a page. They are set using the Properties window. To start your introduction to properties, you will work with some of PageNavBar control's properties. The first property of the PageNavBar control that you will look at is the IncludeHome property. The default value of this property is False, which means that the home page is not included as a link on the navigation bar. You may have noticed this when you looked at your project in the browser. If you wanted to include the home page in the navigation bar, you would set this property's value to True. To experiment with this property and include your home page as part of the navigation bar, use the following steps:

1. Select <u>V</u>iew, View in <u>B</u>rowser. In a few moments, your page displays in your browser. Look at the bottom of the page to locate the navigation bar. You'll find that there are two buttons: Previous and Next (see Figure 6.7). It would be nice to have a Home button as well. The next few steps will add this feature.

2. Close the browser window. You are returned to Visual InterDev.

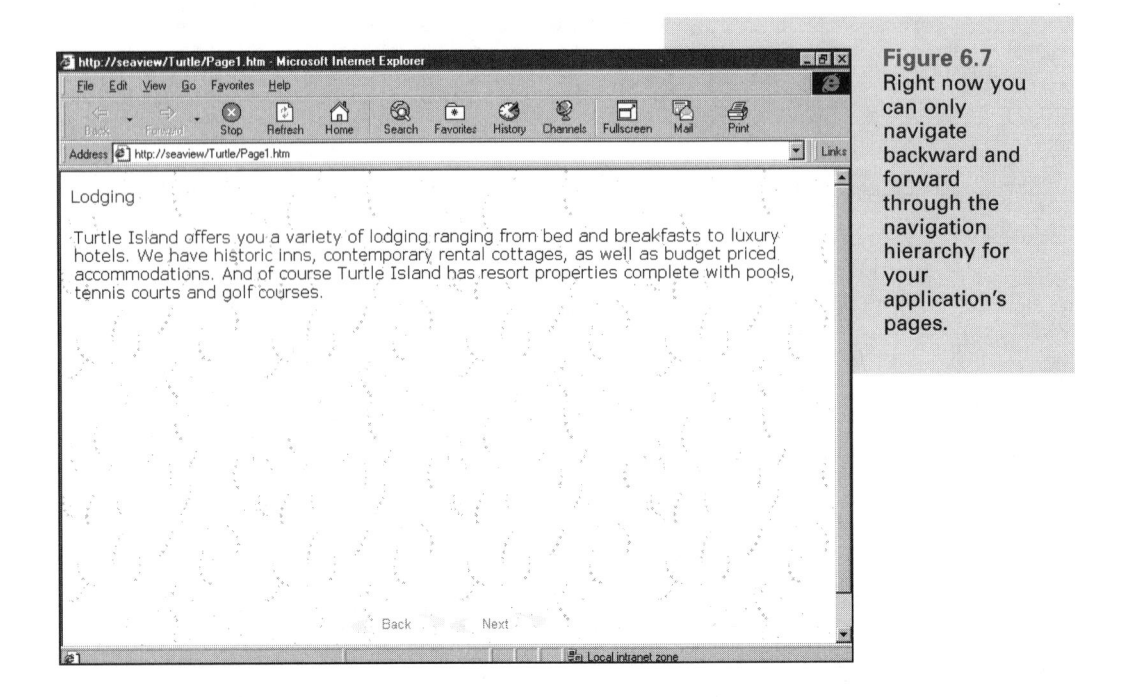

Figure 6.7
Right now you can only navigate backward and forward through the navigation hierarchy for your application's pages.

CHAPTER 6 • BUILDING THE TURTLE ISLAND SOLUTION

3. From the Design window, select the PageNavBar control.
4. Locate and select the IncludeHome property from the Properties window. You will then see a selection button display.
5. Click on the selection button for this property. There are two available settings: True and False.

> **Tip**
> When you are setting a property that has a selection arrow associated with it, you can double-click on the property's value to toggle through the possible options. For example, you can double-click on True to set the property to False and vice versa.

6. Select True. This includes the Home page in the navigation bar.
7. Select File, Save Page1.htm to save the changes you have made.
8. Select View, View in Browser. In a few moments, your page displays in your browser. Look at the bottom of the page to locate the navigation bar. You'll find that a new button has been added to the navigation bar, Home (see Figure 6.8).

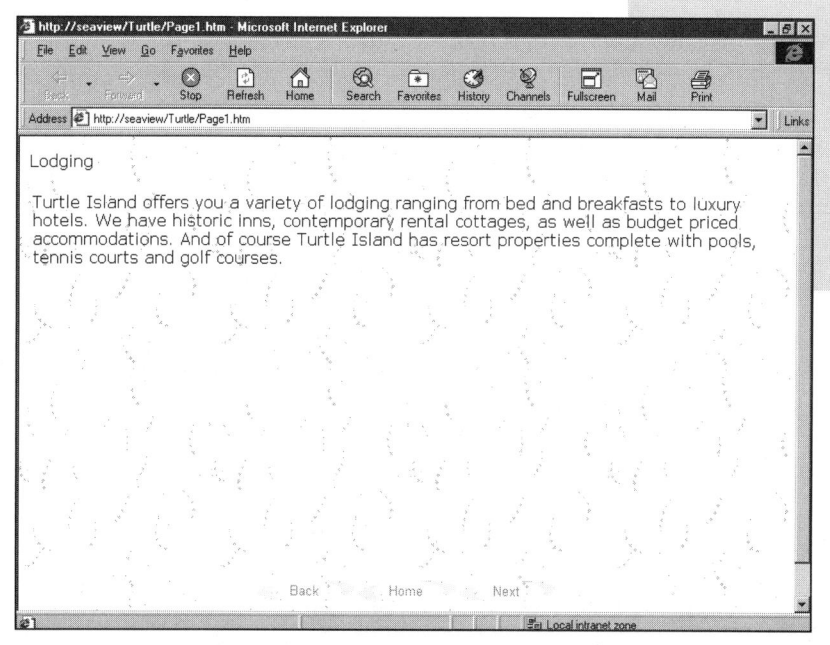

Figure 6.8
By setting the IncludeHome property to True, you've added a link from the navigation bar to the home page.

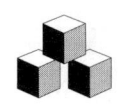

9. Close the browser window. You are returned to Visual InterDev.

The change that you made to the PageNavBar's IncludeHome property only applies to the navigation bar found on Page1. If you wanted to include the home page as part of another navigation bar, you would have to go to that page and set that PageNavBar's IncludeHome property to True. By letting you set properties for each individual PageNavBar control (or any control), Visual InterDev provides you with control and flexibility in your site's design.

You can also set the navigation link structure for your PageNavBar by using its properties dialog box. You may prefer this method because the interface provides you with graphical information about your choice. To access the properties dialog box of the PageNavBar control, complete the following steps:

1. Right-click on the PageNavBar control.
2. Select Properties. The PageNavBar dialog box displays.
3. Select the General tab. The available Type settings display, as shown in Figure 6.9. Also notice that Home and Parent are checked. These two settings equate to the IncludeHome and IncludeParent properties found in the Properties window.
4. Click on the various Type options. You will see that the diagram on the left side of the dialog box changes to reflect the meaning of the current Type setting.

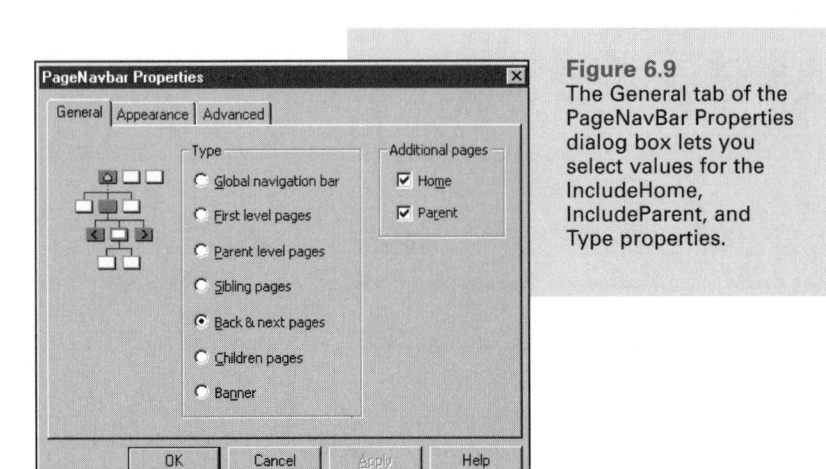

Figure 6.9
The General tab of the PageNavBar Properties dialog box lets you select values for the IncludeHome, IncludeParent, and Type properties.

5. You aren't going to change any of these settings, so click on Cancel to close the dialog box.

The Type property is used to select the type of links the PageNavbar control includes on the navigation bar. These links are based on the navigation structure you defined in the site diagram. There are seven possible values for the Type property, as detailed in Table 6.1.

Table 6.1 Type Property Values

Navigation structure	Description	Setting
Global navigation bar	Displays links for all pages. Included as part of the global navigation bar in the site diagram.	Global
First level pages	Displays links for all child pages of the home page.	First
Parent level pages	Displays links for pages one level above the current page.	Parent
Sibling pages	Displays links for pages at the same level as the current page.	Siblings
Back and next pages	Displays Previous and Next links for pages at the same level as the current page.	Arrows
Children pages	Displays links for pages one level below the current page.	Children Children
Banner	Displays the title of the current page overlaid on a graphic. The theme applied to the page controls the graphic used.	Banner

That covers the discussion of some of PageNavBar's properties. You will find that the IncludeHome and Type properties are the two properties that you work with most for this control.

Using an Editor

Up to this point, you've worked with your project in three views: Site Diagram view, Design view, and Quick view. Design view displays the text of your pages in much the same manner as a word processor. Quick view allows you to preview your .htm files as they would look in Internet Explorer. Another view that you haven't worked with is Source view. Source view lets you see and edit text, HTML tags, and script. This section will build on your previous experience with the HTML editor's views.

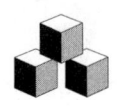

Using Design View

In Chapter 5, you used Design view to add content to your home page. As you know, Design view makes it easy to view and edit HTML text in a format similar to what it will look like in a browser. The real beauty of working in Design view is that you don't have to know HTML. All you need to do is point, click, and type. If you want to change the appearance of text on the page, you simply highlight it and apply formatting as you would in a word processor. As you add text and other objects to your page, the page has a browser-like appearance and displays the formatting that you've applied. Design view also reflects any HTML-style information tags or cascading style sheets, if you are using one. I said earlier that Design view presents your page in a manner similar to a browser. The differences are listed here:

- Links are not live.
- Character and paragraph formatting might look different. This is because each browser often implements formatting differently.
- Comments, unrecognized HTML tags, and some elements can be displayed as glyphs. This allows you to know that they are in the page.
- You have the option to display a border around elements that are invisible when displayed in the browser. With this option activated, you can see where these elements are by clicking on the Visible Borders toolbar button from the Design toolbar.
- Client scripts do not run.

Using Quick View

You've already used Quick view (see Figure 6.10) to get a preview of what an .htm file will look like in Internet Explorer. Because Quick view

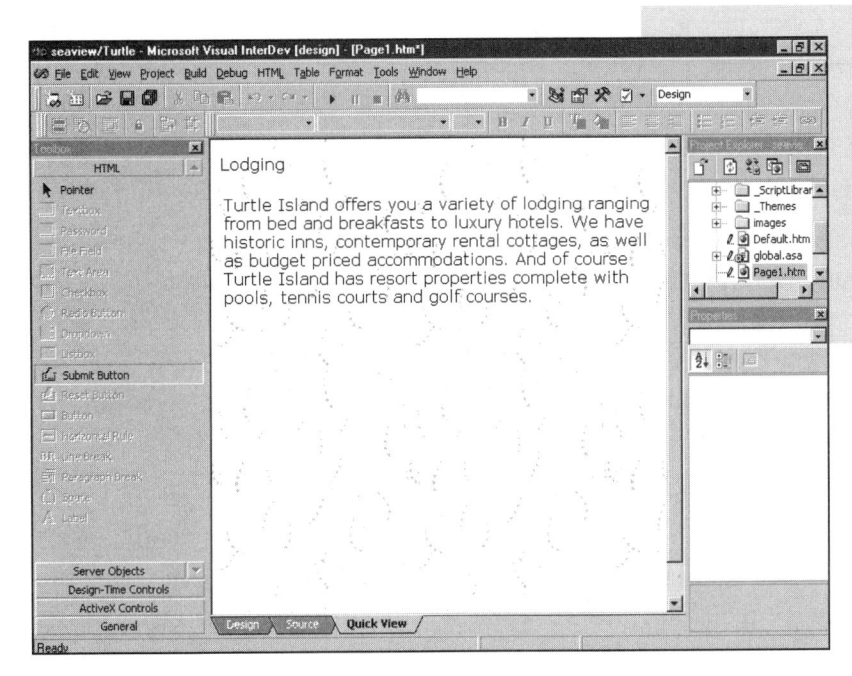

CHAPTER 6 • BUILDING THE TURTLE ISLAND SOLUTION   99

Figure 6.10
Quick view gives you an idea of the layout and appearance of your page, but does not let you test the functionality of the page.

displays your page in a browser, you can't edit or debug the page in this view. The other thing that you'll notice about Quick view is that your navigation bar does not display. You need to view the page in a browser to see the navigation bar.

> **Tip**
> Quick view does not process the page through the server. Because of this, you can't get an accurate view of what .asp files will look like. To preview a document containing server elements, select <u>V</u>iew, View in <u>B</u>rowser.

Using Source View

If you are an experienced HTML jockey, you may prefer to work with the raw HTML of your page. Source view allows you to edit your page's HTML and work directly with script. An interesting feature of Source view is that it gives you the option of graphically representing Visual InterDev design-time controls, ActiveX controls, and Java applets.

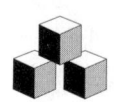

Source view provides you with an advanced HTML editor environment. If you are used to working in Microsoft's other development environments, you'll find Source view comfortably familiar. Visual InterDev uses different colors for the text displayed so that you can easily distinguish script keywords, HTML tags, attributes, comments, and so on.

You can set properties in Source view using the Properties window, just as you did in Design view. You can also set their properties using a custom Property Pages window. Changes you make in the Properties window or in Property Pages dialog boxes are reflected in the HTML source code for those objects. If you aren't familiar with HTML, you can use this feature to learn some of the available HTML tags.

If your page contains scripts, you can see the source code of the scripts in Source view. While in Source view, you can use the Script Outline window to view scriptable elements in your page and to see what scripts are already created. You will start working with scripts later in this chapter.

Working with HTML

This section will give you a quick overview of working with HTML. If you are already familiar with HTML, this section will be a review. I'll try to make it brief and painless!

To display text in a Web page, you simply start a new HTML document (.htm file) or ASP page (.asp file) and enter text onto the page. If you want to format the text or add features such as images or links to your page, you use HTML (Hypertext Markup Language). HTML is built around *tags*, which are formatting instructions embedded in the text. Tags are surrounded by angle brackets (< and >) to separate them from the surrounding text. Tags are usually used in pairs around the text you want to format. The basic format is an opening tag, the text, and a closing tag, which is marked with a slash (/). This is the basic format for a tag:

`<tag>text</tag>`

For example, this line shows how you would format some text as bold:

`<B>Hello</B> World!`

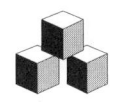

The opening tag (<B>) represents bold. The text that the tag is being applied to is "Hello." The closing tag is identified by its / (</B>). When this line is displayed in a browser, it would look like this:

Hello World!

The type of tag just used is called a *container tag*. The tag itself contains the text to be formatted. The other type of tag available is called an *empty tag*. Empty tags, also called open tags, are used to represent formatting constructs such as line breaks. Tags of this type perform operations that don't apply to specific text. Some commonly used HTML tags are listed in Table 6.2.

Table 6.2 Commonly Used HTML Tags

Tag	Use
<A>	Anchor: source or destination of a link
<B>	Bold
<H1>	Heading level 1
<H2>	Heading level 2
<H3>	Heading level 3
<H4>	Heading level 4
<H5>	Heading level 5
<H6>	Heading level 6
<HEAD>	Document head
<HR>	Horizontal line
<I>	Italic
<IMG>	Image; icon; etc.
<LINK>	Link from this document
<P>	Paragraph
<PRE>	Preformatted text
<TABLE>	Table definition
<TD>	Table data is contained in these tags
<TR>	Each row of a table is contained by this tag

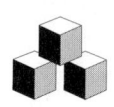

Visual InterDev lets you work with HTML in each of its three views. In Design view, you can format text and paragraphs as you would in a word processor, and the editor will embed the appropriate HTML tags for you. In Source view, you can edit HTML tags directly. In Quick view, you can see what .htm files will look like in Internet Explorer. At any time during the editing process, whether you are using Design view or Source view, you can switch between views to see the effects of edits you are making. Take a few moments to analyze the HTML that has been generated for you by Visual InterDev. Complete these steps:

1. Double-click on your home page file (default or index) from the Project Explorer to open it.
2. Click on the Source tab. The HTML source code for your home page displays (see Figure 6.11).

The first thing you'll probably notice as you look at the code displayed is that different words are in different colors. Visual InterDev uses these

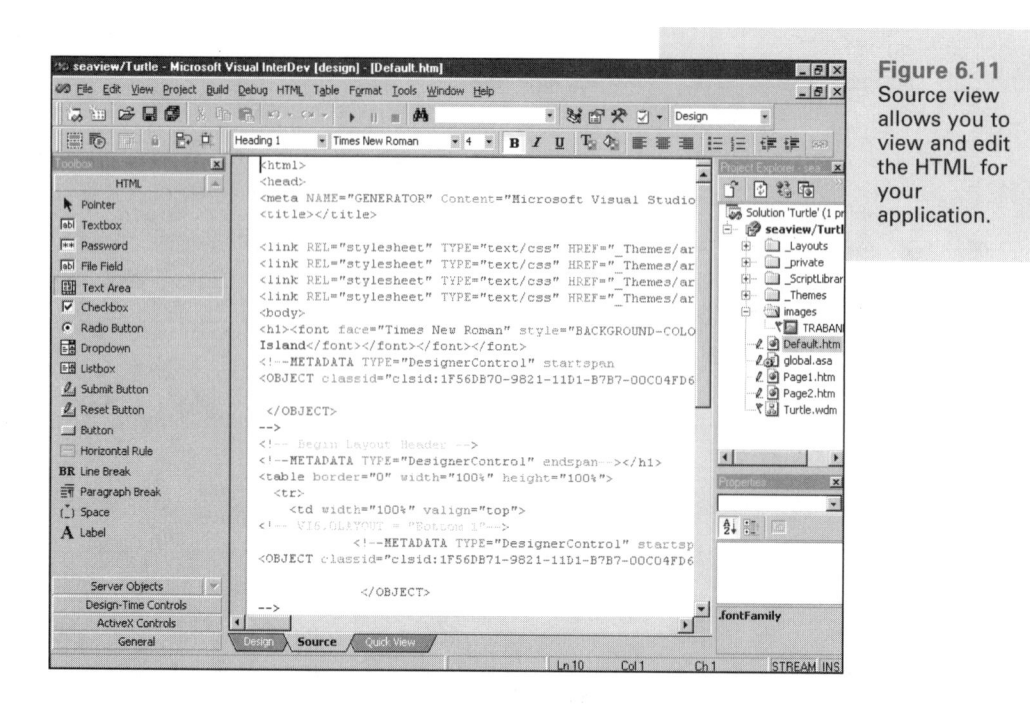

Figure 6.11
Source view allows you to view and edit the HTML for your application.

CHAPTER 6 • BUILDING THE TURTLE ISLAND SOLUTION

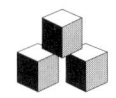

colors to guide you and inform you about the different text components being used. The colors have these meanings:

- Purple: tag names
- Red: attribute names
- Blue: attribute values
- Grey: comments
- Black: HTML text

If you don't like the default colors used by Source view, you can change them using these steps:

1. Select Tools, Options. The Options dialog box displays.
2. From the outline box, click on the plus sign beside Text Editor. The outline expands.
3. Select Font and Colors. The options for fonts and colors display, as shown in Figure 6.12.
4. At this point, you can select a display item and then choose a color. For the sake of this exercise, you are just going to leave this dialog box alone. Click on Cancel.

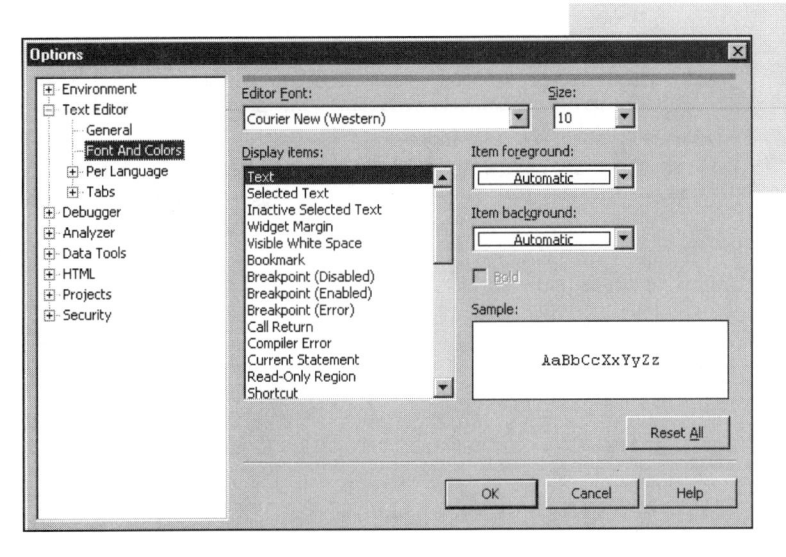

Figure 6.12
Visual InterDev allows you to change the colors used by Source view.

Hands On Project 1 • The Travel Site

The code displayed is as follows:

```html
<html>
<head>
<meta NAME="GENERATOR" Content="Microsoft Visual Studio 6.0">
<title></title>

<link REL="stylesheet" TYPE="text/css" HREF="_Themes/arcs/THEME.CSS" VI6.0THEME="Arcs">
<link REL="stylesheet" TYPE="text/css" HREF="_Themes/arcs/GRAPH0.CSS" VI6.0THEME="Arcs">
<link REL="stylesheet" TYPE="text/css" HREF="_Themes/arcs/COLOR0.CSS" VI6.0THEME="Arcs">
<link REL="stylesheet" TYPE="text/css" HREF="_Themes/arcs/CUSTOM.CSS" VI6.0THEME="Arcs"></head>
<body>
<h1><font face="Arial"><font face="Times New Roman"><font size="4"><font color="green"><font>W</font></font></font></font><font><font color="green"><font size="4">elcome</font></font></font></font><font><font color="green"><font size="4"> to Beautiful
Turtle Island</font></font></font></h1>
<p>
</p>
<table border="0" width="100%" height="100%">
    <tr>
        <td width="100%" valign="top">
<!-- VI6.0LAYOUT = "Bottom 1" -->
<p> Turtle Island is many things. Most know it
            as a beautiful resort destination. Others know it for its rich
            history. It is a rare location that is perfectly suited for all
            types of vacation plans, whether you are single and looking for
            great outdoor activities, a couple looking for a romantic
            getaway, or a family needing a variety of activities to meet
            your family's varied tastes.p>
            <p><img alt src="TRABANNA.GIF" WIDTH="600" HEIGHT="60"></p>
</td>
    </tr>
    <tr>
        <td width="100%" height="80" align="center">
</td>
    </tr>
</table>
<!-- Layout Footer End -->
</body>
</html>
```

The first lines of this code are shown here:

```html
<html>
<head>
```

Chapter 6 • Building the Turtle Island Solution

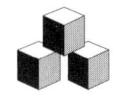

```
<meta NAME="GENERATOR" Content="Microsoft Visual Studio 6.0">
<title></title>
```

The `<html>` statement identifies your document as containing HTML elements. The `<head>` statement starts an area of information about your document. The first piece of this information is provided by the `<meta>` statement. The `<meta>` statement provides information to browsers, search engines, and other applications about your document. The `<title>` statement, which in this case is empty, provides a kind of global title or descriptor for your document. The next series of statements, listed here, are also part of the head section:

> **Note**
> The `<title>` tag is actually very important. Most search engines use it to locate and index documents, and when a user bookmarks a page, the title is used as the identifying text. The `<title>` displays as the browser window name too.

```
<link REL="stylesheet" TYPE="text/css" HREF="_Themes/arcs/THEME.CSS"
VI6.0THEME="Arcs">
<link REL="stylesheet" TYPE="text/css" HREF="_Themes/arcs/GRAPH0.CSS"
VI6.0THEME="Arcs">
<link REL="stylesheet" TYPE="text/css" HREF="_Themes/arcs/COLOR0.CSS"
VI6.0THEME="Arcs">
<link REL="stylesheet" TYPE="text/css" HREF="_Themes/arcs/CUSTOM.CSS"
VI6.0THEME="Arcs"></head>
```

The `<link>` statement specifies relationships between your HTML document and other resources. You can see from these statements that there are links to style sheets. Notice that the last line in this code snippet closes with `</head>`. This closes the head section, leading to the next line, which starts the body of your document:

```
<body>
```

In Chapter 5, you formatted the text for Welcome to Beautiful Turtle Island. Here is the result of that formatting:

```
<h1><font face="Arial"><font face="Times New Roman"><font size="4"><font
color="green"><font>W</font></font></font></font><font><font
color="green"><font size="4">elcome</font></font></font></font><font><font
color="green"><font size="4"> to Beautiful
Turtle Island</font></font></font></h1>
```

```
<p>
</p>
```

The next lines define the format of a table. The text you entered on your home page was actually entered into a table whose width equals the width of the page:

```
<table border="0" width="100%" height="100%">
```

The table has one row, created with the `<tr>` statement:

```
<tr>
```

It also has one cell, which was created using the `<td>` statement:

```
<td width="100%" valign="top">
```

The next two lines are comments. Visual InterDev uses comments to embed the special associations within the page. Comments are enclosed by `<!—  —>` as shown here:

```
<!— VI6.0LAYOUT = "Bottom 1"—>
```

Your actual text is enclosed by paragraph tags (`<p>`) and shown here:

```
<p> Turtle Island is many things. Most know it
        as a beautiful resort destination. Others know it for its rich
        history. It is a rare location that is perfectly suited for all
        types of vacation plans, whether you are single and looking for
        great outdoor activities, a couple looking for a romantic
        getaway, or a family needing a variety of activities to meet
        your family's varied tastes.</p>
```

You also added a graphic to this page. Here is the HTML code that reflects that:

```
<p><img alt="Travel Banner" src="TRABANNA.GIF" WIDTH="600" HEIGHT="60"></p>
The table is closed with these statements:
<!— Layout Footer Begin —>
</td>
    </tr>
```

Another table/text area was set up on this page as a default, even though you didn't use it:

```
<tr>
        <td width="100%" height="80" align="center">
</td>
```

```
    </tr>
</table>
<!-- Layout Footer End -->
```

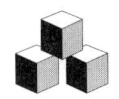

Actually, if you are looking at this code in your own window, you'll notice that the PageNavBar design-time control has been incorporated into this section. Figure 6.13 shows how the control appears in the HTML code. PageNavBar controls appear as objects, even in the Source view. This doesn't mean that the object doesn't have a code equivalent. If you selected the control from the Source view and then copied it, you could paste it in your word processor and see the following:

```
<!--METADATA TYPE="DesignerControl" startspan
<OBJECT classid="clsid:705396F5-3471-11D1-B693-006097C9A884">
    <PARAM NAME="Type" VALUE="4">
    <PARAM NAME="IncludeHome" VALUE="1">
    <PARAM NAME="IncludeParent" VALUE="1">
    <PARAM NAME="Appearance" VALUE="0">
    <PARAM NAME="Orientation" VALUE="0">
    <PARAM NAME="UseTable" VALUE="1">
    <PARAM NAME="UseTheme" VALUE="1">
    <PARAM NAME="HTMLFragment" VALUE="">
    <PARAM NAME="CurrentHTMLFragment" VALUE="">
    <PARAM NAME="UseObjectSyntax" VALUE="0">
    <PARAM NAME="ScriptLanguage" VALUE="0">
    <PARAM NAME="FrameTarget" VALUE="">
    <PARAM NAME="AlternatePage" VALUE="">


    </OBJECT>
-->

<!--METADATA TYPE="NavBar" endspan-->
<!--webbot bot="vinavbar" tag="table" s-type="arrows" b-include-home="true"
b-include-up="true" s-orientation="horizontal" s-rendering="graphics" b-use-
table="true" b-use-theme="true" s-script-lang="VBScript" b-use-object-syn-
tax="false" u-page="" s-target="" s-html-fragment=" "
s-selected-html-fragment=""  -->
<!--METADATA TYPE="NavBar" startspan-->

<!--METADATA TYPE="DesignerControl" endspan-->
```

Finally the body of the document is closed, as is the document itself:

```
</body>
</html>
```

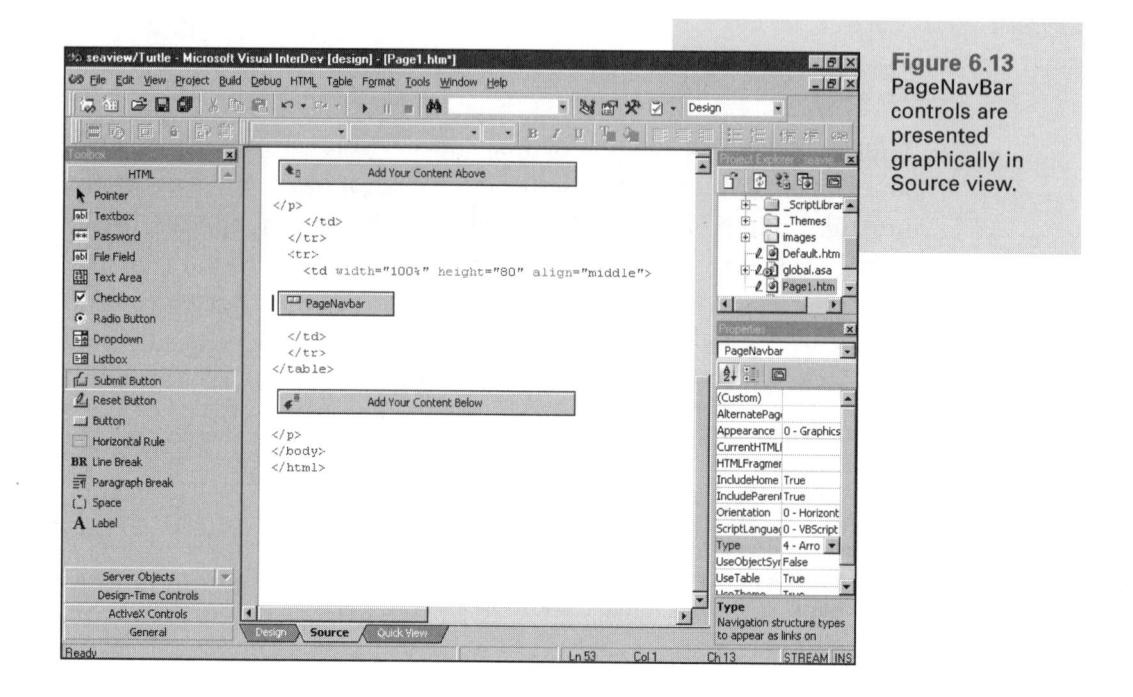

Figure 6.13
PageNavBar controls are presented graphically in Source view.

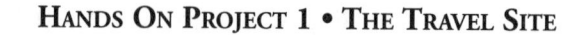

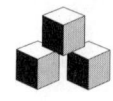

So you've pulled apart your first HTML document. Hopefully you now know that it isn't as scary as it first looks. You'll be doing more with code and scripting later in this book.

Changing Your Default View

When you first create or open a Web page, the page is displayed in Design view. This is because Design view has been set as the default view for HTML pages. If you are more comfortable working in HTML directly, you may want Source view to be your default view. To change the default view, follow these steps:

1. Select <u>T</u>ools, <u>O</u>ptions.
2. In the left pane, select and expand HTML. The HTML options display, as shown in Figure 6.14.
3. In the Initial View area, choose Sou<u>r</u>ce as the default view for HTML (.htm or .html) pages. Click on OK.

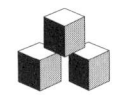

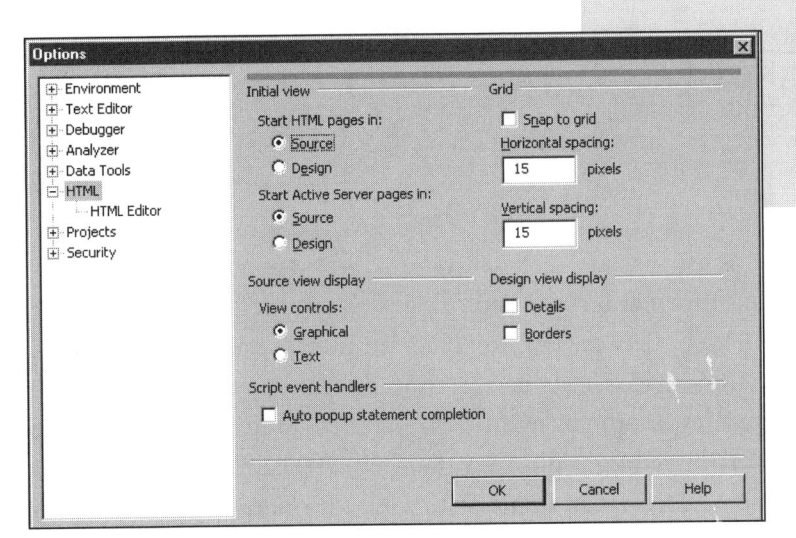

Figure 6.14
You can select different default views for HTML pages and Active Server Pages.

Adding Links from Your Page

You've put text on pages as well as graphics and other objects. How do you know where objects are mapped to? How does your application keep track of this information? This is done by using *links*. And to view these links, you'll use *link diagrams*. Link diagrams provide a graphical view of the links between files so that you can easily maintain the links in your Web application. Lines joining items in a link diagram represent links between the items. Arrows communicate the direction of links, either in or out.

> *In links* are resources that point at the current item, and *out links* are resources that the current item points to.

The main point of using a Link view is to locate broken links. When you create or refresh a link diagram for an item, Link view retrieves information about the links, either from information stored on the master Web server or by searching for external links on the World Wide Web. This process allows Link view to determine the validity of the links. If the item is not valid, the link is defined as *broken*.

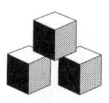

> **Note:** If the information on the master Web server has changed since you created the link diagram, you'll need to execute the Refresh command so that the most current link information is used by your link diagram.

If you have items that are external to your Web application, Link view retrieves link information by searching for the link's destination on the World Wide Web. Because the link diagram information is being pulled from a location that is external to the application, the link diagram tends to take a few moments if you have external items. Also, don't panic when you first open a link diagram that has external links that are broken. Initially, all external items in a link diagram are displayed as unknown. Use the Verify or Expand commands to have Link view determine if the link is valid or broken.

Viewing Links for an Item

When you open a link diagram on an item, a large icon in the middle of the link diagram represents the item. Resource items used by the current item are displayed on the diagram as well. If Visual InterDev cannot process the link to an item, the link is said to be broken. Broken links can occur for several reasons. The destination file may have been deleted or moved, or its location may have been entered incorrectly. To view the link diagram for your home page, follow these steps:

> **Tip:** For detailed information about the legend used in Link view, see "Items in a Link Diagram" in online help.

1. From the Project Explorer, double-click on Page 2. The first thing you do is force a broken link by adding an item that doesn't exist.
2. Add a new line in the section labeled Add Your Content Below.
3. Select HTML, Image. The Insert Image dialog box displays, as shown in Figure 6.15.

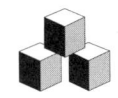

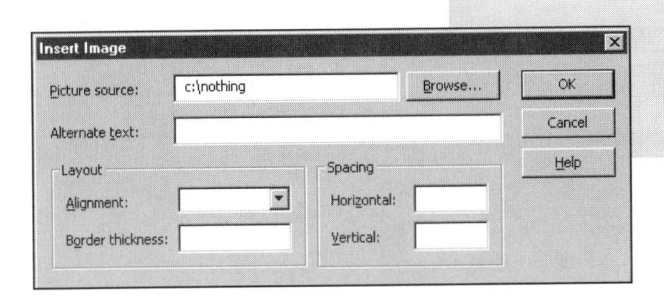

CHAPTER 6 • BUILDING THE TURTLE ISLAND SOLUTION   111

Figure 6.15
To add an image to your page, use the Insert Image dialog box.

4. Type c:\nothing for the Picture Source and press Enter. Obviously you do not have an image on your system with the name c:\nothing, so the link cannot exist. Visual InterDev lets you know that it couldn't find the image by placing a red × on the page where the image should go (see Figure 6.16).

5. Select File, Save Page2.htm. This saves the changes made.

6. Select View, View Links. In a few moments the Link diagram displays, as shown in Figure 6.17. You can see that the icon beside the nothing item has a question mark.

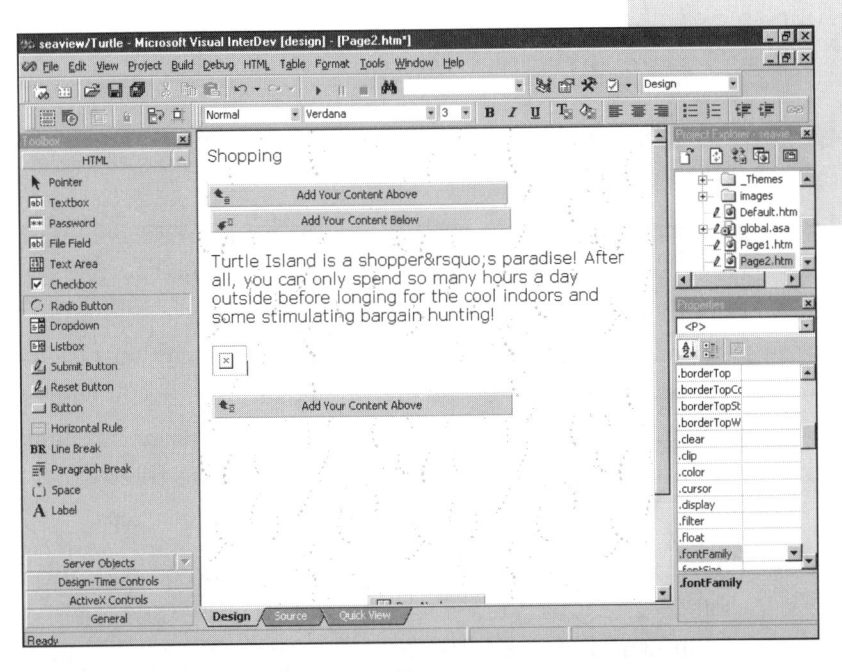

Figure 6.16
A small box with an 'x' in it lets you know that the image could not be found.

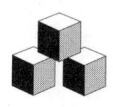

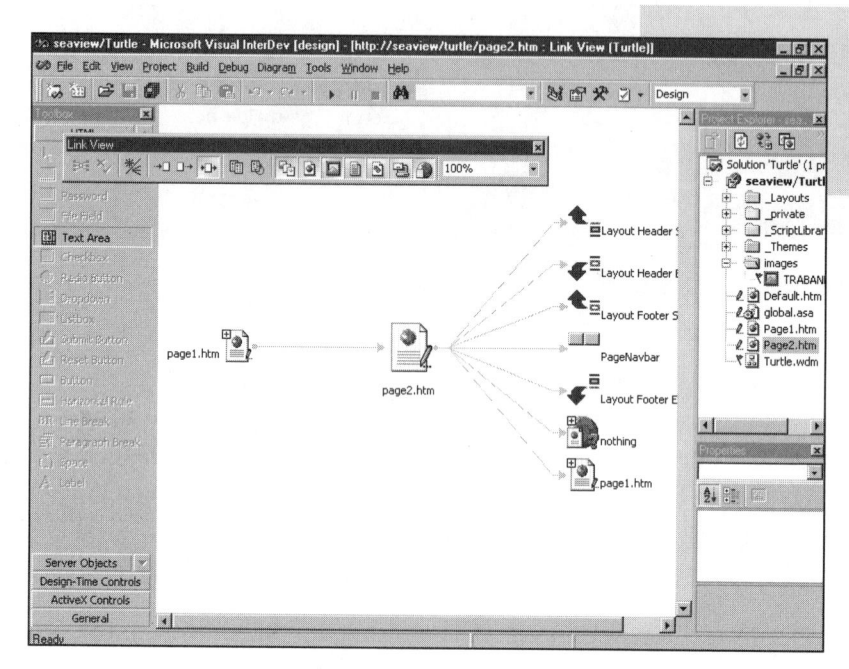

Figure 6.17
The Link diagram is used to analyze links in your project.

7. Click on the plus sign for the nothing item to expand it. This will graphically demonstrate that this link is broken, because Link view will not be able to reconcile this item. It will mark it as broken, as shown in Figure 6.18.

Changing the Layout of the Link View Diagram

Link view uses two layouts for link diagrams: the horizontal layout and the radial layout. Link view's default layout is the horizontal layout. This layout shows both the in links and the out links for an item in a modified linear fashion. The horizontal layout displays both in and out links, with in links appearing to the left of the expanded item and out links appearing to its right. The radial layout shows either in links or out links for an item, but not both at the same time. It is a more filtered perspective on links. To view the different layouts, follow these steps:

1. Click on the Change Diagram Layout button found on the Link View toolbar. The Link View diagram displays using the radial layout, as shown in Figure 6.19.

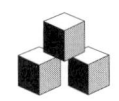

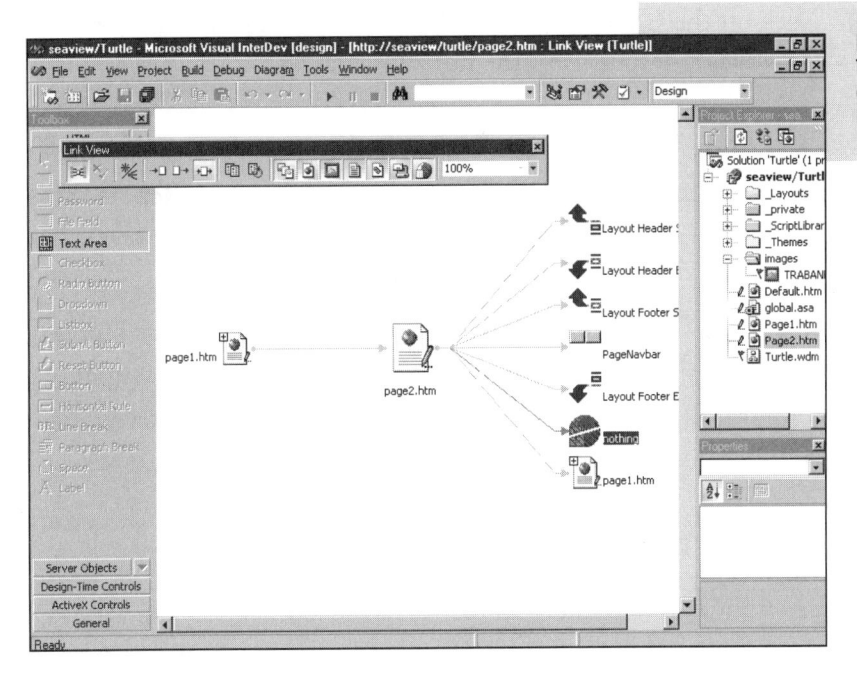

CHAPTER 6 • BUILDING THE TURTLE ISLAND SOLUTION   113

Figure 6.18
This is an example of a broken link.

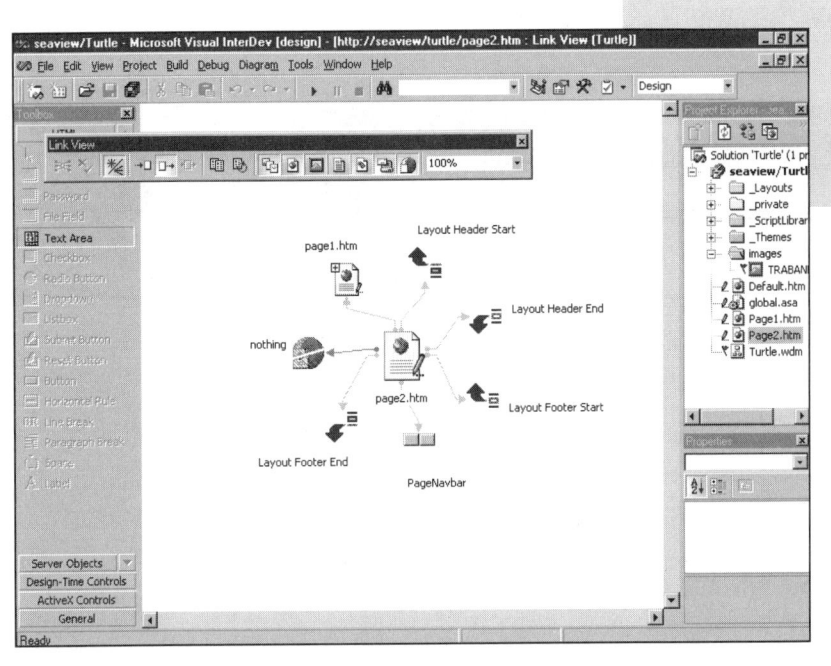

Figure 6.19
The radial layout gives you another way to look at your links.

2. Click on the Change Diagram Layout button again. The Link View diagram returns to the horizontal layout.

Using the Broken Links Report

Another useful tool for link analysis is the Broken Links Report. This report gives you detailed information about link usage and issues in a text format. To view this report, follow these steps:

1. Select <u>V</u>iew, Broke<u>n</u> Links Report. In a few moments the report appears at the bottom of your screen, as shown in Figure 6.20.

2. Scroll through the report's contents. You'll notice an entry saying:

```
Broken external links:
    file://c:\nothing: broken link from page2.htm
```

This is the reference to your broken link.

3. Close the Broken Links Report.

In addition to creating the report you just saw, the Broken Links Report command created a task in your task list. Complete the following steps to see this task:

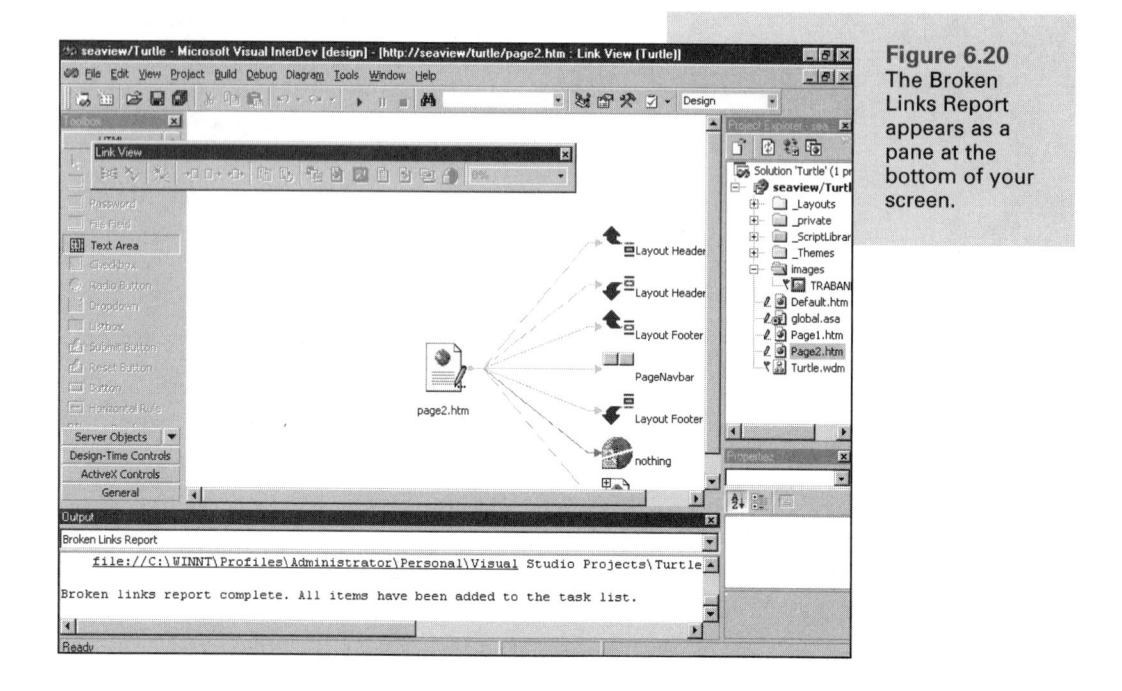

Figure 6.20
The Broken Links Report appears as a pane at the bottom of your screen.

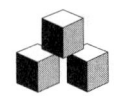

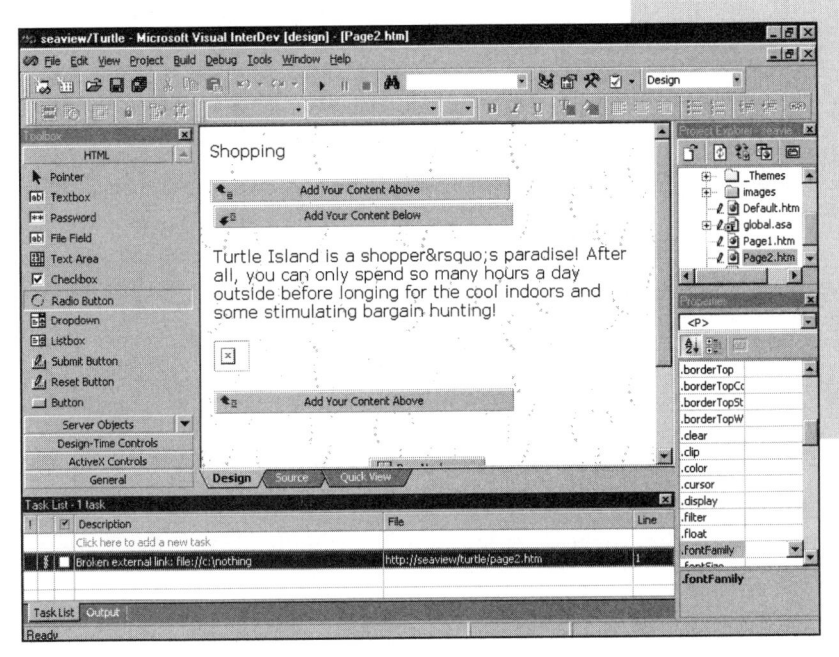

CHAPTER 6 • BUILDING THE TURTLE ISLAND SOLUTION   **115**

Figure 6.21
When you elected to view the Broken Links Report, Visual InterDev automatically added a task to your Task List (shown here at the bottom of the screen). This task reminds you to repair the broken link.

1. Select View, Other Windows, Task List. Figure 6.21 shows the contents of the Task List.
2. Click in the check box associated with the broken link. This marks the task as completed. Since you are going to deal with the broken link in the next section, mark it complete for now.
3. Close the Task List window.

Repairing the Broken Links

Now you'll repair the broken link (in the sense that you are going to delete it) by following these steps:

1. Select Window, Page2. This returns you to the Design view for this page.
2. Click on the control representing the graphic.
3. Press Delete to delete the item.
4. Select File, Save Page2.htm. This saves the changes made. Just deleting the item is not enough. You also have to save the page so

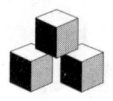

that this information is saved to the project, since Link view pulls its analysis from the project.

5. Select Window, Link View to display Link view. The broken link is still displayed. This is because you need to refresh the view.

6. Select View, Refresh. The Link view is updated, and the broken link is no longer displayed.

> **Tip:** The keyboard shortcut for refreshing your view is Ctrl+R.

In reality, you don't repair most links by deleting them. In practice, you'll more often find the new location for the file the link points to and reset the link to that location. Or if you are like me, you'll just need to correct your typos.

Summary

You've covered a lot of ground in this chapter. Starting with modes, you learned the difference between Master and Local modes and how to switch between these modes. The next topic you covered was expanding your project. You added pages to your application via the site diagram. Then you applied a theme to the pages. At this point, you were introduced to the global navigation bar and used it to add navigation to your application.

After mastering the graphical interface, you were ready to move on to the code side of Visual InterDev. Using Source view, you reviewed the code that was generated as you created pages and items in other views. You saw that HTML is not a difficult language to use. It is, however, very structured.

You wrapped up the chapter with link maintenance. You saw how to identify broken links and deal with them.

In the next chapter, you are going to complete this project. You'll test your application and then update it.

CHAPTER 7

Testing the Travel Site

You are ready to test and deploy your Web application. This chapter discusses what needs to be done to prepare for the deployment of your application to a live Web server, and the various methods of deployment.

How Do You Test a Web Page?

Because of the graphical nature of Visual InterDev, testing is an ongoing process. Every time you look at your work in Quick view or in a browser, you are testing your work. You tested your application at the end of the last chapter when you worked with broken links. Testing actually occurs throughout the development process. You'll find your testing will focus on the following areas:

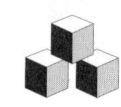

- **Verifying links.** You've already seen how to use a link diagram to determine if your links are broken. This is probably one of the most common forms of testing in Visual InterDev.
- **Debugging code.** In the preceding chapter, you were briefly introduced to HTML code. This will become another area of testing as your project progresses. Unless you are a flawless typist with an incredible memory, you will make mistakes when working with code; testing will help you locate those mistakes.
- **Working with data access.** You'll find that data access is another area that will require testing. You'll need to test to verify that the correct data is presented, and if not, you'll need to test to find out why.

Since this is a relatively small project and you have been testing as you go, there really isn't any further testing to be done at this point. You are ready to deploy your solution.

Deploying Your Solution

You've developed and tested your solution, and now you're ready to deploy it. *Deployment* is the process of moving a Web application from the development server to the production server. In other words, you are moving your application to the real world. Deployment transforms your application from a project to a published Web application.

Since your Web application is actually a set of files, you need to copy the virtual root and its file set to the production Web server. If your pages use the virtual root as the basis for their links, all links should still work. The copy of the Web application created when you deploy it is separate from your master Web application.

This leads to the main advantage of a Web application. Because it is made up of files, it is easy to maintain. Unlike a more traditional development environment, it doesn't require you to recompile and redistribute an entirely new executable file to upgrade it. All you need to do is add new files and replace previous versions. As a matter of fact, during an upgrade, visitors may not even be interrupted while they are working. This is because their browsers use the original copies of the files they downloaded from the Web server. This is why most browsers provide a Refresh button. To find out that a change has been made, a visitor would have to click on the Refresh button to refresh the page.

At times, a visitor to a page may be interrupted as new files are posted to a live Web site. When using ASP-based Web pages, the browser does not cache the page unless the developer specifically adds logic to the application to indicate an appropriate expiration date that allows caching. Also, if a user is currently filling out a form that will be submitted back to a new, recently posted form handler, the results could arrive out of sync for the new handler. Therefore, it may not be safe to post new files to a live Web without concern for users who are currently online. The decision to post live, or not to, has to be made by the developer, as only he knows the impact, if any, of the new code.

You can break the deployment process into three major stages:

- The preparation stage
- Actual deployment to the Web server
- Verification of production server content

The Preparation Stage

The preparation stage actually is an extension of the testing process. You are not prepared to deploy an application until you have tested it. Don't forget to release all working copies of your work to the master Web server to make sure it is up to date.

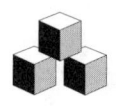

> **Note**
>
> Though I haven't dealt with databases yet, specific issues arise in implementing an application with a database connection. Often you work with a database other than the production database. Typically it contains smaller amounts of data than the production database to speed up the development and testing process. If this is the case, you'll need to make sure the data connection in your project points to the appropriate database for production.

Actual Deployment to the Web Server

Once you have your project ready for deployment, only a few steps remain to make it available to your users. This part of the chapter is more a discussion than an exercise for you to do. Because of the almost unlimited range of locations, Web servers, and such that you could be using, I'm just going to give you the generic steps. You'll need to provide the specifics yourself.

When you deploy your project, several things occur. The first is the specification of a root location on the Web server. Then copies are made and saved of each file used by the application. After that, components marked as server components are registered. Then transaction packages are created for use by Microsoft Transaction Server. Finally the actual copy to the server is performed.

How much you have to do of these tasks is dependent on the deployment method you use. You can use a variety of methods to deploy your application, but the quickest and easiest is copying to the production server through Visual InterDev. However, this requires that your production server have FrontPage Server Extensions installed. Visual InterDev uses the FrontPage Server Extensions to communicate with the production Web server. Your Web application is ready to run as soon as the copy is complete. Here are the available deployment methods:

- Using FrontPage Server Extensions
- Deploying without using FrontPage Server Extensions
- Manually deploying your project

CHAPTER 7 • TESTING THE TRAVEL SITE 121

> **Tip:** Microsoft FrontPage Extensions are free and available for a wide variety of Web servers. You can download them from Microsoft's FrontPage site at `http://www.microsoft.com`.

Deploying with FrontPage Server Extensions

The first procedure, which is the easiest, is the one you can do if you have Microsoft FrontPage Server Extensions installed on your production server. If this is the case, you'll use the following steps to deploy the Web application:

1. In the Project Explorer, select the project you want to deploy.
2. Select Project, Web Project, Copy Web Application. The Copy Project dialog box displays, as shown in Figure 7.1.

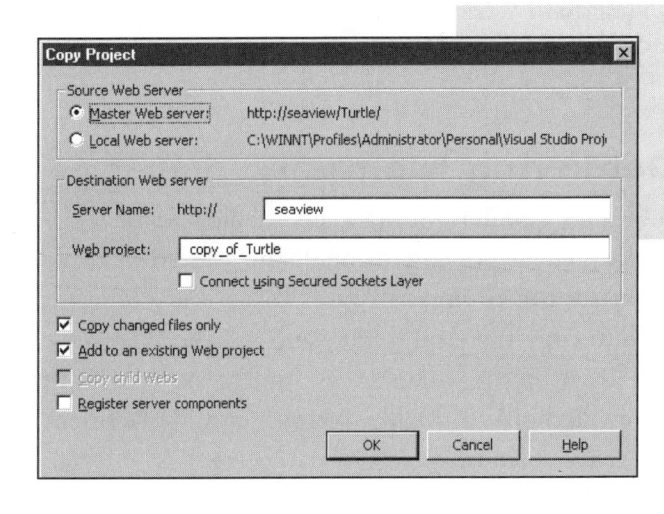

Figure 7.1 The Copy Project dialog box is used in the deployment process.

3. In the Server Name box, enter the name of the destination Web server.
4. In the Web Project box, enter the name you want the users to type for the URL.
5. Clear the Copy Changed Files Only check box.
6. Click on OK. The solution is deployed.

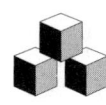

The newly deployed application is created on the destination Web server, and the files in the Web application are copied to that new folder. The name you entered in the Copy Web dialog box becomes part of the application's URL.

Deploying without FrontPage Server Extensions

If your production server doesn't have FrontPage Server Extensions or your application requires special deployment configurations, you can use Posting Acceptor, available with the Visual InterDev Enterprise Edition. You can find out more about this feature in the online documentation that comes with Visual InterDev.

> **Note** You may want to look up information on the Web Publishing Programmer's Reference MSDN Library reference. In the online material, you will find information on the Web Publishing Wizard, Wpwiz.exe, that can also be used to deploy your project.

Deploying Manually

You might prefer to manually deploy some of your files. Manual deployment is possible through the Windows Explorer and your Web server administration software. To do everything manually, you would need to copy files and folders and use the Web server administrator, as well as set up the Web server's application root. Of these three deployment methods, I highly recommend deployment using FrontPage Server Extensions.

Verification of the Production Server Content

You've got your application deployed, and you're ready for the moment of truth. You're ready to view your real, live application in your browser. You'll want to do this on a machine other than the one you use for development to ensure that you aren't looking at a development copy of your work. To verify your deployed application, you'll access your solution as you would any other address on the Web. In the address box of a Web browser, enter the full URL to the application on the production server. And, drum roll please, there is your solution, looking very professional!

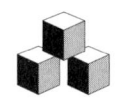

Common Error Messages

I've encountered very few error messages while using Visual InterDev on the Windows NT platform. I started this book using Windows 95 as my operating system. This was, in a word, ugly! Not that Visual InterDev has a problem running on Windows 95 or Windows 98, but I was using Personal Web Server as my development server, and that is not a happy camper on anything other than Windows NT. You can get it to run, but keeping it running is the trick. I even called Microsoft to see if there was anything I could do to optimize Personal Web Server on Windows 95 or 98, and the response was, "Isn't there any way you could run it on Windows NT instead?" It really does make a huge amount of difference to run it on Windows NT.

I've also noticed that if you are running Visual InterDev and Personal Web Server on the same machine, the best friend you can have is RAM. These two together are serious memory munchers. This is definitely not a place for a machine with less than 32MB of RAM.

Troubleshooting: Unable to Connect Remotely to Windows 95 or Windows 98 Web Server

Microsoft Windows 95 and Windows 98 support the Web servers installed with FrontPage or the Windows NT Option Pack. These Web servers are intended for local development. If you want to use a machine as a remote Web server, install Windows NT Server and the Windows NT Option Pack, which includes Microsoft Internet Information Server.

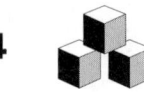

> **Troubleshooting: Cannot access server information for the file <name>**
>
> You're trying to access a file on the server from your project, but information for this file is not available. The file may no longer exist on the server. For example, someone may have deleted a file from the Web server. This error typically occurs when you're trying to check out a file or get the latest version of a file.
>
> To correct this error, use the Refresh command to synchronize your project with the server.

Summary

This chapter focused on two areas: testing and deployment. Testing a Web application is a combination of verifying links, debugging code, and working with data access. Deploying it consists of using FrontPage Server Extensions, not using FrontPage Server Extensions, and manually deploying your project.

Now that you've finished this project, it's time to move on to the next one. In the upcoming project, you will add database functionality to your Web applications.

Project 1 Summary

You've created your first project, added content in the form of text and graphics, and viewed it in your browser. After getting comfortable with the interface and building a simple project, you got the opportunity to work with the various modes of Visual InterDev. You learned the difference between Master and Local modes and how to switch between these modes.

The next topic you covered was expanding your project. You added pages to your application via the site diagram. Then you applied a theme to the pages. At this point, you were introduced to the global navigation bar and used it to add navigation to your application. In conjunction with this topic, you worked with link maintenance. You saw how to identify broken links and deal with them, and finally you learned how to deploy the project.

HANDS ON PROJECT 2

THE DATABASE WEB PROJECT

- Understanding Visual InterDev's data environment
- Creating a project with a database connection
- Using Visual InterDev with SQL Server
- Using the Data View window
- Querying your data
- Viewing the records from your home page
- Adding a Recordset control
- Adding databound controls to your page
- Using Visual InterDev with Access
- Using scripts
- Creating a data form using the FormManager design-time control
- Using breakpoints, just-in-time debugging, watches, and stepping-through-script to test your Web solution
- Debugging server script

Project Overview

The Database Web project is designed to give you hands-on experience designing and building a dynamic Web application. You get the opportunity to add information to your application from both Microsoft SQL Server and Microsoft Access. In this project, you will use a sample SQL Server database, which is included with the SQL server provided with the Professional and Enterprise editions of Visual Studio. You'll also use another sample database called Northwind. This database is an Access database that contains a company's information about suppliers, customers, inventory, and other business essentials.

CHAPTER 8

What Is the Database Web Project?

The Database Web project is designed to give you hands-on experience designing and building a dynamic Web application. You will get the opportunity to add information to your application from both Microsoft SQL Server and Microsoft Access. In this project, you will use a sample SQL Server database that is included in the Professional and Enterprise editions of Visual Studio. This database is designed to model the data needs of a bookstore. You'll also use another sample database called Northwind. This is an Access database that contains a company's information about suppliers, customers, inventory, and related items.

One of Visual InterDev's key features is that it provides you with great flexibility in designing Web applications that interface with databases. You can use any database supported by ActiveX Data Objects (ADO) for which you have drivers, including Microsoft SQL Server, Microsoft

> *Active Data Objects (ADO)* supply an open, application-level data access object model that allows corporate programmers to write database applications to access **OLE DB** data using any language.

FoxPro, and Microsoft Access. Once you've established a connection to a database from within Visual InterDev, you can interact directly with the database.

Requirements for the Database Web Project

As you know, the first thing you need to do before starting any application is review the requirements of the system. This project has two requirements:

- Connect to and retrieve data from a SQL Server database.
- Connect to and retrieve data from an Access database.

Start with the first requirement. Since the database you are working with is one designed for a bookstore, you will perform the following queries:

- Display title and price information.
- Locate books with a price that is less than $10.
- From your Web application, move from record to record.

This may seem like a short list of requirements, but don't let that fool you. A lot must go on in the background to accomplish these tasks. For example, you are going to need to be able to design a query that takes user input and uses that information for its conditions. You are also going to need to display the results of the query.

The second requirement is to connect to an Access database. Using the data in the Northwind database, you will perform the following actions:

- Locate product name, price, and suppliers' company names for inventory items.

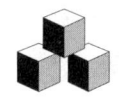

- Display the data on a page and allow a user to navigate from record to record.

Goals of the Database Web Project

How will creating the database project help you to learn Visual InterDev? This project is designed to present Visual InterDev concepts beyond the basics. Your clients, whether they are internal or external, expect database capabilities in applications. And why shouldn't they? Think of the possibilities of combining the flexibility of a database with the broad accessibility of the Internet. You can publish catalogs, sale items, job postings, new products, acquisitions, real estate listings, and more. The list is virtually limitless. And that information is available to the millions of users who have access to the Internet.

Developers who used the first version of Visual InterDev were asked for their feedback on the product, and the majority felt that the integration of database tools was the most important feature of that version. This version improves on these tools and simplifies the process of integrating databases into a Web solution. These concepts, which you should become familiar with, are described in the following sections.

Creating a Database Project

The first step in this process is to create a database project. Database projects are used to create and manage databases and their objects. In Chapters 10 and 11, you will learn how to create this type of project. You will work with two different databases in these chapters. Chapter 10 focuses on SQL Server and Chapter 11 gives you an opportunity to work with Access.

Structured Query Language (SQL) is a widely adopted standard for getting answers to particular questions about your data.

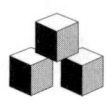

Connecting to a Database

Once you create a database project, the next step is to connect to a database. Chapter 10 will explain this process and discuss the concept of a data source name (DSN).

Using Visual Database Tools and the Data View Window

When designing Visual InterDev, the development team was well aware that Web developers could no longer content themselves with making great Web sites. They also needed the ability to create and modify objects in databases. Visual InterDev offers sophisticated database design tools that make it easier to create and modify database tables, views, stored procedures, and other objects.

The Data View window (described in Chapter 10) is one of these tools. It is a window that gives the developer a live view of the data in the database to which your Web project is currently connected, as shown in Figure 8.1. From the Data View window, you can access a variety of tools to manage your database.

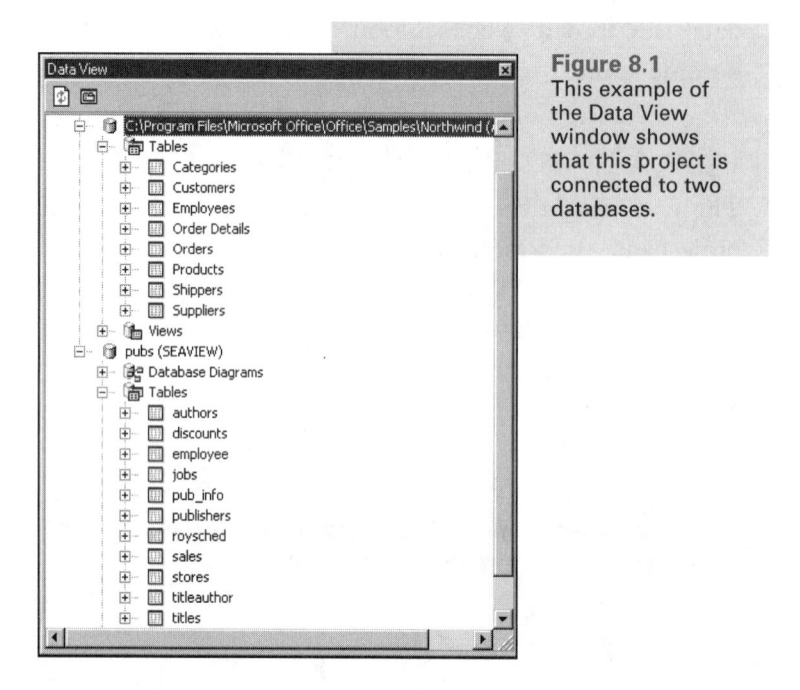

Figure 8.1
This example of the Data View window shows that this project is connected to two databases.

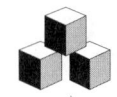

Querying and Displaying Database Information for Your Web Page

One of the key features of Visual InterDev is its ability to query and display records (see Figure 8.2). Visual InterDev has made this process easy. Once you are connected to a database in Chapter 10, you will be ready to specify and display the set of records.

Using FormManager

In Chapter 11, you will learn how to use the FormManager design-time control to create a page that can display, edit, and add records to your database. The FormManager DTC makes creating a page to edit database information easy by generating the necessary scripts for you. Most of the work you have to do involves setting properties for the control.

Debugging Your System

No matter how good you are at software development, you will occasionally make a mistake. This is where debugging comes into play. Debugging

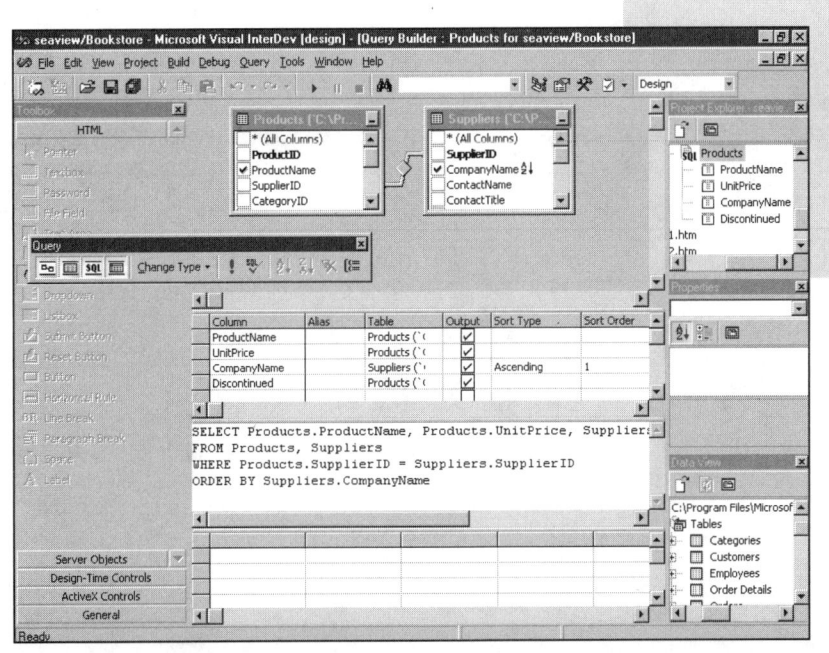

Figure 8.2
Data tools like the Query Builder, discussed in Chapter 10, make it easy to query and display records.

is the process of finding errors. In Chapter 12, you'll learn several debugging techniques, including stepping through individual statements to see line-by-line execution, and stopping scripts by setting breakpoints.

Summary

Your second project will help you to develop many skills that can be used for a variety of Web solutions. One of your goals as a Visual InterDev developer is to create Web sites that are flexible in their presentation of data. This project will give you the hands-on experience you need to integrate a database as part of your Web site. Chapter 9 starts this process by giving you the background information.

CHAPTER 9

Gathering Information for the Database Web Project

The first thing you did in the previous project was gather information for the application; you then analyzed the information and used it in the design process. You're in the same situation now—you need to gather any information necessary to complete the analysis process. You've already identified the goals of the application (see Chapter 8, "What Is the Database Web Project?"), and by reviewing these goals you should be able to identify the forms, controls, queries, and other objects needed to complete the application. This chapter gives you background information about Visual InterDev's data environment and then discusses selecting the database for your site.

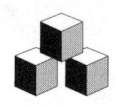

Understanding Visual InterDev's Data Environment

OK, you've created your first application, and you're ready to build on the knowledge you gained through that process. The next giant leap that you are ready to take is to add database functionality to a Web application solution.

Before you can build a Web application with database functionality, you need to understand some of the underlying concepts involved. One of the newer buzz phrases of Internet development is *dynamic Web application*. A dynamic Web application, as the name implies, is one that is not built on static text. To be dynamic, the application relies on a way to allow the contents of the application to change without changing the application itself. Sounds like a job for a database! That's why this type of solution is a called a data-driven solution.

You can connect to data from any ODBC-compliant database with open support for enterprise data sources. This gives you a broad range of databases to work with, including:

- DB/2
- dBase
- Informix
- Microsoft Access
- Microsoft SQL Server
- Microsoft Visual FoxPro
- Oracle
- Paradox
- Sybase

You can interact with your database in the ways that you are used to. You can directly interact with the database using queries, or you can use views. You can even use stored procedures.

The first thing you need to understand, as far as the data environment goes, is that in Web applications that access databases, two server-like functions are occurring. You are already familiar with one of these server functions—the Web server. As you know, the Web server handles requests for pages for your application. The server function that you are adding to this equation is the database server.

When designing your Web solution that is going to have data access, you must first decide how to configure your environment. Here are your choices:

- **The database server is on the same computer as the Web server.** The advantage of this configuration is accessibility. You know you can get to the data if it is on the same system. A drawback to this configuration may be performance. Both servers are competing for the same resources. For this reason, if you are planning to use this configuration, you will want to have a reasonably high-end system, possibly one with multiple processors. On the other hand, any system performance issues may be nullified by the fact that a database and Web server located on the same machine can be much faster than those that are split on the network. The backplane and hard disk bandwidth is much faster than current network technology. A downside is security, as databases on Internet Web servers are targets for hackers.

- **The database server is on a separate computer from the Web server.** This configuration has lots of advantages. The first advantage is performance. By breaking the servers apart onto separate machines, you may increase performance. This configuration lends itself to an environment where multiple Web servers are accessing data from the same database server. The split-server setup provides a slight security advantage, as the separate database server can be better secured against public Internet attacks. Another thing to consider with this type of configuration is the increased cost of purchasing and maintaining multiple machines.

- **The database is on a local computer.** This is not a typical configuration. It is only used in a testing situation.

The next concept you need to address is data connection. Before you can connect to a database, you have to know its name, the type of database you are addressing, and its location. You may also need a user ID and password to gain access. This information is stored and used by a *data connection*.

You aren't limited to just one data connection per project. You can add as many data connections to your project as you need. This gives you enormous flexibility when designing your Web application. Here's an example for you: A major department store has a bridal registry service. When you go in, you can find out what the happy couple has registered for wedding gifts. When you request this information, the application connects to the Internet to gain access to a central bridal registry. The benefit of this approach is that the couple only has to register in one store and someone can go into any store in any state and find out what they want. So that's your first data connection. The second data connection is to the inventory system. When designing the bridal registry, you wouldn't want to store all kinds of inventory information in the database. You only need the inventory number to find detailed information from the inventory database. That is your second data connection.

To make a connection to a database from Visual InterDev, you need to create a data source name (DSN). The DSN is either a file (with an extension of .dsn) or a Windows registry entry.

Another element that you'll need to connect to a database is the appropriate ODBC driver. When you install Visual InterDev, ODBC drivers are installed on your development machine and on your Web server.

So you can connect to a database, but what else can you do? With Visual InterDev, not only can you add data functionality to your applications, you can manage your databases. Depending on the database you are working with, you may be able to add, delete, or modify items from within Visual InterDev, including databases, tables, columns, views, synonyms, relationships between tables, indexes, constraints, triggers, stored procedures, functions, packages, and queries.

> **Note**
>
> You have to have the appropriate permissions in the database you are using to perform these tasks.

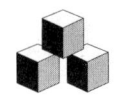

In Visual InterDev, Microsoft provides the tools to make it easy to manage databases. The following list is a brief summary of these tools:

- **Data view.** This is a window that displays all the database objects that you can view.
- **Database Designer.** When you are working with an SQL server or Oracle database, you can use this tool to display your database as a database diagram. When your database is displayed in this manner, you can create indexes, add or change table and column definitions, define relationships between tables, and add constraints.
- **Query Designer.** This designer lets you visually create SQL statements using drag-and-drop techniques to query or modify a database.
- **View Designer.** The View Designer lets you visually create the SQL statement that defines a view.
- **Script Editor.** This window is similar to the Source view. The Script Editor is used for creating SQL scripts.
- **Data-bound controls.** Getting data into controls on your Web page isn't very hard to do, because Visual InterDev provides data-bound controls. These controls include text boxes and option buttons. When you add one of these controls to a page, the control can be bound to a specific field in a database record. Data-bound controls already include the scripts required to make data connections, retrieve data, and write changes to the database, so you can incorporate database functionality into your Web pages with little to no programming.
- **Stored Procedure Editor.** Certain databases, such as SQL Server, use stored procedures, which are SQL procedures that can accept arguments. You can use this editor to create stored procedures.
- **Trigger Editor.** A *trigger* is a procedure that is invoked when a certain event occurs, such as adding or deleting a record. This window can be used to create triggers.

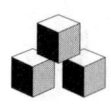

Visual InterDev's data environment has its own object model. You'll use this model when you write scripts to work with data. The data environment object model is based on the ActiveX Data Objects (ADO) object model, but it is simpler to use. In ADO, you work with five main objects: Connection objects, Command objects, Recordset objects, Field objects, and Parameter objects.

When you use ADO, you manipulate data almost entirely using Recordset objects. A Recordset object represents the entire set of records from a table or the results of an executed command (query). The Recordset object itself refers to only the current record at any given time. The next chapter discusses working with ADO objects in depth.

Selecting the Database for Your Site

When you are planning your application, choosing the right database can provide one of the toughest challenges. Visual InterDev only requires that the database be ODBC-compliant. This book is not large enough to compare and contrast all the supported database formats. To walk through the process in this project, I'll use Microsoft Access and Microsoft SQL Server. To determine which database fits your needs, consider several questions:

- How much data will be stored?
- How many users will use the system?
- What type of support is available?
- What existing systems are in place?

How Much Data Will Be Stored?

Although you cannot pinpoint the exact storage requirements for your system, you can get a rough idea. If you know that you'll have 500 records, storage requirements are less of an issue than if you expect to have 500,000 records.

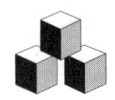

Microsoft Access was developed to provide a user-friendly desktop database. It can serve as its own development environment, or it can be accessed from Visual InterDev. When you use Access as an application development tool, you can store your data and your interface in one file. Access is also capable of storing different objects in separate files and linking them.

If you are working with a lot of data, you should choose to store each table in a separate file, but you still need to keep the database product's limitations in mind. An Access file cannot exceed one gigabyte (GB). Another Microsoft database product, Visual FoxPro, can support a table of up to 2GB.

If you are dealing with greater amounts of data, you need to select another product. Microsoft SQL Server is one such product. It is designed as a client/server database tool. Client/server applications often serve more than one user at a time, which usually means handling a greater amount of data. Microsoft SQL Server can accommodate up to 200GB of information, and this number is predicted to increase in future releases.

> **Note** To get an idea of what size database future versions of SQL Server will be able to support, go to terraserver.microsoft.com on the Internet. The information available through this site is stored in Microsoft SQL Server 7.

If you decide to go with Access and your data needs eventually grow larger than you originally planned, you aren't stuck. Access has a set of upsizing tools to assist you with moving your data to Microsoft SQL Server.

For the application in this project, the data requirements aren't large. This system needs to store simple information about hotels, shops, and the like.

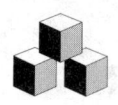

How Many Users Will Use the System?

Depending on how you plan to configure your system, the next concern may be how many concurrent users are on the system. Both Access and SQL Server support multiple concurrent users and offer security, referential integrity, data validation, transaction processing, and replication.

> *Referential integrity* is a set of rules developed to protect the integrity of data. It prevents a user from altering table relationships by adding data to one table in a relationship without adding matching information to the related table. It also prevents the user from deleting data involved in a relationship.

> *Data validation* involves verifying the data entered by a user to make sure that it meets the information needs of the system.

> *Replication* is the ability to make a copy of a database and then synchronize the copy with the original database. This allows for independent accessing of the database with the benefits of a single data source.

> *Security* is a system for a database to establish user access requirements to restrict undesirable actions.

SQL Server is a client/server database tool. It offers better performance than Access as the number of concurrent users increases. SQL Server also offers a more efficient transaction processing system, which is essential for interrelated updates. It keeps a transaction log, which is essential when a system failure occurs. *Transaction logs* are areas reserved by SQL Server to record changes to the database. Each change made to a database is automatically recorded in the transaction log for that database. SQL Server uses transaction logs during automatic recovery.

With Internet applications, it's hard to predict how many people will be connected concurrently. Because your project is a small resort island, it may be safe to assume that only a small number of users will connect concurrently, and in that case, Access will be sufficient.

What Type of Support Is Available?

Another factor that may affect your decision about database products is how much support is available for data administration. Both Access and SQL Server can operate on LANs, and both require some maintenance periodically.

Access files tend to increase in size as activities are performed with the database. This includes not only the addition of records, but the creation of queries and other database-related objects. It is recommended that you periodically compact the database file to eliminate unused space. Performing this task doesn't take an Access expert, but it does require other users to be out of the system.

SQL Server is better designed for a client/server, multiuser database environment. It has many standard database administration tools. It supports data replication, remote operations, e-mail notification, activity monitoring, and online backup.

SQL Server is designed to make administration of the database as painless as possible. The fact that users can remain in the system while most of the maintenance activities are occurring is a plus, especially for systems that need to be available around the clock.

What Existing Systems Are in Place?

Another factor to consider when selecting a database format is the type of databases that are already in use at your location. If many databases are already supported for a particular format, then maintenance routines are already in place. Adding a new database of the same format does not significantly increase the time required for maintenance. Selecting the same format also eliminates the need to learn a new product.

Time also can influence your decision when you're designing a new system. If you're trying to develop a replacement for an integrated system from another database development tool, it might take some time to complete the replacement system. With all the formats supported by

Visual InterDev, you can switch different parts of the system without disturbing the data.

The Choice for Your Application

You could have added another question to your analysis: "What database do you have?" A developer version of SQL Server ships with the Enterprise Edition of Visual Studio. You may also want to consider using Microsoft FoxPro. FoxPro is a component of Visual Studio, and that may sway you from SQL Server or Access.

Because the goal of this book is to give you hands-on experience with Visual InterDev, I elected to use both SQL Server and Access in the project. I did this for a couple of reasons. One reason is that both of these databases are very popular with developers. Another reason is to show you that you can access multiple data sources in one project.

Summary

In the previous chapter, you covered some of the goals and requirements of the database Web project. In that chapter, you discovered that Visual InterDev is surprisingly full-featured when it comes to database accessibility and maintenance.

Because Visual InterDev does provide extensive database accessibility, you have to select what database you want to work with. In this chapter, I discussed that when selecting a database, you need to consider many issues, including how many people need access to the system, how much data needs to be stored, and what resources are already in place.

You'll find in the next few chapters that you'll be able to include a wide range of features in your solution. In the next chapter, you will add a data connection to your project and design a query. You will use the result of that query to display data on your page using the Recordset control and RecordsetNavpage control. Now it's time to start your database Web project!

CHAPTER 10

Designing the System

The last chapter provided you with the concepts you need to start working with database projects. In this chapter, you are going to apply those concepts and actually start creating the database project. This chapter focuses on working with SQL Server, so you must have it installed to complete this project.

This chapter focuses on using a SQL Server database as your data source. This means that you need access to SQL Server to complete this chapter. The Enterprise Edition of Visual Studio comes with a development version of Microsoft SQL Server 6.5. To use SQL Server on your system, you need to have Windows NT as your operating system. SQL Server does not run on Windows 95/98.

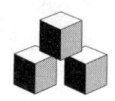

Creating a Project with a Database Connection

The first thing you need to do is create a project with a database connection. One of the best things about connecting to a database from a Visual InterDev project is that the connection allows you to have complete control over your database. This means you have control over its structure as well as its content. The amount of control you have over a database's structure is dependent on the version of Visual Studio you have. The Enterprise Edition offers more control than the Professional Edition. A detailed discussion of the differences between the Professional and Enterprise Editions of Visual Studio as they pertain to data access and manipulation can be found at the end of this chapter. You don't have to leave Visual InterDev to perform maintenance and other chores on your database. Visual InterDev integrates itself with your database.

> **Note**
> Visual InterDev 6.0 is a member of the Microsoft Visual Studio development tools suite. Visual Studio, Professional Edition, features Visual J++, Visual Basic, Visual C++, Visual InterDev, and Visual FoxPro. Visual Studio, Enterprise Edition includes all of the tools found in the Professional Edition plus Visual Database Tools, Visual SourceSafe, Microsoft Repository, Visual Component Manager, Microsoft Visual Modeler, and development versions of SQL Server 6.5, Microsoft Internet Information Server 4.0, Microsoft Transaction Server 2.0, and Microsoft Message Queue Server.

In this project, you will use a sample database that is included with the SQL server provided with the Enterprise edition of Visual Studio. Basically, I've opted to use this database because it already exists and it saves us from having to create a database. It is also a nicely designed database complete with tables, data, views, and stored procedures. This database is designed to model the data needs of a bookstore. To that end, you'll find the following tables in the database:

- Authors
- Discount

- Employee
- Jobs
- Pub_Info
- Publishers
- Roysched
- Sales
- Stores
- TitleAuthor
- Titles

To create a database connection from a project, use the following steps:

> **Tip:** Don't forget to start the SQL Server service before doing these steps. It may start automatically, but it doesn't hurt to check. To verify that the SQL Server service has started, select Services from Control Panel and look for MSSQLServer. The Services dialog box lists whether or not MSSQLServer has been started.

1. Start Visual InterDev, if necessary, and select File, New Project. The New Project dialog box displays.
2. Select the New tab.
3. Select New Web Project and Name it Bookstore.
4. Continue creating the Web project. Use Bottom 1 for the layout and pick any theme you like.
5. Add a site diagram to the project and then open the Home page created with the site diagram.
6. Select Project, Add Data Connection. The Select Data Source dialog box opens (see Figure 10.1).
7. Select MTSSamples and click on OK. The SQL Server Login dialog box displays, as shown in Figure 10.2.
8. If this is the first time you are accessing the SQL Server that shipped with your copy of the Enterprise Edition of Visual Studio, you should see SA in the Login ID box. This is the ID

Figure 10.1
The Select Data Source dialog box allows you to select from existing defined data sources or to create a new one.

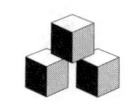

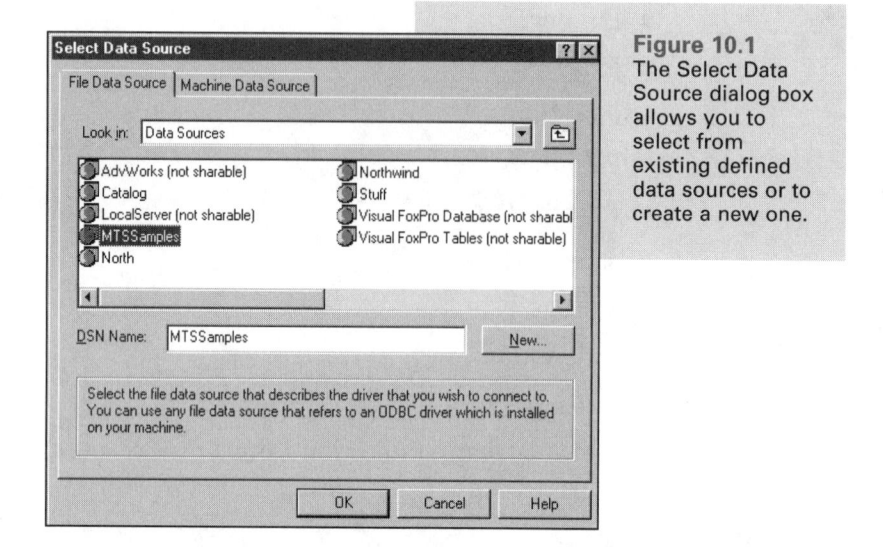

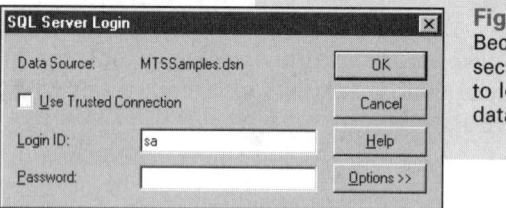

Figure 10.2
Because of SQL Server's security structure, you have to log in to be able to access data.

you will use. This ID doesn't require a password. If you are connecting to an existing SQL server, you may need to use another ID and password. Click on OK. The Connection1 Properties dialog box displays (see Figure 10.3).

9. Set the Connect Name to SelectTitles and press Enter. The connection to SQL Server is made. The Data View window opens in the lower-right corner, as shown in Figure 10.4.

Using the Data View Window

The Data View window provides a live view of the data to which your database or Web project is currently connected. This window provides a graphical interface for creating, viewing, and editing the database objects.

CHAPTER 10 • DESIGNING THE SYSTEM   149

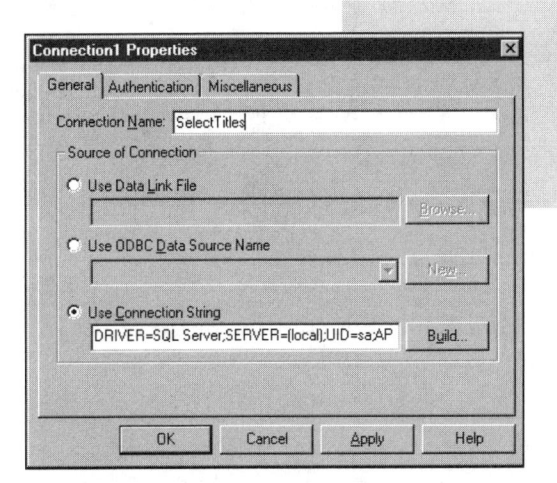

Figure 10.3
Use the connection's Properties dialog box to assign a descriptive name to the connection.

Figure 10.4
The Data View window shows you the database that you are connected to.

You can see by looking at the Data view that you are connected to a database named Pubs. You may have expected the name to be MTSSamples. MTSSamples is the name of the data source. The data source name is the collection of information used to connect your application to an ODBC database. It is not a database. The database that was connected to it is named Pubs. A database is represented in the Data view by a small yellow drum. To view the objects within the connection, perform these steps:

1. Click on the plus sign beside the Pubs database object. The view expands. You'll see that four items are displayed: Database Diagrams, Tables, Views, and Stored Procedures (see Figure 10.5).

Tip

To make it easier to see the information contained within the Data view, I recommend dragging the Data View window to the center of the screen and resizing it if necessary.

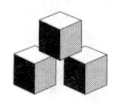

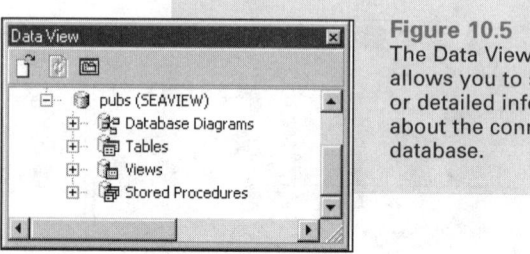

Figure 10.5
The Data View window allows you to see high-level or detailed information about the connected database.

2. Expand the Tables folder. A list of the tables in the database displays (see Figure 10.6).

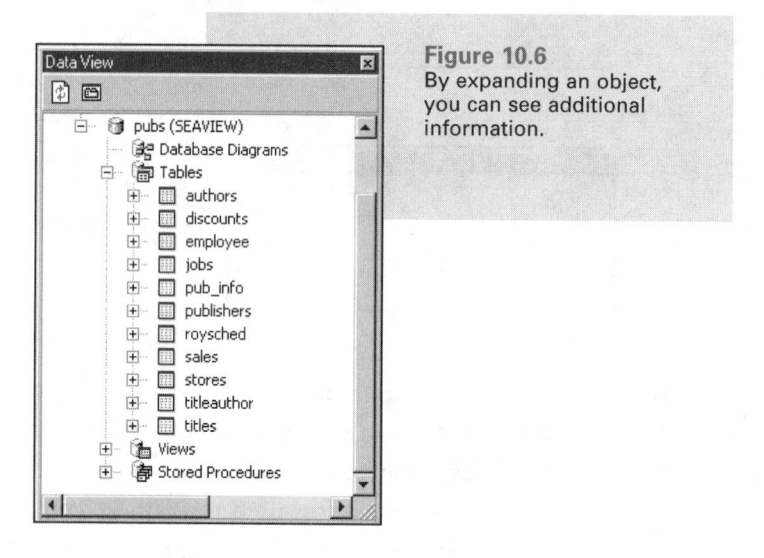

Figure 10.6
By expanding an object, you can see additional information.

3. Collapse the Tables folder.
4. Expand the Views folder. You can see that one view has been created for this database.

> A *view* is a subset of columns from one or more tables used to present data to a user. For example, you have a table about employees that contains such fields as name, department, phone number, and salary. You would probably want to create a view that showed all the fields in this table except the salary field, since salary information is not something that the average user should have access to.

5. Collapse the Views folder.

CHAPTER 10 • DESIGNING THE SYSTEM   151

6. Expand the Stored Procedures folder. Several stored procedures are defined.

> A *stored procedure* is a set of SQL statements (SQL Server also supports flow control statements in stored procedures) that are stored under a procedure name so that the statements can be executed as a group by the database server.

7. Collapse the Stored Procedures folder.
8. Expand the Tables folder. A list of the tables in the database displays.
9. Expand the Authors table. You can see a list of columns (fields) that are part of this table's definition.
10. Select the au_lname column object. The properties for that column display in the Properties window. (I know that you were probably expecting a dialog box to display, but Visual InterDev displays the properties in the standard Properties window, as shown in Figure 10.7.) You can see that the column has a data type of varchar and a length of 40 characters.

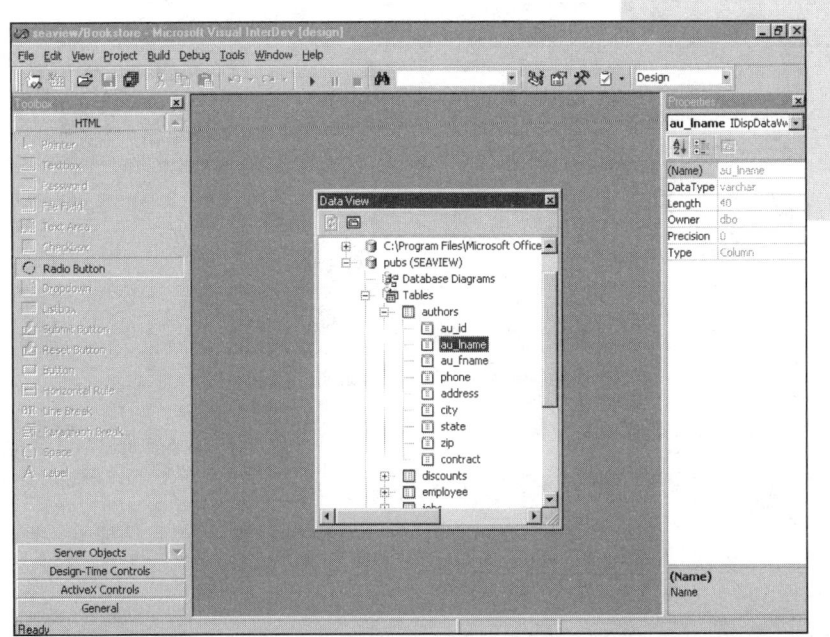

Figure 10.7
You can view information about database objects in the Properties window.

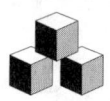

Viewing the Contents of a Table

If you aren't familiar with the database you are using, you may want to look at the contents of its tables. This is easily done using the Data View window by completing these steps:

1. Right-click on the Authors table. A pop-up menu displays.
2. Select <u>O</u>pen. In a few moments, the rows of the Authors table display (see Figure 10.8).

> **Tip**
>
> Depending on how many rows the table has, this operation could take a while. Unless you have huge amounts of RAM, you may want to avoid having extra applications running when you are working with data in Visual InterDev. Otherwise, you may get messages about your system's resources running low.

3. Close the window displaying the table's contents.

Figure 10.8
Because of the integrated database tools provided, you can look at your data without leaving Visual InterDev.

Querying Your Data

You may or may not be familiar with using SQL (Structured Query Language). If you haven't ever created a query using SQL, don't worry. Visual InterDev provides you with an easy way to create queries using a drag-and-drop tool called the Query Designer. Even if you are familiar with SQL, you may still want to use the Query Designer because it is so easy to use. Just in case you aren't familiar with SQL, I'll briefly discuss what a query is and how SQL comes into play.

What Is a Query?

Once upon a time, in the early days of relational database systems, a language was created called SQL. SQL was and still is a standard for the retrieval of records according to criteria. You query, or question, the database management system about your tables, and the database management system responds to your query by returning the records that match your query. Queries are not limited to just finding records. Queries are also used to modify and analyze your records.

> *Queries* are used for the retrieval and manipulation of a subset of a table's records.
>
> *Structured Query Language (SQL)* is a widely adopted standard for getting answers to particular questions about your data.

The most common type of query you'll use is a *select query*. A select query retrieves data from one or more tables according to your requirements. Select queries let you do a variety of tasks beyond just the simple display of records:

- Display only the desired fields.
- Sort records.
- Group records.
- Perform calculations such as sum, average, count, or evaluate your own expression.

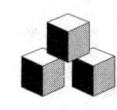

Accessing the Query Designer

Create a simple query that finds all the books that cost less than ten dollars. When viewing the results of this query, you only want to see the name of the book and its price. An easy way to create a query is to use the Query Designer. To do this, perform the following steps:

1. Expand your project from the Project Explorer. The connection displays.

> **Tip**
> You may need to expand Global.asa and then DataEnvironment to locate the connection.

2. Right-click on the connection. A pop-up menu displays.
3. Select Add Data Command. The Command1 Properties dialog box displays, as shown in Figure 10.9.

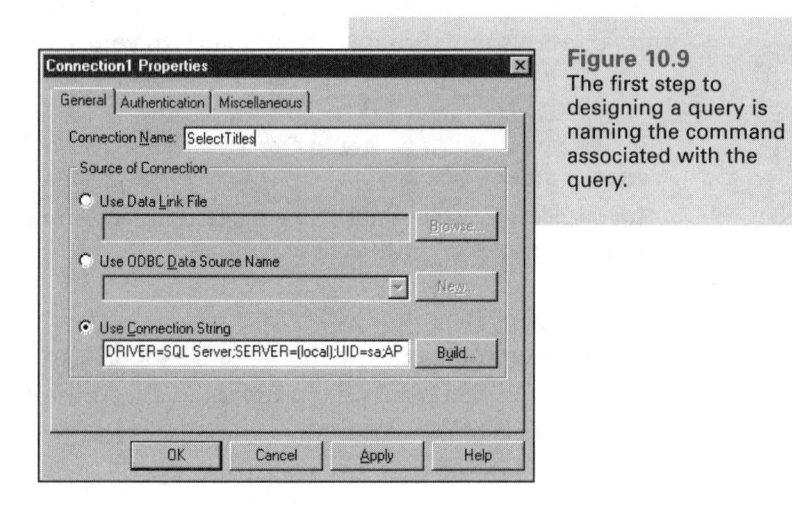

Figure 10.9
The first step to designing a query is naming the command associated with the query.

4. Enter CheapBooks for the Command Name.
5. Select SQL Statement. You could enter a SQL Statement here, but you are going to use the Query Designer.
6. Click on SQL Builder and then on Open. The Query Designer displays, as shown in Figure 10.10.

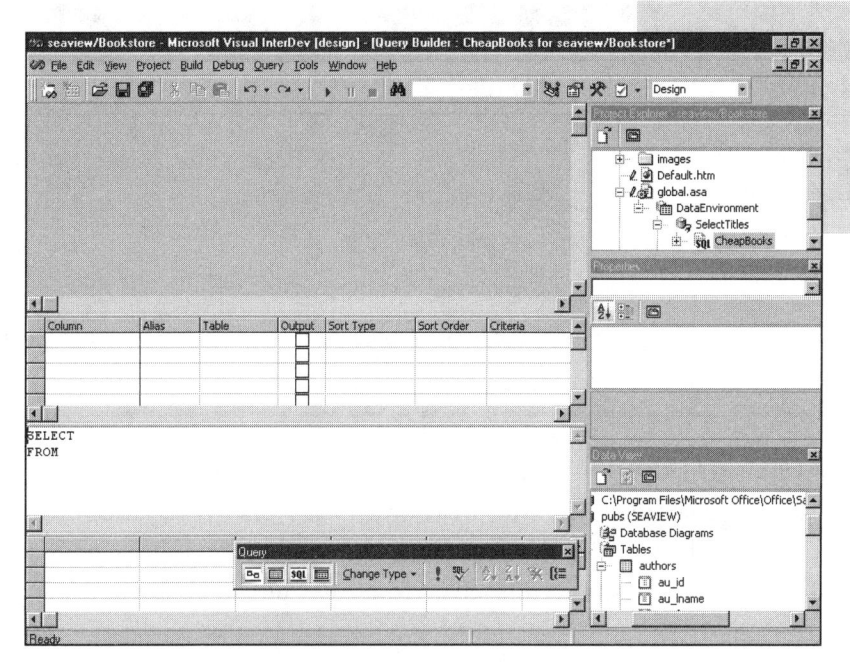

Figure 10.10
The Query Designer allows you to use drag-and-drop techniques to build a query.

The Query Designer is broken into four parts. The top pane is called the Diagram pane. This pane will hold the table listings for the query you are designing and will illustrate the relationships (joins) between tables. The pane below the Show Diagram pane is the Grid pane. The Grid pane is used to add criteria to your query to get more detailed results.

> A *relationship* is a connection between two tables accomplished through common fields.
>
> When two or more tables are linked by a similar field or fields (typically a key field), the tables are said to be *joined*.

To effectively use criteria in your queries, you have to be aware of what operators you use to create expressions that make up your criteria. These operators are called *comparison operators* and are used to compare values and expressions. Table 10.1 lists the comparison operators. Using these comparison operators, you can create criteria such as "price < 10.00."

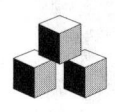

Table 10.1 The Comparison Operators

Symbol	Name
=	Equal to
<	Less than
<=	Less than or equal to
>	Greater than
>=	Greater than or equal to
<>	Not equal to

The third pane is the SQL pane. This pane will contain the SQL statement that is generated as a result of your actions. The final pane is the Result pane. When a query is executed, the result (the answer to the query) is displayed in the Result pane. To create the query, follow these steps:

1. If needed, expand the Tables folder in Data view.
2. Drag the Titles table to the top pane of the Query Designer. The table is added to the query, as shown in Figure 10.11. When the table is added to the Diagram pane, its name, in this case Titles, is added to the SQL pane. As you can see, this table has quite a few columns in it. You only need the name of the book and its prices. You can choose which columns you want to see in the result set of your query.
3. Place checks beside the title and price columns to add these columns to the query, as shown in Figure 10.12. The first thing you may notice is that these two column names are added to the Grid pane. Also, look at the SQL pane. You can see the query being built. Currently the query is as follows:

```
SELECT title, price
FROM titles
```

4. Scroll the Grid pane over until you see the Criteria column. Position your pointer in the cell for the Price row.

CHAPTER 10 • DESIGNING THE SYSTEM 157

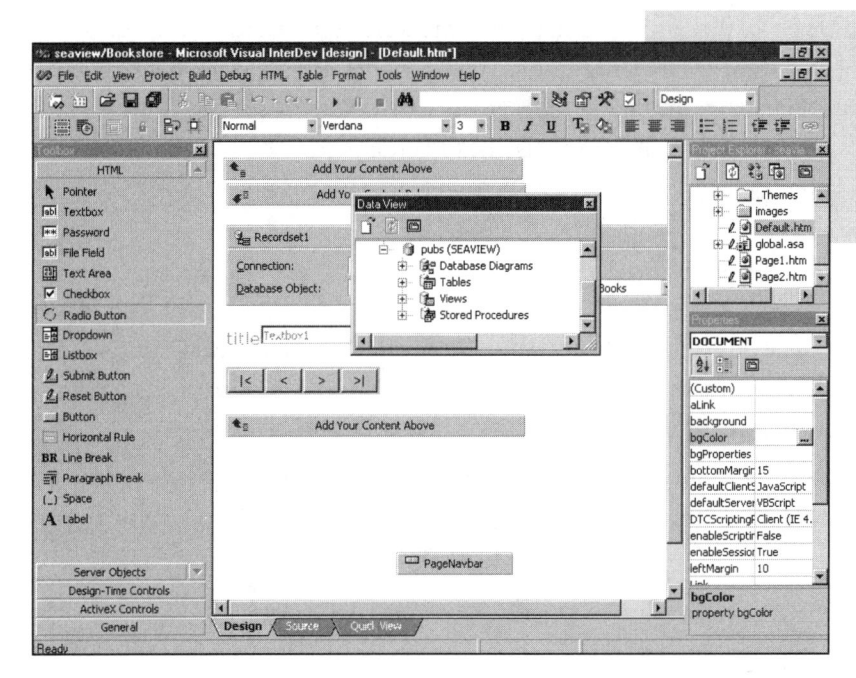

Figure 10.11
To build a query, you need to select the table or tables you want to work with.

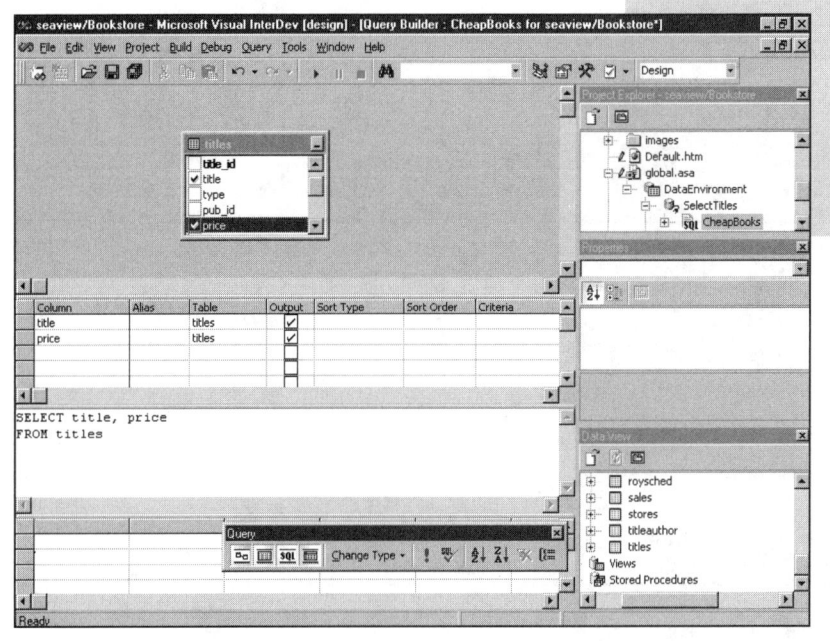

Figure 10.12
The selection of columns in the Diagram pane is reflected in the Grid pane and the SQL pane.

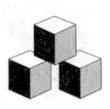

5. Type <10 and press Enter. You are adding a criterion that says you want to see only books whose prices are greater than ten dollars. Again, take a look at the SQL pane to see the query being built. A *Where* clause has been added. The SQL statement now looks like this:

```
SELECT title, price
FROM titles
WHERE (price < 10)
```

6. Click on the Run Query button located on the Query toolbar. The results of the query are shown in the Results pane, as shown in Figure 10.13.

You can build more complex queries than the one you just created. However, this example demonstrates the basic skills you need for query design.

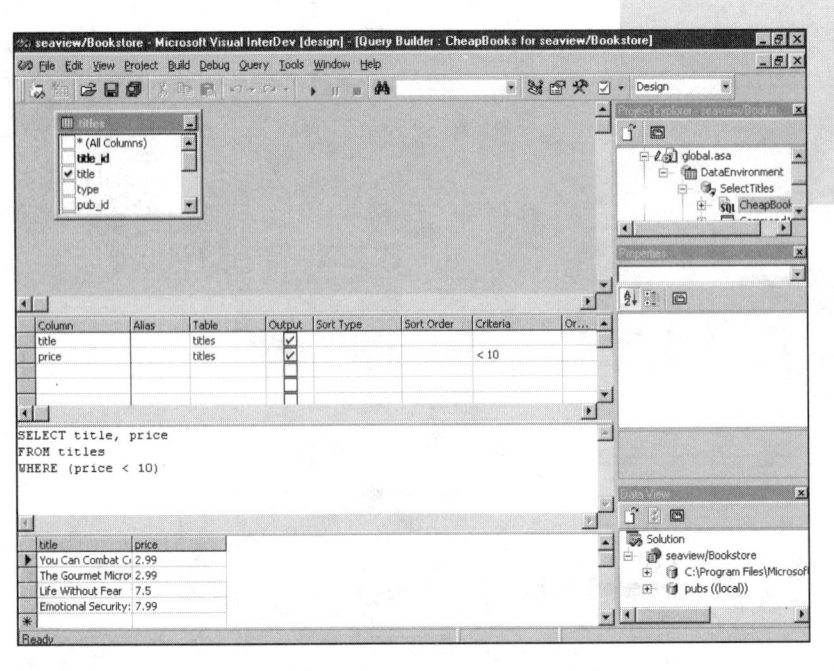

Figure 10.13 Four records meet the criteria that were set for the query.

Saving the Query

Next, you need to save the query. You can't use the query with your project until you save it. To save the query, select File, Save CheapBooks. You know the query has been saved because the columns used by the query are listed in the Project Explorer window.

Viewing the Records from Your Home Page

To use the results of the query you created, you need to do three things: First, you must add a Recordset control to your page. Second, you must add bound controls to the page. Finally, you must add record navigation to your application.

Adding a Recordset Control

To gain access to data from your page, you have to add a Recordset control to the page. A Recordset control is bound to a particular database using a database connection. It acts as a pointer that says, "Hey, I want to use these records." The Recordset can be bound to a table, a stored procedure, or a command. To add a Recordset control to your page, complete the following steps:

1. Close the Query Builder window and open the Default page from Project Explorer.
2. Select Design-Time Controls from the Toolbox.
3. Drag the Recordset control from the Design-Time Controls tab of the Toolbox onto the page, below where it says Add Your Content Below. A Recordset control is added to the page, as shown in Figure 10.14.
4. Right-click on the Recordset control. A pop-up menu displays.
5. Select Properties. The Recordset Properties dialog box displays, as shown in Figure 10.15.

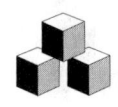

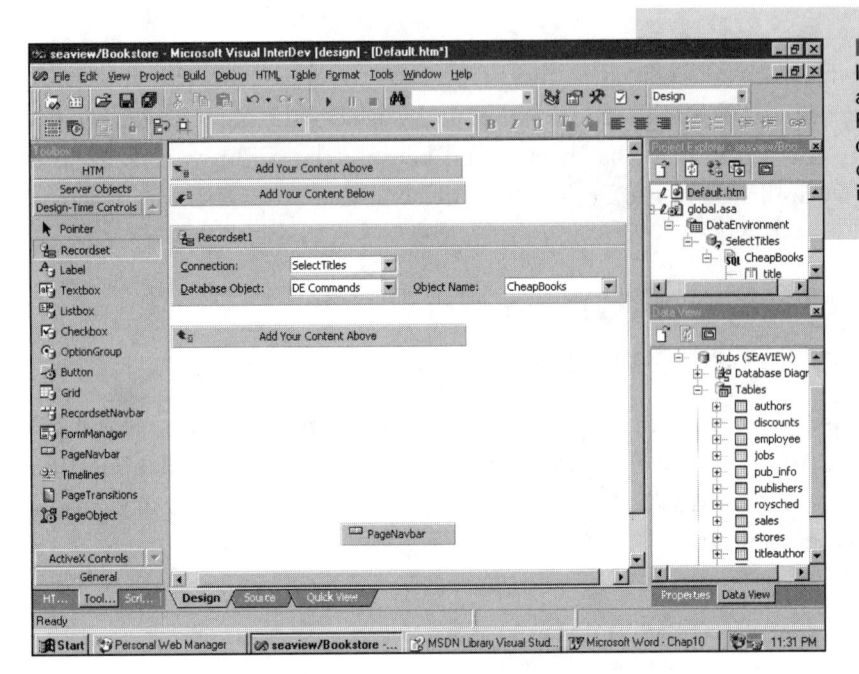

Figure 10.14
Information about the Recordset control displays on the control itself.

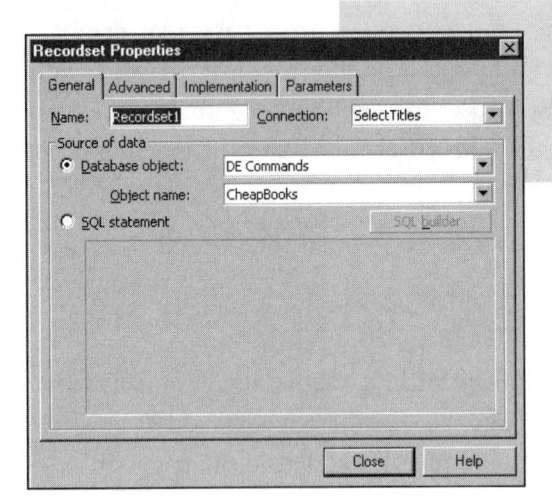

Figure 10.15
By setting the properties of the Recordset control, you'll connect it to the query you created.

6. Set Database object to DE Commands.

> **DE commands** are Data Environment commands. In this case the DE command is the query you just created.

CHAPTER 10 • DESIGNING THE SYSTEM   161

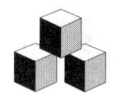

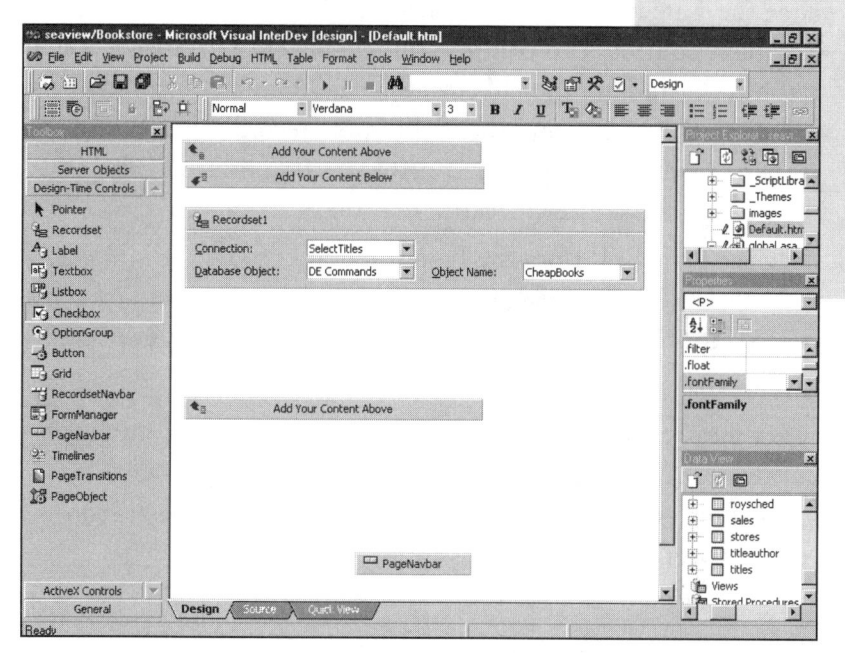

Figure 10.16
The Recordset control displays information about its Connection, Database Object, and Object Name settings.

7. Set Object Name to CheapBooks and click on Close.

The Recordset control is now bound to the query you created earlier (see Figure 10.16).

Adding Databound Controls to Your Page

Once you have the Recordset control created on your page, you can use drag-and-drop editing to add the fields to your page. Complete the following steps:

1. Add a blank line after the Recordset control.
2. If needed, expand CheapBooks in the Project Explorer window.

> **Tip**
> If you don't see the field names you selected when you created your query listed in Project Explorer, you didn't save your query. Open the query again and save it.

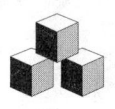

3. Drag the Title field from the Project Explorer to underneath the Recordset control. Two controls are actually created, a label and a text box. Each dragged field creates a data-bound control that will display the data from that field in the record set. Text and numeric fields create Textbox controls. Yes/No or True/False (Boolean) fields create Checkbox controls.//

4. Drag the Price field from the Project Explorer so that it is beside the Title field in the Design view. Another label and text box are created. Your page should look similar to the one in Figure 10.17.

5. Save the page.

6. Select the Quick View tab. As you can see, the controls display, but the text boxes are empty (see Figure 10.18). To actually see the text boxes with data in them, you need to view the page in your browser.

Note: You may receive a Debug dialog when attempting this step. If this is the case, dismiss the debug offer.

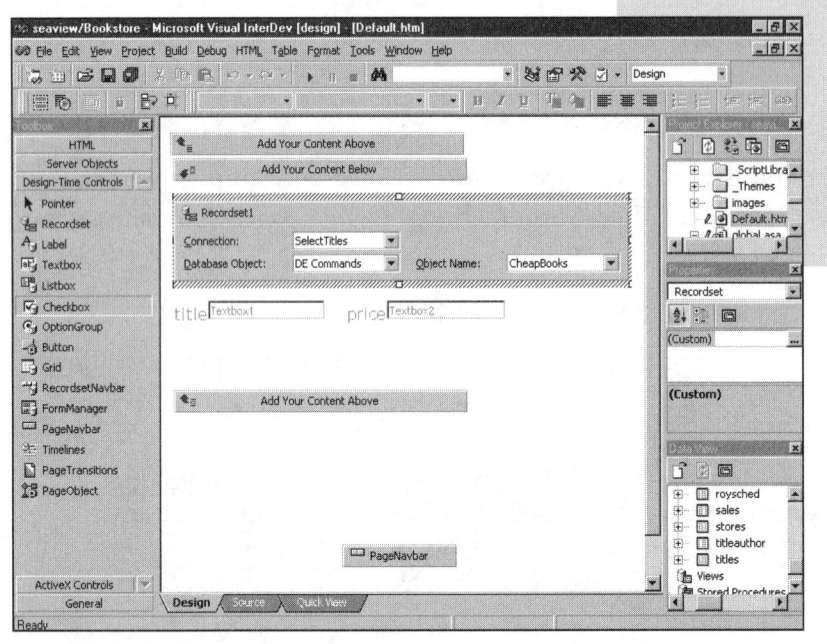

Figure 10.17 Add bound controls simply by dragging columns from the Project Explorer to the page in Design view.

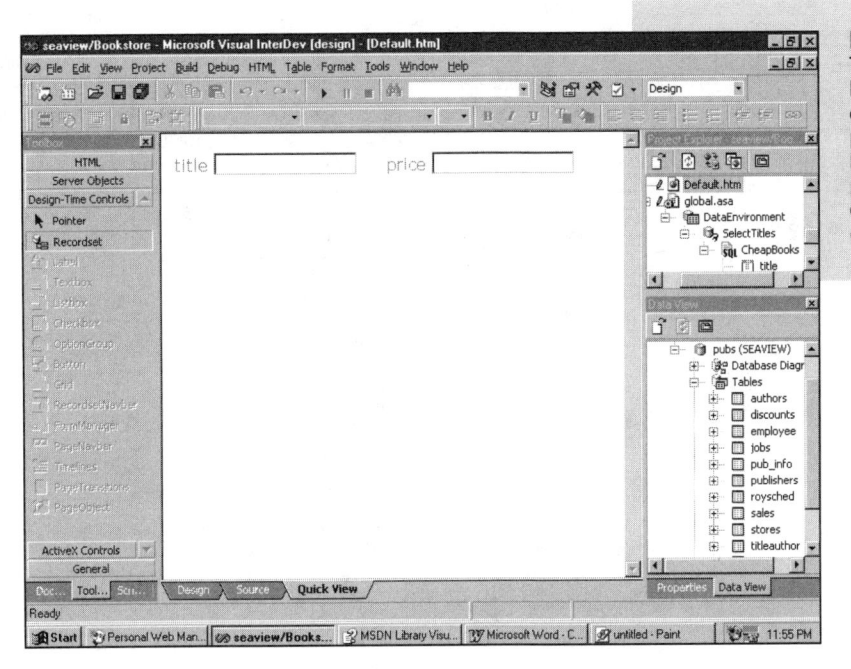

Figure 10.18
The Quick View lets you see control placement, but does not populate the controls with data.

7. Select View, View in Browser. You can see the data in the text box controls.
8. Close the browser window.
9. Select the Design tab to access the Design view.

You may have noticed that you can't read the whole title of the book. You can, if you wish, resize the title text box control once you return to the Design view.

Adding Record Navigation

Great! You've got data displaying on your Web page. You've officially entered the world of dynamic Web applications. But there's one little problem. Your user can only get to one record. This won't get you into the Internet Hall of Fame! You need to add a RecordsetNavbar control to your application. This control provides record navigation for your page. To add the RecordsetNavbar to your page, use the following steps:

1. Add a blank line after your bound controls.

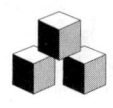

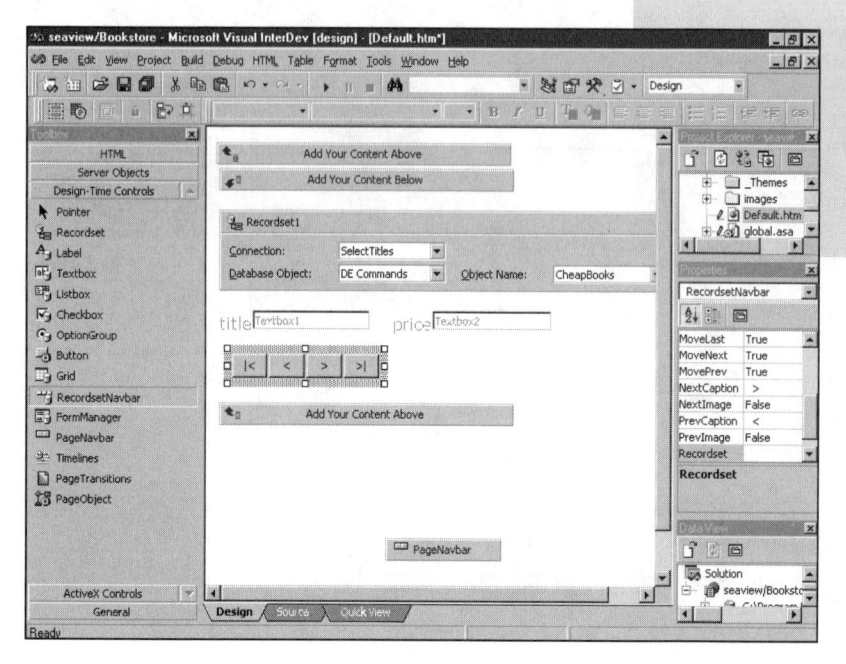

Figure 10.19 The RecordsetNavbar control contains four buttons that are used for record navigation.

2. Drag the RecordsetNavbar from the Toolbox to the newly created blank line. The control is added to the form, as shown in Figure 10.19.

3. Right-click on the new control and select Properties. The Properties dialog box displays.

4. Set the Recordset property to Recordset1 and click on OK.

5. Save the page.

6. Select View, View in Browser. You can see the data in the text box controls and the added navigation bar with four buttons. From left to right, the first button takes you to the first record in the record set. The second button takes you back to the previous record. The third button moves to the next record. And the last button moves you to the last record in the record set.

7. Click on the third button in the record navigation bar. The next record displays.

8. Click on the last button in the record navigation bar. The last record in the record set displays.

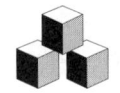

9. Click on the first button. The first record displays.
10. Close the browser window.

The Professional Edition versus the Enterprise Edition

Now that you've had a little hands-on experience with the Data view and Query Designer, you are probably curious about the relevant differences between the Professional and Enterprise Editions of Visual Studio as they pertain to data access and manipulation. Table 10.2 illustrates these differences.

Table 10.2 Data Access and Manipulation Differences between Editions of Visual Studio

Feature	Professional	Enterprise
Create new tables	No	Yes
Create new views	No	Yes
Create new stored procedures	No	Yes
Create queries	Yes	Yes
Create new triggers	No	Yes
Create new database diagrams	No	Yes
Edit database diagrams	No	Yes
Edit table structures	No	Yes
Edit queries	Yes	Yes
Edit stored procedures	No	Yes
Execute stored procedures	Yes	Yes
Debug stored procedures	No	Yes

As you can see from Table 10.2, if you plan to do extensive development using data access that requires you to create new database objects, you may want to invest in the Enterprise Edition of Visual Studio. If you are just going to work with data that is maintained by a database administrator, the Professional Edition will meet your needs.

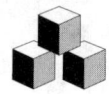

Summary

You've covered a lot of material in this chapter. You've added a data connection to your project and designed a query. You've used the result of that query to display data on your page using the Recordset control and RecordsetNavpage control. In other words, you've created a dynamic Web application.

In the next chapter, you will work with a Microsoft Access database instead of a SQL Server database to give you more experience working with dynamic data.

CHAPTER 11

Building the Database Web Project

In the last chapter, you worked with gaining access to data that resided on SQL Server. You saw that this is an easy process to accomplish. This knowledge is useful if you are using SQL Server as your database system, but what if you aren't? What if you are using Microsoft Access or Microsoft FoxPro? The good news (and there's no bad news) is that you use the same steps that you used to work with SQL Server.

Because of Visual InterDev's user interface, it doesn't matter which ODBC-compliant database you are connecting to, as long as it is ODBC-compliant. In this chapter, you are going to do many of the steps that you did in the last chapter, but you are going to use Access as your data source. If you don't have SQL Server installed, you'll be able to get hands-on experience using data access in a project. If you were able to do the steps in the last chapter, you'll get an opportunity to further experiment with data connections.

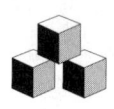

You'll also be introduced to scripting in this chapter. This introduction to this language will act as a foundation when you delve deeper into VBScript later in this book.

This chapter gives you a chance to work with a number of design-time controls. You'll use a grid to display data and the FormManager to create a feature-rich dynamic form. You will use Button and Textbox design-time controls while creating this form.

Using Visual InterDev with Access

You start with the key concept, which is really the only concept you need to consider in using Access with Visual InterDev: Access is an ODBC-compliant database. Of course, you need to know how to connect to a database, query it, and conduct other procedures, but if you read the previous chapter, you already know how to do this.

In this chapter, you will create a data source from scratch. Not that you have to—if you did a full install of Access on your system, the data source is already defined on your system. But just for the thrill of learning and because you might need to know how in the future, you are going to go through the steps.

Connecting to an Access Database

You will to connect to a database called Northwind. This database ships as part of Access and is designed as a sample database for you to experiment with. First I'll take you through the steps to show you that a data source has already been defined for this database object. Then you'll ignore that fact and create your own! To connect to the Northwind Access database, follow these steps:

> **Note:** To complete this exercise, you will need to have the Northwind database installed on your system. The Northwind database is a sample database that ships with Microsoft Access.

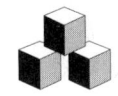

CHAPTER 11 • BUILDING THE DATABASE WEB PROJECT   169

1. Start Visual InterDev and open the Bookstore project.
2. Using the Site Diagram, add another page to your Bookstore project.
3. Open the newly created page by double-clicking on it from the Site Diagram.
4. Right-click on *servername*/Bookstore (where *servername* is the name of your Web server) and select Add Data Connection. The Select Data Source dialog box displays. Earlier I said that you didn't really have to create a new data source because one named Northwind already exists. Remember that you are doing this as an exercise.
5. Click on New. The Create New Data Source dialog box displays, as shown in Figure 11.1.
6. Select Microsoft Access Driver from the list and click on Next. The next Create New Data Source dialog box displays, as shown in Figure 11.2.

Note

If you were connecting to FoxPro, you would select the Microsoft FoxPro Driver for this step instead. This holds true for any of the database applications listed. The process is virtually the same once you select your driver.

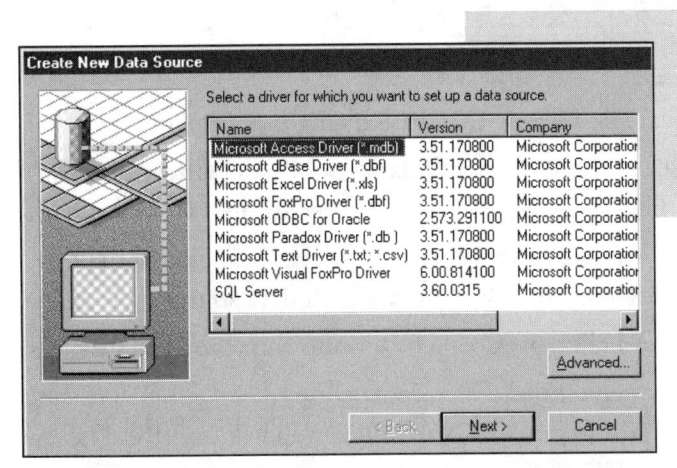

Figure 11.1
The Create New Data Source dialog box prompts to select a driver for the data source.

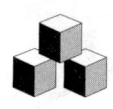

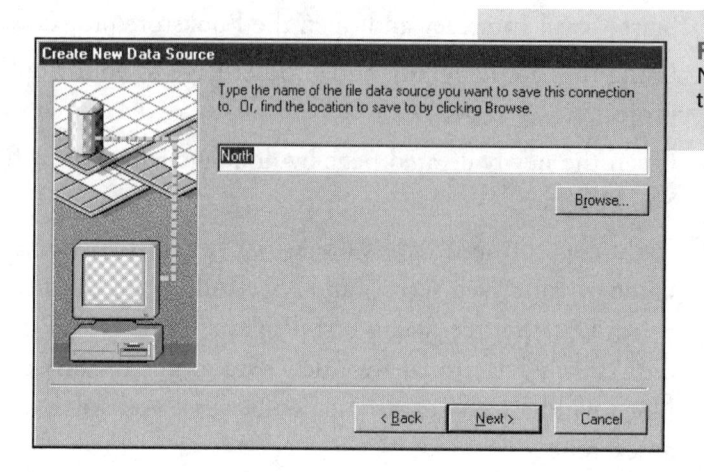

Figure 11.2 Next, you name the connection.

7. Type **North** and click on **N**ext. The next dialog box displays.
8. Click on Finish. The ODBC Microsoft Access 97 Setup dialog box displays (see Figure 11.3).

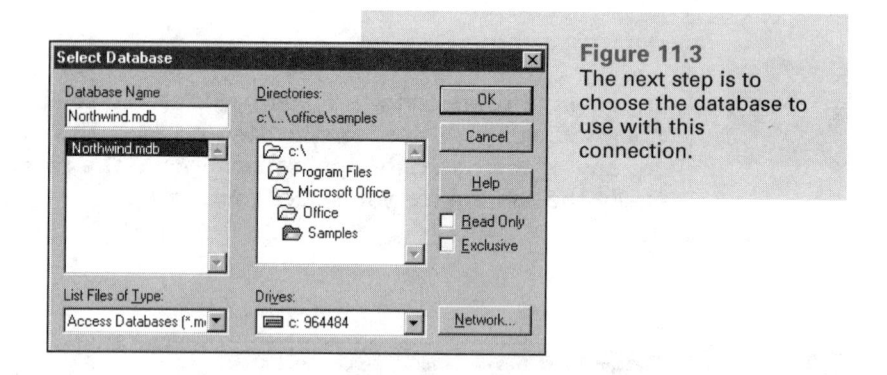

Figure 11.3 The next step is to choose the database to use with this connection.

9. Click on **S**elect. The Select Database dialog box displays.
10. Locate and select the Northwind database. By default, it installs in \Program Files\Microsoft Office\Office\Samples. Click on OK.
11. Click on OK. You are returned to the Select Data Source dialog box. Notice that your newly created North data source is listed.
12. Select North and click on OK. The Connection Properties dialog box displays.
13. Set the Connection **N**ame to NorthDC and click on OK. The

CHAPTER 11 • BUILDING THE DATABASE WEB PROJECT

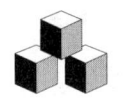

data connection has been added to Project Explorer, and you can see that Northwind.mdb has been added to the Data view.

14. Expand Northwind.mdb from the Data view. You'll see that two folders are listed, Tables and Views.

15. Right-click on NorthDC in Project Explorer. Select Add Data Command. The Properties window displays.

16. Enter Products for the Command Name.

17. Select SQL Statement and click on SQL Builder. In a few moments the Query Designer displays. In the last chapter you used only a single table in your query. In this chapter you are going to use multiple tables.

18. Drag the Products table from the Data View window to the Diagram pane.

19. Drag the Suppliers table from the Data View window to the Diagram pane. Notice that a line connects the two tables in the Diagram pane. The line goes from SupplierID in Products to SupplierID in Suppliers. Because of these like fields, the tables relate to one another. This relationship forms a *join*.

20. In the Products table, check ProductName and UnitPrice.

21. In the Suppliers table, check CompanyName.

22. In the Grid pane, set the Sort Type for CompanyName to Ascending.

23. When you are done, you should see this statement in the SQL pane:

```
SELECT Products.ProductName, Products.UnitPrice, Suppliers.CompanyName
FROM Products, Suppliers
WHERE Products.SupplierID = Suppliers.SupplierID
ORDER BY Suppliers.CompanyName
```

On the first line of this Select statement, you see the columns that are being retrieved. Notice that they are prefixed with the name of the tables that they reside in. The Where clause shows which fields relate to each other. The Order By clause lets you know that the results of this query will be sorted on the CompanyName field.

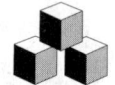

24. Click on the Run Query toolbar button to see the results of the query.

25. Select File, Save Products, and close the Query Builder window.

Displaying the Results of an Access Query

Okay, you've created the query you want to use. Do you remember the next step? You need to add a Recordset control to your page. A Recordset control is bound to a particular database using a database connection. The Recordset can be bound to a table, a stored procedure, or a command. To add a Recordset control to your page, complete these steps:

1. Open Page1 from Project Explorer.
2. Select Design-Time Controls from the Toolbox.
3. Drag the Recordset control from the Design-Time Controls tab of the Toolbox onto the page, below where it says Add Your Content Below. A Recordset control is added to the page.
4. Right-click on the Recordset control. A pop-up menu displays.
5. Select Properties. The Recordset properties dialog box displays.
6. Set Database Object to DE Commands.
7. Set Object Name to Products and click on Close.

The Recordset control is bound to the query you created earlier. Now that you have the Recordset control created on your page, you can use drag and drop to add the controls to your page. Complete these steps:

1. Add a blank line after the Recordset control.
2. If needed, expand Products in the Project Explorer window.

> **Tip**
> If the column names you selected when you created your query are not listed in Project Explorer, you didn't save your query. Open the query again and save it.

3. Drag CompanyName from Project Explorer to beneath the Recordset control.

CHAPTER 11 • BUILDING THE DATABASE WEB PROJECT   173

4. Add a blank line after the control.
5. Drag ProductName from Project Explorer onto the blank line you just added.
6. Add a blank line after the control.
7. Drag UnitPrice from Project Explorer onto the blank line you just added.
8. Save the page.

The last thing you need to do is add record navigation. To add the RecordsetNavbar to your page, follow these steps:

1. Add a blank line after your bound controls.
2. Drag the RecordsetNavbar from the Toolbox to the newly created blank line. The control is added to the form.
3. Right-click on the new control and select Properties. The Properties dialog box displays.
4. Set the Recordset property to Recordset1 and click on OK. The completed page should look like the one in Figure 11.4.

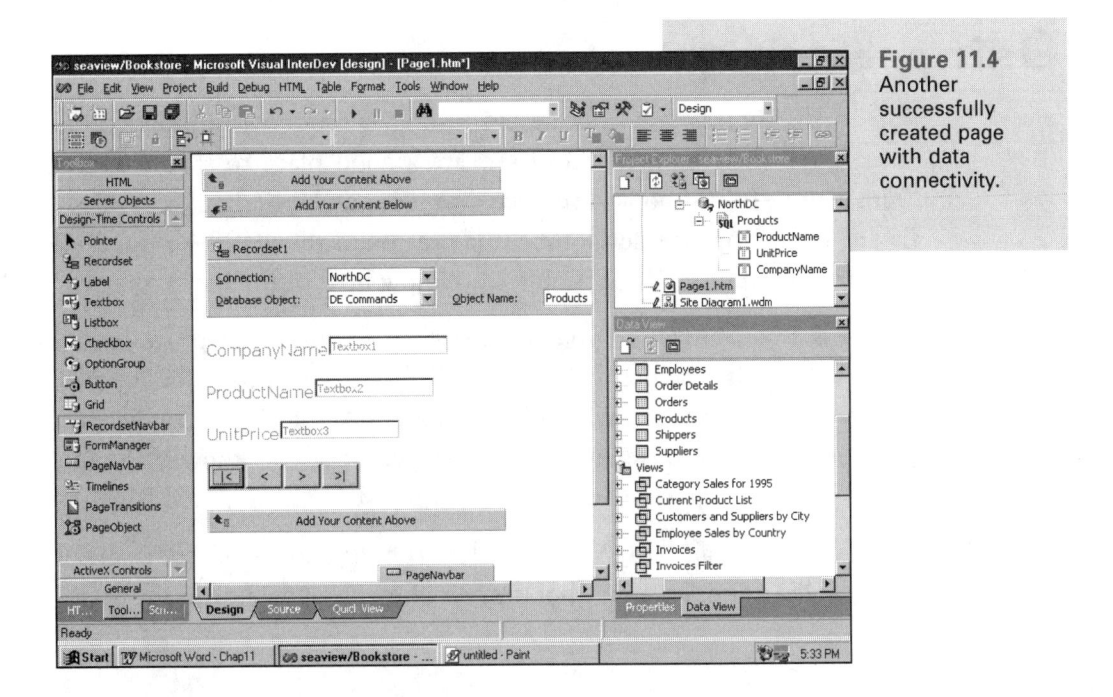

Figure 11.4
Another successfully created page with data connectivity.

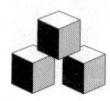

5. Save the page.
6. Select <u>V</u>iew, View in <u>B</u>rowser. You can see the data in the text box controls and the added navigation bar with four buttons. The first button takes you to the first record in the record set. The second button takes you back to the previous record. The third button takes you to the next record. And the last button moves you to the last record in the record set.
7. Click on the third button in the record navigation bar. The next record displays.
8. Click on the last button in the record navigation bar. The last record in the record set displays.
9. Click on the first button. The first record displays.
10. Close the browser window.

I know that you may have found that these steps are repeated in Chapter 10, but by completing this exercise, you will realize that working with an Access database is just like working with a SQL Server database, and vice versa.

Using Scripts

Up to this point, you've done everything without writing any code. Because of their nature, record sets are a good place to start working with scripts. In this book, I've elected to focus on VBScript. Visual Basic is one of the top five development languages in the world, so there are hundreds of thousands of people who know how to use it.

There is an advantage to you as well, even if you haven't programmed with Visual Basic before. By learning VBScript, you'll have the foundation you need to work with Visual Basic or Visual Basic Application Edition through transference of knowledge. Since you know VBScript, you'll be able to quickly learn and use other versions of Visual Basic.

Another advantage to VBScript for the developer is that all of Microsoft's examples use VBScript, so copying and pasting into your application makes development quicker than translating the code snippets into a different language.

> **Visual Basic, Application Edition** is the automation language for Microsoft's Office suite of products. It can be used to automate tasks in Word, Excel, Access, PowerPoint, and Project.

Note: VBScript is also the automation language for Microsoft Outlook.

Working with Objects, Properties, and Methods

You need to know three very important concepts in the VBScript world before you can begin using scripts with record sets. These concepts are objects, properties, and methods.

What Is an Object?

VBScript is a structured, English-like language. In this language, the items that are worked with and manipulated are *objects*. Basically, if you can name it, it's an object. If you wish, you can think of objects as the nouns of the VBA world.

What Is a Method?

Objects have actions that have been defined for them to perform. These actions are called *methods*. Some people like to think of methods as VBScript's verbs. Here is the structure of a method statement:

```
Objectname.methodname arg1, arg2, argn
```

where `Objectname` is the name of the object whose method is being used; `methodname` is the name of the method itself; and `arg1`, `arg2`, and `arg3` represent required and optional arguments that can be used with the method.

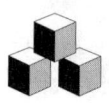

What Is a Property?

One of the things that you'll find yourself doing frequently in a VBScript procedure is working with properties. A *property* is an attribute of an object that defines one of the object's characteristics, behaviors, and other settings. To continue comparing VBScript to the English language, properties would act a lot like adjectives. You've actually worked with properties already through the Properties window and through properties dialog boxes.

This syntax structure is used for setting a property:

```
Objectname.propertyname = somevalue
```

In this case, `Objectname` is the object that you are manipulating, `propertyname` is the specific property you are working with, and `somevalue` is the value you are setting the property to. To see an example of how to work with setting properties, you will create a simple form that has a label on it, and you'll use properties to change its appearance.

Understanding What Happens When You Open a Page

When you open your page in a browser, the record set script object opens the table or executes the query specified in its properties. Then it creates a record set. A pointer is placed at the first record in the record set, which becomes the current record. All this happens in the background on the server.

Viewing Data Using a Script

In the previous exercise, you used design-time controls by dragging the column names to your form. These controls, because they are bound to the data, automatically update to reflect database values. You are not required to use design-time controls to display data. You can use some of the controls found on the HTML tab of the Toolbox.

If you did want to use a non-data-bound control to display data from a database, you would have to use a method called `getValue`. If, for exam-

CHAPTER 11 • BUILDING THE DATABASE WEB PROJECT   177

ple, you wanted to get the value of the `UnitPrice` field and place it in a Text control on your page, you would use code like this:

```
txtPrice.value = Recordset1.fields.getValue("UnitPrice")
```

In this example, `txtPrice` is the name of the Text control. `Value` is the property you are setting. The `getValue` method applies the fields available through the `Recordset1` Recordset control. And the field you are retrieving data from is `UnitPrice`.

Now use this example in your project. Say you wanted to show a price that is discounted ten percent. To do this, complete these steps:

1. Add a blank line above the navigation bar on the page.
2. Type **Discounted**:
3. Select the HTML group from the Toolbox.
4. Add a text box next to the text you just entered. Your completed page should look like the one in Figure 11.5.
5. Go to the Properties window and select the text box.

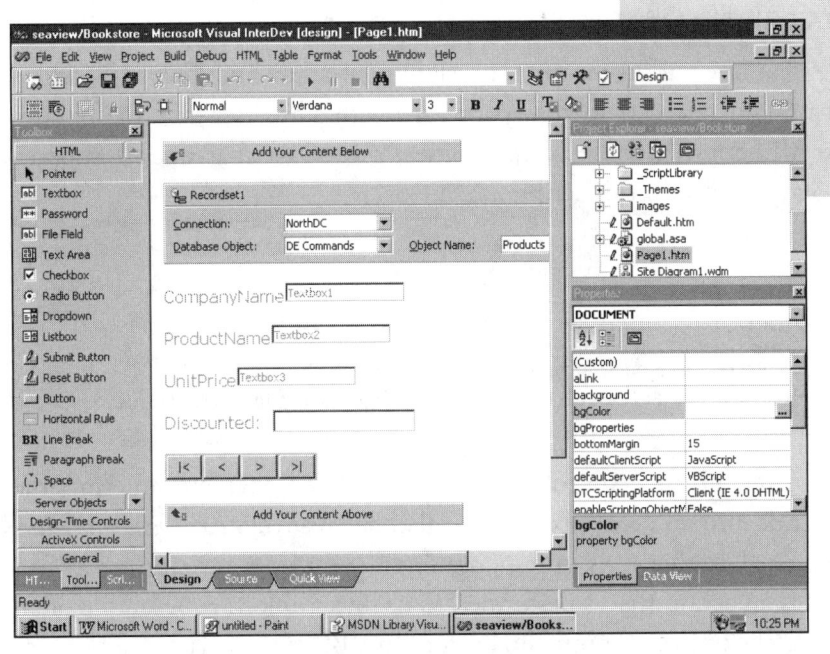

Figure 11.5
This page contains a control that will be populated using a script.

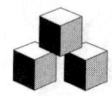

6. Set the (ID) property to txtDiscountedPrice. This property is the very first property in the Properties window.
7. Go to the Source view.
8. Add the following code below the Link tags at the top of the page:

```
<script LANGUAGE="VBScript">
<!—
function Recordset1_onrowenter()
       txtDiscountedPrice.value = Recordset1.fields.getvalue("UnitPrice") * .90
end function
//—>
</script>
```

Before you view what you have done in the browser, take a moment to understand what you've entered.

The first line indicates a script starting for client-side execution and sets the scripting language. By default, the scripting language is JavaScript. Because you are using VBScript, you need this statement:

```
<script LANGUAGE="VBScript">
```

The next line and its termination statement a few lines down are added in case someone tries to view your page with a browser that doesn't support VBScript. Because of these lines, a browser that doesn't support VBScript will skip this script:

```
<!—
//—>
```

The procedure you are writing actually starts on the next line:

```
function Recordset1_onrowenter()
    txtDiscountedPrice.value = Recordset1.fields.getvalue("UnitPrice") * .90
end function
```

The name of the control is Recordset1, and you are entering the VBScript into an event procedure called onrowenter. An *event procedure* is a procedure that runs in response to an event on a form or report. An event is an action that is performed to or by an object. An example of an event is clicking on a command button. In VBScript terms, the click event of the button occurs. Whatever code has been entered for that event exe-

CHAPTER 11 • BUILDING THE DATABASE WEB PROJECT

cutes when the event occurs. So what you are doing here is getting the value of the `UnitPrice` field every time a new record displays. Then you take the value and multiply it by .90 to discount the price by ten percent. You place the result in the text box named `txtDiscountedPrice` by setting the object's value property. The final line ends the scripting:

```
</script>
```

Bet you are dying to see the results of your first scripting attempt! To see the results, follow these steps:

1. Select View, View in Browser. A message box displays. Click on Yes to save your work. In a moment, your page displays (see Figure 11.6).
2. Click on the Next button on the record navigation bar. The next record displays, and the discounted price is calculated and displayed.
3. Close the browser window.

Did you expect scripting to be hard? It's not too bad, is it? VBScripts can get more complex than this, but you've got the basic concept now.

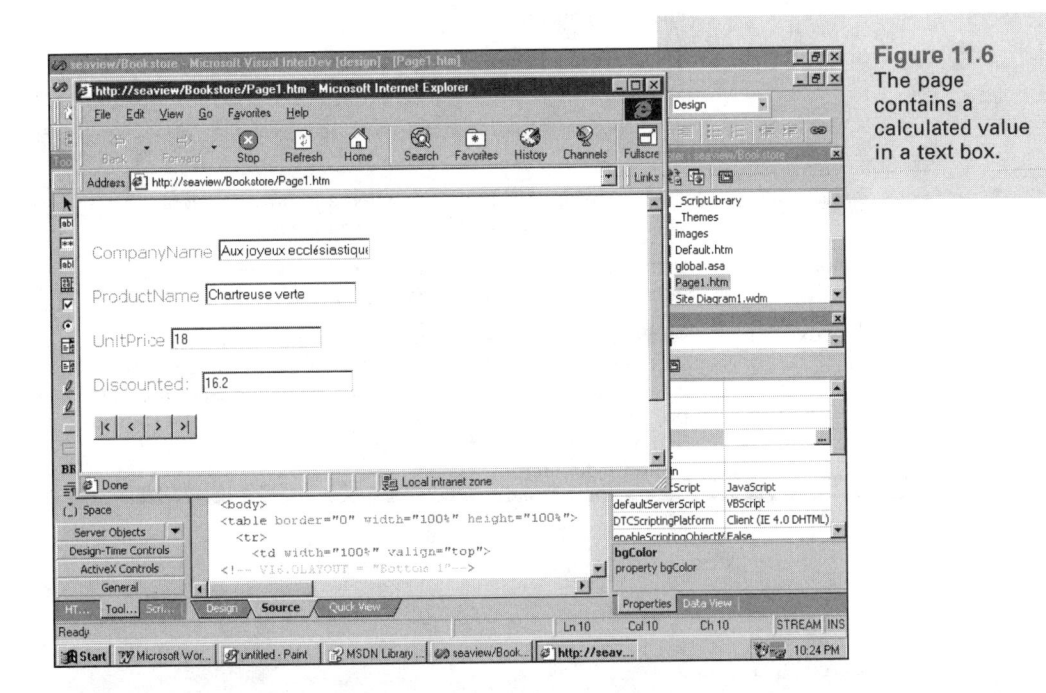

Figure 11.6
The page contains a calculated value in a text box.

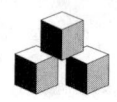

Working with Other Design-Time Controls

You've worked with one design-time control at this point, the DTC text box. This control was created when you dragged column names onto your page. You've probably noticed that there are a lot more design-time controls than just a text box. Take a look at some of these other controls.

An Overview of Other Data-Bound Design-Time Controls

Visual InterDev provides you with several data-bound design-time controls to make it easy to display data on your forms. Table 11.1 lists these controls.

Table 11.1   Data-Bound Design-Time Controls

Control	Description
Check box	Check boxes are used to display Boolean values (yes/no, true/false). These controls act as toggles, in that when one is clicked, a check is placed in the box. Click on it again, and the check is removed.
Grid	This control lets you display data from a database in an HTML table.
Label	A label is used to present text to a user in a static or unchangeable way.
Text box	Text boxes are used to display text and provide users with a visual clue that the text is changeable.
OptionGroup	Sets of mutually exclusive choices. For example, you can be either male or female. These choices are mutually exclusive.
List box	This control is similar to an OptionGroup in functionality in that the choices are typically exclusive. This is a good choice when you have a lot of options for a field. For example, a list box would be a good way to present states (as in the states in the United States of America). You would not want fifty OptionGroup items!

Chapter 11 • Building the Database Web Project

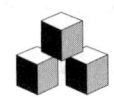

Using the Grid Control

The Grid control is a personal favorite of mine. The Grid control allows you to display data from a record set in a grid or table-like format. The best way to learn about grids is to use one, so complete these steps:

1. Add an HTML page to your project.
2. Add a Recordset control from the Design-Time Controls page of the Toolbox.
3. Right-click on the Recordset control on the page and select Properties.
4. Select NorthDC for the Connection.
5. Select Tables for the Database Object.
6. Select Products for the Object Name and click on Close.
7. Add a Grid control to the page.
8. Right-click on the Grid control and select Properties.
9. Select the Data tab. The Data page displays, as shown in Figure 11.7.

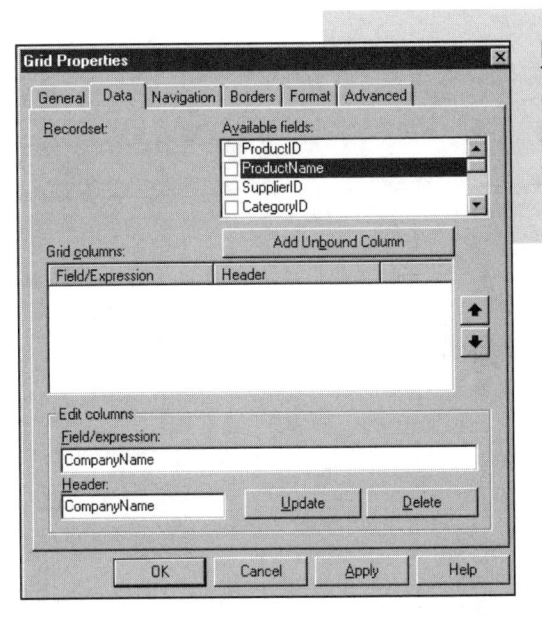

Figure 11.7
The Data page of the Grid Properties dialog box allows you to pick and choose the fields you wish to view in your grid.

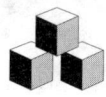

10. From the Available Fields list box, select ProductName, UnitPrice, and UnitsInstock.

11. Click on OK. The grid will show the column names you have selected.

12. Select View, View in Browser. A message box displays, prompting you to save your work.

13. Click on OK. The page with its grid display is shown in Figure 11.8. Doesn't the grid look great! And the best part is that it didn't take a lot of work!

14. Close the browser.

Besides being an easy control to use and a great medium to display data, the Grid control is a very flexible control. One of the nice features of the Grid control is its ability to create an unbound column. An example of how you may want to use an unbound column is to display a calculated value. In the example, you may want to multiply the unit price by the units on hand to get a cost of stock. To do this, follow these steps:

1. Right-click on the Grid control and select Properties.

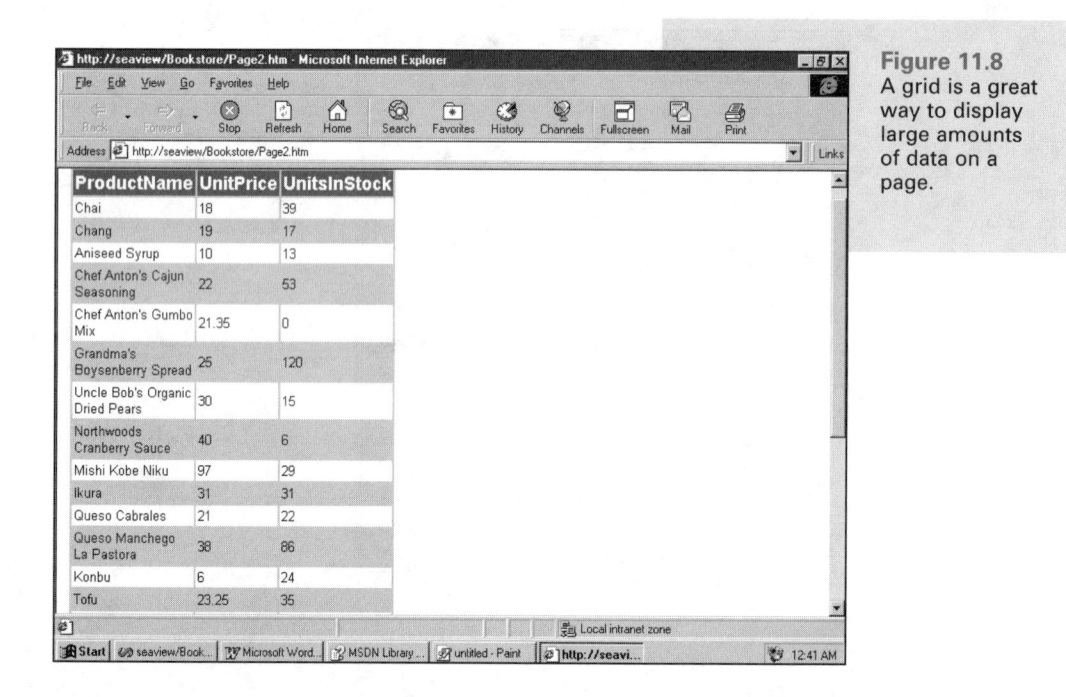

Figure 11.8
A grid is a great way to display large amounts of data on a page.

CHAPTER 11 • BUILDING THE DATABASE WEB PROJECT   183

2. Select the Data tab.
3. Click on Add Unbound Column. A column is added to the Grid Columns list box.
4. In the Field/Expression box, type

   ```
   Indent code
   =[UnitPrice] * [UnitsInStock]
   ```

   An expression has to start with an equal sign. This expression multiplies the UnitPrice field by the UnitsInStock field. Notice that field names are in square brackets.
5. Type **Cost of Stock** in the Header box and click on Update. The change is saved.
6. Select Cost of Stock from the Grid Columns list box. It doesn't make sense to have this as the first item displayed in the grid. Use the down-arrow button to the right of the list box to move the Cost of Stock column to the last column in the grid.
7. Click on OK.
8. Select View, View in Browser. A message box displays, prompting you to save your work.
9. Click on OK. You can see the calculated value in the new column.
10. Close the browser.

You are probably feeling pretty happy with your grid. But wait, there's more! You can change the appearance of the grid. This is done through the Properties dialog box using these steps:

1. Right-click on the Grid control and select Properties.
2. Select the General tab. The General page displays (see Figure 11.9).
3. Select Basic Maroon from the Style Name list box. A preview of the format displays.
4. Spend a moment checking out the different formats.
5. Select Teal Titles 3D.
6. Select the Format tab. The Format page displays (see Figure 11.10).

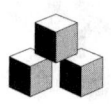

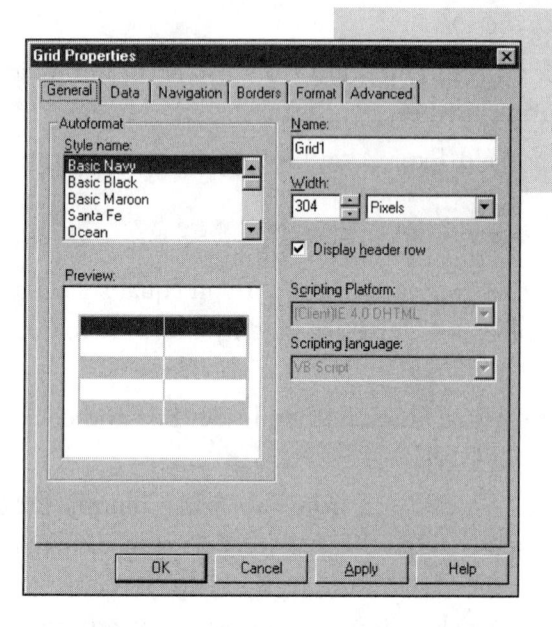

Figure 11.9 Visual InterDev provides several Autoformats for your use.

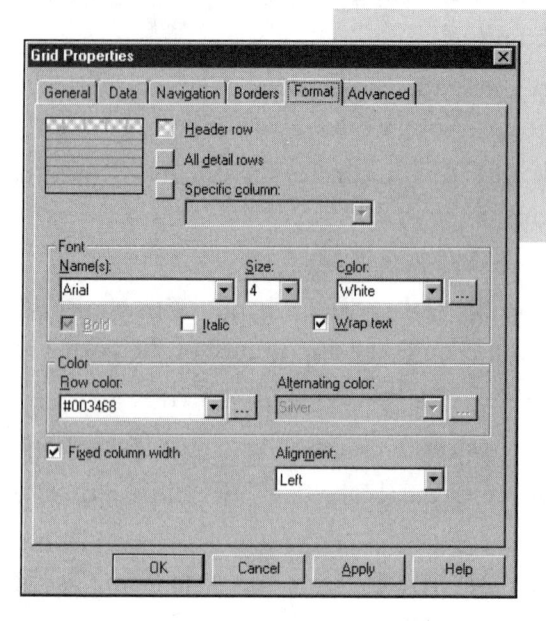

Figure 11.10 The Format tab allows you to do additional formatting beyond what is provided by an Autoformat.

7. Click on the Header Row button.
8. Change the Font Color to Black.
9. Click on OK. The grid reflects some of the changes.

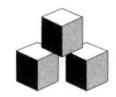

CHAPTER 11 • BUILDING THE DATABASE WEB PROJECT   **185**

10. Select <u>V</u>iew, View in <u>B</u>rowser. A message box displays, prompting you to save your work.
11. Click on OK. You can see your format change.
12. Close the browser.

The last thing you are going to do to this grid is change the number of rows being displayed. Complete these steps:

1. Right-click on the Grid control and select P<u>r</u>operties.
2. Select the Navigation tab. The Navigation page displays (see Figure 11.11).
3. Set <u>R</u>ecords/Page to 10.
4. Click on OK.
5. Select <u>V</u>iew, View in <u>B</u>rowser. A message box displays, prompting you to save your work.
6. Click on OK. As expected, the Grid control displays only 10 rows at a time.
7. Close the browser.

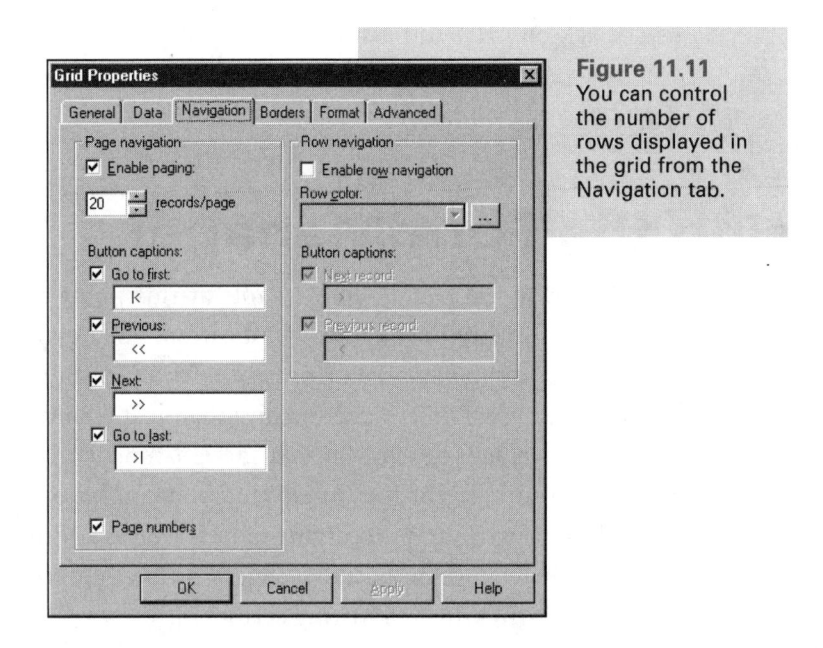

Figure 11.11
You can control the number of rows displayed in the grid from the Navigation tab.

Using a Check Box

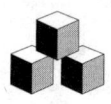

Another control you'll probably want to use is a check box. The Products table has a field named Discontinued. Using a check box, you could display this information in your project using these steps:

1. Open Page 1.
2. From Project Explorer, right-click on Products found under NorthDC. Select SQL Builder. The Query Designer opens.
3. Put a check beside Discontinued in the Products table.
4. Select File, Save Products.
5. Close the Query Designer window.
6. Add a blank line above the record navigation bar.
7. Drag the Discontinued column from Project Explorer to the blank line on the page. A check box displays. Visual InterDev examined the data in the column and determined that a check box was the best way to display it!
8. Select View, View in Browser. A message box displays, prompting you to save your work.
9. Click on OK. You can navigate through the records and see how the value of the check box changes.
10. Close the browser.

Using the FormManager

Hopefully you are feeling comfortable at this point about adding data access functionality to your Web application. So far, you have given your users the ability to view data from your Web site. But what if you need to allow your users more functionality than just record viewing and navigation? InterDev's FormManager design-time control generates the needed run-time script for you so that you can have one page that can be used for viewing and modifying data as well as adding records to your database. By setting the FormManager's properties, you add functionality to your form without writing script.

CHAPTER 11 • BUILDING THE DATABASE WEB PROJECT

Before creating the data entry page that you want to use FormManager with, you must complete the following tasks:

- Create a Web project.
- Add a data connection.
- Add an ASP file to the project with the Scripting Object Model enabled.

You are in luck. You have already done two of these three steps. You already have an existing Web project. You are just going to use the Bookstore project that you are currently working with. You already have a data connection. As a matter of fact, you have two in this project: SelectTitles and NorthDC. So all you have to do is add an ASP file to the project and enable the Scripting Object Model using the following steps:

> The *Scripting Object Model (SOM)* simplifies Web development by introducing a familiar object-oriented programming model to HTML and script programming. The Scripting Object Model is discussed in detail in Chapter 16.
>
> *Active Server Pages (ASP)* are HTML files that include embedded scripts that are executed on the Web server. The output of the scripts is included as part of the HTML that is downloaded to the browser.

Note The FormManager DTC uses both client- and server-side scripting. Thus, you must use an ASP page to enable the server-side logic.

1. Select Project, Add Item. The Add Item dialog box displays.
2. Select ASP Page.
3. Type Form Example for the Name and press Enter. The Form Example page is added to the page. Open the new page in Source view, as shown in Figure 11.12.
4. Right-click on the page away from any controls. A pop-up menu displays.

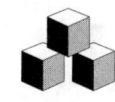

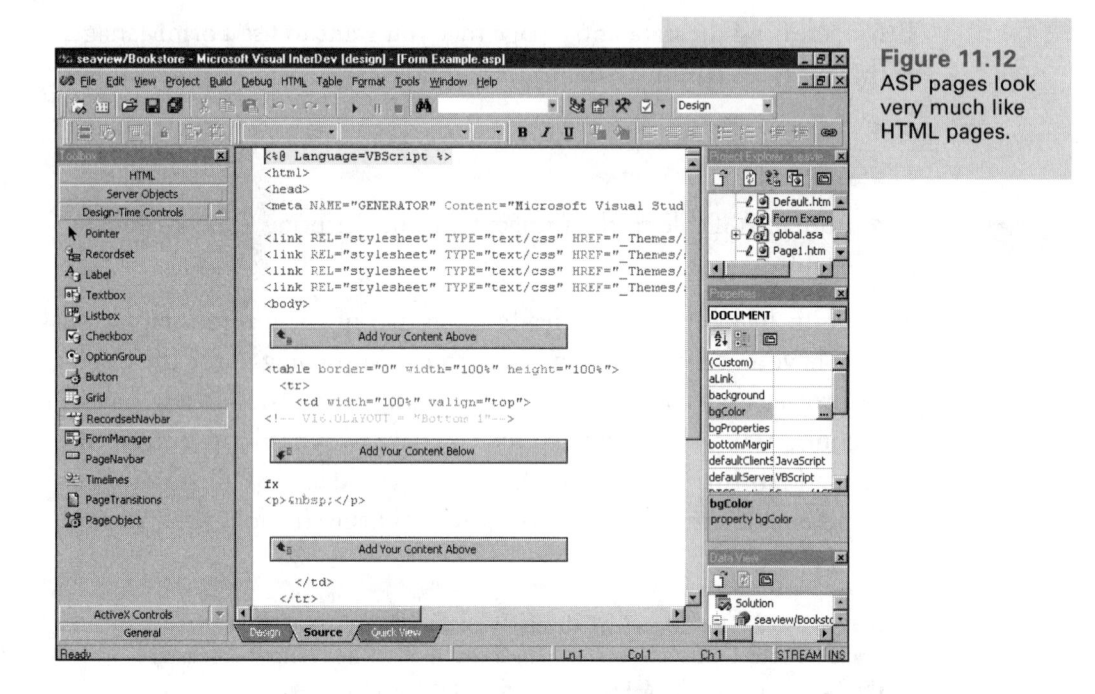

Figure 11.12
ASP pages look very much like HTML pages.

5. Select Properties. The Properties dialog box displays, as shown in Figure 11.13.
6. Check Enable scripting object model and click on OK.

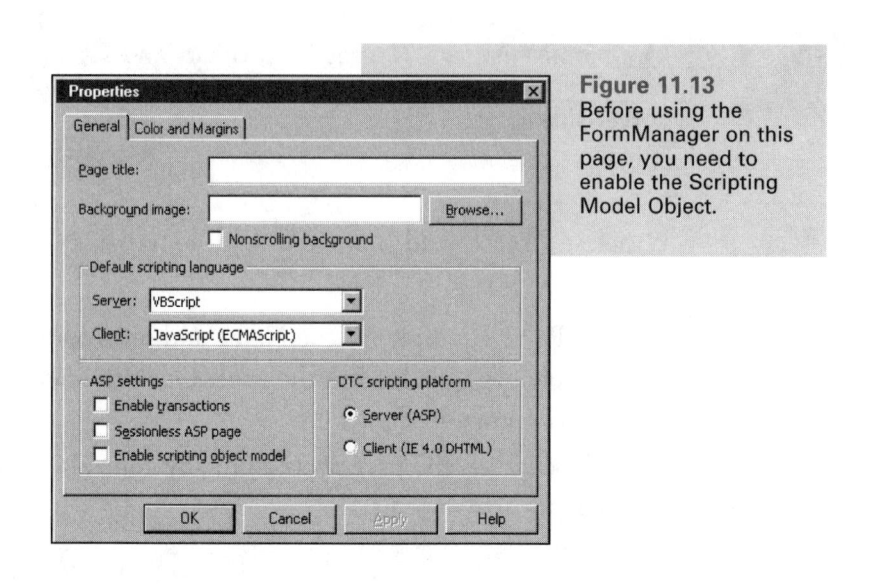

Figure 11.13
Before using the FormManager on this page, you need to enable the Scripting Model Object.

CHAPTER 11 • BUILDING THE DATABASE WEB PROJECT

Now that you've enabled the scripting object model, you are ready to start working with the FormManager design-time control.

> **Tip:** Before adding modes, make sure you have all of the controls you need on the form. For example, you may need to add buttons, such as an Edit button for moving to the Edit mode, and a Save button for triggering transition events in that mode.

If you decide to add more controls, you can do that later, but adding controls before adding the modes makes them readily available to the FormManager control. This also applies to functions and methods you want to script in the page. Here is the next series of steps you need to complete:

- Add a Recordset design-time control to your form.
- Set the source for the Recordset control. Also make sure that the lock type used is optimistic so that the form can update records.
- Add the necessary controls to display the fields you want to show the user and to make changes to the records.

These are steps you've done before in this chapter using an Access database, and in Chapter 10 using a SQL Server database. You have yet to add the Recordset control and a couple of other controls. You are going to create a very detailed form because you have worked with these concepts already. Complete the following steps:

1. Select the Design-Time Controls tab from the Toolbox.
2. Drag the Recordset control from the Design-Time Controls tab of the Toolbox onto the page, below where it says Add Your Content Below. A Recordset control is added to the page.
3. Right-click on the Recordset control. A pop-up menu displays.
4. Select Properties. The Recordset properties dialog box displays.
5. Set the Connection to NorthDC.
6. Set Database Object to Tables.
7. Set Object Name to Products and click on Close.

8. On a blank line under the Recordset control, type **Item:**
9. Add a text box beside the text you just typed.
10. Right-click on the newly added text box and select Properties from the pop-up menu.
11. Set the Name to txtItem, Recordset to Recordset1, and Field to ProductName. Set the Enabled property to False. When this form is complete, it will be initially shown in display mode, and therefore this field should not be available for editing.
12. Click on OK to close the Properties dialog box.
13. Add a blank line after the line that contains the text box.
14. On a blank line under the Recordset control, type **Price:**
15. Add a text box beside the text you just typed.
16. Right-click on the newly added text box and select Properties from the pop-up menu.
17. Set the Name to txtItemDesc, Recordset to Recordset1, and Field to UnitPrice. Also set the Enabled property to False.
18. Click on OK to close the Properties dialog box.
19. Add a blank line after the text box you just created.
20. Add a RecordsetNavBar control to the form on the new blank line.
21. Set the RecordsetNavBar's Recordset property to Recordset1. The completed form should look similar to the one in Figure 11.14.

The only thing left to do before adding the FormManager control is to add the command buttons that a user needs to work with this form. This form will have a total of four command buttons:

- **Display:** When this button is selected, the form is placed in a read-only mode.
- **Edit:** When this button is clicked on, the form is placed in a read-write mode.
- **Save:** To actually save your work, click on this button.
- **Cancel:** To abort a change, select this button.

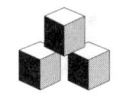

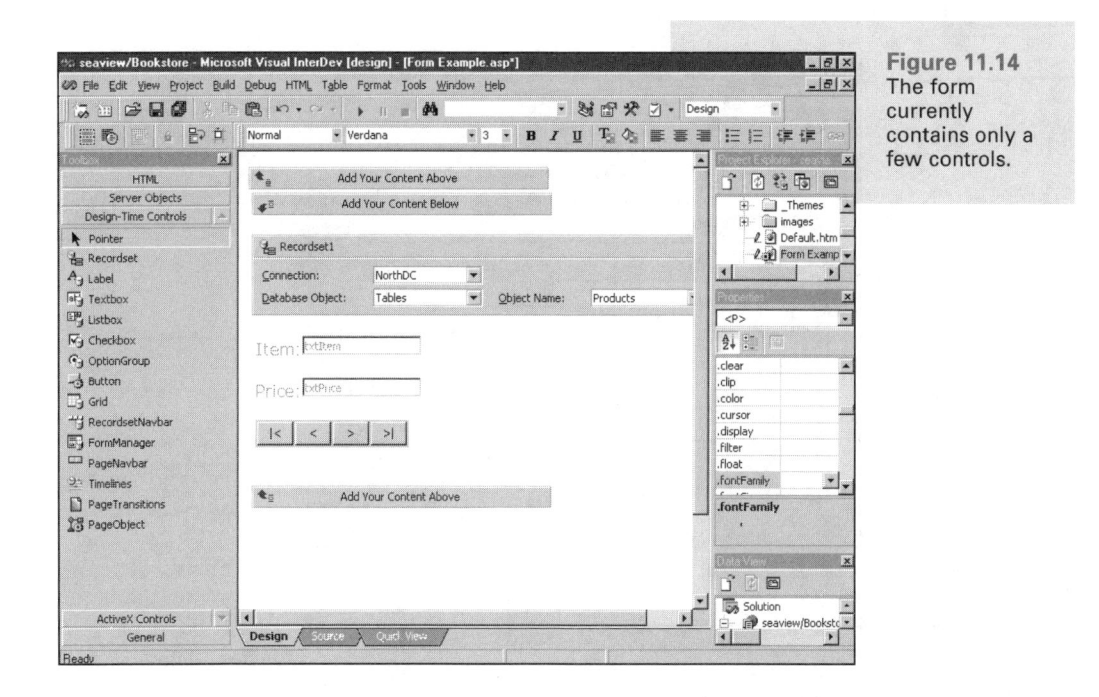

Figure 11.14
The form currently contains only a few controls.

There are two ways you can add these buttons to your form. One way is to create them by dragging onto the form and then visually aligning them. Or you can do it the easy way: Using a table to hold the buttons, you can let Visual InterDev do the work of aligning them using the following steps:

1. Add a blank line above the first text box.
2. Select Table, Insert Table. The Insert Table dialog box displays (see Figure 11.15).
3. Set Rows to 1 and Columns to 4. Click on OK to add the table.
4. Drag a Button design-time control from the Toolbox and drop it in the first cell of the table.
5. Repeat this process until each of the remaining three cells of the table holds a button.
6. Right-click on the first button and select Properties. The Button Properties dialog box displays, as shown in Figure 11.16.

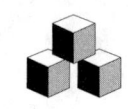

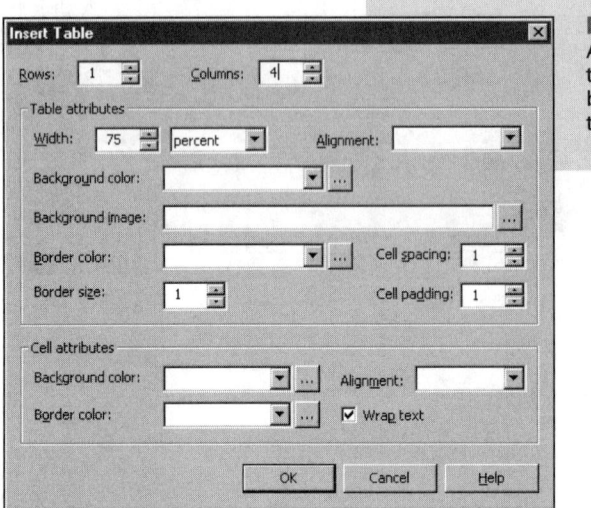

Figure 11.15
A table is created to hold the buttons needed by the form.

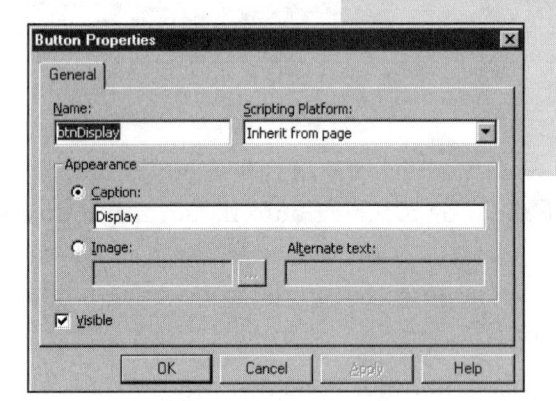

Figure 11.16
Button design-time controls have a limited number of properties that you can set.

7. Set the Name to btnDisplay, set Caption to Display, and place a check in Visible. Click on OK.

8. Right-click on the second button and select Properties. The Button Properties dialog box appears again.

9. Set the Name to btnEdit, set Caption to Edit, and place a check in Visible. Click on OK.

10. Right-click on the third button and select Properties. The Button Properties dialog box appears once more.

CHAPTER 11 • BUILDING THE DATABASE WEB PROJECT   193

11. Set the Name to btnSave, set Caption to Save, and remove the check from Visible. Click on OK. This button needs to be visible when the project is first shown because the form is going to be in Display mode.

12. Right-click on the fourth button and select Properties. The Button Properties dialog box appears again.

13. Set the Name to btnCancel, set Caption to Cancel, and remove the check from Visible. Click on OK. This button does need to be visible when the project is first shown because the form is going to be in Display mode. The completed buttons can be seen in Figure 11.17.

And now the moment you have been waiting for—adding the FormManager control! Using the FormManager control, you can specify modes for your form without writing script. This form is going to have two modes, Display and Edit. I selected these names for the modes, but I could have just as easily named them Show and Change if I wanted

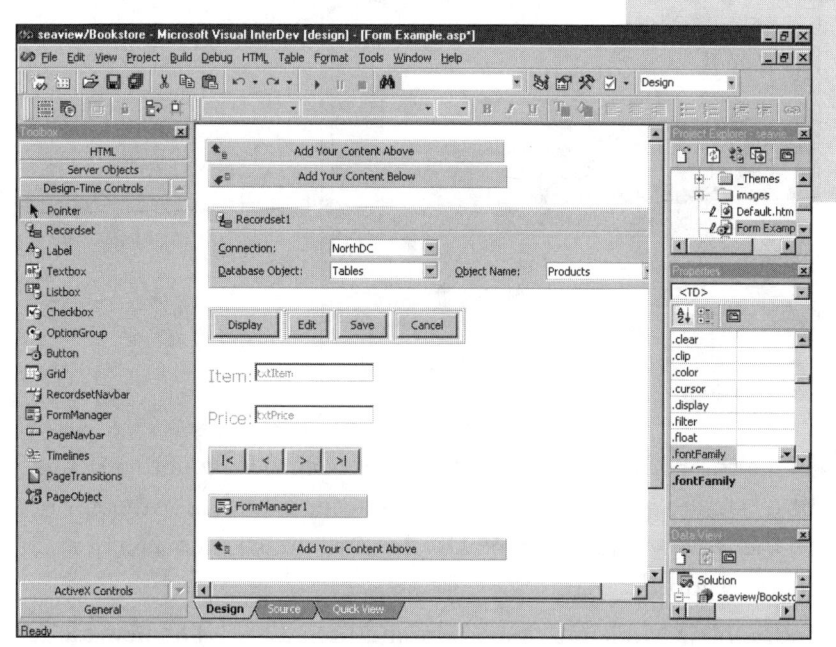

Figure 11.17
The four added buttons are neatly organized in a table.

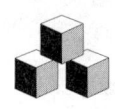

to. When the form is in Display mode, the text boxes are disabled and the Save and Cancel buttons are not visible. Once clicked on, the Display button will be disabled. When the form is in Edit mode, the opposite occurs. The text boxes are enabled. The Save and Cancel buttons are visible. And once clicked on, the Edit button is disabled.

Start by adding the FormManager control to the form using the following steps:

1. Add a blank line on the form under the RecordsetNavBar control.
2. Drag a FormManager control from the Toolbox to the newly created blank line.
3. Right-click on the FormManager control and select Properties. The FormManager Properties dialog box displays (see Figure 11.18).

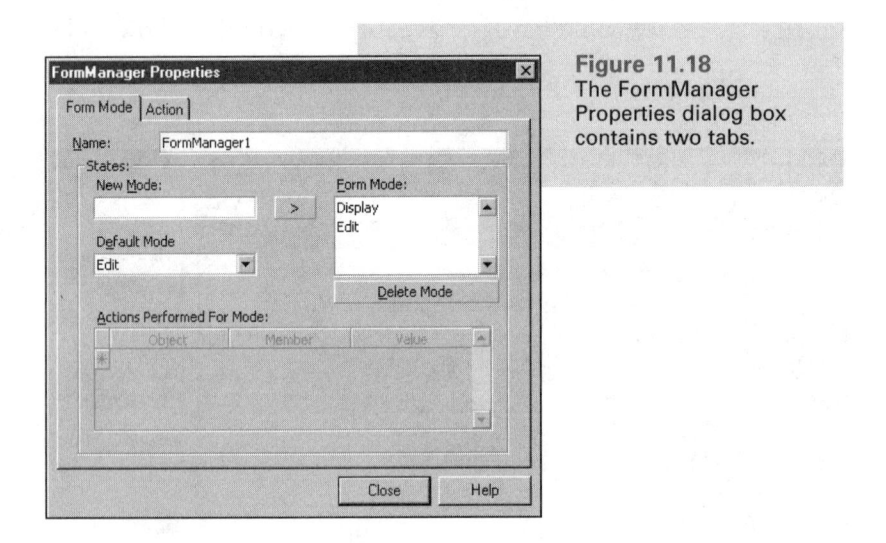

Figure 11.18
The FormManager Properties dialog box contains two tabs.

4. Using the Form Mode tab of the FormManager Properties dialog box, you are going to create the two needed modes for this form. In the New Mode box, type **Display** and press Enter. The new mode is added.
5. In the New Mode box, type **Edit** and press Enter. The new mode is added.

6. From the Default mode list box, select Display. This sets Display as the default mode for this form.

The next thing you need to do is assign the actions that the controls on the form will perform for each mode. For the modes that you are working with, you need to assign the following actions:

- Disabled
- Show
- Hide

When Disabled is set to true, the control is not available for use. Show and Hide are used to set whether the control will be visible on the form for a particular mode. To be honest, setting the actions performed for a mode is the most tedious and difficult part of this process. It's not that the steps themselves are hard; it is the thought process involved. You need to go through the controls and your form and ask yourself, "Should users be able to work with this control in this mode and if not, should they be able to see it?" On this form, this task isn't too bad, but on a form with a couple dozen controls, it can be challenging. When I'm working with a detailed form, I print a copy of the form for each mode. Then I write on the form the actions that I need to set beside each control. This gives me an organized approach to this step. To set the actions performed for the modes, use these steps:

1. Select Display from the Form Mode list box.
2. Select the first cell in the blank row of the Actions Performed for Mode grid.
3. Click on the down arrow selection button for the cell. Select btnDisplay. This selects the first object you are working with.
4. Select the next cell in the row.
5. Click on the down arrow selection button for the cell. Select Disabled.
6. In the cell under the Value column, type **true**. If you want to disable the control, its disabled property needs to be true, which is the case here. This is because once the button has been clicked on and the form is in Display mode, you shouldn't be able to

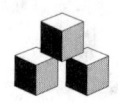

click on the Display button again. Also note that the value is case-sensitive. You need to enter true in all lowercase letters.

7. Continue setting actions using the values in Table 11.1.

Table 11.1 Actions Performed for the Display Mode

Object	Member	Value
btnDisplay	show	()
btnEdit	disabled	false
btnEdit	show	()
btnSave	disabled	true
btnSave	hide	()
btnCancel	disabled	true
btnCancel	hide	()
txtItem	disabled	true
txtItem	show	()
txtPrice	disabled	true
txtPrice	show	()
RecordsetNavBar1	show	()

8. Select Edit from the Form Mode list box.
9. Continue setting actions using the values in Table 11.2.

Table 11.2 Actions Performed for the Edit Mode

Object	Member	Value
BtnDisplay	disabled	false
btnDisplay	show	()
btnEdit	disabled	true
btnEdit	show	()
btnSave	disabled	false
btnSave	show	()
btnCancel	disabled	false
btnCancel	show	()

Chapter 11 • Building the Database Web Project

Object	Member	Value
txtItem	disabled	false
txtItem	show	()
txtPrice	disabled	false
txtPrice	show	()
RecordsetNavBar1	hide	()

You are almost done. The last thing you need to do is assign form mode transitions. For example, before you click on the Display button, the form is in Edit mode. Therefore when the OnClick event for the Display button occurs, the mode becomes Edit mode. You need to assign transitions for each of the four buttons using the following steps:

1. Select the Action tab. The Action page displays, as shown in Figure 11.19.

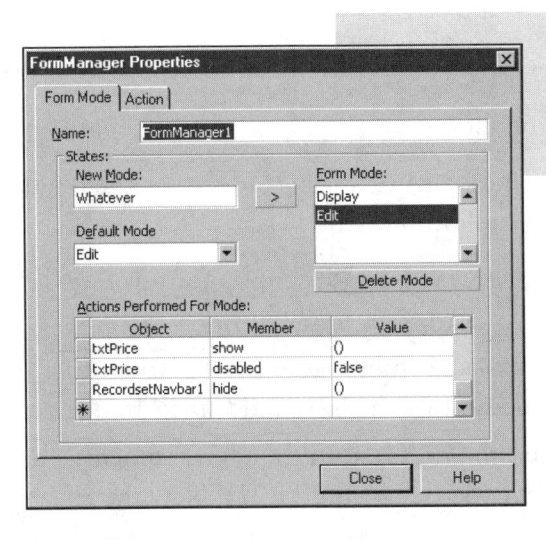

Figure 11.19
The Action tab is used to assign form transitions.

2. Select the first cell of the Form Mode Transitions grid.
3. Click on the down arrow selection button for the cell and select Display.
4. Select the next cell in the row.
5. Click on the down arrow selection button for the cell and select btnEdit. This is the first button you will work with.

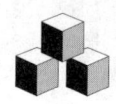

6. Select the next cell in the row.
7. Click on the down arrow selection button for the cell and select onclick for the event. This means the transition occurs when the button is clicked on by the user.
8. Select the next cell in the row.
9. Click on the down arrow selection button for the cell and select Edit. After the button is clicked on, the form is placed in Edit mode.
10. Continue entering transition settings using Table 11.3.

Table 11.3   Transition Settings

Current Mode	Object	Event	Next Mode
Edit	btnDisplay	onclick	Display
Edit	btnSave	onclick	Display
Edit	btnCancel	onclick	Display

11. Click on Close.

Believe it or not, you are finally ready to see the result of all your work. Complete the following steps:

1. Select File, Save Form Example. Your work is saved.
2. Select View, View in Browser. In a few moments the form displays, as shown in Figure 11.20. Notice that the text boxes are disabled and that the Save and Cancel buttons are hidden.
3. Click on the Edit button. In a few moments, the form is loaded in Edit mode (see Figure 11.21). Now the text boxes are enabled and the Save and Cancel buttons are shown. The Display button has been disabled. Also, the navigation bar is hidden.
4. Replace the value in the Price text box with 20.
5. Click on the Save button. The value is written to the record, and the form is in Display mode because of the transition you set earlier.

CHAPTER 11 • BUILDING THE DATABASE WEB PROJECT

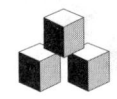

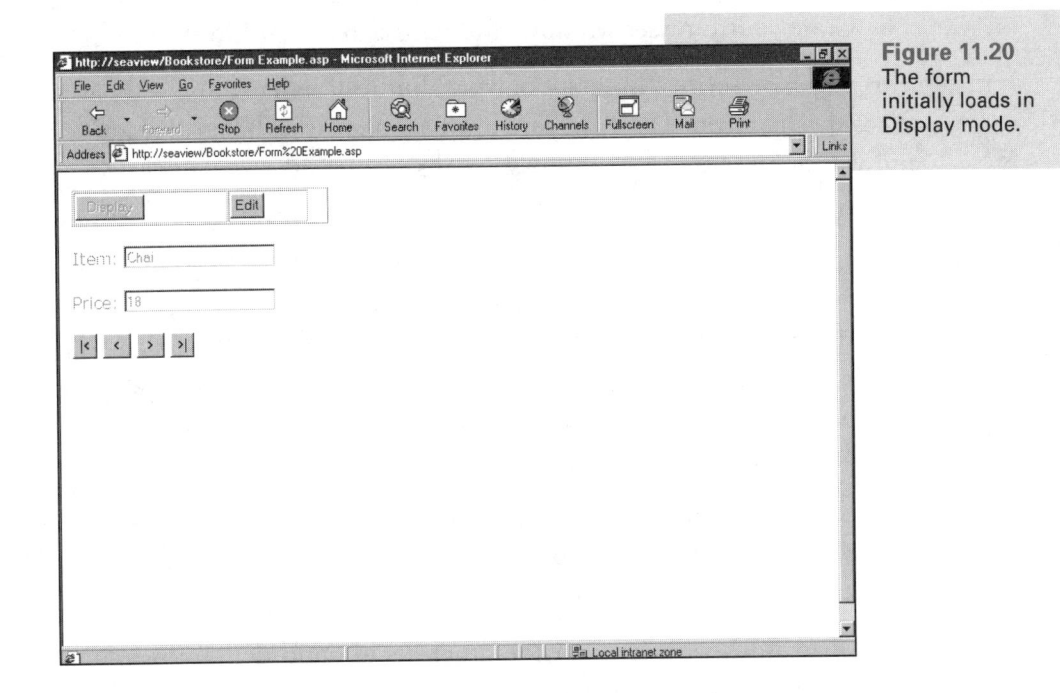

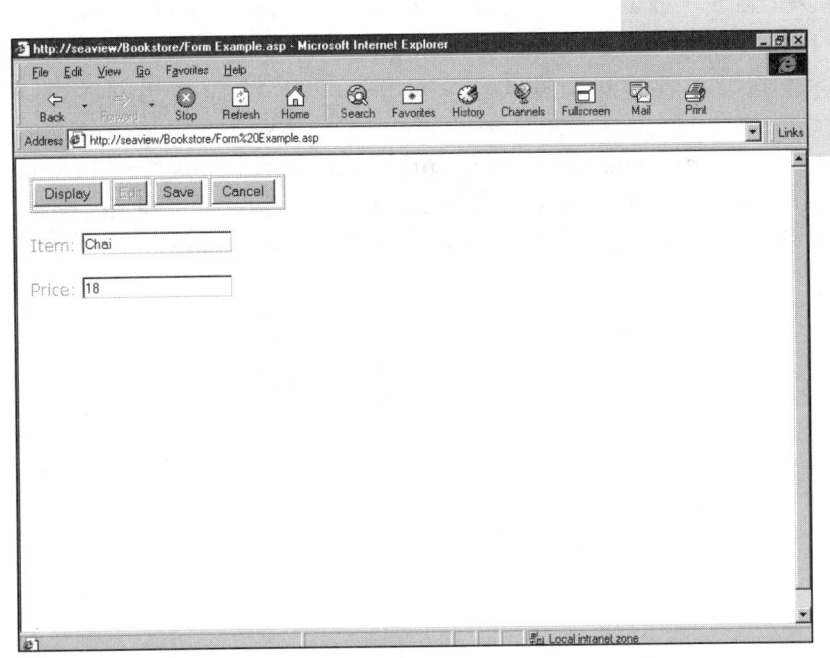

Figure 11.20
The form initially loads in Display mode.

Figure 11.21
The form as it appears in Edit mode

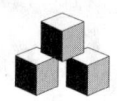

6. Close your browser window. You return to Visual InterDev.

This may have seemed like a lot of work, but realize that you mostly just selected values from lists. And you now have a form with lots of features, and you did it without writing a single line of script!

Summary

One of the most significant things you saw in this chapter was that you can display data from an Access database in exactly the same way you did from SQL Server. In conjunction with this, you learned how to create a data source.

This chapter introduced scripting. You saw how you could expand on what Visual InterDev could do by using code. Scripting will be covered in more detail in Chapter 16.

You got to work with some of the other data-bound design-time controls in this chapter, as well. You saw that the Grid control, one of my favorite controls, is a great way to display large pieces of data. The chapter's final major topic was another design-time control, FormManager. Using this control, you created a form that allowed you to display data in a read-only mode as well as edit data in a read-write mode. And you did it all without having to write script. In the next chapter, you'll complete this project. Chapter 12 also introduces you to some of the basic debugging techniques available for you to test your application.

CHAPTER 12

Testing the System

In the last chapter, you had a brief introduction to the world of scripting. In that chapter, you wrote a very short procedure that, hopefully, ran correctly on the first try. But what if it didn't? If you were writing code on your own, how would you begin to find the problem? Visual InterDev provides several tools for finding problems with your code. By the way, in case you are new to the world of coding, the process of finding and correcting errors in your code is called *debugging*. Some of the tools available to you for debugging script are as follows:

- **Breakpoints.** Breakpoints pause your script's execution at a designated point. When you pause a procedure, its source is displayed and you can test it.
- **Watches.** Watches are expressions that you want to track in your script.

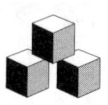

- **Stepping through a procedure.** You can execute your code line-by-line and watch the effect each line has on your application.

In this chapter, you are going to use two of these tools to debug your code, breakpoints and stepping. This will give you the opportunity to gain familiarity with the debugging environment. You'll build on this knowledge later in this book.

The Debugging Process

Visual InterDev has a tool called the debugger that you use to test the scripts you are creating for your Web solution. These scripts can be written in either VBScript or JScript. If you have worked with Microsoft development environments such as Visual Basic, you'll find that the techniques used to debug scripts are familiar to you. However, there are differences between debugging Visual InterDev solutions and debugging in traditional development environments. Some of these differences are listed here:

- You can have both VBScripted and JScripted procedures in the same Web solution.
- Your scripts are mixed with HTML text.
- Some of your scripts will reside on the client in .htm files, and some will reside on the server in .asp files, the Global.asa file, and .css files.
- The automation components of your Web solution are not limited to scripts, but can include Java components such as applets and COM objects.

The good news is that the Visual InterDev debugger allows you to debug in all of these scenarios.

> **Tip** Microsoft highly recommends that you do not use Active Desktop mode of Microsoft Internet Explorer 4.0 when you are debugging.

Types of Errors

Up to this point, the only mistakes you may have made with this application have been typos. These typos are known as syntax errors. Three basic types of errors are possible in programs:

- **Syntax errors**. As was already pointed out, syntax errors arise when you use the script language incorrectly.
- **Run-time errors**. A run-time error is any error that causes a program to stop running. Sometimes run-time errors are the fault of the programmer. For example, you might have mistyped the name of a procedure when you called it from another procedure. At other times, they result from a user action that you cannot control or predict. For example, if your program needed to save something to a floppy drive and the user failed to insert a disk, a run-time error would result.
- **Logic errors.** Logic errors are the result of programming errors. Logic errors typically have to do with your approach to a situation. Logic errors occur when you are setting up conditional tests. Somewhere in the test is a mistake that produces a wrong result. Sometimes logic errors are the result of mistakes in calculations. If unexpected results occur during your application, but the application continues to run, you have a logic error.

You'll find that most of your debugging efforts will deal with logic and syntax errors.

Using Breakpoints to Test Your Web Solution

Often when you are trying to find an error in your code, you know where the problem is. Rather than dealing with all of your code, you can mark where you think the problem is using a *breakpoint*. A breakpoint is a line of code that, when encountered, will pause execution of your application. This allows you to run the part of your application that is executing fine and work with just the problem portion. Once you get to the line where the breakpoint is set, you can use a variety of troubleshooting techniques to determine exactly what is going on. There are several ways to break program execution:

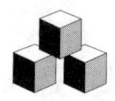

- Select the statement to set as a breakpoint and select the Debug, Insert Breakpoint menu.
- Select the statement to set as a breakpoint and press F9.
- Select the statement to set as a breakpoint and click in the margin indicator bar of the Code window.

The line that has been set as a breakpoint changes color according to the settings you have set for the Editor format in Tools, Options. To set a breakpoint in your application, follow these steps:

> **Caution:** You must be using Internet Explorer 4.0 or newer to debug client scripts in Internet Explorer. Debugging must also be enabled in Internet Explorer. This is a default setting for Internet Explorer.

1. If it isn't open, open the Bookstore project.
2. Open Page 1.
3. View the page using Source view.

> **Note:** You can't work with the debugger in Design view or Quick view of the HTML editor. To debug, switch to Source view.

4. The page you are debugging needs to be made the project's start page. Right-click on Page1.htm in the Project Explorer and select Set as Start Page.
5. Locate the following line of code toward the top of the page:
   ```
   txtDiscountedPrice.value = Recordset1.fields.getvalue("UnitPrice") * .90
   ```
6. Click on the gray margin bar beside this line. A dot appears in

CHAPTER 12 • TESTING THE SYSTEM   205

the margin beside the line, as shown in Figure 12.1. This is the notation for a breakpoint. Just for fun, remove the breakpoint.

7. Select Debug, Remove Breakpoint. This is one way to remove the breakpoint. You could have removed the breakpoint the same way that you inserted it, by clicking on the margin bar. Enough with the fun and games, you need to insert the breakpoint and use it.

8. With the line of code selected, press F9. This is yet another way to set a breakpoint.

9. Select Debug, Start. A message box displays, asking if you want to enable debugging for .asp pages. Since you are debugging an .htm page, click on No. In a few moments, the application displays in Internet Explorer.

> **Tip**
>
> The keyboard shortcut alternative to selecting Debug, Start is pressing F5.

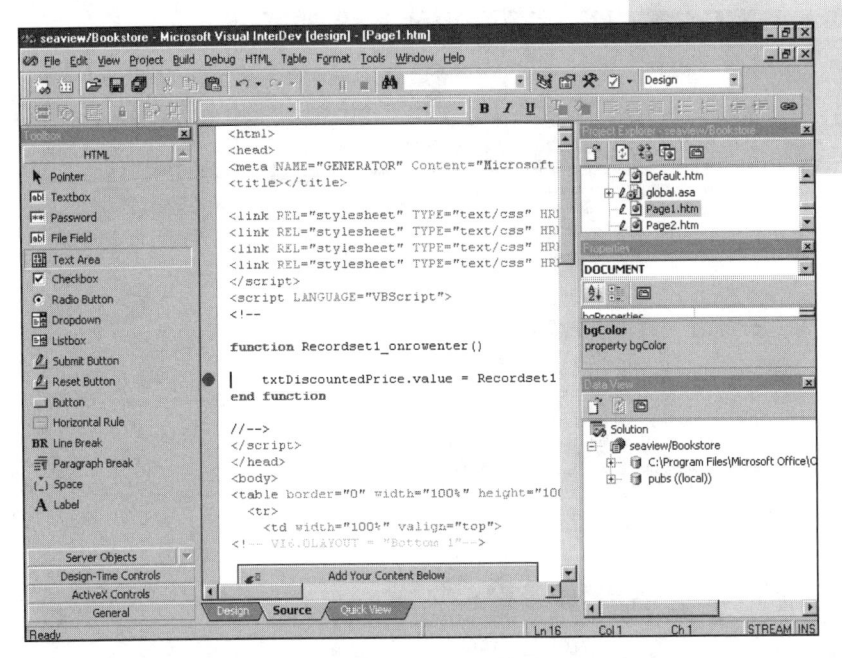

Figure 12.1
A breakpoint is denoted by a large dot in the margin bar.

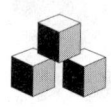

10. When your browser reaches the breakpoint, it stops and displays the source code in the editor window. You'll see the line with the breakpoint highlighted in Source view, as shown in Figure 12.2.
11. In the lower-left corner of the screen, you should see a window with three tabs. Click on the Immediate tab. The Immediate window displays. The Immediate window is an "on the spot" debugging area.
12. In this window, type

    ?Recordset1.fields.getvalue("UnitPrice")

    and press Enter. The value 18 is returned. This is the current value for the UnitPrice field.
13. Click on the dot in the margin bar to remove the breakpoint.
14. Select Debug, End. This ends the application's run and closes Internet Explorer. If you wanted to, you could have continued the program's run by selecting Debug, Restart (or by pressing Ctrl+Shift+F5). You've seen enough, so end the application run.

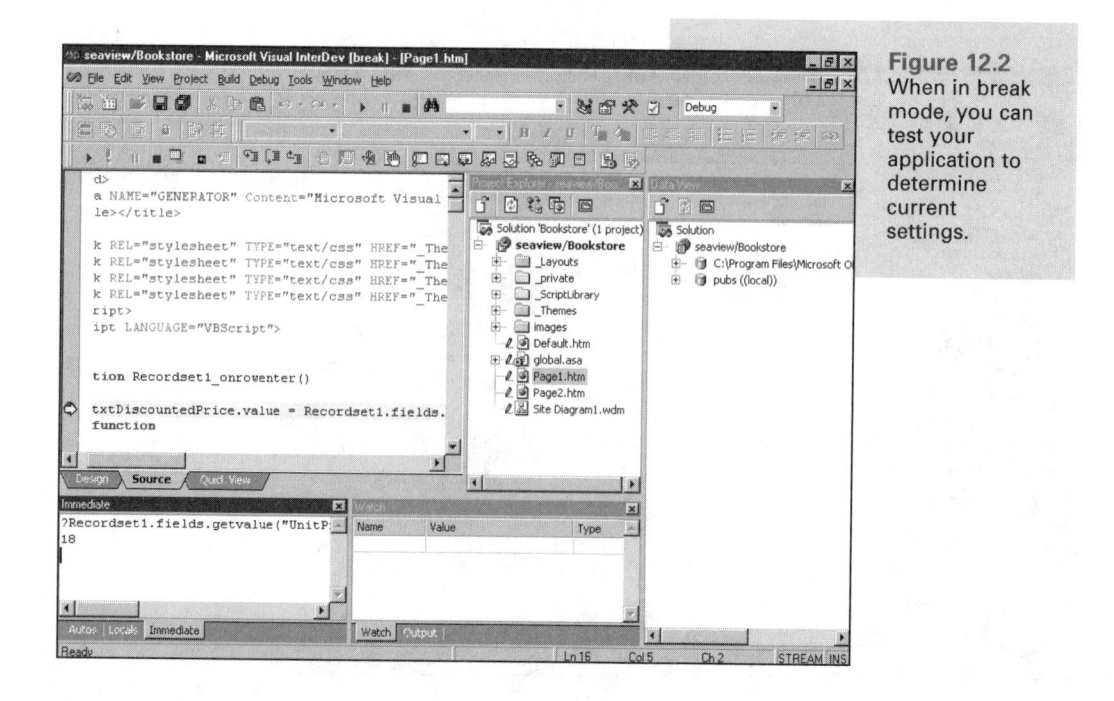

Figure 12.2
When in break mode, you can test your application to determine current settings.

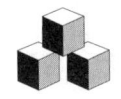

> **Tip**
> The keyboard shortcut for ending an application's run is Shift+F5.

> **Note**
> If you did this to find an error in a real situation, you would have fixed it at this point. Then you would save the file. If you didn't have a working copy of the file, you would right-click on the name of the file in the Project Explorer and choose Get Latest Version before you made modifications.

This was just a brief demonstration of using breakpoints. You'll find that you'll use them more when you have more complex scripts.

Using Just-in-Time Debugging

Just-in-time debugging refers to debugging a client script in response to an error or debugger statement. If Internet Explorer encounters a syntax or run-time error, you can use just-in-time debugging to find and fix it. You can launch the debugger in response to an error or debugger statement only if just-in-time debugging is enabled. To enable just-in-time debugging, follow these steps:

1. Select Tools, Options. The Options dialog box displays.
2. Select Debugger from the list box. The Debugger options display, as shown in Figure 12.3.
3. Select Just-in-Time debugging from the Script section.
4. Click on OK.

To demonstrate what happens when you enable just-in-time debugging, complete these steps:

1. Edit the line of code by dropping the "s" in "fields" so that the line matches this one:

    ```
    txtDiscountedPrice.value = Recordset1.field.getvalue("UnitPrice") * .90
    ```

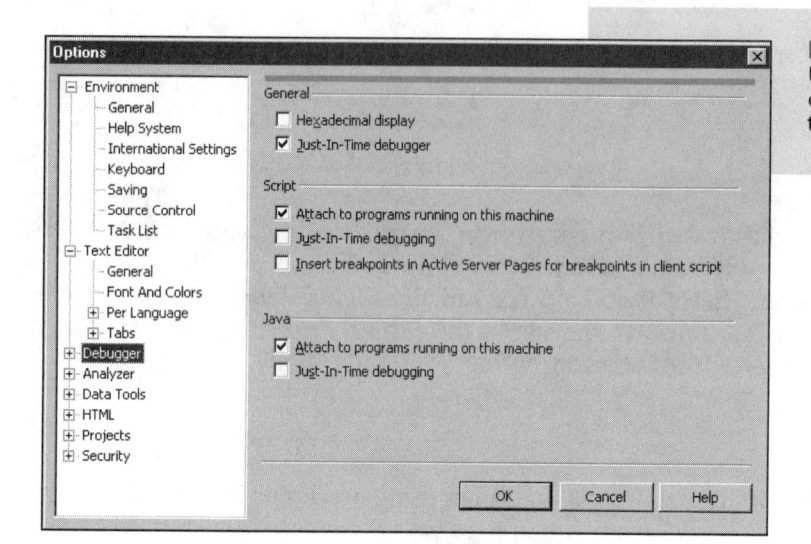

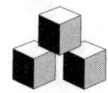

HANDS ON PROJECT 2 • THE DATABASE WEB PROJECT

Figure 12.3
Use the Debugger options to set just-in-time debugging.

2. Press F5 to run the application. In a few moments, you'll see an error message about the error you caused, as shown in Figure 12.4.

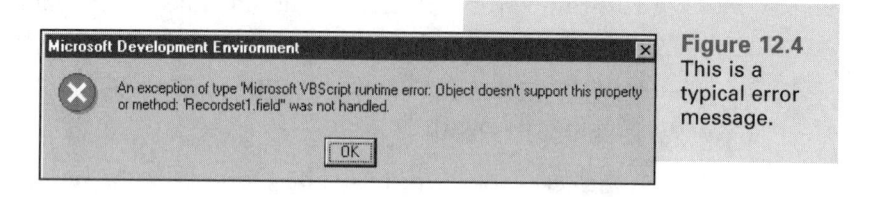

Figure 12.4
This is a typical error message.

3. Click on OK. The offending line is highlighted in Source view (see Figure 12.5).

4. Select Debug, End. Internet Explorer ends, and the application ends.

5. Correct the offending line:

    txtDiscountedPrice.value = Recordset1.fields.getvalue("UnitPrice") * .90

CHAPTER 12 • TESTING THE SYSTEM   209

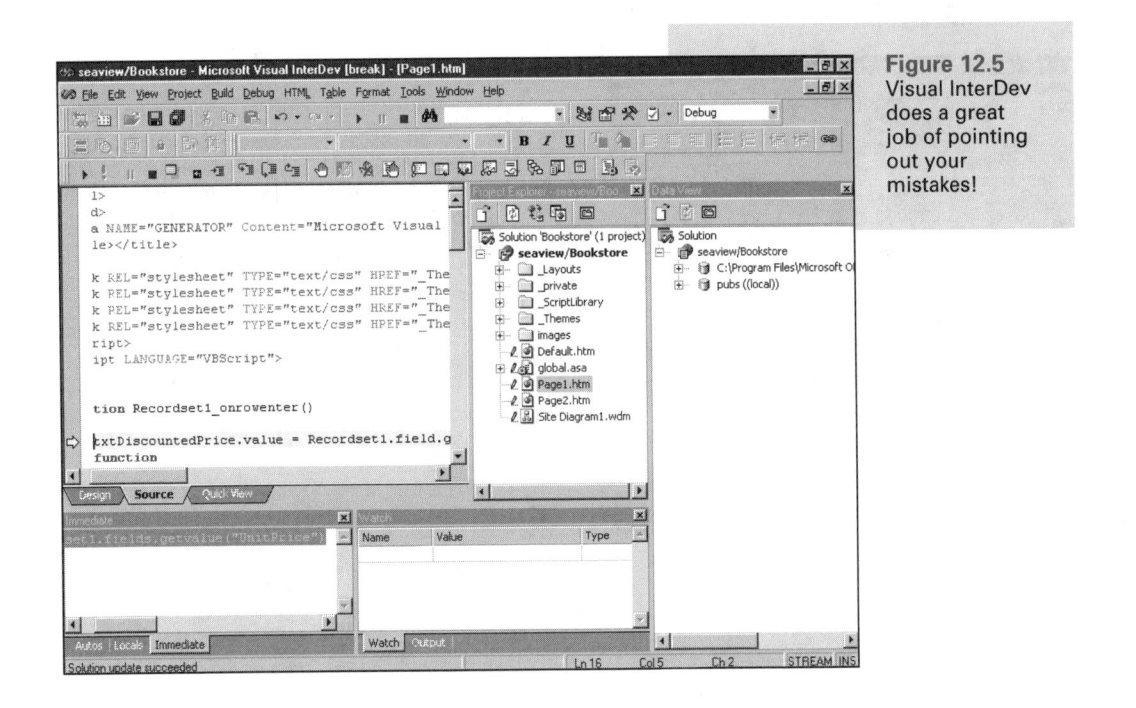

Figure 12.5
Visual InterDev does a great job of pointing out your mistakes!

Using Watches

Before you correct the problem, however, try one more debugging technique called *watch expressions*. Watch expressions are user-defined expressions that let you observe the behavior of a variable or an expression. Watch expressions are created by selecting Debug, Add Watch at design time or in break mode at run time. A watch expression can be any valid script expression. To add a watch for debugging your script, use the following steps:

1. Highlight txtDiscountedPrice.Value. This is the expression that you are going to add a watch for.
2. Select Debug, Add Watch. The Watch window opens with the watch listed, as shown in Figure 12.6.

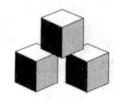

Hands On Project 2 • The Database Web Project

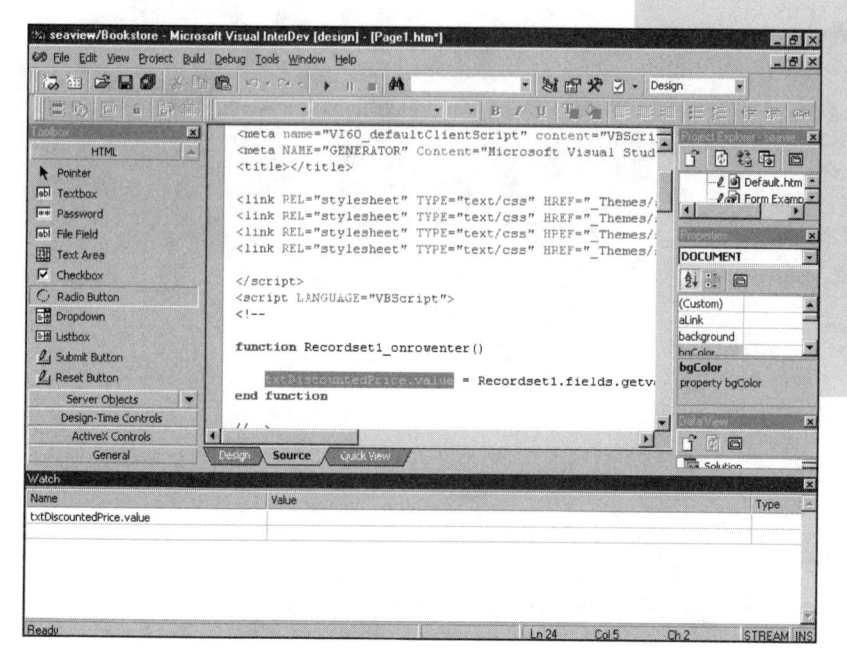

Figure 12.6
The Watch window, located at the bottom of the screen, currently doesn't display any information other than the watch name because the script isn't running.

> **Tip**
> The keyboard shortcut for setting a watch is Shift+F9.

3. Set a breakpoint for this line, too.
4. Press F5 to run the application. When your browser reaches the breakpoint, it stops and displays the source code in the editor window. You'll see the line with the breakpoint highlighted in Source view.

> **Tip**
> If the Watch window is not open, select <u>V</u>iew, Debug Windows, <u>W</u>atch.

5. Look at the Watch window. You'll notice that the value of txtDiscountedPrice.value is " " (see Figure 12.7). This is because the breakpoint pauses the script before the line's execution.

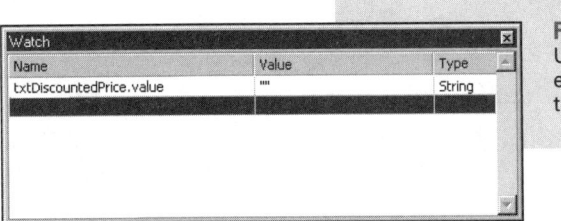

Figure 12.7
Until the line executes, the value of this watch is empty.

6. Press F5 to continue the script's execution. The value in the Watch window changes to reflect the line's completion (see Figure 12.8).

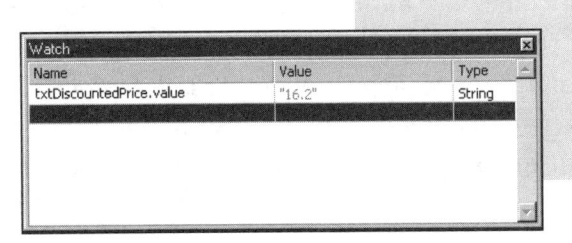

Figure 12.8
As the script progresses, the contents of the Watch window update.

7. Close the browser window.
8. Remove the breakpoint from the script.

Once you are through using a watch expression, you can delete it by right-clicking on it in the Watch window and selecting <u>D</u>elete Watch.

Stepping through Lines in a Script

In the earlier section, you set a breakpoint in the procedure. A breakpoint stops execution of the application before executing the line that contains the breakpoint. You next want to step though your code starting with this line to observe what happens. There are four ways of doing this:

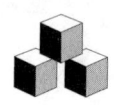

- Step Into
- Step Over
- Step Out
- Run to Cursor

Step Into and Step Over allow you to see line-by-line execution of the application so that you can trace the flow of logic statements, such as If statements, and to test variable and property values. Step Out executes all remaining code in a procedure and exits to the next statement in the procedure that initially called the procedure. Run to Cursor allows you to select a statement in your code where you want the execution to stop. This lets you "step over" sections of code.

There is a difference to the types of stepping done by Step Into and Step Over. If you are debugging a procedure that calls another procedure and you do not want to step through the called procedure, use Step Over. Step Over skips doing line-by-line execution of the called procedure. If you want to observe line-by-line execution of all statements, including the ones in called procedures, use Step Into. To step through your procedure, follow these steps:

1. Select Debug, Step Into. Internet Explorer starts, as does your application. You'll see the line of code that is being executed in Source view (see Figure 12.9).
2. Press F11. This is the keyboard shortcut key for Step Into. The next line is executed.
3. Press F11 several times to see the code being executed.
4. Select Debug, End. This ends the run of the application.

You've already seen that when debugging your solution, you may combine different debugging techniques. Earlier you set a breakpoint in conjunction with using a watch. You may also combine watches with stepping; combine stepping with breakpoints; and use watches, breakpoints, and stepping all at the same time.

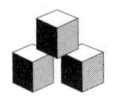

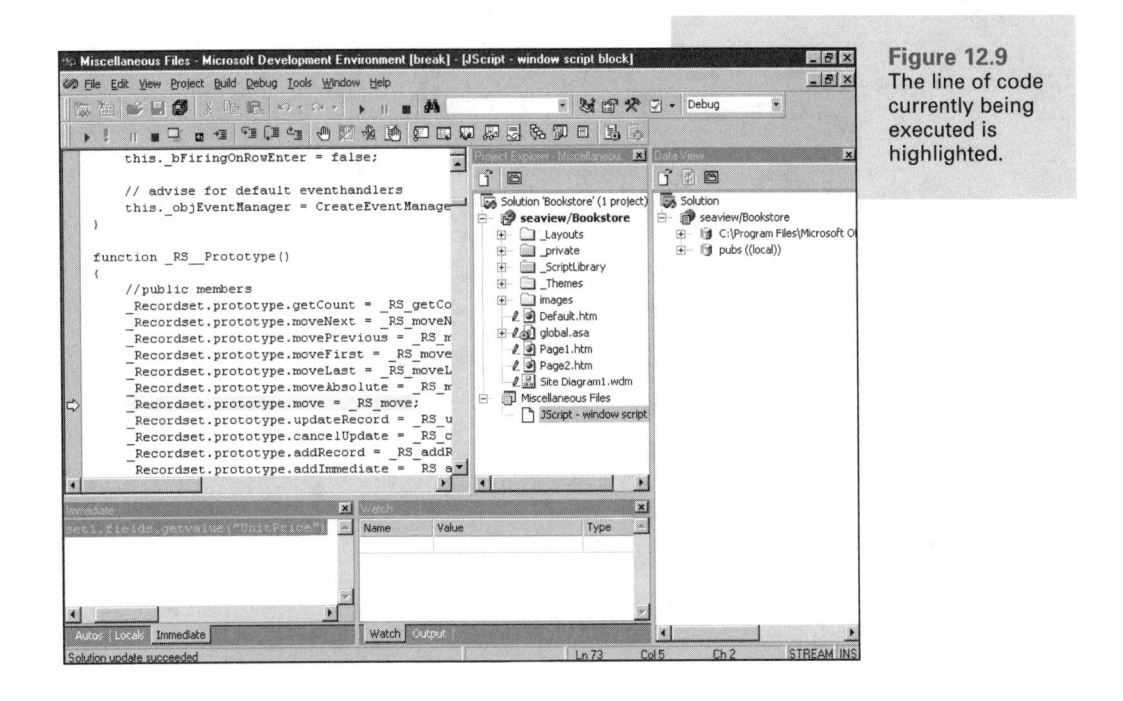

Figure 12.9
The line of code currently being executed is highlighted.

Debugging Server Script

Debugging server script is very much like debugging client script. Typically you will set a breakpoint in the server script and then start debugging from there. Before you can debug client script in ASP pages, you must enable debugging. To enable script debugging in ASP pages, complete the following steps:

> **Note:** To interactively debug script in ASP pages, you must be running version 4.0 or later of Microsoft Internet Information Server (IIS).

1. Right-click on the project in the Project Explorer.
2. Select P<u>r</u>operties. The Property Pages dialog box displays.
3. Select the Launch tab to display the Launch page, as shown in Figure 12.10.

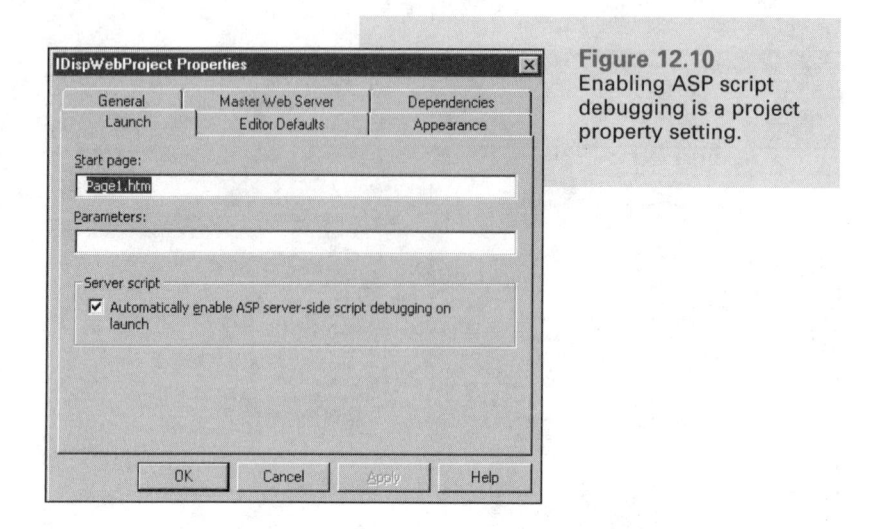

Figure 12.10
Enabling ASP script debugging is a project property setting.

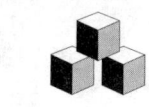

4. Check Automatically Enable ASP Server-Side Debugging on Launch.
5. Click on OK.

Understanding the Colors in Source View

Now that you are getting familiar with looking at code, you may become more curious about what you are looking at. Source view provides you with colored text to give you a clue as to the type of text in each line. This is a list of the default colors for the Source View editor:

- **Red**: HTML attribute name, HTML entity
- **Blue**: HTML attribute value, HTML tag delimiter, HTML string, HTML operator
- **Gray**: HTML comment
- **Burgundy**: HTML element name
- **Pink**: HTML tag text
- **Bolded Blue**: keyword

CHAPTER 12 • TESTING THE SYSTEM   **215**

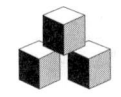

You can redefine the colors used in the Source view using the following steps:

1. Select Tools, Options. The Options dialog box opens.
2. Expand Text Editor. Select Font and Colors. The Font and Colors options display (see Figure 12.11).

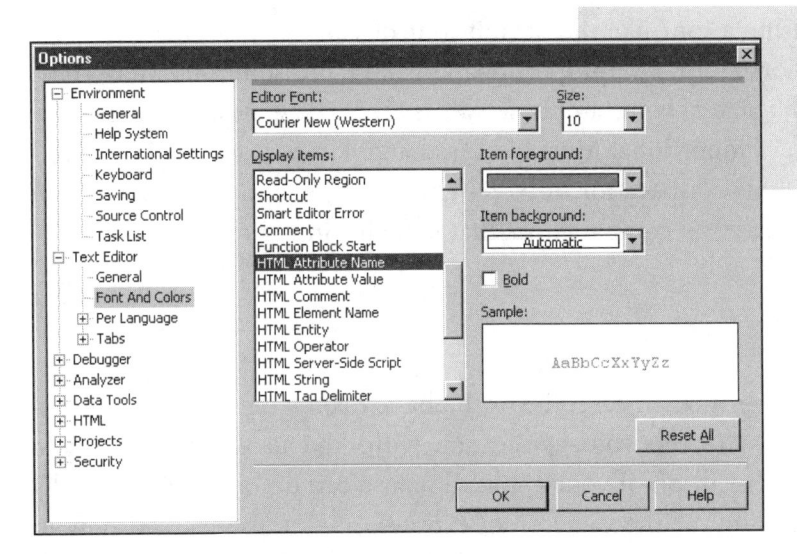

Figure 12.11
You can select the colors (and fonts) for the text editor to display.

3. Locate and select HTML Attribute Name from the Display Items list box. Currently, the color used for displaying this type of text is red.
4. From the Item foreground drop-down list box, select pink. The selection is previewed in the Sample box.
5. Click on OK.
6. You can see that the color change has been made. All HTML attribute names are now pink. Change it back to red now.
7. Select Tools, Options. The Options dialog box opens.
8. Expand Text Editor. Select Font and Colors. The Font and Colors options display (see Figure 12.11).

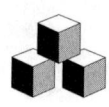

9. Locate and select HTML Attribute Name from the Display items list box.
10. From the Item foreground drop-down list box, select red. The selection is previewed in the Sample box.
11. Click on OK.

Color and font settings are a matter of personal preference. I recommend using a font like the default font of Courier New that is a nonproportional font. Nonproportional fonts use the same amount of space for all characters. For example, a "W" is given the same amount of space as an "I." Proportional fonts like Arial and Times Roman allow different amounts of space for different characters. A nonproportional font makes it easier to compare lines that contain similar text.

Summary

This chapter focused on some of the basic debugging techniques available for you to test your application with. You used a breakpoint to pause the execution of your application at a certain point. You added a watch to monitor the value of an expression. You also learned how to step through code to get a line-by-line view of code execution.

In the next project, you will learn more about coding in Visual InterDev. You'll also learn about the features that are available to you to make working in multiple-developer environments easier.

Project 2 Summary

This project gave you the hands-on experience you need to integrate a database as part of your Web site. You added a data connection to your project and designed a query. You used the result of that query to display data on your page using the Recordset control and the RecordsetNavpage control. You got to work with some of the other data-bound design-time controls and saw that the Grid control is a great way to display large pieces of data. You used the FormManager design-time control to create a form that allowed you to display data in a read-only mode, as well as edit data in a read/write mode.

This project introduced Scripting. You saw how you could expand on what Visual InterDev could do by using code, and you worked with some of the basic debugging techniques available for you to test your application. You used a breakpoint to pause the execution of your application at a certain point, and you added a watch to monitor the value of an expression. You also learned how to step through code to get a line-by-line view of code execution.

HANDS ON PROJECT 3

THE CORPORATE WEB SITE

- Setting up Visual SourceSafe
- Adding source control to your project
- Adding multimedia to your site
- Working with Active Server Pages (ASPs)
- Understanding the difference between client and server scripts
- Working with the Scripting Object Model
- Adding to your VBScript knowledge
- Record navigation using script
- Using the Immediate window to debug scripts
- Error handling
- Setting up security

Project Overview

This project focuses on presenting the tools employed by developers in a corporate environment. You will learn answers to such questions as "What happens if two people try to work on the same file?" and "How do I move my project from my local machine to the Web?"

The other focus of this chapter is scripting. It presents additional VBScript programming topics. You get the chance to create scripts that perform database record navigation and new record creation.

CHAPTER 13

What Is the Corporate Web Site?

This next project has two goals. One is to present topics related to working in a multideveloper environment, and the other is to present new programming topics. Remember, in the computer world, we don't have pretend things, we have virtual things! Accordingly, think of this as a virtual learning environment, where you are one among many developers.

Requirements of the Corporate Web Site

Unlike the other projects in this book, you are not going to have clear-cut system requirements. Instead, this project focuses on presenting the tools employed by developers in a corporate environment. You will learn answers to such questions as "What happens if two people try to work on the same file?" and "How do I move my project from my local machine to the Web?" This project is really designed to give you hands-on experience with a variety of techniques.

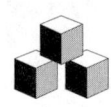

In an enterprise such as a corporation, you are not an island unto yourself. As a team member, you may be working on one or two of the files associated with a Web project, rather than all the files of the project. How do all the team members keep from stepping on each other's toes, and how do you manage the big picture? This project will show you.

Using Visual SourceSafe

You may be familiar with Visual SourceSafe if you have used some of Microsoft's other development tools, such as Visual Basic or Visual C++. As you will see in Chapter 15, Visual SourceSafe manages files by saving them to a database. This structure allows a developer to share files and maintain version control. Team members can see the newest version of any file, modify the file, and save the changes. Another advantage of Visual SourceSafe is that when you update a file, it automatically creates a backup of the previous version of that file. This allows for recovery of an old version as a safety net in case you decide you don't want to keep the changes you made.

When you install Visual SourceSafe, you'll need to install the Visual SourceSafe server on the same machine that the Web server is located. You'll need to run the Visual SourceSafe setup program. Chapter 15 discusses the steps to install Visual SourceSafe on the Web server.

Adding Multimedia to Your Site

When people visit your site, they expect to see bells and whistles. The unofficial corporate term for bells and whistles is the use of multimedia. In the part of the project covered in Chapter 16, you'll learn how to add a background sound to your Web page and how to embed video into a Web page.

Setting Up Security

The accessibility of your information on the World Wide Web is definitely a double-edged sword. On the one hand, it is great because you can make your information available to a huge audience. On the other hand, among that audience are people who wish to hack into your system and do evil things; hence the need for security. Chapter 17 discusses the issues surrounding security and how to implement it.

Utilizing Visual InterDev's Programming Features

Yes, Visual InterDev is a wonderful product; yes, it can help you perform many of the tasks you need to create your Web solution; but no, it cannot do it all. At this point you'll turn to scripting to overcome some limitations of Visual InterDev. You may want to use scripts, for instance, to control what happens when a user clicks a button or to collect and store user information so that you can dynamically customize your Web application. Various scripting languages are available, including VBScript, which is discussed in Chapter 16.

Chapter 16 also presents information about the two differences between client and server scripts. One difference lies in where the script is processed, and the other has to do with the script's physical location.

Using the Immediate Window

Another tool that Visual InterDev provides for debugging is the Immediate window. In Chapter 17, you will learn how to use the Immediate window to perform tasks such as displaying variable and property values, and changing the value of a variable or property while an application is running.

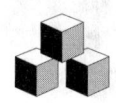

Error Handling

Whereas debugging is the process of handling errors and identifiable problems with your scripts, error handling is setting up a mechanism to deal with script errors and problems once the script is deployed with your solution. Chapter 17 will show you how to set up error handling for your application.

Summary

The purpose of this project is to expose you to the features of Visual InterDev that are geared to the multideveloper environment. You'll also have the opportunity to create scripts to extend the functionality of the Web applications that you create using Visual InterDev.

The following chapter starts this process by giving you the background information that you need to plan and gather information to work with Web projects in a multiple-developer environment. Upon completion of the project, you'll have the essential skills to use Visual SourceSafe, integrate security as part of your solution, and add additional scripting functionality to your projects.

CHAPTER 14

Gathering Information for the Corporate Web Site

Your current project has three main areas of focus. One area gives you experience in working with Visual SourceSafe. The second area builds on your VBScript background. And the final focus introduces you to the security concerns of Web application development.

Using Visual SourceSafe

Although Microsoft Visual SourceSafe is frequently used in a multideveloper environment, you can track and save your changes to files with Visual SourceSafe whether you are working on a team or by yourself. Visual SourceSafe is a product that you may already have on your system if you are using Visual Basic or Visual C++. Visual SourceSafe comes with the Enterprise Edition of Visual Studio. It does not come with Visual InterDev or the Professional Edition of Visual Studio. Using this application will require that you set up source control on your Web server.

For this stage of the project, you need to know just two things: where your master Web server is and where your Visual Studio CD-ROM discs are. If you are going to do the installation, you need to have the appropriate permissions to do the installation. Once you install Visual SourceSafe, the next thing you'll need to do is grant permissions to users in Visual SourceSafe. You need to grant read/write permissions to all users that you want to author files using Visual InterDev or Microsoft FrontPage. You'll need to grant yourself these permissions for this project.

Once Visual SourceSafe is installed and set up, you can enable source control for your Web application. The information that you need to perform this step is the name of the project that you are adding the source control to, which is the Bookstore project.

After a Web application has source control enabled, you check your files in and out instead of getting and releasing working copies as you did before. When checking out a file, you need to decide if you want to check it out using exclusive checkout or multiple checkouts. When you are working with a project, you'll need to ask yourself whether you are actually going to make changes to the file or you are going to preserve the file as it is for reference. The answer to this question determines whether you need to open the file as an exclusive checkout or a multiple checkout (see Figure 14.1).

Development team members check files in and out through the Web projects in Visual InterDev. Thus they gain more control over when the

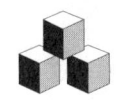

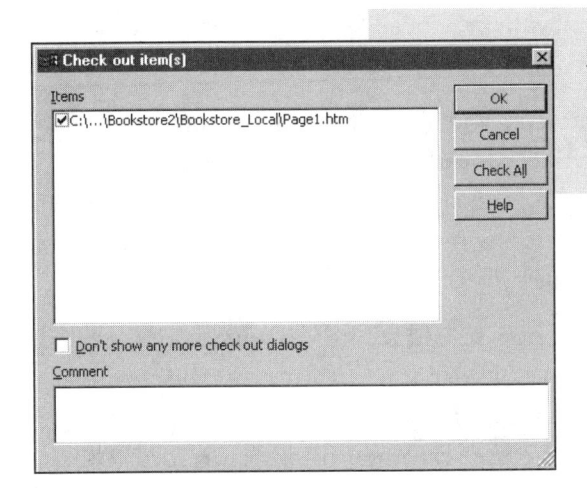

Figure 14.1
The Check Out Item(s) dialog box is used to check out files so that you can work with them.

Exclusive checkout allows only one user to check out a file at a time.

Multiple checkout allows more than one person to check out the same file at one time.

master Web application and Visual SourceSafe repository are updated with newer versions from local Web applications. In other words, you won't be stepping on each other's feet!

Writing VBScript Code

This project will definitely involve more VBScript code than the preceding one. In the last project, you wrote a one-line procedure. In this project, you are going to write multiple procedures. Many of the procedures you are going to write involve manipulating database record sets, for which you'll need to gather some information. That is to say, you'll need more knowledge of VBScript.

One of the series of procedures you'll be writing will teach you how to navigate through records using a script. You'll learn how to move between records in the record set by calling navigation methods. These methods are `moveNext`, `movePrevious`, `moveFirst`, `moveLast`, `moveAbsolute`, and `move`.

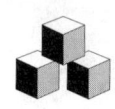

In the last project, you read about allowing updating by setting the RecordsetNavBar control's updateOnMove property. As was noted, using that method can significantly affect performance. Another way to update information is by using a script. You'll learn how to update the current record using VBScript.

You'll also learn how to add records to your record set. When you work with a record set object in a script, you can add records to the database in two ways. The first is a two-step process. First you initialize a new, blank record. The user can then fill in the record. When the record is complete, the user can click on a Save button (or something similar) to write the current record to the database, just as if an existing record had been updated. This strategy is useful when you are working with a form in which users can edit existing records or add new ones. Another way to do this is to create a new record and populate it in a single operation. This is referred to as *adding immediately*. The opposite of adding records is deleting them. This is done using the record set's `delete` method. To complete this part of the project, you need to answer the following questions:

- Are you going to use an existing page in your project to add these features, or are you going to create a new page?
- Which table from which database are you going to work with?
- What controls are going to be added to the form to complete these tasks?

Start with the first question. Are you going to use an existing page in your project to add these features, or are you going to create a new page? You are going to add a new page to the project. You could modify one of the existing pages, but I thought that it would be nicer for you to have this code located on its own page for your own future reference. That way, if you want to add the completed page to one of your own projects, you will have the basic script already done.

Next you need to decide which database and table you are going to work with. The database you are going to work with is the Northwind database. Just as a reminder, this is an Access database with client, inventory, order, and other information. The table you'll use from this database is Categories. This is one of the smaller tables in the Northwind database, so it will be easy to work with. This is not to say the techniques you are using are only usable with small tables. The knowledge you'll gain in Chapter 16 is transferable to any size table.

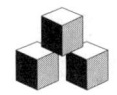

The final item to address is what controls are going to be added to the form to complete these tasks. You will need to add text boxes for the field information, a Recordset control to access the information, and a series of command buttons to perform tasks. The text boxes you'll need to create are these:

- txtCategoryID
- txtCategoryName
- txtDesciption

The buttons you need to add to the form have to do with navigation and adding and saving records. The buttons you will need are these:

- btnFirst
- btnPrevious
- btnNext
- btnLast
- btnNewRecord
- btnSave

Security

You covered some of the things that you will do via VBScript code, such as adding and deleting records. Did this set off any flags for you?

The coolest thing about creating and deploying a Web solution on the World Wide Web is that millions of people have access to your information. The scariest thing about creating and deploying a Web solution on the World Wide Web is that millions of people have access to your information. Security controls how those millions of people work with

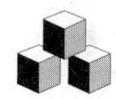

Web application files. Security also controls the access to the system that houses the files of your Web applications.

Security is a complex topic to say the least. This is because security can be set at several levels in several different ways. Here is a list of the locations at which you can set security:

- The operating system
- Folders
- The Web server
- The virtual root
- A database
- A Web application
- A page
- Through source control

When creating a Web application, you need to decide how much (or how little) security you need and where to implement the security. This project discusses some of these topics.

Summary

In this chapter, you divided this analysis stage of your project into three tasks: using Visual SourceSafe with your project, adding VBScript for record navigation and other database tasks, and implementing security.

With the analysis stage complete, you are ready to start working with the features of Visual Studio that are geared at the multiple-developer environment. The next chapter shows you how they apply to the Visual InterDev environment.

CHAPTER 15

Working in the Corporate Web Development Environment

The scenario for this project is that you are working with several other developers on the same project. Visual InterDev facilitates this environment by allowing each developer to work on his or her own local copy of the Web project and then to copy that work to the master Web server. Visual InterDev tries to resolve any conflicts that it may encounter.

A more sophisticated tool for managing files in a multideveloper environment is called Visual SourceSafe. Visual SourceSafe is a source control tool that has been used by developers in other Microsoft development environments, including Visual C++ and Visual Basic. In this chapter, you will set up Visual SourceSafe for use with your Visual InterDev projects.

Setting Up Visual SourceSafe

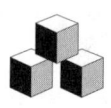

Setting up Visual SourceSafe to work with your Visual InterDev projects takes several steps. Part of the installation is done on the Web server, part of it is done in Visual SourceSafe itself, and part of it takes place in Visual InterDev. Here is a list of the individual procedures that will need to be completed:

> **Note** Visual SourceSafe is a product that you may already have on your system if you are using Visual Basic or Visual C++. Visual SourceSafe comes with the Enterprise Edition of Visual Studio. It does not come with Visual InterDev or the Professional Edition of Visual Studio.

- Install Visual SourceSafe on the master Web server.
- Grant permission to users in Visual SourceSafe.
- If you are using a Web server on Windows NT, add permissions to the anonymous user account.
- Share source control between Web projects.

Installing Visual SourceSafe on the Master Web Server

When you install Visual SourceSafe, you'll need to install the Visual SourceSafe Server on the same machine where the Web server is located. You'll need to run the Visual SourceSafe setup program. Complete these steps to install Visual SourceSafe on the Web Server:

> **Note** This procedure assumes that you have Internet Information Server and FrontPage Server Extensions already installed on your master Web server.

1. Run the Visual Studio Setup program from your Visual Studio Enterprise Edition CD-ROM. The first dialog box of the Installation Wizard displays (see Figure 15.1).

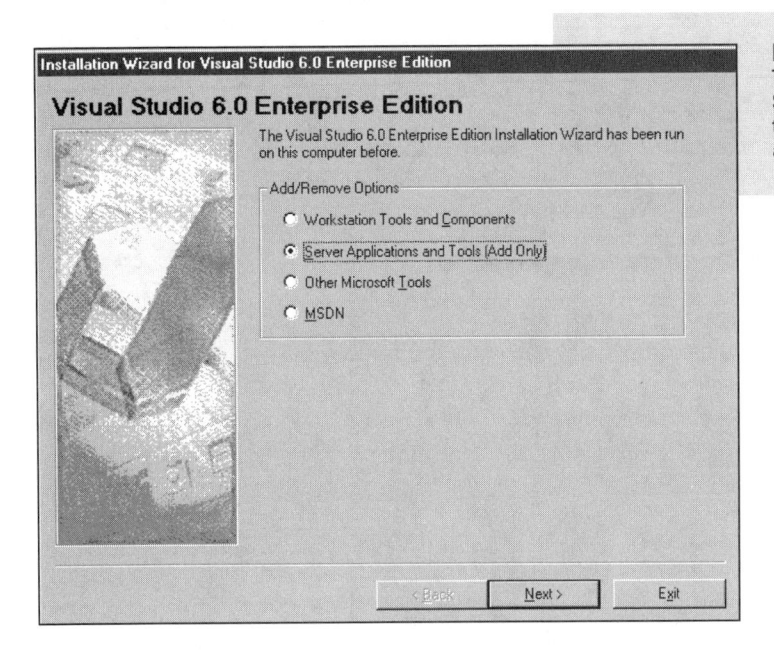

CHAPTER 15 • WORKING IN THE CORPORATE WEB ENVIRONMENT   **233**

Figure 15.1
To install Visual SourceSafe, you'll select the Server Applications and Tools option button.

2. Select Server Applications and Tools. Click on Next. The Server Setups dialog box of the Installation Wizard displays, as shown in Figure 15.2.
3. Select Visual SourceSafe Server and click on Install. You'll be instructed to insert CD-2.
4. Insert CD-2 and click on OK. The Visual SourceSafe Server welcome screen displays. Click on Continue. Your product ID number displays.
5. Click on OK. The start installation message box displays (see Figure 15.3). Click on the large button to start the installation. A message box displays, letting you know that the files are being copied.
6. When the installation is through, you may be notified that you have to restart Windows to complete the installation. If you are asked, click on Restart Windows. In a few moments, Windows will restart.
7. Click on Finish when the Installation Wizard displays.

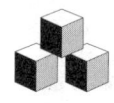

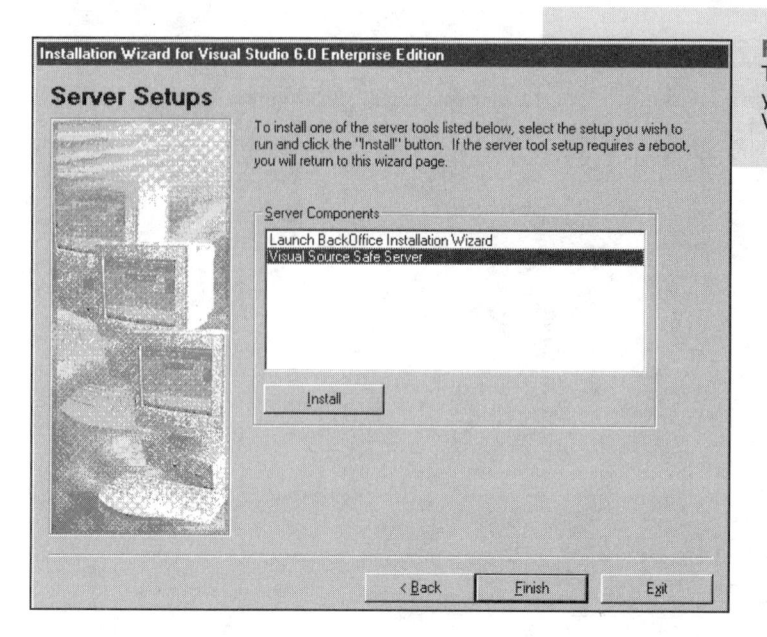

Figure 15.2
The server component you are installing is Visual SourceSafe.

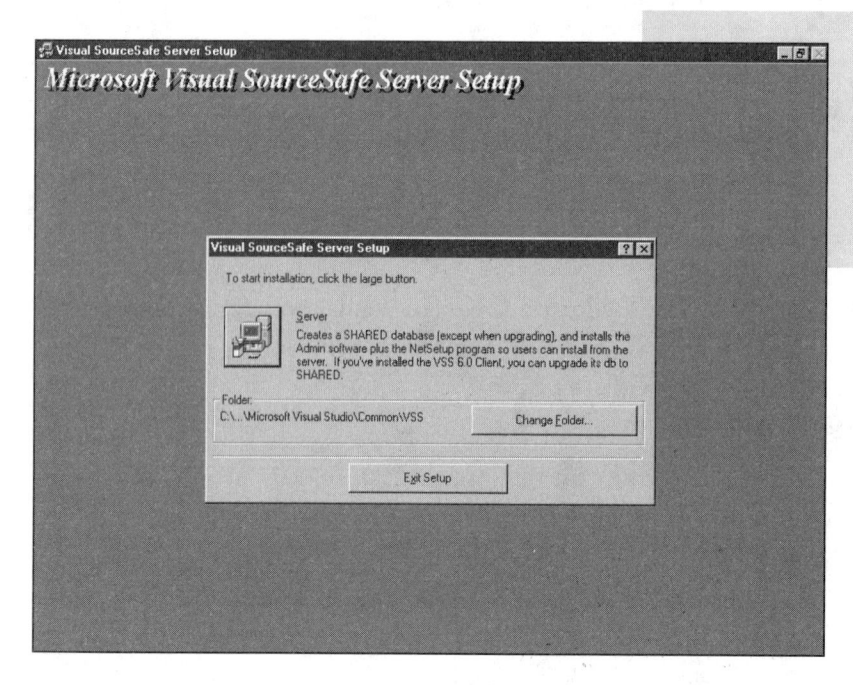

Figure 15.3
To start the Visual SourceSafe installation, just click on the big button with the computer icon.

CHAPTER 15 • WORKING IN THE CORPORATE WEB ENVIRONMENT   **235**

Now that you've installed Visual SourceSafe Server, you need to grant read/write permissions to all users that you want to be able to author files using Visual InterDev or Microsoft FrontPage. This is done using the Visual SourceSafe Administrator:

1. From the Start menu, select Programs, Microsoft Visual Studio 6.0, Microsoft Visual SourceSafe, Visual SourceSafe 6.0 Admin.

2. Because this is the first time you run this program, you'll be notified that the Admin user doesn't have a password. Click on OK.

> **Tip**
>
> For this example, you will not assign a password to the Admin user. In the real world, this would leave you wide open to anyone who wanted to hack Visual SourceSafe. When you are using Visual SourceSafe as part of your real development environment (instead of the virtual world of training!), you will need to go into the Visual SourceSafe 6.0 Admin program and assign a password to the Admin user by selecting Users, Change Password. The Visual SourceSafe Administrator window is shown in Figure 15.4.

Figure 15.4
Use Visual SourceSafe Administrator to add users to the Visual SourceSafe environment.

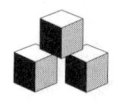

3. Select Users, Add User. The Add User dialog box displays (see Figure 15.5).

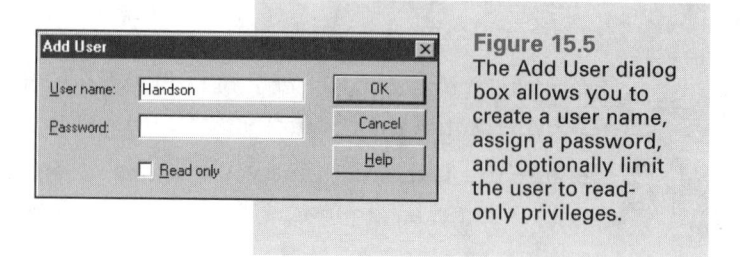

Figure 15.5
The Add User dialog box allows you to create a user name, assign a password, and optionally limit the user to read-only privileges.

4. Enter HandsOn for the User name. Don't enter a password.
5. Verify that the Read-Only option is not selected and click on OK.
6. Exit from the Visual SourceSafe Admin application.

> **Note** You may need to perform additional steps depending on your operating system. Please refer to the online documentation for more information.

If you have installed Visual SourceSafe on a Windows NT machine, then you must perform an additional procedure. You also have to add permissions for the Anonymous user account following these steps:

> **Note** In the online Microsoft documentation, it is implied that these steps only need to be done on a Windows NT server system. I have found that they need to be done on a Windows NT workstation as well.

1. From the Start menu, select Programs, Windows NT 4.0 Option pack, Microsoft Personal Web Server, Internet Service Manager. The Microsoft Management Console displays (see Figure 15.6).

CHAPTER 15 • WORKING IN THE CORPORATE WEB ENVIRONMENT

Figure 15.6
Use the Microsoft Management Console to set up the Anonymous user account.

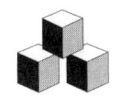

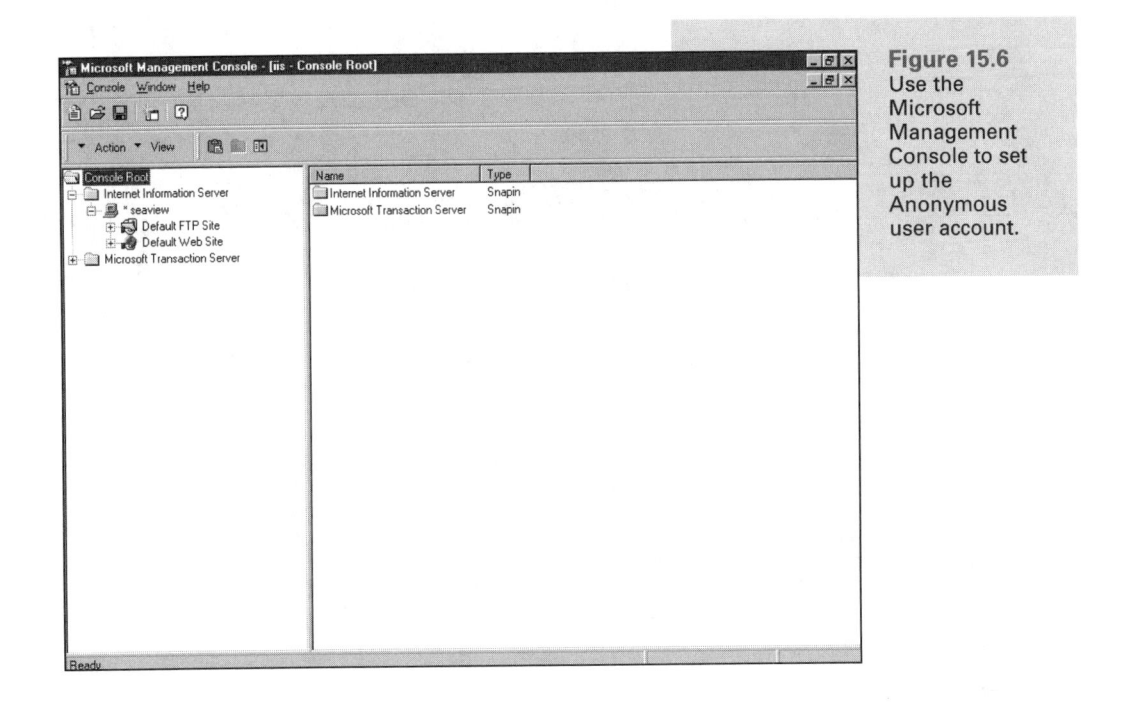

2. Expand Internet Information Server.
3. Expand the server that is running Visual SourceSafe.
4. Right-click on Default Web Site and select Properties. The Properties dialog box displays.
5. Select the Directory Security tab. The Directory Security page displays, as shown in Figure 15.7.
6. Click on Edit. Click on Edit again. The Anonymous User Account dialog box displays (see Figure 15.8). You need to know the name of the account so that you can add it to Visual SourceSafe.
7. Highlight the contents of the Username box and press Ctrl+C to copy the contents.
8. Click on Cancel. Click on Cancel again. Click on Cancel one more time.

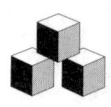

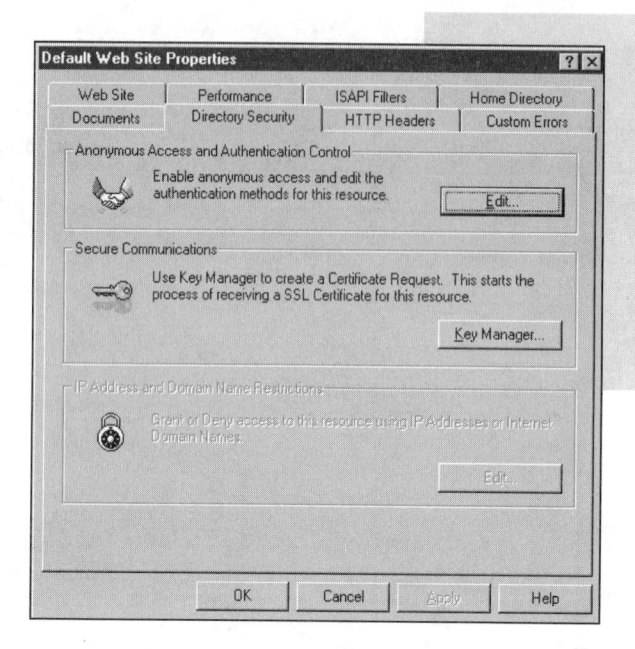

Figure 15.7
The Directory Security page of the Default Web Site Properties dialog box is used to access the settings needed to add permissions for the Anonymous user account.

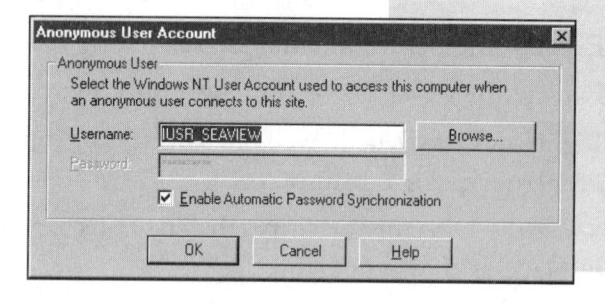

Figure 15.8
You need to add the username displayed in the Anonymous User Account dialog box to the Visual SourceSafe environment.

9. Close the Microsoft Management Console.
10. From the Start menu, select Programs, Microsoft Visual Studio 6.0, Microsoft Visual SourceSafe, Visual SourceSafe 6.0 Admin.
11. Select Users, Add User. The Add User dialog box displays.
12. Select the User name box and press Ctrl+V to paste the value from the Microsoft Management Console. Don't enter a password.

CHAPTER 15 • WORKING IN THE CORPORATE WEB ENVIRONMENT   **239**

13. Verify that the Read-Only option is not selected and click on OK.
14. Exit from the Visual SourceSafe Admin application.

The administrator has only two levels of access rights to choose from when adding new users to the Visual SourceSafe environment. One level of access is read-only. This means that the user can see everything in Visual SourceSafe but can't change anything. The other level of access is read/write. When a user has read/write rights, he can see and change anything in the Visual SourceSafe database.

Adding Source Control to Your Project

Once you've installed Visual SourceSafe, you can add source control to your project. To enable source control for your Web application, complete these steps:

1. Open the Bookstore project in Visual InterDev.
2. Select the project from the Project Explorer.
3. Select Project, Source Control, Add to Source Control. A message box displays, asking if you want to add the whole solution or just the selected project. Choose Selection. The Enable Source Control dialog box displays (see Figure 15.9).

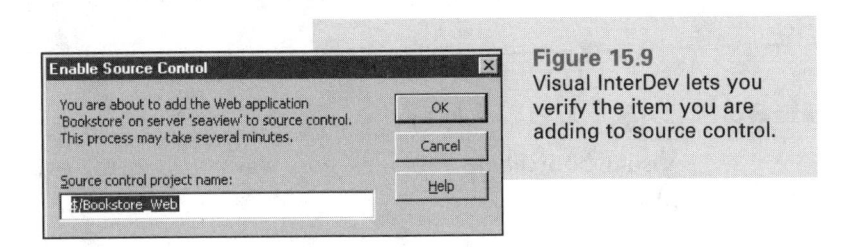

Figure 15.9
Visual InterDev lets you verify the item you are adding to source control.

4. Verify that the correct project is referred to in the dialog box and click on OK. It may take a few minutes to add the project to source control.

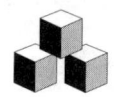

5. When the project has been added to source control, a message box displays (see Figure 15.10). Click on OK. You're done!

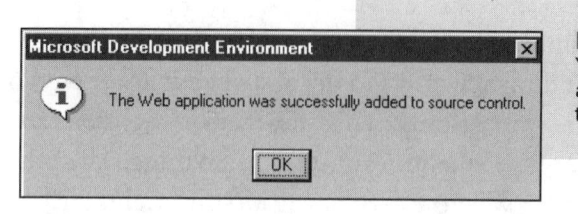

Figure 15.10
You've successfully added source control to your project.

Working with Source Control

After you've added source control to your project, you are ready to check files in and out of the project. As you have probably figured out, Visual SourceSafe uses a public library as its analogy. Just as in a library, if you want to use something, you have to check it out. While you have the item checked out, no one else can change it. Anyone who requests a local copy of a file that someone has checked out gets a message saying that another user has the file and only read-only copies of the file are available. Once you return the file or check it in, it is writable again.

> **Note** Visual SourceSafe allows you to set source control so that multiple people can check out the same object, but this is not the default setting.

Checking Files Out

Visual SourceSafe provides two ways to control checking out source files:

- **Exclusive checkout**. This is the default option. Exclusive checkout allows only one user at a time to check out a file.

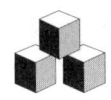

CHAPTER 15 • WORKING IN THE CORPORATE WEB ENVIRONMENT

- **Multiple checkouts**. This option allows more than one person to check out the same file at one time.

In this section, you are going to check out files using exclusive checkout. Later in this chapter, I'll show you how to set up source control to allow multiple checkouts. To check out a file, follow these steps:

1. Select Page1.htm from the Project Explorer. Currently a lock icon is displayed by this file.
2. Right-click on the file and select Check Out Page1.htm. The Check Out Item(s) dialog box displays (see Figure 15.11).

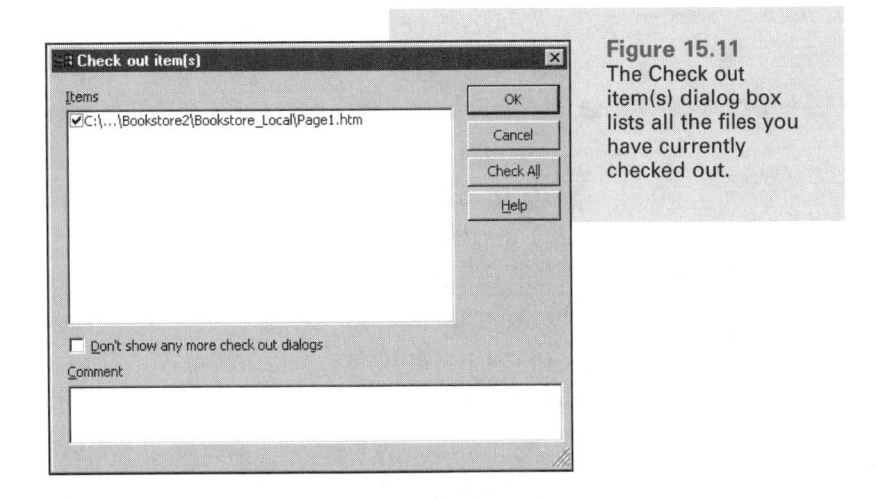

Figure 15.11
The Check out item(s) dialog box lists all the files you have currently checked out.

3. Click on OK. The lock icon is replaced with a check mark.

Tip

You can check out multiple files at the same time by clicking on the first file you want to check out and holding down the Ctrl key while clicking on the other files you want to check out. Then right-click on one of the selected files and select Check Out.

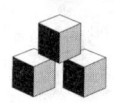

Adding Files to a Source Control-Enabled Web Application

Once you've enabled source control for a Web application, any files that you create or add to that Web application are added automatically to the Visual SourceSafe project. These include files that you create in other applications, such as Microsoft FrontPage, and add to a Web project. If you have a file in your Web project that for some reason is not under source control, you can add it manually using these steps:

1. Select the file that you want to add to source control in the Project Explorer.
2. Select Project menu, Source Control, Add to Source Control.

Getting the Master Version of a File

At times, you will want to review the latest version of a file without making changes to it. For example, you need to look at a page to see if its content is going to affect what you are doing with the page that you are working on. In this case, you can get a copy of the master version of a file without checking the file out. When you get the latest version of a file, you are getting a read-only copy of the master file onto your local Web server. To get a copy of the master version of a file, follow these steps:

1. Right-click on Form Example.asp from the Project Explorer.
2. Select Get Latest Version of Form Example.asp. The Get Latest Version dialog box displays (see Figure 5.12).

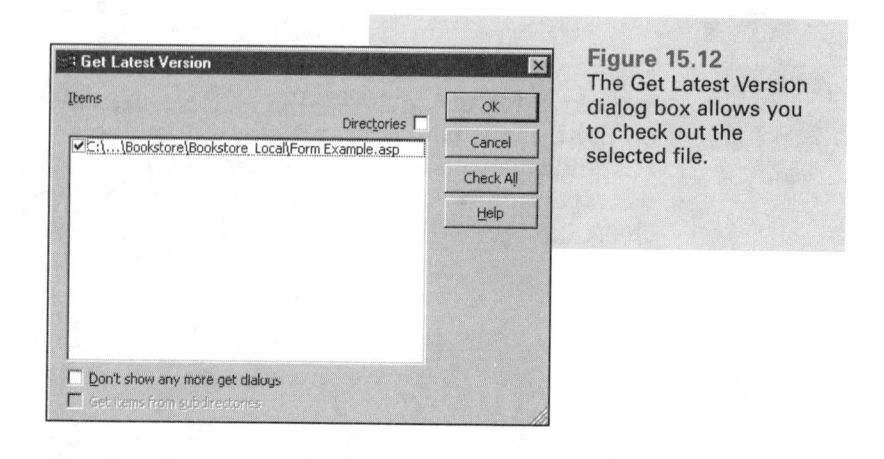

Figure 15.12
The Get Latest Version dialog box allows you to check out the selected file.

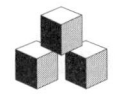

CHAPTER 15 • WORKING IN THE CORPORATE WEB ENVIRONMENT   243

3. Click on OK.

> **Caution**
> If the local directory is not synchronized with the master Web directory, the Get Latest Version command may fail. If this happens, select View, Refresh, to synchronize the project with the Web directory and then try the command again.

Checking Files In

When you are through with a file, check it back in to make it available to other team members. When the file is checked in, the version of the file you are checking in replaces the current version of the file in Visual SourceSafe. Visual InterDev automatically interacts with Visual SourceSafe to check the file in. Follow these steps:

1. Right-click on the Page1.htm in the Project Explorer.
2. Select Check In Page1.htm. The Check In Item(s) dialog box displays (see Figure 15.13).

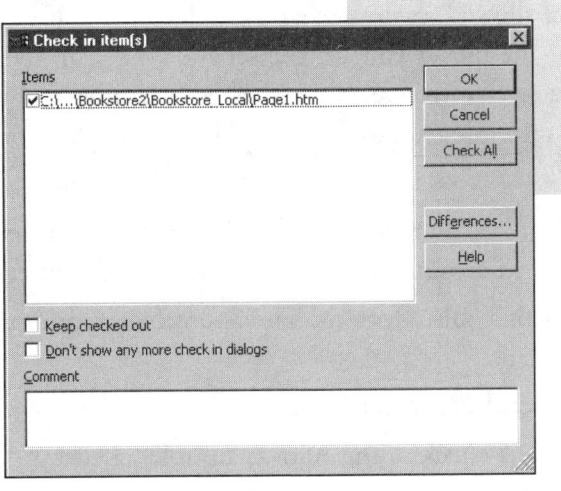

Figure 15.13
The Check in item(s) dialog box looks similar to the Check out item(s) dialog box.

3. Click on OK. A lock icon appears next to Page1.htm in the Project Explorer.

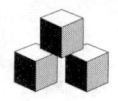

Discarding Changes to a File

If you checked out a file, made changes to it, and then decided that you didn't want the changes, you can undo checkout of the file. This results in changes to the file being discarded. To discard changes made to a checked-out file, follow these steps:

1. Check out Page1.htm. You are checking a file out so that you have something to undo the checkout with.
2. Right-click on Page1.htm from the Project Explorer.
3. Select Undo Checkout of Page1.htm. The Undo Checkout dialog box displays.
4. Click on OK. A message box displays, letting you know that your version of the file will be replaced with the current version under source control. Click on Yes.

Enabling Multiple Checkouts

The default setting for Visual SourceSafe is to let only one person have a particular file checked out at a time. If you want, you can allow multiple people to check out a file at the same time. When multiple checkouts are allowed, each user who checks out the file gets a write-enabled copy of the file. If you are the second person to check the file in, you can review the differences and choose to merge the two versions. To enable multiple checkouts for a Visual SourceSafe project, follow these steps:

1. From the Start menu, select Programs, Microsoft Visual Studio 6.0, Microsoft Visual SourceSafe, Visual SourceSafe 6.0 Admin.
2. Select Tools, Options. The SourceSafe Options dialog box displays.
3. Select the General tab.
4. Place a check in the Allow Multiple Checkouts check box.
5. Click on OK.
6. Exit Visual SourceSafe Admin.

I said earlier that if you are the second person to check the same file in, you have the option of resolving merge conflicts. When you check a file in that has been modified by another user, Visual InterDev detects the merge conflicts and displays the Merge dialog box for you to review the two different versions.

If you and Sally check out the same file, the process would go something like this: Sally makes changes to the file and promptly checks the file back in. Sally's version of the file becomes the master version. You've made changes as well, but you check your file in after Sally has checked hers in. When you check in your copy of the file, the Merge dialog box displays. This dialog box allows you to merge the two versions and save the merged file as the latest version. This situation can't be simulated on a single machine, so I'll outline the process here:

1. Right-click on the file in the Project Explorer and select Check In. The Merge dialog box displays.
2. Select the conflict area you want to resolve in the bottom pane of the dialog box.
3. Right-click on the conflict. Choose the changes you want to merge.
4. Click on Close.
5. Click on Save.

Both the master and local copies reflect the changes you saved. Don't forget to let Sally know that she should get the latest version of the file, as her local copy doesn't have the changes that you made!

Disabling Source Control

You may have wondered, "What if I don't want to use source control anymore?" No problem, you can disable source control at any time. Because you don't need source control, you can go ahead and disable it for the rest of this project by completing these steps:

Note: When you disable source control for a Web application, the Visual SourceSafe project created when you first enabled source control for your Web project remains on the Visual SourceSafe server. This feature allows you to re-enable source control for your Web project at a later time.

Tip: If you want to remove the Visual SourceSafe project from your system, delete it from within Visual SourceSafe Explorer. This is a good thing to do if you've disabled source control for a project and then made significant changes to the file structure of the project.

Caution: Re-enabling source control after disabling it may cause some unexpected results. The most typical "unexpected result" occurs when you've disabled source control, deleted files, and then re-enabled source control. Magically, your deleted files reappear. This is because the files were deleted outside source control and the original Visual SourceSafe project still shows them as part of the project. Other unexpected results include renaming files that you changed the names of.

1. Select the Bookstore project in the Project Explorer.
2. Select Project, Source Control, Disconnect Web Project. A message box displays, letting you know that you are about to disconnect your Web project from source control.
3. Click on Yes. In a few moments you'll see a message that lets you know that the project has been successfully removed from source control.
4. Click on OK.

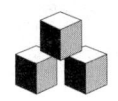

Summary

Once you get it set up, source control is easy to add to your application and easy to use. And once you've set up source control for a Web project, you aren't stuck with it; you can disable it if you wish.

In the next chapter, you will work with code to enhance the appearance and functionality of your Web Project.

CHAPTER 16

Building the Corporate Web Site

You've been climbing the hill of Visual InterDev knowledge, and in this chapter you are going to reach the climax. This chapter puts heavy emphasis on coding skills, and you are going to get a decent primer on the VBScript language. Before you jump into VBScript, I'll teach you some ways to enhance your current pages using sound and video. This chapter also introduces security, a topic that is often foremost in the mind of corporate Web solution implementers.

Building on an Existing Page

In the first project, you did two things for the appearance of your Web site: you added text and graphics. This chapter expands on these concepts by adding sound and video to your graphics.

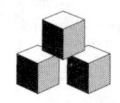

Adding Multimedia to Your Site

Multimedia is all the rage on the Web these days, and for good reason. You are competing with millions of other pages on the Internet for everyone's attention. How are you going to make someone want to come to your site? With bells and whistles, that's how. In this section, you will learn how to add a background sound to a Web page and embed a video on a page.

Adding a Background Sound

To add a background sound, you will use an HTML tag. The tag you are using is BGSOUND. BGSOUND lets you create pages with background sounds or "sound tracks." This element can be used only within the HEAD tag. Complete these steps:

1. Add this file to the project:

    \Program Files\Microsoft Visual Studio\VIntDev98\Samples\Gallery\content\mmedia\utopia.wav

    You will need to change the file type choice to Audio Files to be able to locate this file.

2. Add a new HTML page to the project named Page 3. Open Source view for Page 3.

3. Add this line below the <Title> tag:

    <BGSOUND SRC=Utopia.wav>

4. Set Page 3 as the start page.
5. Press F5 to start the application. Check out the sound!
6. Close Internet Explorer.
7. Press Shift+F5 to end the application run.

You may have expected to be able to drag the Utopia file from the Project Explorer and drop it on Page 3 and then have Visual InterDev deal with it. I tried dragging it to both the Design and Source views with undesired results. It created a link to the audio file instead of creating a background sound tag.

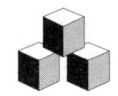

Adding a Video File to Your Application

Now that you have sound, you're ready to move on to video. This is another tag that you'll insert into your document.

1. Add this file to the project:

   ```
   \Program Files\Microsoft Visual Studio\VIntDev98\Samples\Gallery\content\mmedia\globe.avi
   ```

2. Open Source view for Page 3.
3. Add this line within the <Body> tag:

   ```
   <IMG DYNSRC="Globe.avi" LOOP=Infinite>
   ```

4. Press F5 to start the application. Check out the video!
5. Close Internet Explorer.
6. Press Shift+F5 to end the application run.

This line is the trick:

```
<IMG DYNSRC="Globe.avi" LOOP=Infinite>
```

The `LOOP` argument keeps the video going. `DYNSRC` is an Internet Explorer extension to the `IMG` statement.

Using Visual InterDev's Programming Features

In the last project, you created a very simple procedure. In this project, you are going to expand on the introduction to programming that you received. You'll start by working with Active Server Pages. Then you'll be presented with additional language constructs.

Two kinds of scripts are available in Visual InterDev. One is the kind that you wrote in the last project; it is called a *client script*. Since a client script is part of a page, when a user requests a page, the client script is sent to and run by the browser. The other type of script is a *server script*.

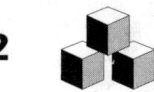

Working with Active Server Pages (ASPs)

Server scripts are also part of a page, but are not sent to the browser. Instead, they are run by the server after the page is requested, but before it is passed to the browser. When the page is sent to the browser, the server has already run the server script and replaced it with its output. Server scripts are saved in Active Server Pages (ASPs).

Active Server Pages aren't strictly processed from top to bottom, in that the server first locates and processes any server script that may reside in the page. After the server script is processed, it is replaced with its output and the remainder of the file is sent to the browser. Any client script in the file is processed by the browser, which treats the .asp file as it would an .htm file.

When you write a server script in an .asp file, you have to identify it as such. This can be done using either of these techniques:

- Use the delimiters <% and %>.

    Any text between these two tags is processed as inline server script by the server.

- Use the <SCRIPT> tag.

    The <SCRIPT> tag used with the RUNAT=SERVER attribute sets the procedure or procedures as server script. The format for this command is as follows:

    `<SCRIPT RUNAT=SERVER>`

    And don't forget the </SCRIPT> end tag after your server-side script.

In Source view, server script is colored yellow to make it stand out from client script.

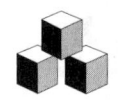

Creating an Active Server Page

The technique you will use to add server script to your application uses the delimiters <% and %>. You are going to write a simple script that determines the day of the week and outputs it to the HTML page. Don't forget that you add an ASP page to your project just as you would an HTML file.

Unlike client script, server script is generally not event-driven. When the ASP page is requested, the server reads the page and processes all server script from top to bottom. The script evaluates all expressions and variables and performs whatever calculations and database access you wrote in the order found in the file.

If the server script produces some output—if, for example, it displays the value of a variable or displays some records retrieved from a database—you can place the output on the page using the Response.Write method (or using the abbreviated form, the <%= operator) in inline script. For example, the following simple page shows server script that calculates the current time and puts it into a variable. Later in the page, the value of the server script variables are integrated into some HTML text:

```
<HTML>
<BODY>
Happy <%Response.Write Date%>!
</BODY>
</HTML>
```

When the page is processed, the server evaluates the expression following Response.Write and places its value at that point in the HTML page.

The first step to creating server script is to create an ASP page. The .asp extension that an Active Server Page has lets your Internet Information Server (which may be a Personal Web Server) know that the page may contain server script. When IIS reads the page, it looks for server script and processes it. Create an ASP page using these steps:

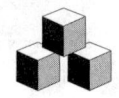

1. Select Project, Add Item. The Add Item dialog box displays.
2. Select ASP Page. Enter Happy for the Name and click on Open. The page is added to the project.
3. In the Source view, add a blank line under the `<body>` tag.
4. Enter this statement on the blank line:

   ```
   Happy <%Response.Write Date%>!
   ```

5. Set Happy.asp as the project's start page.
6. Press F5 to run your application. You'll see the page display with the word "Happy" followed by the date, as shown in Figure 16.1.
7. Close Internet Explorer.
8. End the run of the application.

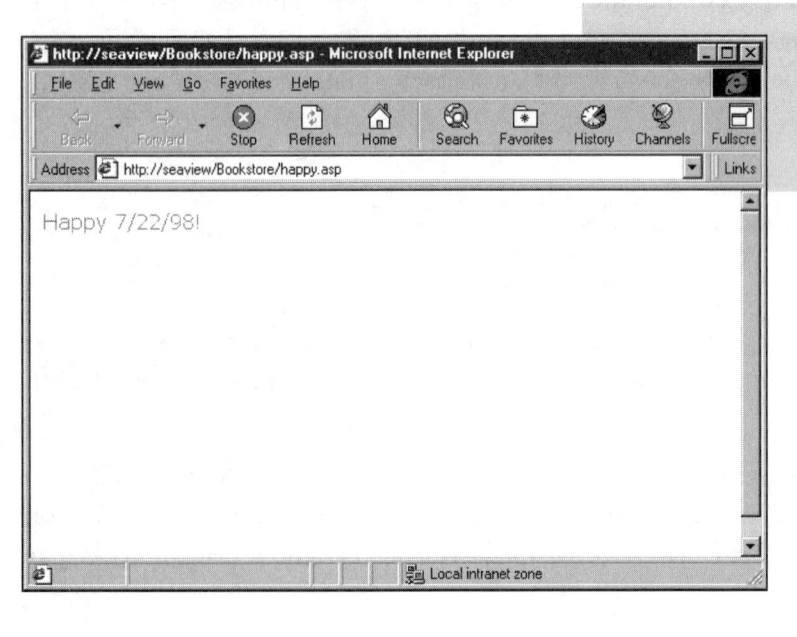

Figure 16.1
Server script can be used to add dynamic content to your pages.

Setting Your Page Language

Your page has a default language, as denoted by the `<%@ LANGUAGE= %>` tag. In Source view, look at the very first line of code in the Happy page. You'll find this line:

```
<%@ Language=VBScript %>
```

This `<%@ LANGUAGE=VBScript %>` tag specifies VBScript as the default scripting language. This doesn't mean that you have to restrict yourself to VBScript on this page. Your page can contain a mix of VBScript and JScript. If you are using a language on the page other than the page language, use the `<SCRIPT LANGUAGE = "language">` (where *language* is the language you wish to script in) at the beginning of the script block.

Table 16.1 provides you with a listing of keywords that you can use to access VBScript or JavaScript.

Table 16.1   Script Keywords

Keyword	Sets To
vbscript	VBScript
Vbs	VBScript
javascript	JavaScript
Jscript	JavaScript

Understanding the Difference between Client and Server Scripts

Before going further with scripting, you should understand the two differences between client and server scripts. One lies in where the script is processed. Client scripts are part of a page and are sent to and run by the browser when a user requests the page.

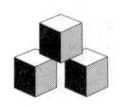

In contrast, server scripts are also part of a page, but they are not sent to the browser. Instead, they are run by IIS after the page is requested, but before it is passed to the browser. When the page is sent to the browser, the server has already run the server script and replaced it on the page with its output.

The other difference between client and server scripts is their location. Client scripts can reside in either HTML or ASP pages. Server scripts can only reside in ASP pages.

> **Note** ASP pages are supported by Microsoft Internet Information Server (IIS) and Personal Web Server.

The Scripting Object Model

As far as programming languages are concerned, you aren't hip if you don't do objects! Since Visual InterDev is obviously hip, its scripting languages use objects. Microsoft names Web objects using the *scripting object model*, which introduces the familiar object-oriented programming model to HTML and script programming. The scripting object model defines a set of objects with events, properties, and methods that you can use to create and script your application. It allows you to create Web applications in much the same way you create applications in environments such as Visual Basic and Microsoft Excel.

Understanding Objects

Before you go further, you need to understand the concept of objects. All the components you work with in the Windows environment are objects. Record sets are objects, command buttons are objects, and so are option buttons, check boxes, and list boxes. If you can point to something, it's an object. Objects are everything you control and interact with through your application.

Objects have events. An event is a specific run-time action, such as the user's selecting a menu or clicking on a button. Events are tied to code via event procedures. To name an event procedure, add the name of the event to the name of the object. For example, if you had a record set object named, originally enough, Recordset1, and you wanted to write a procedure that would run when the onrowenter event occurred, you would name the procedure `Recordset1_onrowenter`. Don't worry about knowing all the events associated with an object. You'll use the Script Outline tool to help you in this area.

All objects have properties. Properties control the appearance and behavior of objects. They can be set with code, which is referred to as setting properties at run time, or through the Property window or Property pages. Setting them using the Property window or Property pages is called setting properties at design time.

Objects also have methods. Methods tell an object to do something and can be thought of as object-specific functions. You'll see several examples of methods as you progress through this chapter.

You already used the scripting object model when you created the simple procedure in the preceding project. Take a look at that procedure:

```
</script>
<script LANGUAGE="VBScript">
<!--
function Recordset1_onrowenter()

    txtDiscountedPrice.value = Recordset1.fields.getvalue("UnitPrice") * .90
end function
//-->
</script>
```

The first thing you'll identify is the event. In this case it is onrowenter. This means that every time as the record set moves to a new row, this procedure will execute. Can you identify the objects you are using in this procedure? There are two, `txtDiscountedPrice` and `Recordset1`. Actually there is a third, in the form of a collection named `fields`. How about properties? Only one property is referred to in this procedure, value. Do you think there are any methods? Yes, `getvalue` is a method of the `fields` collection.

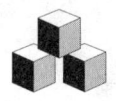

> A *collection* is a group of related objects.

Enabling the Scripting Object Model

Before you can use the scripting object model, you have to enable it. In this case, you already enabled the scripting object model and didn't even know it. Design-time controls require the scripting object model, and you added a design-time control when you added the record set control. You were prompted briefly at that time to enable the scripting object model, and you said yes. If you need to enable the scripting model for a page, you would use these steps:

1. Right-click anywhere in the page away from an object or control.
2. Select Properties.
3. Select the General tab.
4. Check Enable Scripting Object Model.
5. Click on OK.

When you complete this procedure, Visual InterDev adds the following code to your page:

```
<% ' VI 6.0 Scripting Object Model Enabled %>
<!--#include file="_ScriptLibrary/pm.asp"-->
<% if StartPageProcessing() Then Response.End() %>
<FORM name=thisForm METHOD=post>
```

Visual InterDev Objects

The scripting object model has several objects for your programming pleasure. One that is high up in the object hierarchy is the page object. A page object is simply a Web page. If you needed to refer to the current page in your script, you would use an object called `thisPage`. Page objects can be referenced from other pages. Other objects are contained within Page objects.

Some of the other objects that you'll work with are the controls that are found in the Toolbox. Other languages, such as COBOL or FORTRAN, provide only one tool for creating an interface: the keyboard. Visual InterDev provides you with a palette of controls to create your application's interface.

Each control has a specialized purpose. For example, when a user sees a group of option buttons, he knows that he can only select one from the group. If a user sees a group of check boxes, however, he knows he can select multiple items. The type of control communicates these selection options to the user. Because of this, it is important to select the right tool when requesting input from a user. There is a standard for interface design called *Common User Access (CUA)*. If you have used Windows, you can quickly learn to use OS/2, a Macintosh, or a Sun Microsystems computer. This is because they have similar interfaces. For example, if you know how to use a command button on one system, you know how to use one on all systems.

By placing controls on your pages, you are creating your user interface. Controls provide a mechanism for you to request information from and present information to your user.

An example of an object (control) that you've already used on a page is a text box. You used a text box in the last project to display the value of a field from a record set. A text box is used to hold text that the user either entered or changed. At design time, you typically set the values of two properties for text box controls: ID and Text. The Text property controls the text displayed by the control.

> **Note**
>
> **An object's ID property must start with a letter. It can include numbers and the underscore (_) character. It cannot include spaces, punctuation marks, or special characters.**

> **Note:** The conventional prefix to use when naming text boxes is .txt.

Another object you've used is a check box. A check box has two uses. One is as a toggle selection. If a check box has a check mark at run time, then the user has set something to True. If the check box has no check mark, then the user has set the item to False. The check box is sometimes used to present users with multiple options from which they may select one or more.

> **Note:** The conventional naming prefix used for a check box is .chk.

Use OptionButtons to display multiple choices for an item. OptionButtons allow a user to select only one available option. To see an example of OptionButtons, select File, Print. The Range Frame contains a group of OptionButtons, from which you can select only one. Typically, OptionButtons are placed within frames so that, if you need more than one group of OptionButtons on a form, your application knows which OptionButtons are related.

> **Note:** The conventional prefix to use when naming OptionButtons is .opt.

Option buttons provide users a way to select from among several choices. The list box control is used to display a list of items from which a user can choose. It can be used to replace option buttons. A general rule of thumb as to when to use option buttons and when to use a list box is if you need more than three option buttons, convert them to a list box.

> **Note** The conventional naming prefix used for a list box is .lst.

A special form of the list box is the drop-down list box. A drop-down list box is basically a list box that shows one line of information. To see more information, you select the down arrow button so that a list drops down from the control. The advantage of a drop-down list box over a plain list box is that the drop-down form takes up less "screen real estate."

Buttons are a frequently used control. You should be able to name a common command button, an OK button for instance, without really thinking. Buttons are used to prompt a user to select an action. For example, you may have a form with the following command buttons on it: Yes, No, and Cancel. A user clicks on the desired button, and the associated action is initiated.

> **Note** The conventional naming prefix used for command buttons is .cmd or .btn.

This is just a sampling of some of the controls, also known as objects, that you'll be working with when developing your application. Even though I've compared working with objects, properties, methods, and such to using objects in other development environments, some things about working with script and objects in Visual InterDev are unique to Visual InterDev.

One is that you have to consider the target platform, which specifies where scripts run and therefore dictates what your scripts can do. When the target platform is the server, you can use the scripting object model and the ASP programming model, including IIS objects. If your target platform is the client, you are using the scripting model to extend the document object model provided by Dynamic HTML (DHTML). You may not think this is a big deal until you consider where you run your script controls and what you can do with that script.

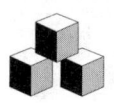

You may be familiar with a function named `MsgBox`. The `MsgBox` function displays a message box on a screen. If you used the `MsgBox` function in a client script, there would be no problem. If you tried to use the `MsgBox` function in a server script, however, you would have a problem. Visual InterDev would try (and probably fail) to display the message on the server rather than to the user, because the script was processed by the server. Client scripts can display messages to the user. So to borrow a phrase from the real estate industry, what's important to know about where you are writing script is location, location, location.

Working with Properties

I've talked about and used properties. Just to make sure you understand their usage in code, take a moment to consider how they are referred to in a script. To use a property, you first type the name of the object, followed with a period, and then the property name, as shown:

```
Objectname.propertyname
```

For example, if you had an object named `txtDiscountedPrice` and you wanted to set its `Value` property, you would use this line:

```
TxtDiscountedPrice.value = 18
```

> **Tip** Object and property names are case-sensitive in JScript and JavaScript.

Using Methods and Functions

The syntax for using a method is very much like that of a property. You use the object's name followed by a period and then the method. An example of a method is `getvalue`. `Getvalue` is a method of the fields collection and allows you to retrieve the value of a specific field. The field whose value you want is passed to the `getvalue` method through

CHAPTER 16 • BUILDING THE CORPORATE WEB SITE

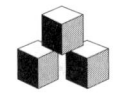

an argument. This value can be returned to a property or to a variable. Here is an example of using a method:

```
Recordset1.fields.getvalue("UnitPrice")
```

> **Tip:** Method names are case-sensitive in JScript and JavaScript.

Setting Your Client Script Language

You can choose your scripting language for your project. In this case, you need to set it to VBScript. Use these steps to do this:

1. Open Page 3 in Source view.
2. Right-click anywhere in the page away from an object or control.
3. Select Properties. The Properties window displays (see Figure 16.2).
4. Select the General tab.
5. Select VBScript from the Client drop-down list.
6. Click on OK.

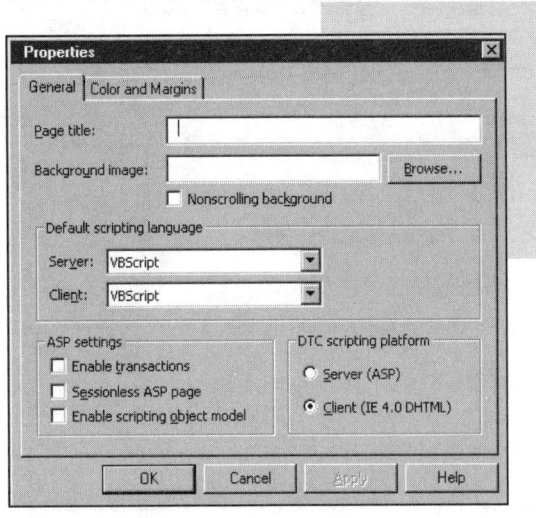

Figure 16.2
The Properties window of a page allows you to set your server and client script language.

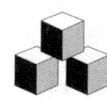

Using the Script Outline

The Script Outline lists objects and their events. You can use the Script Outline window to create event handlers. In the Script Outline window, expand the node for the object you are working with, and then double-click on the name of the event you want to write a handler for. To see an example of this, follow these steps:

1. Select View, Other Windows, Script Outline. The Script Outline window opens. You may need to take a few moments to arrange your desktop so that you can see both the Script Outline and Page 3 (see Figure 16.3).
2. Expand Window in the Script Outline. Its events are displayed.
3. Double-click on OnLoad. The following code is added to your page:

   ```
   Sub window_onload
   End Sub
   ```

4. Select Edit, Undo, to remove the added code.

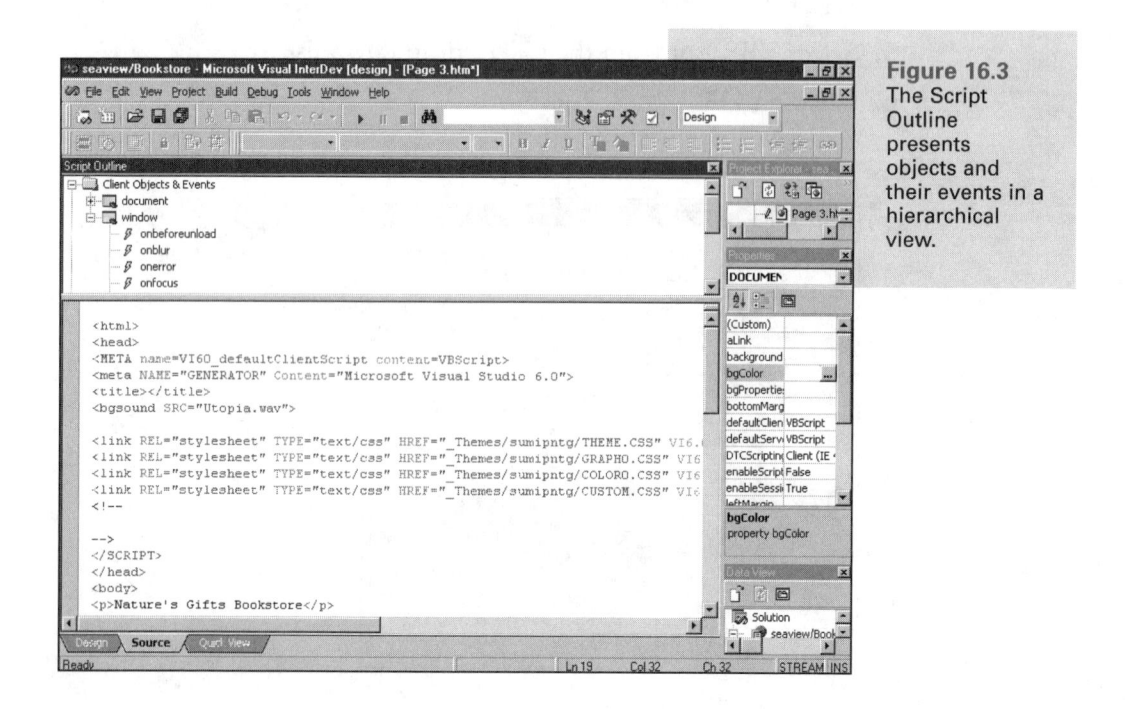

Figure 16.3
The Script Outline presents objects and their events in a hierarchical view.

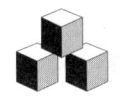

I already said that a browser, such as Internet Explorer, processes client scripts. And you know that client scripts are placed between `<SCRIPT>` and `</SCRIPT>` tags. You are not limited in the number of script blocks you can have on your page. Have you thought about the fact that your application may not run on a browser that doesn't understand the script language you are using? In this case, you can embed the script within HTML comment tags so that non-script-capable browsers ignore it. You may have noticed that the following tags were added to your page when you worked through the last procedure:

`<!—`

`—>`

These comment tags instruct non-script-capable browsers to skip this part of the page.

Building Your VBScript Knowledge

You've selected VBScript as your client scripting language; you've learned about objects, events, properties, and methods. What now? You are going to build on your VBScript knowledge.

Understanding Variables

Times will arise when you need to temporarily hold data for use later in an application. This data is stored in *variables*. A typical application has several variables, which store text, numbers, dates, time, and property values. Here is a list of things you may want to store in variables:

- The result of a calculation
- User input
- Data from one form that you want to use on another form
- A changing date such as the current date

The two key concepts associated with the concept of a variable are that it is temporary storage, meaning that it is removed from memory when the application ends, and that it is dynamic data. Variables are used because the data stored in them can be different from application session to application session and even within a single session. To use variables, you must know how to declare them and how to assign values to them. This is what you are learning in the next sections.

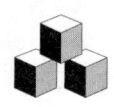

Declaring Variables

Declaring a variable is the process of creating a variable and setting memory aside for it. To declare a variable, you use the `Dim` statement, which stands for dimension. The `Dim` statement's syntax is listed here:

```
Dim variablename
```

This form of variable declaration is called *explicit declaration*. You can also declare multiple variables on the same line by separating each variable name with a comma. Here is an example of declaring multiple variables:

```
Dim Fname, Lname, City, State
```

Variable names must start with an alpha character. The variable name can be up to 255 characters in length, and it cannot contain spaces or special characters or be a keyword.

You can also use the reserved words `Public` and `Private` to declare variables. These statements will be discussed later in this section.

You can declare a variable implicitly by simply using its name in your script. Although nothing is technically wrong with doing this, it is considered poor programming practice. Many organizations require that their developers use explicit declaration. To ensure that you use explicit declaration, enter `Option Explicit` as the first statement in your script. This statement forces Visual InterDev to verify that each variable used by your application is declared using a `Dim` statement. If it finds a variable that does not have a `Dim` statement associated with it, it generates an error.

If you have worked with other programming languages, you are used to having a set of data types for use with your variables. This is not the case with VBScript. VBScript has only one data type, called a *Variant*. A variant data type variable is a variable that can hold any type and size. It varies itself based on the data it is holding. Because Variant is the only data type in VBScript, it's also the data type returned by all functions in VBScript.

Assigning a Value to a Variable

Assigning a value to a variable is done with the assignment operator (=). After declaring the variable, you can assign a value to the variable with this operator. You can assign different values to the same variable at different points of a program's execution. Here are examples of variable assignment statements:

```
City = "Atlanta"
FirstName = "Mark"
NumberOfStudents = 12
TaxRate = .065
```

Constants

Whereas variables contain changeable data, *constants* are placeholders for static data. There are two main reasons for using constants. One reason is to make your program more readable. Which is easier for you to interpret: .065 or SALESTAX? Obviously SALESTAX is more readable. Another reason for using constants is make it easier to make certain changes in your application. Sales tax is a perfect example. If you entered the number of the current sales tax every time your application needed it for a calculation, you would have to find every line of code that used that number when the sales tax increased. If you used a constant instead, you would only need to change one line of code.

The Const keyword is used to define constants. Here are examples of defining constants:

```
Const SALESTAX = .065
Const GROUPDISCOUNT = .1
```

When naming constants, use the same rules as for variables. A convention for naming constants is to make them all caps so that they are easily differentiated from variables.

Scope

The last topic concerning variables and constants is the concept of *scope*. Where and how you declare variables and constants determines where you can use them. There are three levels of scope:

- Local
- Global
- Script level

The most commonly used scope is local. *Local variables* are local to, or owned by, the procedure they were created in. Local variables only exist when the procedure they were created in is running. Once the procedure is through running, its local variables are removed from memory. These variables are typically declared at the top of a procedure using the Dim statement. Variables with local scope are called procedure-level variables. If you declare a variable outside a procedure, you make it available to all the procedures in your script. This is a *script level variable,* and it has script level scope. These rules of scope also apply to constants.

Using Message Boxes and Input Boxes to Receive User Input

The first way you are going to use variables is in conjunction with message boxes and input boxes. These are two tools for getting information from your user through a dialog box interface.

The message box you probably have seen most often is the one that displays when you try to exit an application without saving your work. Through a message box (a specialized form of a dialog box) you're prompted with a question like "Do you want to save your work?" You can click on Yes, No, or Cancel. Message boxes are created in Visual InterDev with the MsgBox function.

The MsgBox function allows you to display a message in a dialog box. When a user clicks on one of the buttons available in the message box, an integer representing that button is returned. The syntax for this function is as follows:

> **Note:** The syntax statements in this book place optional items in square brackets ([ ]).

```
MsgBox(prompt[, buttons] [, title] [, helpfile, context])
```

The prompt argument is required. It is a text string representing the message that is to be displayed in the message box. The maximum length of prompt string is approximately 1,024 characters.

The buttons argument is optional and is a numeric value that tells Visual InterDev the number and type of buttons to display in the message box, the icon style to use, which button is the default button, and the modality of the message box. Table 16.2 lists the values for this argument.

Table 16.2 MsgBox Buttons Argument Values

Value	Constant	Description
Button Group		
0	vbOKOnly	OK button only
1	vbOKCancel	OK and Cancel buttons
2	vbAbortRetryIgnore	Abort, Retry, and Ignore buttons
3	vbYesNoCancel	Yes, No, and Cancel buttons
4	vbYesNo	Yes and No buttons
5	vbRetryCancel	Retry and Cancel buttons
Icon Group		
16	vbCritical	Critical Message icon
32	vbQuestion	Warning Query icon
48	vbExclamation	Warning Message icon
64	vbInformation	Information Message icon

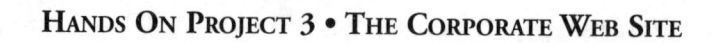

Table 16.2 MsgBox Buttons Argument Values (continued)

Value	Constant	Description
Default Group		
0	vbDefaultButton1	First button is default
256	vbDefaultButton2	Second button is default
512	vbDefaultButton3	Third button is default
768	vbDefaultButton4	Fourth button is default
Modal Group		
0	vbApplicationModal	Application modal
4096	vbSystemModal	System modal

To build the value of the buttons argument, you can pick one from the button group, one from the icon group, one from the default group, and one from the modal group. Here are examples of MsgBox statements with acceptable buttons argument values:

```
Dim Response
MsgBox "This is a test."
Response = MsgBox("Do you wish to continue?", vbYesNo)
Response = MsgBox("Do you want to save your work?", 
vbYesNoCancel+vbQuestion+vbDefaultButton1)
```

If you do not provide a value for the buttons argument, it is set to 0. This means you get a message box with one button, the OK button, and no icon.

Another optional argument is title. This is the text used in the title bar of the dialog box. If you do not provide a value for the title argument, the name of the application is used.

The optional helpfile argument is a string that identifies the Help file to use to provide context-sensitive help for the dialog box. The optional context argument works in conjunction with the helpfile argument by providing a numeric expression that is the help context number assigned to the appropriate help topic by the help author. If a value for the context argument is provided, a value for the helpfile argument must also be provided.

When a user clicks a message box's button, it returns an integer value. These return values can be used to test which button was clicked by the user. The statements for doing this are discussed later in this chapter. The return values are listed in Table 16.3.

Table 16.3 MsgBox Return Values

Value	Constant	Description
1	vbOK	OK
2	vbCancel	Cancel
3	vbAbort	Abort
4	vbRetry	Retry
5	vbIgnore	Ignore
6	vbYes	Yes
7	vbNo	No

You are going to create a simple procedure that displays a message box when a user clicks a button. Follow these steps:

1. Add a new HTML page to the project named VB Examples.
2. Drag a button control from the HTML Toolbox to the page in the Add Your Content Below area.
3. Set the (ID) property to btnTalkToMe. Set the Name property to btnTalkToMe as well. The ID property is used when referring to the object in client scripts, and the Name property is how the object's value is tagged when the browser submits the user's input back to the server. To make things easy on me, I always set these two properties to be the same.
4. Click on the text that appears on the button. Delete this text and type Talk to Me.
5. Go to Source view.
6. Set the client script language to VBScript.
7. Locate btnTalkToMe in the Script Outline.

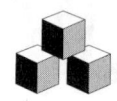

8. Double-click on onclick. This adds the event procedure to the Source view.
9. Position your insertion point between the `Sub` and `End Sub` lines.
10. Type `MsgBox` followed by a space. When you do this, you'll see a small box (see Figure 16.4) pop up that contains the basic syntax for the `MsgBox` function. This helper is called IntelliSense and is a form of help.
11. Complete the statement so that it matches this one:

    ```
    MsgBox "This is an example of a message box."
    ```

12. Modify the code until it matches this:

    ```
    sub btnTalkToMe_onclick()
        MsgBox "This is an example of a message box."
    End sub
    ```

    Don't forget to add the () at the end of the sub line.

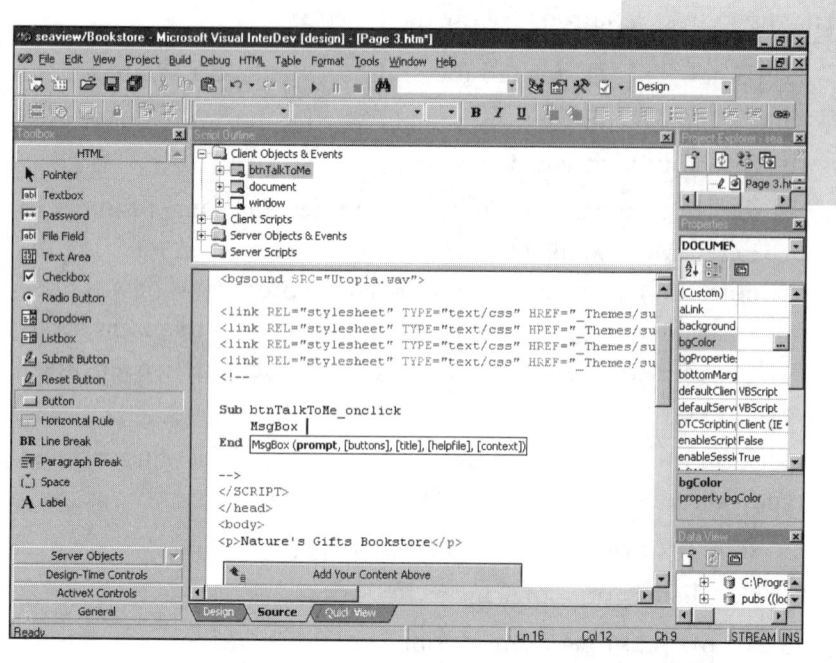

Figure 16.4 The IntelliSense feature provides you with syntax information.

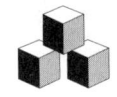

13. Select File, Save.
14. View the page in the Microsoft Internet Explorer browser.
15. Click on the Talk to Me button. You'll see the message box you created (see Figure 16.5).

Figure 16.5
The MsgBox statement is a great tool for communicating with a user.

16. Close Internet Explorer.

In real life, you wouldn't be popping up messages all over your application. An example of when you would use a message box is when a user is getting ready to modify or delete a record in a database.

Another way to display a message box is by using the window object's `alert` method. To do this, complete these steps:

1. Add this line after the end sub statement:

    ```
    window.alert("Hi!")
    ```

2. Save the page.
3. View the page in the Browser. The message box pops right up!
4. Close Internet Explorer.

Using Conditional Logic

Now, add the actual functionality of this application. A lot of this functionality is done with *conditional logic*. Conditional logic controls the flow of program code. For example, say you added a message box to your application that has three buttons on it: Yes, No, and Cancel. How are you going to know which button a visitor has clicked, and once you find out, what are you going to do about it? This is where conditional logic comes into play. Conditional logic allows you to select different program paths based on a variable value, user response, function calculation, or property setting.

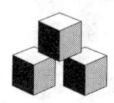

Using Conditional Operators

When you are using conditional logic, you are going to create a test, and based on the results of that test, you are going to perform an action. For example, you may want to take one action if a user selects "Georgia" and another if the user selects "Florida." Or you may want to do one thing if the user enters a value greater than 5 and another if the user enters a value less than 3. To do this type of test, you need to use *comparison operators*. The result of a test using a comparison operator is either True, meaning it met the test condition, or False, meaning it did not meet the test condition. Table 16.4 lists the available comparison operators.

Table 16.4 Comparison Operators

Comparison Operator	Meaning
=	Equal to
< >	Not equal to
>	Greater than
<	Less than
> =	Greater than or equal to
< =	Less than or equal to

Go through some examples to demonstrate the concept of comparison operator usage. If you had a variable that was equal to five and you were using it with the following comparison operators, you would get the results listed in Table 16.5.

Table 16.5 Using Comparison Operators to Test a Variable (`HighFive`) with the Value of 5

Statement	Result
HighFive = 5	True
HighFive > 6	False
HighFive > 5	False
HighFive >= 5	True
HighFive < 7	True
HighFive < 5	False

Sometimes you may need to test if a value meets multiple conditions. You may need, for example, to test to see if a user lives in Hollywood, Florida. There are multiple Hollywoods, so you need to test for both Hollywood and Florida. To do this, you use *logical operators* to combine test condition requirements. Table 16.6 lists Visual InterDev's logical operators. Table 16.7 uses examples to illustrate the use of these operators.

Table 16.6 Logical Operators

Logical Operator	Meaning
And	If both conditions are True, then the result is True.
Or	If either condition is True, then the result is True.
Not	If the conditional expression is False, then the result is True. If the conditional expression is True, then the result is False.
Xor	If one and only one of the conditions is True, then the result is True. If both are True or both are False, then the result is False.

Table 16.7 Examples of Logical Operators

Statement	Result
State = "Florida" And City = "Hollywood"	Both conditions have to be met to result in a true statement.
State = "Florida" Or City = "Hollywood"	Either of these conditions needs to be met to result in a true statement.

Using the If Statement to Validate User Input

One of the primary tools you will use to build conditional logic into your applications is the If statement. An If statement lets you test a condition and perform an action based on the results of the conditional test. Visual InterDev supports two forms of the If statement. The simple version of the If statement is referred to as an If...Then statement. This form allows you to test a single condition. The format of this statement is as follows:

```
If condition Then statement
```

Condition is a conditional expression such as State = "Florida". Statement is any valid Visual InterDev statement. This format only allows for one statement. If you need to execute several statements, use this syntax:

```
If condition Then
    statement1
    statement2
    ...
    statementn
End If
```

This format of the If statement must be terminated with an End If. Notice the indention in this syntax statement. The indention is not required but makes the If statement easier to read. Here are some examples of using the If statement:

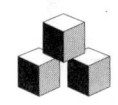

> **Note:** When writing VBScript, you can add comments to explain your code by starting the commenting line with a single quote.

```
'This example tests to see if the customer lives in Alabama.
'If they do they need to pay a $5.75 handling charge.
If State = "Alabama" Then Cost = Cost + 5.75
'This example tests to see if the customer lives in Georgia.
'If they do they pay an extra 10% for shipping and a message displays.
If State = "Georgia" Then
     Cost = Cost * 1.1
     MsgBox "An extra 10% has been added to this shipment due to state
requirement."
End If
```

There will be times when you need to test for multiple conditions. To do this, you'll use an If…Then…Else statement. This form of the If statement allows you to test for different conditions. The syntax for this form is as follows:

```
If condition1 Then
[statements]
[ElseIf condition-n Then]
[elseifstatements] ...
[Else]
[elsestatements]]
End If
```

When Visual InterDev sees an If…Then…Else statement, it tests *condition1* first. If that test results in False, then it goes to the next test condition. If none of the test conditions result in True, then the statements found in the Else block execute. There are variations of this statement. It can have multiple ElseIf statements. It can have ElseIf statements and no Else statement. It can also have no ElseIf statements and have an Else statement. The following code illustrates some variations on the If…Then…Else statement:

```
'In this example, Alabama pays 5.75 for shipping and handling.
If State = "Alabama" Then
```

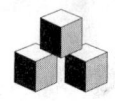

```
Cost = Cost + 5.75
'Georgia pays 10% of the cost for shipping and handling.
ElseIf State = "Georgia" Then
    Cost = Cost * 1.1
    MsgBox "An extra 10% has been added to this shipment due to state requirement."
'All other states pay a flat fee of $2 for shipping and handling.
Else
    Cost = Cost + 2
End If
'In this example, the If statement is used to determine what the sales tax will be for
'an item. This example demonstrates the use of multiple ElseIf statements.
Dim cSalesTax As Currency
If Department = "Snacks" Or Department = "Cookies" Or Department = "Candy" Then
    cSalesTax = .03
ElseIf   Department = "Personal Hygiene" Or Department = "Baby" Then
    cSalesTax = .04
ElseIf   Department = "Produce" Or Department = "Meat" Or Department = "Dairy"
    cSalesTax = 0
Else
    cSalesTax = .05
End If
'This example demonstrates the use of an If statement without ElseIf.
If bContribution = True Then
    cAmount = 25
Else
    cAmount = 0
End If
```

When testing for multiple conditions, it is important to design your If statement for maximum performance. You should try to place the most likely condition to be met as the first condition. This way once the condition is met, the statements are performed without unnecessary additional testing.

If you need to have an additional test within a conditional test, you can nest If statements. Here is an example of nested If statements:

```
If State = "Georgia" Then
    If City = "Atlanta" or City = "Valdosta" Then
        cShipping = 5
        MsgBox "This city has an additional $2 shipping charge."
    ElseIf City = "Athens" or City = "Macon" or City = "Albany" Then
        cShipping = 4
        MsgBox "This city has an additional $1 shipping charge."
```

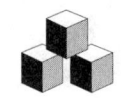

```
        Else
            cShipping = 3
        End If
ElseIf State = "Florida" Then
    If City = "Miami" or City = "Orlando" Then
        cShipping = 5
        MsgBox "This city has an additional $2 shipping charge."
    ElseIf City = "Jacksonville" Then
        cShipping = 4
        MsgBox "This city has an additional $1 shipping charge."
    Else
        cShipping = 3
    End If
Else
    cShipping = 2
End If
```

As you can see from this example, indention can make a nested If statement a lot easier to read. Also note that in nested If statements, each If block needs its own End If statement. In your example, you are going to use the response to a message box to determine what message to display next. To add an If statement to your application, complete these steps:

1. Delete the Window.Alert statement on this page.

2. Modify the btnTalkToMe_onclick procedure to match this one:

   ```
   sub btnTalkToMe_onclick()
       Dim response

       response = MsgBox ("Do you like scripting?", vbyesno)
       IF response = vbyes then
           window.alert "You said yes!"
       Else
           window.alert "You're so negative."
       end if
   End sub
   ```

3. Save the page.

4. View the page in the browser.

5. Click on the Talk to Me button. A message box displays.

6. Click on Yes. You'll see the Yes message box. Click on OK.

7. Click on the Talk to Me button again. A message box displays.

8. Click on No. You'll see the No message box. Click on OK.
9. Close Internet Explorer.

Record Navigation Using Script

The Recordset object has several methods that are used for record navigation. These methods are as follows:

- `moveNext`

  Moves to the next record in the record set.

- `movePrevious`

  Moves to the previous record in the record set.

- `moveFirst`

  Moves to the first record in the record set.

- `moveLast`

  Moves to the last record in the record set.

- `moveAbsolute`

  Moves to a given record number in the record set.

- `move`

  Moves a certain number of records from the current record in the record set. The `move` method lets you pass it an argument that tells it how many records to move.

These methods replace the need for a record navigation bar on your page. Start by creating the page and its controls. You need a Recordset control to access data from the page and a series of text boxes to display field information. In Chapter 14, you identified the needed text boxes. Use the following steps to create the page and add the Recordset and Textbox controls:

1. Add an HTML page to your project named Data Script.
2. Enable the scripting object model for the page and set VBScript as its default client script language.
3. Open the page in Design view.

4. Right-click on the NorthDC data connection from the Project Explorer. Select Add Data Command. The Command1 Properties dialog box displays.
5. Set the Command Name to Categories.
6. Set the Database Object to Table and Object Name to Categories. Click on OK to create the command.
7. Select the Design-Time Controls tab from the Toolbox. Add a recordset control to the page.
8. Right-click on the newly added Recordset control and select Properties. The Recordset Properties dialog box displays.
9. Set the Name to rsCategories. Verify that Connection is set to NorthDC, Database Object to Table, and Object Name to Categories. Click on Close.
10. Turn to the Add Your Content Below section.
11. Type **Category ID**:
12. Beside Category ID, add a text box.
13. Right-click on the newly added text box and select Properties to display the Textbox Properties dialog box.
14. Set Name to txtCategory, Recordset to rsCategories, and Field to CategoryID. Click on OK.
15. Add a blank line after the text box.
16. Type **Category Name:**
17. Beside Category Name, add a text box.
18. Right-click on the newly added text box and select Properties to display the Textbox Properties dialog box.
19. Set Name to txtCategoryName, Recordset to rsCategories, and Field to CategoryName. Click on OK.
20. Add a blank line after the text box.
21. Type **Description:**
22. Beside Description, add a text box.

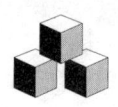

23. Right-click on the newly added text box and select P‌roperties to display the Textbox Properties dialog box.

24. Set N‌ame to txtDescription, R‌ecordset to rsCategories, and F‌ield to Description. Click on OK.

In Chapter 14, I also identified a series of buttons that you would need. Use the following steps to add the buttons to the page:

1. Under the Add Your Content Below section, add a blank line.
2. On this line, create a table with one row and six columns.
3. Drag a button from the toolbox to each of the cells in the table.
4. Use Table 16.8 to set the properties of the buttons you added.

Table 16.8 Button Property Settings

Button	Caption	ID
Button1	First	btnFirst
Button2	Previous	btnPrevious
Button3	Next	btnNext
Button4	Last	btnLast
Button5	New Record	btnNewRecord
Button6	Save	btnSave

5. Select File, S‌ave Data Script.htm. The completed page should look similar to the one shown in Figure 16.6.

The first procedure that you are going to write is for btnPrevious using the `movePrevious` method. Complete the following steps:

1. Open the page in Source view.
2. Select V‌iew, Oth‌er Windows, S‌cript Outline. The Script Outline window opens.
3. Expand Client Objects and Events.
4. Expand btnFirst.
5. Double-click `onclick`. The btnFirst_onclick procedure is added to the page.

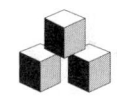

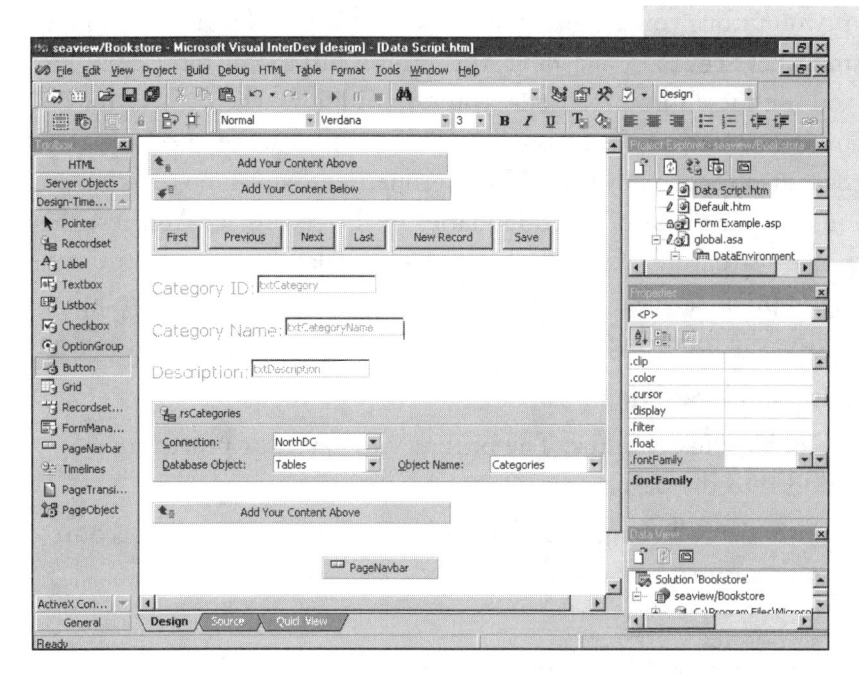

Figure 16.6
Now that the controls have been added to the page, you can write the scripts for the buttons.

6. Enter the following code for the btnFirst_onclick procedure so that it matches this code:

```
Sub btnFirst_onclick()
    thisrsCategories.moveFirst
End Sub
```

7. Expand btnLast.

8. Double-click onclick. The btnLast_onclick procedure is added to the page.

9. Enter the following code for the btnLast_onclick procedure so that it matches this code:

```
Sub btnLast_onclick()
    rsCategories.moveLast
End Sub
```

10. Save the form.

As you can see, the script you are writing replaces the need for a record navigation bar. This allows you to give your page a custom look. The next two buttons you are going to work with are the Previous and Next buttons. For `Previous` and `Next`, the script is just a little more complex. As you use these move methods, you do not know when you've hit the beginning or end of the record set. This requires some checking. The `Recordset` object has BOF and EOF properties that can be tested to see if you're beyond one of the boundaries of the record set. You test this with an `If` structure. If you are beyond a boundary, your code can issue the appropriate `MoveFirst` or `MoveLast` method to correct the situation. Complete the following steps:

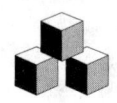

1. Expand btnPrevious.
2. Double-click `onclick`. The btnPrevious_onclick procedure is added to the page.
3. Enter the following code for the btnPrevious_onclick procedure so that it matches this code:

```
Sub btnPrevious_onclick()
rscategories.MovePrevious
If rscategories.BOF Then rscategories.MoveFirst
End Sub
```

4. Expand btnNext.
5. Double-click `onclick`. The btnNext_onclick procedure is added to the page.
6. Enter the following code for the btnNext_onclick procedure so that it matches this code:

```
Sub btnNext_onclick()
rscategories.MoveNext
If rscategories.EOF Then rscategories.MoveLast
End Sub
```

7. Set Data Script.htm as the startup form.
8. View the form in your browser. In a few moments your page displays, as shown in Figure 16.7.
9. Click on the Next button. The next record displays.
10. Click on the Next button again. The next record displays.
11. Click on the Previous button. The previous record displays.

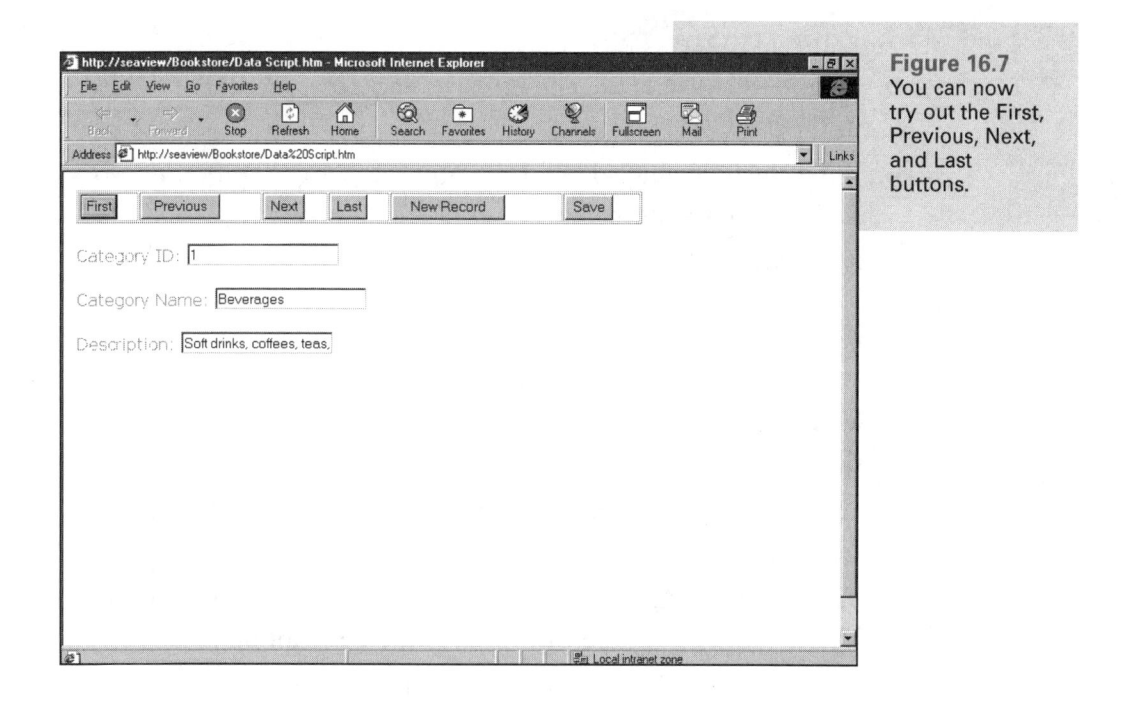

Figure 16.7
You can now try out the First, Previous, Next, and Last buttons.

12. Click on the First button. The first record displays.
13. Click on the Last button. The last record displays.
14. Close the browser window.

VBScript makes this kind of functionality easy to add to your application. All that is left to do is to add the script for the New Record and Save buttons. You are going to use two methods for the remainder of the script, `addRecord` and `updateRecord`. Complete the following steps:

1. Expand btnNewRecord.
2. Double-click `onclick`. The btnNewRecord_onclick procedure is added to the page.
3. Enter the following code for the btnNewRecord_onclick procedure so that it matches this code:

```
Sub btnNewRecord_onclick()
Rscategories.addRecord
End Sub
```

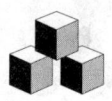

4. Expand btnSave.
5. Double-click `onclick`. The btnSave_onclick procedure is added to the page.
6. Enter the following code for the btnSave_onclick procedure so that it matches this code:

```
Sub btnSave_onclick()
rscategories.updateRecord
End Sub
```

7. Save Data Script.htm.
8. View the page in your browser. In a few moments, the page displays.
9. Click on the New Record button. The text is emptied from the text boxes.
10. Type **99** in the Category ID text box. Type **Test** for the Category Name and type **testing purposes** in the Description box.
11. Click on Save. The record is added to the record set.
12. Close the browser window.

That's all there is to it! You now know how to write your own record navigation routine and can add and save new records.

Summary

This chapter concentrated on giving you additional scripting skills. You now know how to display messages to your user. You also know how to use conditional logic so that you can test user input and perform appropriate actions based on that input. You also know how to use the move methods of the Recordset object and use `addRecord` and `updateRecords` to work with new records. The examples given in this chapter showed you the strength of VBScript and its ease-of-use when working with methods and properties.

The development of this application is almost finished. You're ready to test and debug the application.

Chapter 17

Testing the Corporate Web Site

Testing is the process of guessing everything your user can do to your application. During testing, you want to verify that, for example, when a user clicks on a certain button, the expected result occurs. You are looking for the unexpected, such as incorrect results from a calculation or an inappropriate response to an action—especially things that might result in the premature termination of the application.

There are several ways to minimize these types of mistakes in your application. The first way is to spend time, as you did in earlier chapters, carefully designing the application. Understanding the goals and features of the application gives you a clear picture of the events you need to support in the application, and how to respond to those events.

Consistent naming conventions for variables and objects will help you debug, support, and maintain your application. (For more information on naming conventions, see Appendix A, "Recommended Naming and Programming Conventions.") Another thing that helps you maintain your application is adequate commenting. Comments make your approach easier to understand, and they act as aids if you need to analyze your code. When deciding where to comment, assume that you will not be the one supporting the application in the future. Add the type of comments you would want to see in an application you were supporting but did not write. In other words, the Golden Rule applies.

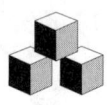

Debugging Scripts

In Chapter 12, you used several ways to debug script, including the following:

- You set a breakpoint to pause program execution and test the state of the application.
- You responded to a syntax or run-time error in a script.
- You stepped through code.
- You ran a page, by using the Debug menu or pressing F5, containing a script. This automatically started the debugger.

Note Microsoft recommends that you do not use Active Desktop mode of Internet Explorer when you are debugging.

You can use other tools to debug too. You can, for example, use message boxes as a debugging tool. You can, periodically in your script, use a message box to display the value of a variable. Just be sure to take the message boxes out of your script before you deploy your solution!

You will use the If statement you created in the previous chapter to experiment with debugging techniques. There isn't an error in it, but it will provide you with a way to get hands-on experience using these tools.

Using the Immediate Window

In Chapter 12, you were briefly introduced to the Immediate window. The Immediate window is automatically opened and displayed below the Code window when the application enters break mode. Tasks you can do with the Immediate window include these:

- Display variable and property values while an application is running.
- Change the value of a variable or property while an application is running.
- Type new statements and immediately execute them.
- Copy and paste existing code lines and immediately execute them.
- Call a procedure as you would in program code.
- View debugging output while an application is running.

Printing Values in the Immediate Window

When you're running an application, you can, as you saw earlier, learn the value of a variable by positioning your pointer above the variable name while in break mode. Another way to track the value of a variable (or a property) is by using the Immediate window. To print values to the Immediate window, you can:

- Use the Print method in the Immediate window.
- Use a question mark (?) in the Immediate window (this is shorthand for the Print method).

Using the Print Method in the Immediate Window

You can use the Print method (or the question mark) to test the values of variables and properties. To print the value of the Response variable in the Immediate window, use the following steps:

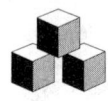

1. Place a breakpoint on the line that says:

   ```
   IF response = vbyes then
   ```

2. Press F5 to run the application. When the page displays, click on the Talk to Me button.
3. Click on Yes. You are taken to Visual InterDev in break mode.
4. In the Immediate window, type **?Reponse** and press Enter. The value 6, which is the value of the VB constant vbYes, displays (see Figure 17.1).

> **Tip**
> If you want to execute a statement that has been previously used in the Immediate window, move the insertion point to the end of that line and press Enter.

5. End the run of the script using the Debug menu.

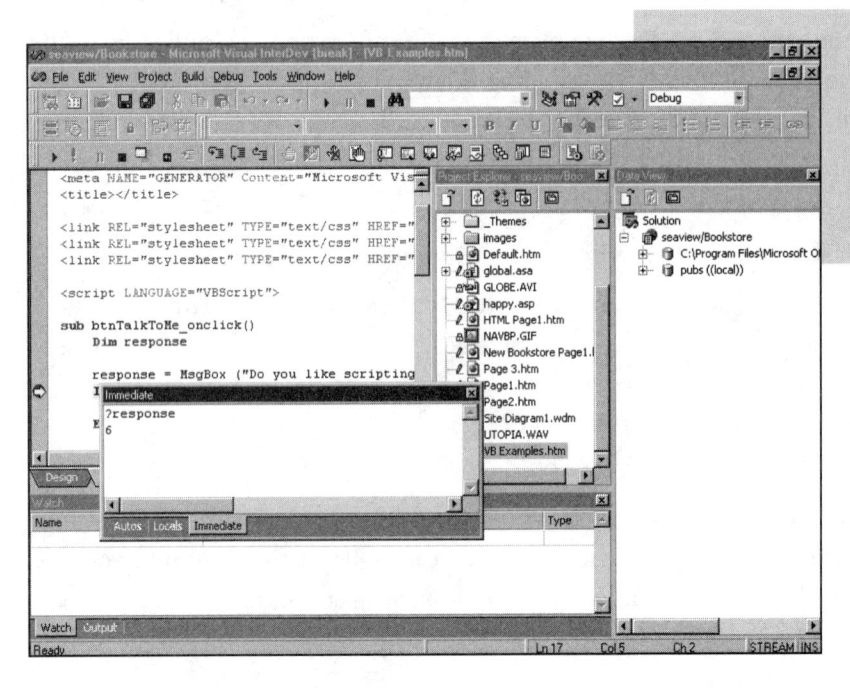

Figure 17.1
The Immediate window, as its name implies, allows you to immediately interact with your script.

This was just a quick little demo, but it gives you a good example of what you can do with the Immediate window.

Error Handling

Debugging is the process of dealing with all the problems you can predict and correct. But what about things you cannot control and cannot predict? Unless your application is very small, there's no way for you to predict every possible thing that can happen while your application runs. You definitely cannot control the user. To paraphrase a popular saying, users do the darnedest things!

To set an error trap, you need to use the `On Error` statement in each procedure that might encounter errors. The `On Error` statement tells Visual InterDev what to do in the case of an error. Only one error trap at a time can be enabled in a given procedure. The syntax for the `On Error` statement is as follows:

```
On Error Resume Next
```

If you don't use an `On Error Resume Next` statement, any run-time error that occurs is fatal. That is, an error message is displayed and execution stops. Needless to say, users hate this!

`On Error Resume Next` causes execution to continue with the statement immediately after the statement that caused the run-time error. By basically skipping the line that caused the error, execution is allowed to continue despite a run-time error.

The `Err` object contains information about run-time errors. You can use two of its properties to display information in an error message, `Number` and `Description`. Here are examples of some simple error handling statements:

```
On Error Resume Next
MsgBox ("Error: " & CStr(Err.Number) & " " & Err.Description)
Err.Clear
```

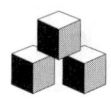

A Testing List

It's a good idea to create a testing list for yourself. To test your Web solution thoroughly, do the following things:

- Set the correct start page.
- Make sure all navigation bars are correct and all pages in the application are accessible.
- Proof all display text for typos.
- Verify that all graphics, video clips, audio clips, and so on display and/or work.
- Test all database connections and make sure the correct set of records displays.
- Click on all buttons to make sure you get the correct result.

You'll probably want to add additional items to this list, but it should give you a foundation to work with. You may also want to print each of the pages and put them into a binder as documentation. On each printed page, write information such as:

- File name
- Any linked file names
- Any data connections
- Which page(s) a user should be able to get to from this page

You may also want to include printed copies of all scripts in your binder. I know that documentation is the last thing (literally) that anyone wants to do, but on the day that you need it because of some kind of crisis or disaster, you'll be glad it's there!

Setting Up Security

In Chapter 14, I pointed out that the coolest thing about creating and deploying a solution on the World Wide Web is that millions of people have access to your information. Likewise, the scariest thing about creating and deploying a solution on the World Wide Web is that millions of people have access to your information. To control how those millions of people work with Web application files and gain access to the system that supports them requires security.

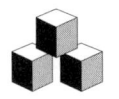

Security for Web applications is complex, to say the least. This is because it can be set at several levels in several different ways. The choices depend on the system and servers used and the needs of the Web application.

Security Locations

What makes security so complex is all the places that you can set security. For example, there's the security that your operating system provides, and then there's the security your network provides. And there's security provided through your Web server. And there's more! Here is a list of the locations you can set security:

- **Operating system.** This applies to Windows NT and other operating systems.
- **Folder.** Most operating systems offer folder security.
- **Web server.** As you've already seen, you can set up user accounts and server properties in the Microsoft Management Console.
- **Virtual root.** This is controlled via Microsoft Management Console.
- **Database.** If you are using SQL Server, the administrator has extensive control over user accessibility. Many other popular databases offer security structures as well.
- **Web application.** You can set Web application properties, which are stored in a session, through Visual InterDev.
- **Page.** This refers to server scripts written in Visual InterDev.
- **Source control.** Since you have user accounts and permissions specified in Visual SourceSafe Administrator, it is another point of security.

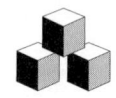

When planning which security options to use for your Web application and where you want to set those options, you need to consider the following four possible access scenarios:

- Allow any Web visitor to execute Active Server Pages (ASPs) and read HTML pages at run time.
- Force users to access as registered Web visitors at run time.
- Restrict Web administration to certain authorized users.
- Let Web developers and authors write to your files at design time.

Operating System-Level Security

What kind of security does your operating system provide? That depends on what operating system you are using. Windows NT has significantly more system-level security than Windows 95 or 98. As a matter of fact, when someone asks me what the difference is between Windows 95/98 and Windows NT, I always start my answer with security. Since Windows NT provides you with the guest user account, you don't have to worry about authenticating individual users. You do have the option of setting up individual user accounts if you need to track who is coming and going from your site.

Another thing to consider at the operating system level is your file system. Windows 95/98 uses a form of file allocation table (FAT). FAT is as old as DOS itself. Doesn't sound very secure, does it? By contrast, Windows NT gives you the option of using the NT File System (NTFS). This file system allows you to control access to each individual file and folder on your system.

Web Server-Level Security

Once you've dealt with security issues at the operating system level, address the Web server's security (these issues are also hidden from the user). The Web server can authenticate the user's identity and control access at run time. The anonymous user set up by Internet Information Server is similar to an Internet guest account defined in Windows NT

User Manager. If you have set the anonymous account access to the requested file, Internet Information Server allows access to the file and honors the request. Otherwise, the request is rejected, an error is returned, and a message is displayed to the user that the request has been denied. You've probably encountered this scenario yourself on your Internet travels.

Database-Level Security

In the last project, you added data access to your project. How does that affect the security of your Web solution? For file-based database systems such as Microsoft Access, you can control security through the sharing permissions available on the folders and files for the operating system. SQL Server, on the other hand, has its own security system, which is administered by the database administrator. Even though SQL Server provides you with different kinds of security, the one that is recommended is standard security. Standard security requires a login ID and a password to access the server. Since this information is part of your data connection information, your users don't need to provide any additional identification.

Using Source Control Security

In the last chapter, you set up source control for your application. Part of that process was creating users. Since Visual SourceSafe controls can check out and modify files in the Web application, it can be considered another point of security.

Web Application-Level Security

Another way to add security to your application is by using the security features provided through FrontPage server extensions and through the Global.asa file processing available with Active Server Pages. If your operating system is Windows NT with the NTFS file system, the FrontPage Server Extensions manage access for administrators and authors using file ACLs (Access Control Lists) for the DLLs in Table 17.1.

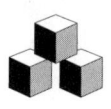

Table 17.1	DLLs Used by the FrontPage Extensions
DLL	Function
Admin.dll	Administrative (e.g., setting Web permissions)
Author.dll	Authoring (e.g., opening a file)
Dvwssr.dll	Browsing (e.g., viewing links)

FrontPage Server Extensions can only control access when a hacker attempts to use the extensions to fetch and post files. If the Web files themselves are not secure, FrontPage Server Extensions will not prevent someone from altering the pages through conventional means.

Using Global.asa File Processing for Security

Up to now, you have worked with .HTM files. A good time to get introduced to .asp (Active Server Pages) files is in conjunction with security. Since the Global.asa file is automatically processed at the start of a new session and is never seen by your user, you can use it to control access to your Web application.

Adding Security Pages

Using .asp files as part of your security is actually just a part of the puzzle. You'll need a combination of an HTML form, a database table, and scripts. I won't go into detail on every step that you need to accomplish this, but I will cover the basic steps. You may want to refer to online help for detailed information on this topic. The detailed information could take a chapter all by itself! Here is a typical way to implement security by using security pages:

1. In a database, add a table that stores the user identification and password information.
2. Add an HTML form to your site's home page that requests user identification and password information.

3. In the site's home page, add a script to verify that the values were entered in the form. This is often referred to as *validation*.
4. In the project, add a connection to the database and table that you created in step 1.
5. Create an ASP page that retrieves a record based on the user input and compares the input with the values in the database.
6. Add a server script that deals with failed logins and successful logins that link to the site. Display the appropriate messages.

You already know how to do some of these steps, such as step 5, making the data connection. You'll learn how to carry out other steps as you progress through this chapter.

Setting a Web Application's Permissions

Typically, a Web project inherits its permissions from its root Web application. You can override this and then set user and group permissions. Unique permissions must be set for a Web application before you can modify its users and groups. Complete these steps:

1. Select the project you want to set permissions for in the Project Explorer.
2. Select Projects, Web Project, Web Permissions. The Web Permissions dialog box displays.

> **Note** Web Permissions are only available on Windows NT systems using the NTFS file system.

3. Select the Settings tab.
4. Select Use Unique Permissions for This Web Application.
5. Click on Apply and OK.

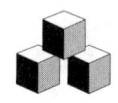

After you have set your project to use unique permissions, you can add individual users and control their permissions.

1. Select the project you want to set permissions for in the Project Explorer.
2. Select Projects, Web Project, Web Permissions. The Web Permissions dialog box displays.
3. Select the Users tab.
4. Click on Add.
5. Select a domain from the Obtain List From box.
6. Select users from the Names box.
7. In the New Users Can box, select the permission you wish the user to have.
8. Click on Apply and OK.

Summary

In this chapter, you covered some additional debugging techniques. You were also introduced to error handling. And you wrapped up this chapter by covering security.

In this project, you tackled such advanced topics as security and VBScript. You've gone from creating very simple pages with just text to adding automation, graphics, and multimedia to your pages.

Project 3 Summary

This project exposed you to the features of Visual Inter-Dev that are geared at the multideveloper environment. You set up Visual SourceSafe for use with your Visual InterDev projects and used it to manage files.

You gained additional scripting skills in this project. You know how to display messages to your user. You also know how to use conditional logic so that you can test user input and perform appropriate actions based on that input. You also know how to use the move methods of the Recordset object and use the addRecord and updateRecords methods to work with new records. You also covered additional debugging techniques, as well as error handling.

CHAPTER 18

Creating Your Own Visual InterDev Templates and Themes

When you first create a project, one of the very first things that you do is select a theme. What if you don't want to use one of the built-in themes? No problem, create your own! This chapter will cover the steps required to create a theme.

When you create a Web solution, you add a lot of HTML and ASP pages to your project. You can also create your own template for these types of pages.

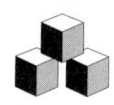

Creating Themes

Themes provide the visual appeal of a Web solution. Some of the visual settings provided by themes are:

- Background images
- Bullet styles
- Fonts
- Font sizes
- Font colors
- Graphics
- Paragraph formats

The elements of a theme should work together to present a professional, visually appealing look. The goal of a theme is not only to make your Web solution visually appealing, but also to make it visually consistent. Each page in your solution will have a similar look and feel because of its theme.

There are several reasons why you might want to create your own theme. The first and most basic is because you have your own creative vision. You know how you want your site to look. Another reason is to promote corporate identity. If your company is known for a certain color or graphic or font, you'll want to create a theme that reflects this. Creating a custom theme is basically just the process of providing files in the right places. To create a custom theme, use the following steps:

1. Create a directory named after your theme in the ...\VinterDev98\Themes directory. You'll notice other directories in that folder, including Arcs, Arty, Blitz, and Travel. The name of the directory becomes the name of the theme.

    Later, when you are applying the theme to a project, Visual InterDev will look in the Themes directory and include your custom theme as a selection. As an added bonus, you'll be able to preview your theme just like other themes.

2. Apply a theme to your project.
3. Make any changes you need to the Cascading Style Sheet in the CSS Editor. Define the font, name, size, and other attributes of tags as well as specifying image files to use with bulleted lists and horizontal rules. For example, if you are designing a Web site for an airline, you may want little planes for the bullets, and for a college, perhaps its mascot.
4. Save the style sheet.
5. Copy or move it to your theme's directory.
6. Add your images to the theme directory. By default, Visual InterDev references images in the Themes directory. Copy all images that you want to include in your theme into your custom theme directory.

Microsoft predicts that there will be a market for third-party themes. You'll be able to purchase these professionally designed themes and add them to your system, giving you even greater flexibility.

Designing Templates

If you've used products like Microsoft PowerPoint or even Microsoft Word, you are already familiar with the concept of templates. Templates act as a model for new pages. The most obvious benefit of using templates is to save time. They also give your Web site a consistent look and feel. You can create a page that contains the graphics such as logos and copyright information you want for your site and then create the other pages in your application using that page as a template.

Any existing HTML or ASP page can be saved as a template for creating new identical pages. When an HTML or ASP page is used to create a new page, it is called a template.

Files need to be stored in the \Program Files\Microsoft Visual Studio\VintDev98\Templates directory to be considered templates by Visual InterDev. To create a template, follow these steps:

1. Select the page you want to use as a template.
2. Select File, Save As.
3. Select

   ```
   \Program Files\Microsoft Visual Studio\VintDev98\Templates\Web Project Items
   ```

   as the directory and save the file.

Now that you've created the template, you can use it. But there is a catch. You'll need to exit from Visual InterDev and restart it to see the new template. To use the custom template to create a new page, follow these steps:

1. Exit from Visual InterDev, saving your work.
2. Start Visual InterDev.
3. Open the project where you want to use the template.
4. Select Project, Add Item. The Add Item dialog box displays, complete with an option for the new template (see Figure 18.1).

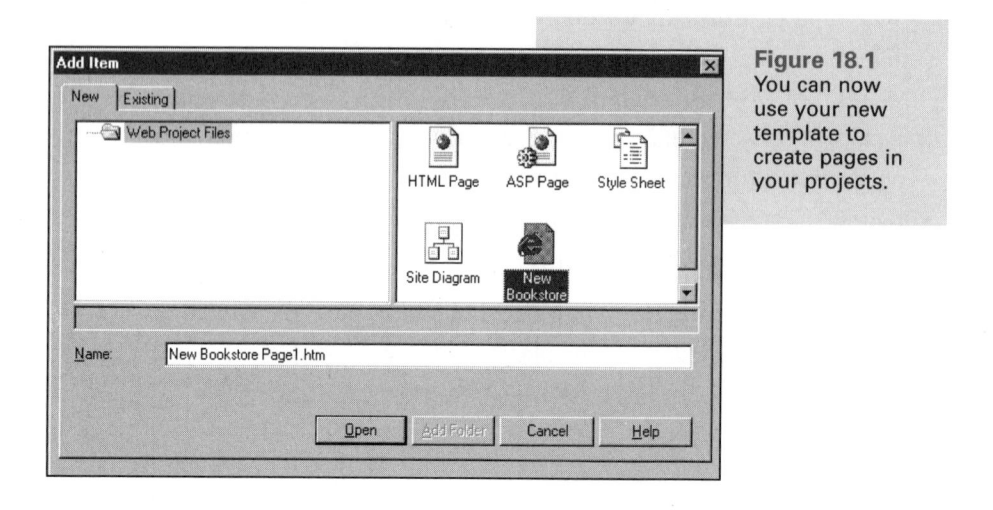

Figure 18.1
You can now use your new template to create pages in your projects.

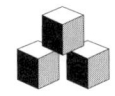

5. Enter the name of the new file and click on Open. The new page displays.

Something that you may want to do to further customize your template is add prompts for the user to answer when creating a new file. To do this, use the delimiters (<%# and #%>) in the template to create a parameter. The parameters that you are creating can be up to 100 characters long and are case-insensitive. The Template Wizard recognizes the parameter and prompts the user for the desired information.

For example, to prompt users to enter the name of their company, you would add this prompt:

```
<%#Company Name: #%>
```

If the user types "Acme Co." then the new file would contain this line:

```
Acme Co.
```

Visual InterDev has reserved some parameters for itself. Here is a list of those parameters:

- `<%#DataConnection#%>`

    When Visual InterDev sees this parameter, it prompts the user to select one of the existing project data connections.

- `<%#FilenameWithExtension#%>`

    This is a great parameter. This parameter automatically inserts the template's file name and extension into the new .htm or .asp page.

- `<%#FilenameWithoutExtension#%>`

    This is basically the same as the previous parameter but without the file's extension.

- `<%#ThemeName#%>`

    This prompts for one of the available themes.

For more information on creating templates, see the "Creating Custom Templates" topic in online help.

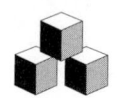

Summary

Themes control the look and feel of a Web solution. Because of their high visibility, you'll want to experiment with creating your own. In this way, your Web solutions can have the maximum impact. And as you know, it doesn't matter how great the text and other data is on your page if no one comes to read it.

Templates allow you to customize page creation. You can customize graphics, text, and script and save them to a reusable template.

CHAPTER 19

Working with Cascading Style Sheets

As you create projects, you rely on themes to control the look and feel of your application. That's good if you like everything about the theme you are using. But what if you want to use a different font or color of text for your headings? You can go through and individually change the font settings for each heading of each page in your application. This isn't too bad of a job if you have only a few pages in your application. On the other hand, if you have several pages, this can be quite a large task. So you go through and change all the headings to Arial, bold, italic, and blue. Then you show it to someone who makes a comment that green would have been nice or who doesn't like the look of italic. So you get to change everything again. As you can imagine, this gets old quickly! Instead of manually changing each occurrence of the heading, you can change the style for the text. This is done through *cascading style sheets (CSS)*.

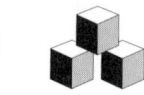

What Are Cascading Style Sheets?

Cascading style sheets (CSS) give you the ability to create and use a set of styles that override a browser's standard method for rendering HTML. Each of Visual InterDev's approximately 60 themes contains one or more style sheets. Style sheets allow you to define attributes such as font, border, and justification properties. These settings are saved to a name such as Heading 1 and are applied as a paragraph format. When you select a paragraph format for your text, an HTML tag is added to your page's source code. To get some hands-on experience working with styles, complete these steps:

> **Caution**
>
> Not all browsers support the use of cascading style sheets. At the time of this book's printing, Microsoft Internet Explorer 4.0 and Netscape Navigator 4.0 support CSS 1 (the version of cascading style sheets implemented by Visual InterDev 6). Internet Explorer 3.0 supports a subset of CSS 1.
>
> Typically, browsers that don't support cascading style sheets ignore them. This means that pages that use cascading styles are still readable by these browsers.

1. Start a new project. Name the project CSS1. Select Bottom 1 for the layout and Construction Zone for the theme.
2. Add a new HTML page to your project and view it in Design view.
3. At the top of the page, above the Add Your Content Above bar, type **This is a title**.
4. Click on the selection button from the Paragraph Format box found on the HTML toolbar.
5. Select Heading 2. The style is applied to the text, as shown in Figure 19.1. You'll notice that the text is larger and has a different color now that the style has been applied.

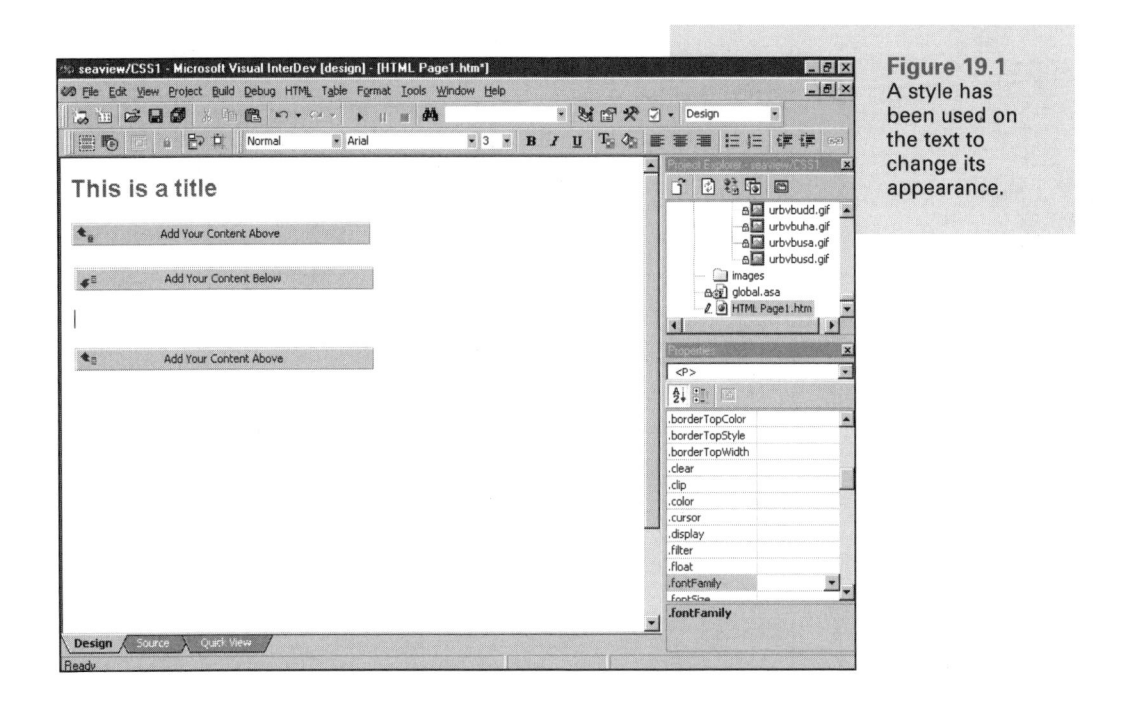

Figure 19.1
A style has been used on the text to change its appearance.

6. Using the Paragraph Format box found on the HTML toolbar, select Heading 1 for the style of the paragraph. The text is now even larger.

That was your quick introduction to using styles. From this point forward, you will work with modifying styles.

Using the CSS Editor

Visual InterDev includes a CSS editor. This editor allows you to modify style properties. Style sheet information is saved in a .css file.

The CSS Editor window, shown in Figure 19.2, is broken into two main sections: the Selector tree and the property options. You'll use the Selector tree to choose the HTML tag, class, or unique ID to modify. You can also add new HTML tags, classes, or unique IDs. Then you modify the settings for the selected HTML tag, class, or unique ID using the property options pane.

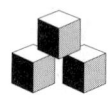

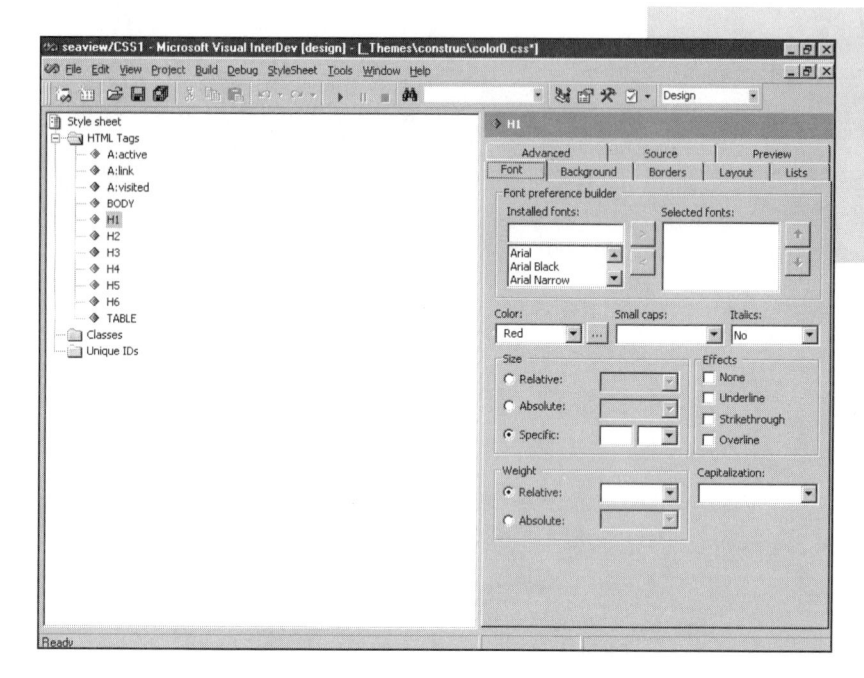

Figure 19.2
The CSS Editor provides a graphical interface that is used to work with cascading style sheets.

A *class* contains certain properties that you apply to a specific tag or make available to all tags.

Unique IDs are used like classes except that they can be used only once per page.

Editing a Cascading Style Sheet

To edit a style sheet, you need to open it. When opened, it is displayed in the CSS Editor. To open a cascading style sheet, follow these steps:

1. Expand the Themes folder in the Project Explorer window.
2. Expand the Construc folder.
3. Right-click on color0.css file and select Open. If prompted, choose Get Working Copy. Color0.css is opened, and the CSS Editor displays, as shown in Figure 19.3.

CHAPTER 19 • WORKING WITH CASCADING STYLE SHEETS

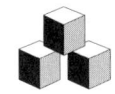

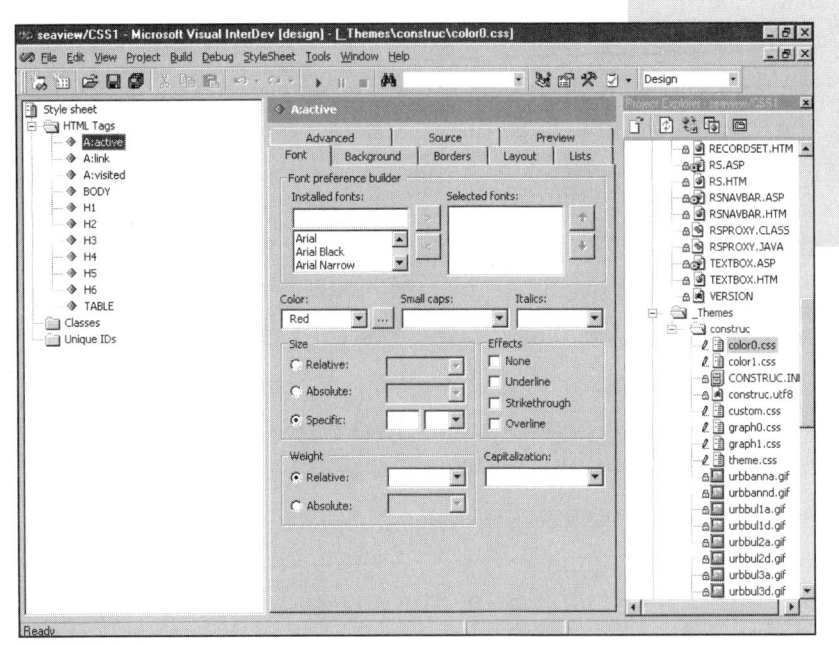

Figure 19.3
The settings found in the color0.css file are graphically represented in the CSS Editor window.

> **Tip**
>
> You may wonder how I knew to select the color0 cascading style sheet. I couldn't find any documentation on the roles of the different style sheets, so I used the old-fashioned method of setting different properties in each style sheet until I got the results I was looking for!

The Font Tab

The tab that displays as a default when you open a style sheet in the CSS Editor is the Font tab. This tab is used to set a specific font or generic font family for the style. It is also used to set the color, size, and style of text. To modify the settings of the Font tab, follow these steps:

1. Select H1 from the Selector tree.
2. Select a font from the Installed Fonts list box. Installed fonts are the text fonts currently installed on your machine.

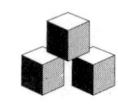

3. Click on the right arrow button to place the font in the Selected Fonts list box. You may want to add several fonts to this list box. The order in which fonts are listed here determines the order of the fonts to be tried when displaying the page. For example, if you have Arial, Times New Roman, and Modern as your selected fonts, the .css file will first try to use Arial as the display font and then Times New Roman and then Modern. You can use the Up and Down arrows to order the font names by preference.

4. Select Red from the Color drop-down list box.

   Leave the Small Caps drop-down list box blank. This means the style will inherit this setting from the parent element. If you do not want to inherit this setting, set this to Yes or No.

5. Set the Italics drop-down list box to Yes so that the text will appear in italics.

6. Select File, Save _Themes/construc/color0.css to save the changes you have made.

7. Use the Window menu to go to your HTML page.

8. The changes you made aren't displayed on the page. To correct this, select View, Refresh. The changes you made to the style are reflected in the view of the page, as shown in Figure 19.4.

You can see the immediate impact of using and modifying styles. The changes you made affect all text that uses the Heading 1 style on all pages in your project. Using the Window menu, return to the color0 style sheet.

Using the Font tab, you can also control the size of the text. The size can be set one of three ways: relative, absolute, or specific. By selecting the Relative option button, you can set the font size smaller or larger in relation to the font size of the parent element. By selecting the Absolute option button, you can set the font size to scale according to the browser font setting preferences. When using Absolute sizing, you can choose from xx-small, x-small, small, smaller, medium, large, x-large, and xx-large. The last option available is Specific. Use Specific when you want to set a particular font size and unit. For example, use this option if you want to set a particular point size for your text.

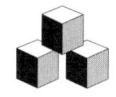

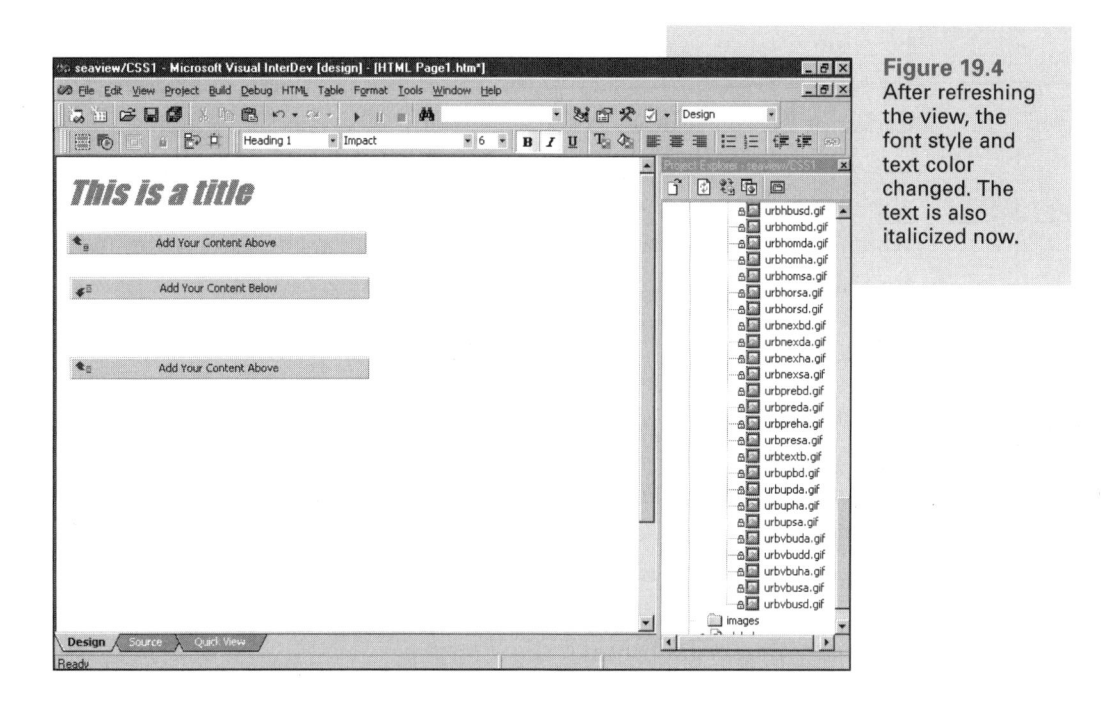

CHAPTER 19 • WORKING WITH CASCADING STYLE SHEETS

Figure 19.4
After refreshing the view, the font style and text color changed. The text is also italicized now.

Next to the Size group box is the Effects group box. Several check boxes are located in the Effects group box:

- **None**
  Select this to specify that any text effects inherited from the parent element or any text effects associated with a normal HTML tag are removed.

- **Underline**
  Select this check box when you want to place a line beneath the text.

- **Strikethrough**
  Use this effect to place a line through the center of text.

- **Overline**
  Specify whether to place a line above the text.

Located below the Size group box is the Weight group box. The options in this group box allow you to control the degree of lightness or darkness of the text. This is described as "weight of text," although you may be more used to speaking of "boldness of text." You have two options for setting weight. The first option is Relative. This lets you set the text darker or lighter, relative to the weight of the parent element. The other option is Absolute. This allows you to set the degree of boldness to be applied to the font text. The setting for this option ranges from 100, which gives you a very light font, to 700, which produces a very bold font. The normal font weight is 400.

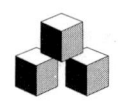

> **Note:** The weight of a font is also controlled by the font itself. For example, Arial Black is heavier than just plain Arial.

Last but not least is Capitalization. Using this drop-down list box, you can specify whether text is all uppercase, text is all lowercase, or only the first letter of the first word is capitalized. As you can see, you can control many properties through the Font tab.

The Background Tab

The Background tab is used to set a background color or a background image for an element. It is also used to specify the position and display of background images. To get an idea of how to use the settings on the Background tab, follow these steps:

1. Display color0 using the Window menu. If it isn't already selected, select H1 from the Selector tree.
2. Select the Background tab. The Background settings display (see Figure 19.5).
3. Select Black for the Background color.
4. Select File, Save _Themes/construc/color0.css to save the changes you have made.
5. Use the Window menu to go to your HTML page.
6. Select View, Refresh. The changes you've made to the style are reflected in the view of the page, as shown in Figure 19.6.
7. Return to the color0 style sheet using the Window menu.

Chapter 19 • Working with Cascading Style Sheets

Figure 19.5
The Background tab allows you to modify the settings for background color and background image.

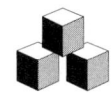

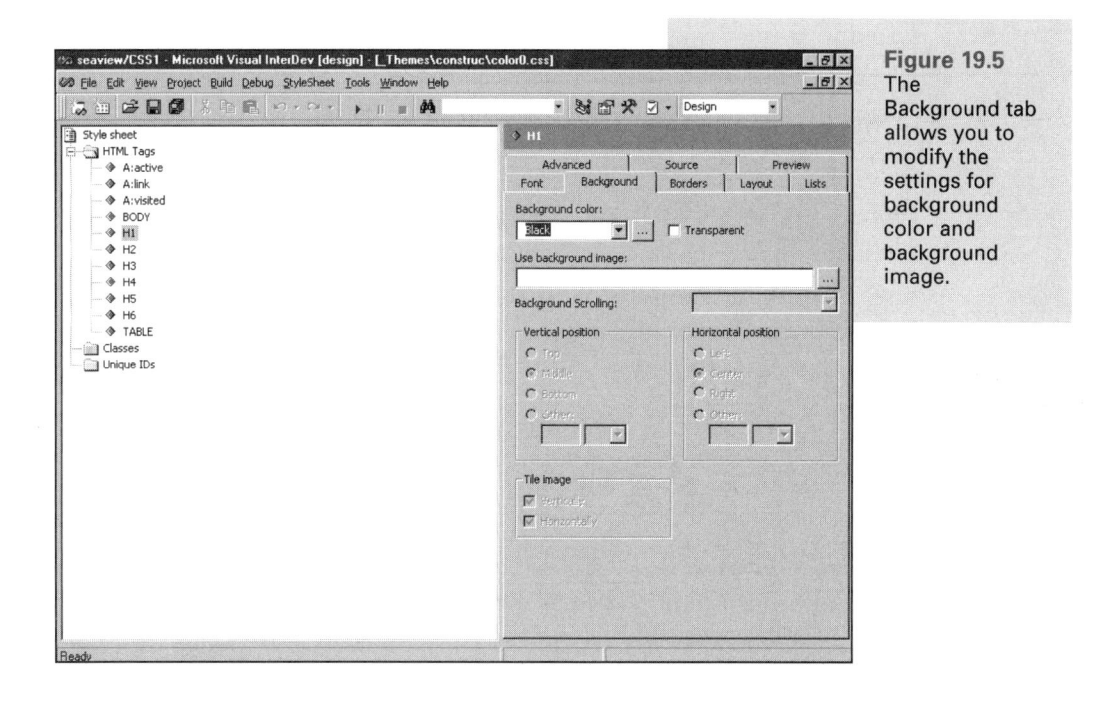

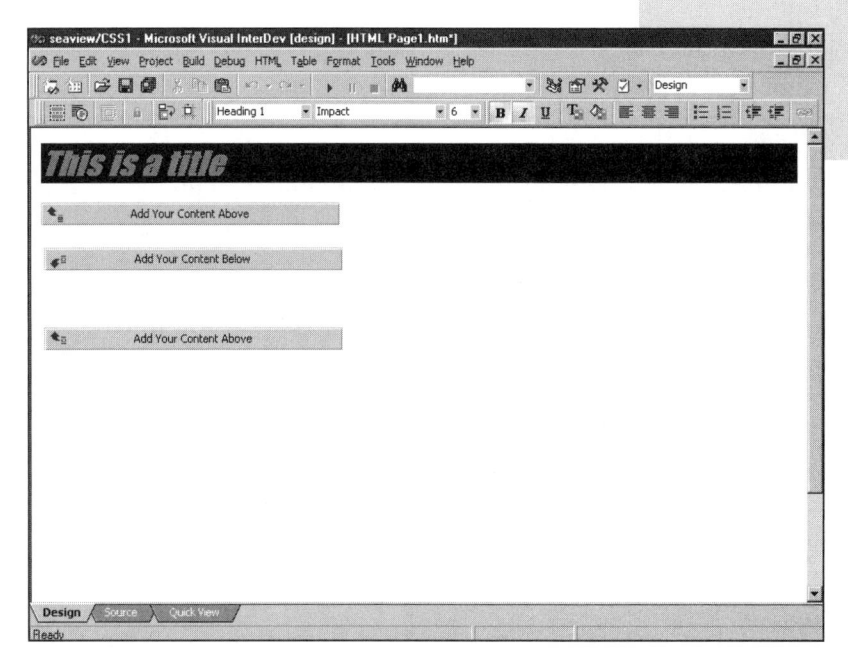

Figure 19.6
This style now applies a black background.

Looking at the Background page, you'll notice that there is a check box labeled Transparent. If you place a check in this check box, the background of the element will appear transparent.

Below the Background color drop-down list box is the Use Background Image drop-down list box. This option allows you to enter a path and file name for a graphic file that is to be used to overlay behind the element. If you don't want to type the path and file name, you can use the Browse button to locate the file.

The next option is Background scrolling. You must have a background image selected to make this option available to set. If you do not want the image to scroll with the page content, select Fixed. If you want the image to scroll with the page content, select Scroll.

The check boxes in the Vertical Position group box allow you to set the initial top-to-bottom position of the background image. You have to have a background image selected to make these options available for you to set. The Vertical Position group box contains these option buttons:

- **Top**
  Positions the background image in the top section of the element.

- **Middle**
  Positions the background image in the middle or center section of the element.

- **Bottom**
  Positions the background image in the bottom section of the element.

- **Other**
  Allows you to set a percentage value or other unit value for the vertical position of the background image. Negative values can be used.

After setting the vertical position, set the horizontal position using one of the option buttons found in the Horizontal Position group box. You have to have a background image selected to make these options available. The Horizontal Position group box contains these option buttons:

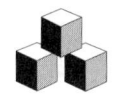

- **Left**

  Positions the background image in the left section of the element.

- **Center**

  Positions the background image in the center of the element.

- **Right**

  Positions the background image in the right section of the element.

- **Other**

  Allows you to set a percentage value or other unit value for the horizontal position of the background image. Negative values can be used.

The last group box on the Background page is the Tile Image group box. You have to have a background image selected to have these options available for you to set. There are two check boxes in this group box, Vertically and Horizontally. If both Vertically and Horizontally are selected, the background image tiles across the entire page. If just Vertically is selected, the background image repeats from top to bottom on the page. If just Horizontally is selected, the background image repeats from left to right on the page. If neither Vertically nor Horizontally is selected, the background image will not repeat on the page.

The Borders Tab

The Borders tab is used to select the size, style, and color of a border. It is also used to set the margin size and padding for an element. Follow these steps to set some of the properties on the Borders tab:

1. Select the Borders tab. The Borders page displays (see Figure 19.7).
2. Click on the Border All Around button located at the bottom-right corner of the Borders page. This button looks like a black square.

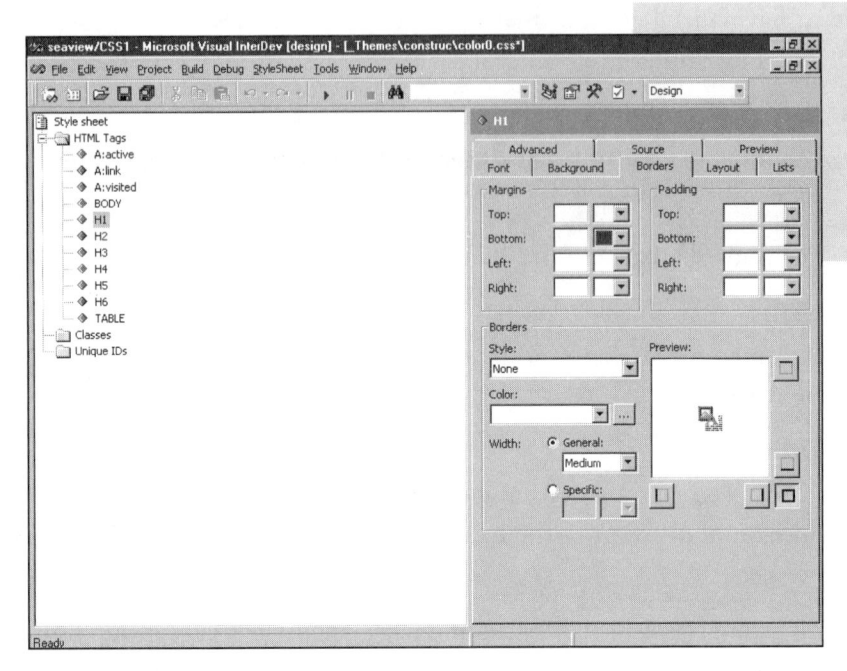

Figure 19.7 Adding a border to an element through the Borders tab can really make it stand out.

3. For Style, select Double.
4. For Color, select Red. Notice that the Preview box changes to reflect the settings.
5. Select File, Save _Themes/construc/color0.css to save the changes you have made.
6. Use the Window menu to go to your HTML page.
7. Select View, Refresh. The changes you made to the style are reflected in the view of the page as shown in Figure 19.8.
8. Return to the color0 style sheet using the Window menu.

By using the settings available through the Borders page, you quickly added a border to your element. You could have also added values for the margins of the element using the Borders page. You can set margins for the top, bottom, left, and right of the element. Margin settings allow negative values.

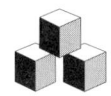

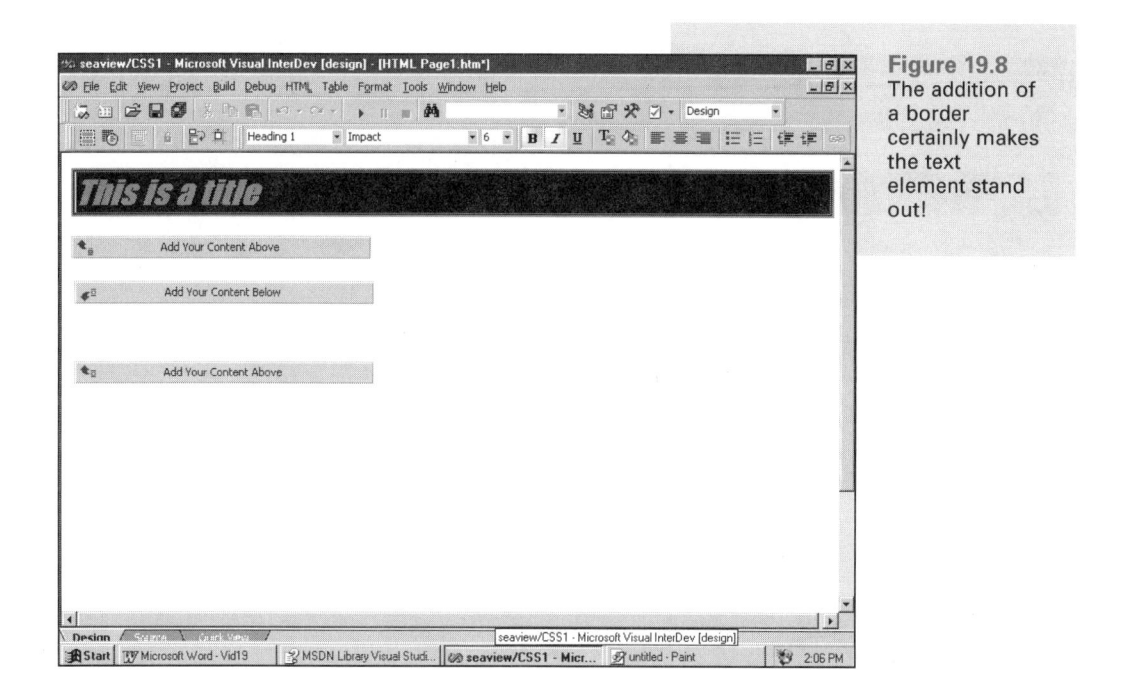

CHAPTER 19 • WORKING WITH CASCADING STYLE SHEETS   319

Figure 19.8
The addition of a border certainly makes the text element stand out!

Another thing that you can set is padding. *Padding* is the amount of space between the border and the content of the element. Padding settings do not allow negative values. You can set padding for the top, bottom, left, and right of an element.

The CSS Editor allows you to control the width of the border. You can elect to choose a thin, medium, or thick border. You also have the option of specifying a particular border size and unit. Width values cannot be negative.

You are not required to have a border on all sides of your element. You may, for example, just want a border on the bottom of the element. To add a border to only the bottom of the element, follow these steps:

1. Select None for the Style.
2. Click on the Bottom Border button.
3. Select Double for the Style.

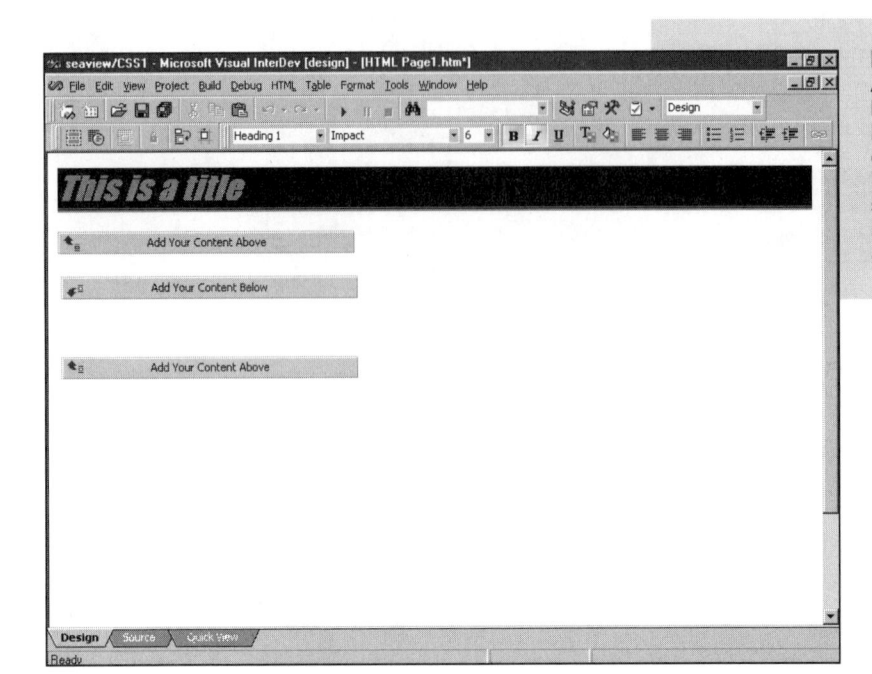

Figure 19.9
Adding a border at the bottom of an element imparts a more subtle look than having one on all sides.

4. Select File, Save _Themes/construc/color0.css to save the changes you have made.
5. Use the Window menu to go to your HTML page.
6. Select View, Refresh. The changes you made to the style are reflected in the view of the page, as shown in Figure 19.9.
7. Return to the color0 style sheet using the Window menu.

The Layout Tab

The Layout tab allows you to control some of the more subtle visual settings of your elements. This tab lets you size, align, indent, and set spacing for your elements. To experiment with these settings, follow these steps:

1. Select the Layout tab. The Layout page displays (see Figure 19.10).

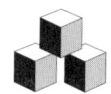

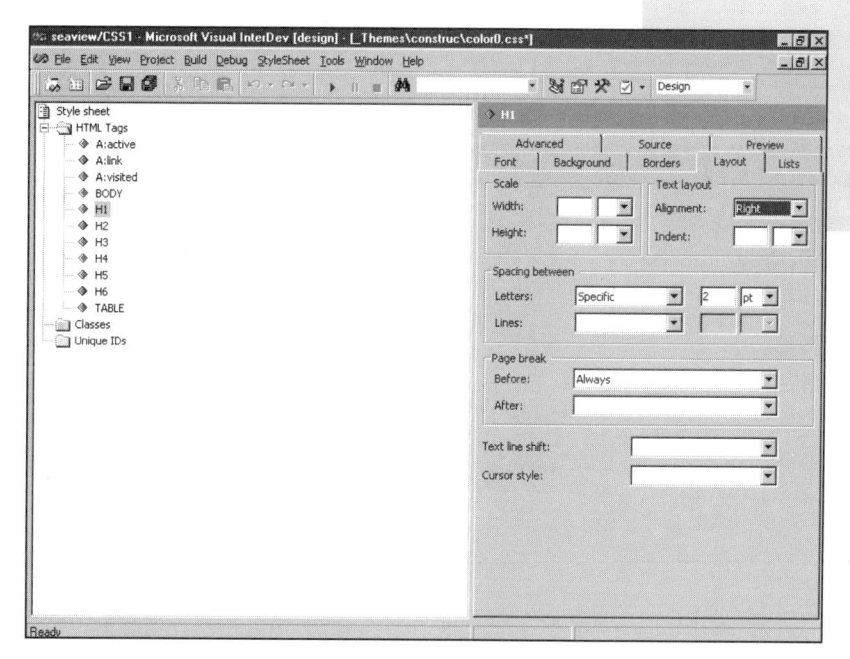

CHAPTER 19 • WORKING WITH CASCADING STYLE SHEETS

Figure 19.10
The Layout tab is used to control the positioning of objects and their spacing.

2. Select Right for the Alignment.
3. For Letters, select Specific from the drop-down list box. In the box to the right of the drop-down list box, enter 2. Select pt from the last drop-down list box on the row. This sets additional spacing between text letters.
4. Select Always for the Before page break.
5. Select File, Save _Themes/construc/color0.css to save the changes you have made.
6. Use the Window menu to go to your HTML page.
7. Select View, Refresh. The changes you made to the style are reflected in the view of the page, as shown in Figure 19.11.
8. Return to the color0 style sheet using the Window menu.

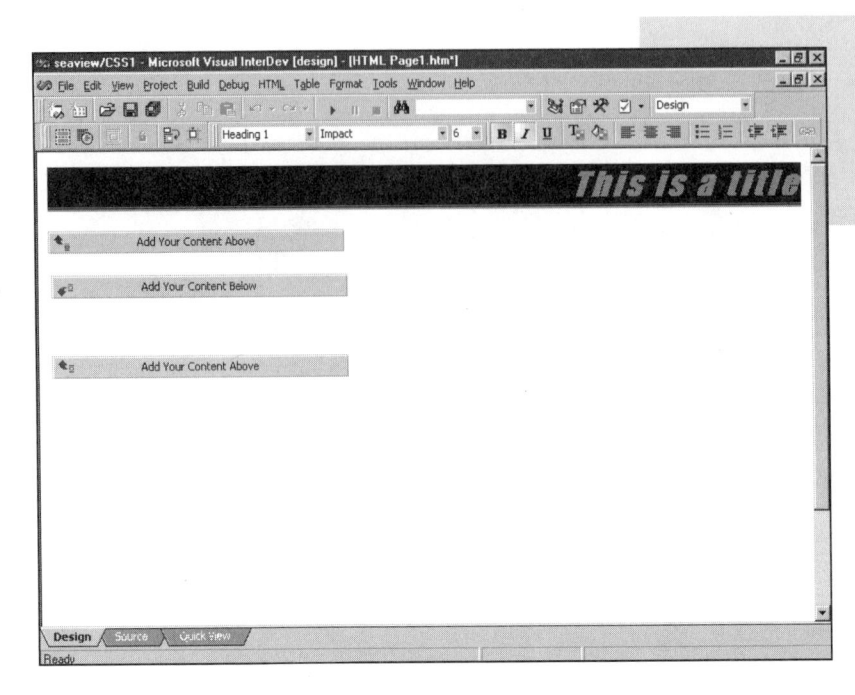

Figure 19.11 The Heading 1 style is right-aligned and has more spacing between letters.

Other options that you can set using the Layout page include scale. An element's width and/or height can be scaled to fit the specified width or height.

In the previous steps, you set the Alignment to Right. You could have also chosen Left, Center, or Justified. The Indent option allows you to set the indent that appears before the first formatted line in a paragraph. Indent accepts negative values.

Toward the bottom of the page, you'll find the Text Line Shift drop-down list box. This is used to set the vertical position of text elements. Your two options are Subscript and Superscript.

The final option on this page is Cursor Style. This allows you to set the type of cursor that displays for the mouse pointer. I recommended that you select Auto. Auto displays the correct cursor type based on the current context. This should ensure that users see the cursor that they expect to see.

CHAPTER 19 • WORKING WITH CASCADING STYLE SHEETS   323

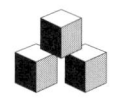

The Preview Tab

An easy way to view your changes is to use the Preview tab. This tab lets you see the effects of the CSS settings on a sample page. Follow these steps to demonstrate the use of the Preview tab:

1. Select the Preview tab. The Preview page displays (see Figure 19.12).
2. Scroll down until you find <H1> Heading 1. This shows you how the Heading 1 style currently looks.
3. Select the Layout tab. The Layout page displays.
4. Set the Spacing between Letters to 12 pts.
5. Select the Preview tab. You can see that the spacing is much larger between letters now.

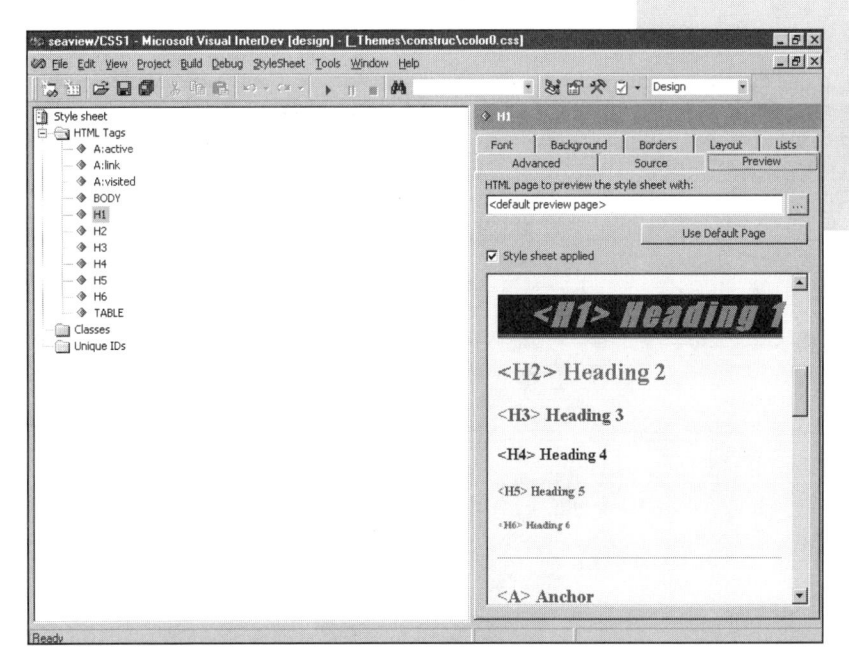

Figure 19.12
The Preview tab allows you to quickly view the impact of your setting changes.

The Lists Tab

To access the Lists options (see Figure 19.13), select the Lists tab, which is used select the placement and type of bullet used in lists. The first group box on this page has three option buttons to control how a list item is displayed:

- **Inherited**

    If you wish the list items to inherit the list item marker from the parent element, select this option.

- **Unbulleted List**

    Displays list items without bullets.

- **Bulleted List**

    Displays list items with bullets. Select the bullet type in the Standard bullets drop-down list or choose an image by selecting the Use Image option.

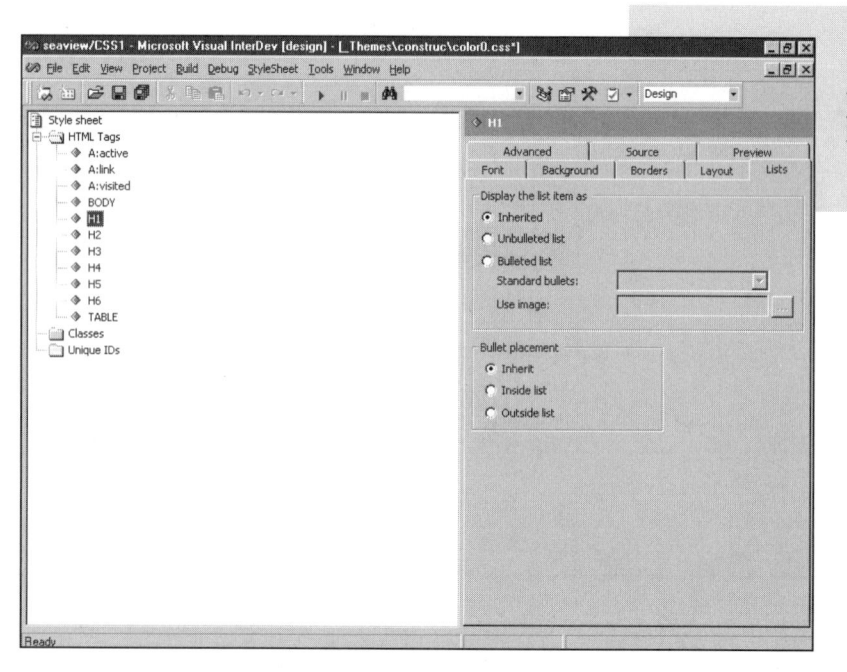

Figure 19.13 Use the Lists tab to change the properties for bulleted and numbered lists.

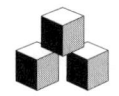

There are several standard bullets to select from. These bullets types are listed here:

- Disc
- Circle
- Square
- Decimal (1 2 3 4)
- Lower-roman (i ii iii iv)
- Upper-roman (I II III IV)
- Lower-alpha (a b c d)
- Upper-alpha (A B C D)

Once you've selected your bullet style, you can select the bullet placement. You can select one of the following options when working with bullet placement:

- **Inherit**
  Positions the bullet using the bullet position of the parent element.

- **Inside List**
  Indents the bullet position. If the text following the bullet goes beyond the length of the line, the text wraps under the bullet.

- **Outside List**
  Positions the bullet flush with the margin. If the text following the bullet is beyond the length of the line, the text wraps under the text above it.

The Advanced Tab

Use the Advanced tab to position elements on the page. To view these settings, select the Advanced tab (see Figure 19.14).

The first group box, Positioning, lets you enter specific coordinates for elements. Normally elements are positioned according to the order they

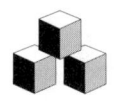

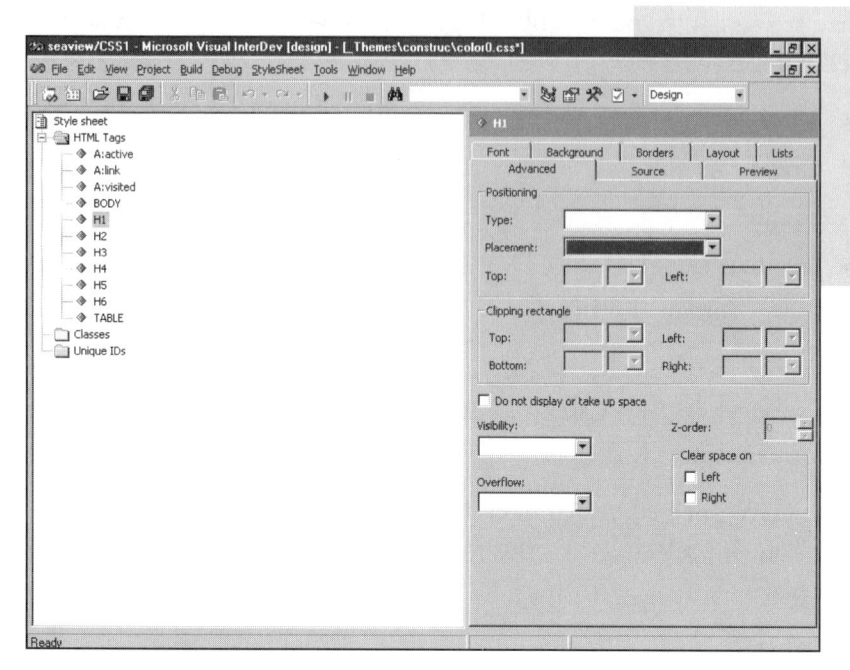

Figure 19.14 The Advanced tab allows you to set a variety of position settings such as the stacking order (z-order) of objects.

appear in the HTML source. The Advanced tab gives you more control over element positioning. By selecting a Type, you set the position of the element on the page. There are three options for the Type setting:

- **Static**

    This is the default setting. This means that there are no special positioning instructions. The layout rules of HTML are obeyed.

- **Absolute**

    Positions an element regardless of the layout of the surrounding elements.

- **Relative**

    Positions an element with respect to the preceding content on the page.

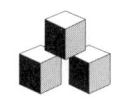

The next drop-down list box, Placement, allows you to specify whether text flows around the object. Select from Do Not Float, Float on Left, or Float on Right.

The Top and Left fields allow you to specify the position of the element relative to the top or left of the document. Top and Left accept negative values.

Using the settings associated with the Clipping Rectangle group box, you can specify the visible portions of positioned elements. The portion of the element outside of the clipped area is transparent. You have to select Absolute in the Type option to use this option. If you have selected Absolute, you can control what parts of the element are visible using these fields:

- **Top**

    Specifies the top portion of the element visible on the page.

- **Bottom**

    Specifies the bottom portion of the element visible on the page.

- **Left**

    Specifies the left portion of the element visible on the page.

- **Right**

    Specifies the right portion of the element visible on the page.

The next setting on this page is the Do Not Display or Take Up Space check box. Place a check in this box if you do not want the element to be visible and do not want space reserved for the element on the screen. The Visibility drop-down list box allows you to select to set whether the content of a positioned element is visible.

The Overflow drop-down list box allows you to select how to handle the content of a positioned element if the content exceeds the height and width of the element. There are four available options for the Overflow setting:

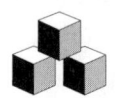

- **Scroll**

  Makes content overflow accessible by scroll bars.

- **Hidden**

  Displays only the content that fits into the height and width of the element.

- **Visible**

  Displays all of the content of the element and disregards the height and width settings for the element. This is the default setting.

- **Auto**

  Allows the default HTML rules to apply.

Z-order is a concept that you may or may not be familiar with. The Z-order controls the stacking order of the positioned element if the element's position overlaps with another element. Absolute or Relative needs to be selected as the type to make this option available.

The last group box on this page is Clear Space On. This has two check boxes, Left and Right. When the Left check box is selected, the element doesn't allow floating elements to the left of the element. The element then appears below floating elements on the left. When the Right check box is selected, the element doesn't allow floating elements to the right of the element. The element then appears above floating elements on the right.

The Source Tab

The Source tab lets you view the source generated by the style sheet based on the CSS settings you've selected. To view the sources code, follow these steps:

1. Select the Source tab. The Source page displays, as shown in Figure 19.15.

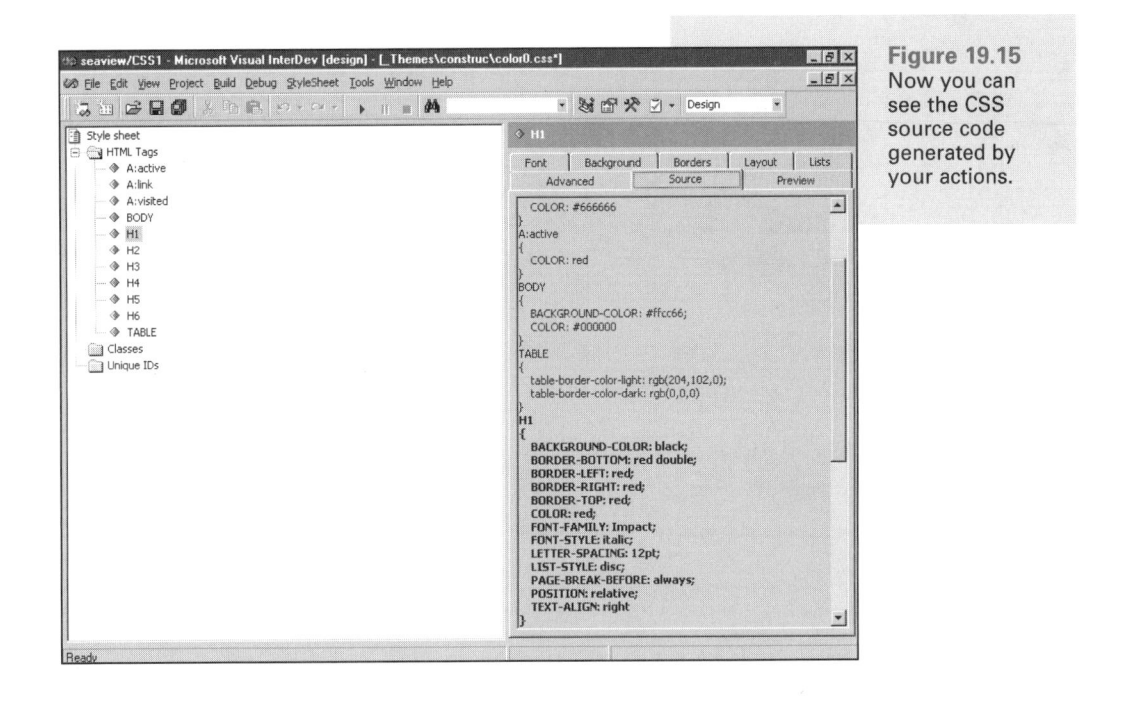

Figure 19.15
Now you can see the CSS source code generated by your actions.

2. Scroll through the source code. Take note of the H1 code.
3. Select File, Save _Themes/construc/color0.css to save the changes you have made.
4. Use the Window menu to go to your HTML page.

Summary

Now you're a real cascading style sheet guru! Don't forget to refresh your view in Design view, or your view may not reflect the changes. Now you can experiment on your own!

APPENDIX A

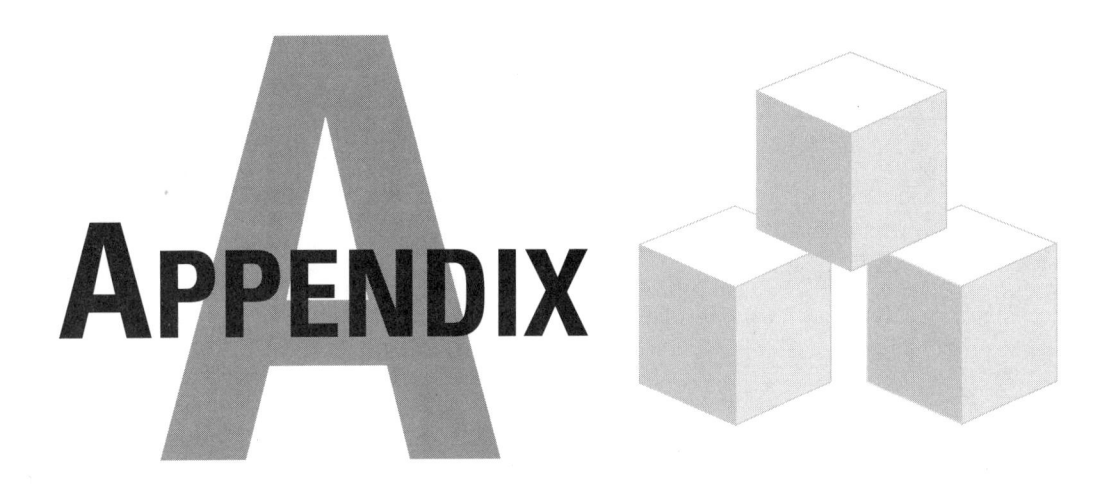

Recommended Naming and Programming Conventions

This book uses naming conventions when naming objects and variables. This makes reading and maintaining code easier for you and for others who may work with your code in the future. This section presents a recommended list of naming conventions and programming standards.

Naming Prefixes

Naming prefixes of the types shown in Tables A.1 through A.6 make your code easier to read and help you organize your variables and controls.

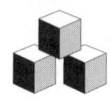

Table A.1

Object Type	Prefix
Animated Button	ani
Application	app
Checkbox	chk
Combo Box	cbo
Command Button	cmd
Grid	grd
Horizontal Scroll Bar	hsb
Image	img
Label	lbl
Line	lin
List Box	lst
Slider	sld
Spin	spn
Spin Button	spn
Text Box	txt
Recordset	rs
RecordsetNavBar	rn
Vertical Scroll Bar	vsb

Table A.2 Variable and Procedure Naming Prefixes

Datatype	Short Prefix	Long Prefix
Array	a	ary
Boolean	b	bln
Byte	byt	byt
Date/Time	dt	dtm or dat
Double	d	dbl
Err	err	err
Integer	i	int

Appendix A • Naming and Programming Conventions

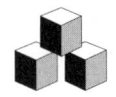

Datatype	Short Prefix	Long Prefix
Long	l	lng
Object	o	obj
Single	f	sng
String	s	str

Use the qualifiers shown in Table A.3 when naming certain variables and procedures. Examples of their use: `iFirstValue`, `sGetLastItem`, `sSaveName`.

Table A.3 Qualifiers for Variables and Procedure Names

Qualifier	Description
Cur	Current item in set
Dst	Destination
First	First item in set
Last	Last item in set
Max	Largest value in set
Min	Smallest value in set
Next	Next item in set
Prev	Previous item in set
Save	Preserve another variable that must be reset later
Src	Source
Tmp	Temporary variable

Table A.4 Variable Naming Prefixes for Scope

Scope	Prefix
Procedure	none
Script	s

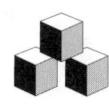

Table A.5 ADO Object Naming Prefixes

Object Type	Prefix
Container	cnt
Containers	cnts
Database	db
Databases	dbs
DBEngine	dbe
Document	doc
Documents	docs
Error	err
Errors	errs
Field	fld
Fields	flds
Group	grp
Groups	grps
Index	idx
Indexes	idxs
Parameter	prm
Parameters	prms
PrivDBEngine	pdbe
Property	prp
Properties	prps
Query	qry or qdf
Queries	qrys or qdfs
Recordset	rst
Recordsets	rsts
TableDef	tbl or tdf
TableDefs	tbls or tdfs
User	usr
Users	usrs
Workspace	wrk
Workspaces	wrks

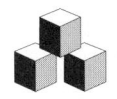

Table A.6 Naming Prefixes for Database Objects

Object Type	Prefix
ODBC Database	db
ODBC Dynaset	ds
Field Collection	fdc
Field Object	fd
Index Collection	ixc
Index Object	ix
QueryDef	qd
Snapshot	ss
Table	tb
TableDef	td

Naming Constants

Constants should be named using all-uppercase letters. Use the underscore (_) character to represent spaces. The following are examples of constant names:

```
SALESTAX
SALES_TAX
MINIMUM_WAGE
```

You can use the scope naming prefixes with constants if you wish. For example, if SALESTAX were a public constant, you would name it gSALESTAX.

Commenting Code

You should begin each of your procedures with a brief comment describing the purpose of the procedure. Follow the statement of purpose with a description of any arguments used by the procedure. If the procedure is a function and returns values, also describe the return values. You may also want to include the developer's name and the date the procedure was created and last modified in this section.

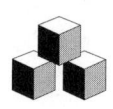

Comments should appear above the line they are documenting. The thought behind this placement is that the reader should read the comment and then read the program.

Every important variable declaration should include an inline comment describing the use of the variable being declared. At the beginning of your script, you should include an overview that describes the script, enumerating objects, procedures, algorithms, dialog boxes, and other system dependencies. Sometimes a piece of pseudocode describing the algorithm is helpful.

Use of Capitalization

HTML tags are not case-sensitive. However, most programmers prefer to use all uppercase characters for tags. Argument values used with tags are usually mixed case.

VBScript is typically done in mixed-case. Variable names are typically named using lowercase or mixed-case characters. Other items such as properties, events, and methods also use mixed-case. Object names have their prefixes in lowercase with the first character of the descriptive portion of the name in uppercase. For example, a Cancel button would be btnCancel.

APPENDIX B

Tables Relationships

The projects in this book used two databases, pubs and Northwind. This appendix illustrates the table relationships for these databases.

The Northwind Database

The Northwind database is an Access database that is provided as a sample to experiment with many Access features. It models an environment that tracks sales, inventory, customer, and supplier information. Figure B.1 illustrates how its tables relate.

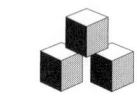

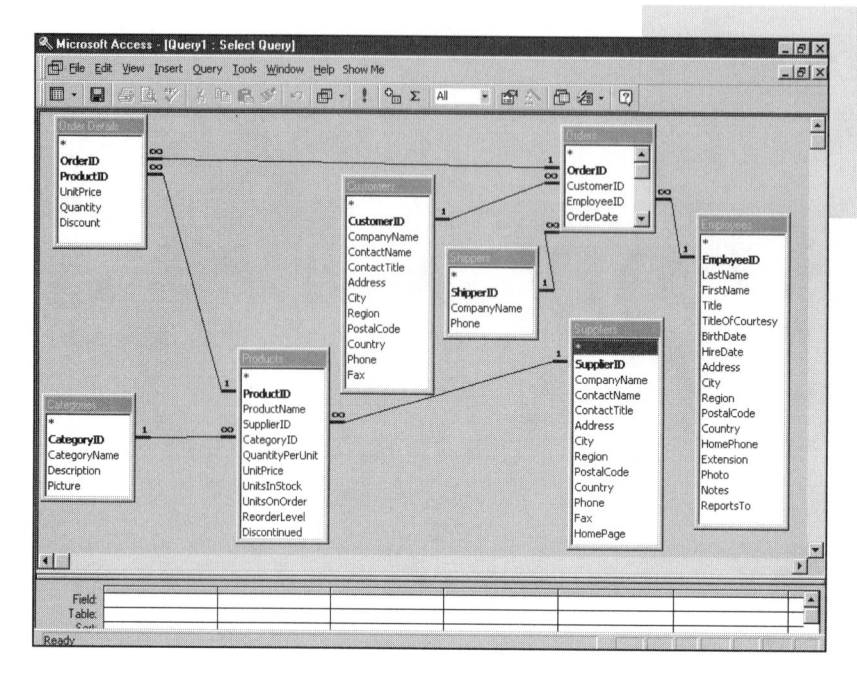

Figure B.1
The lines in this diagram indicate the relationships between tables.

The Pubs Database

The Pubs database is a SQL Server database designed to model a bookstore environment. Pubs is provided with SQL Server as a sample database for training and for experimenting with SQL Server's features. Figure B.2 illustrates how its tables relate.

APPENDIX B • TABLES REATIONSHIPS

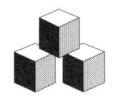

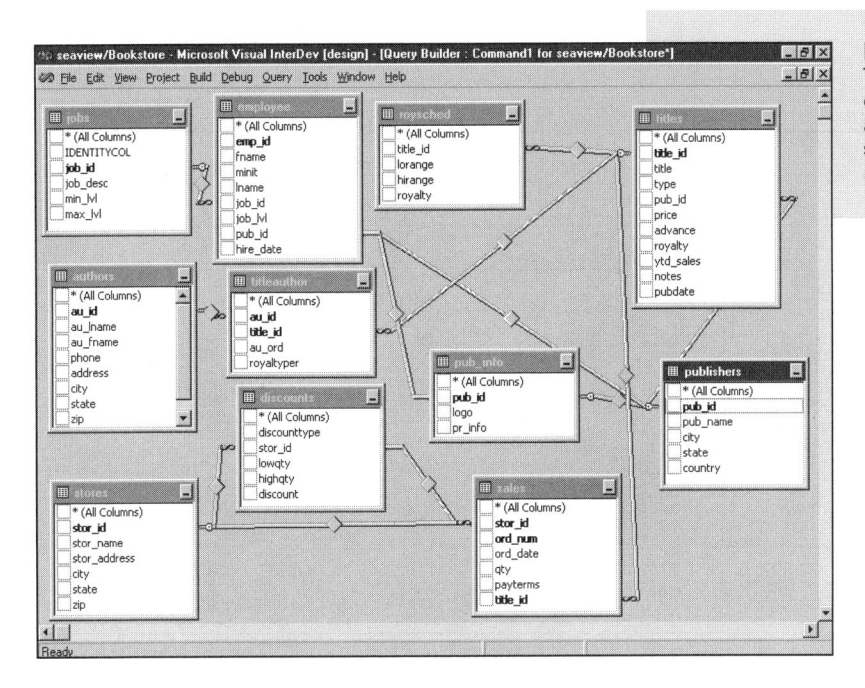

Figure B.2
The Pubs database has an intricate series of table relationships.

APPENDIX C

The Timelines Design-Time Control

You have worked with many DTCs throughout this book. For example, in Chapter 10, you worked with the Recordset and RecordsetNavbar design-time controls. In Chapter 11, you used the Grid and FormManager DTCs. This appendix will provide you with information on the Timelines design-time control.

Adding a Timelines Design-Time Control

Use the Timelines control to assign times for events to occur. The events you specify in the Timelines control perform the following types of tasks:

- Execute scripts.
- Call ActiveX controls, applet objects, Dynamic HTML objects, and intrinsic controls methods.

- Set properties of ActiveX controls, applet objects, Dynamic HTML objects, and intrinsic controls properties.

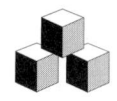

You may want to use a timeline control to execute a procedure that displays an animated sequence or a different message about a product every so often on your page. Follow these steps to add a Timelines DTC to your page:

1. Select the Design-Time Control tab from the Toolbox.
2. Drag the Timelines control to your page.

> **Note** You can only add one Timelines control per page.

3. Right-click on the newly added control to display its pop-up menu.
4. Select Properties. The Timelines Properties dialog box displays (see Figure C.1).

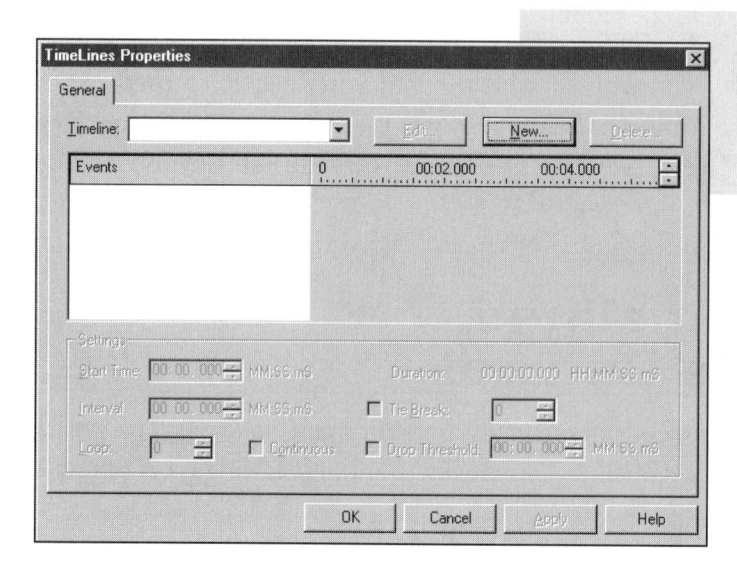

Figure C.1
The Timelines Properties dialog box is used to add, modify, and delete Timeline items.

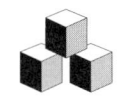

Adding a Timeline

Once you add the Timelines control to your page, you need to add a timeline. Follow these steps to add a timeline:

1. Click on New. The New Timeline dialog box displays, as shown in Figure C.2.

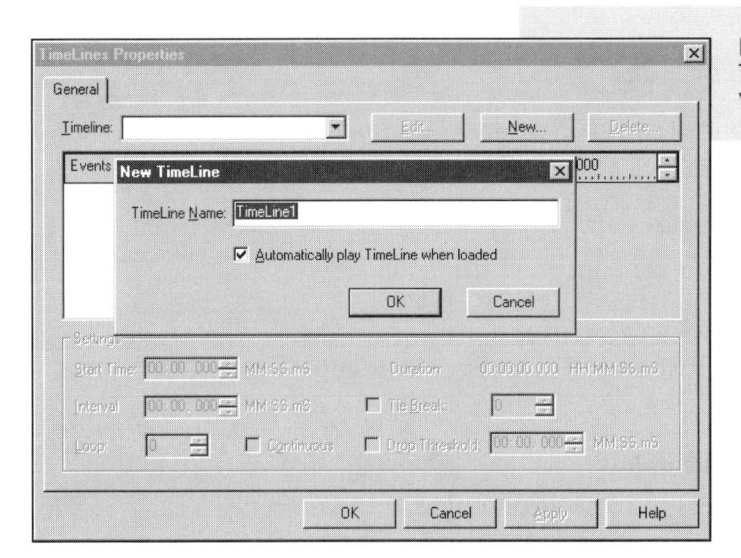

Figure C.2
To add a timeline, you must name it.

2. Enter a name for the new timeline.

> **Note:** A timeline's name must be unique for the page and can be up to 64 characters in length. The name cannot contain spaces.

3. If you want the timeline to play as soon as the page is loaded, place a check in the Automatically Play Timeline When Loaded check box.

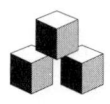

> **Note:** If you don't place a check in this check box, you need to reference the timeline and its play method in the script on your page.

   4. Click on OK. The timeline is added.

Adding Events

The next step is to add an event for your timeline. You can specify three types of events within a timeline:

- **Discrete events**

  These events play once and then stop.

- **Looping events**

  These events play multiple times for a limited period within the timeline.

- **Continuous events**

  These events play for the duration of the timeline.

Each timeline can have multiple events defined for it. For example, you may have a series of functions and procedures that you want to run whenever a user first accesses your page. To add an event to your timeline, follow these steps:

   1. Click on the cell in the Event column that says Click Here to Add New Event.
   2. Type the name for the event.

> **Note:** Event names can be up to 64 characters in length and cannot contain spaces.

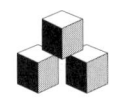

3. Press Enter. The event is added.

After you add the event, set the options found in the Settings group box located at the bottom of the Timeline Properties dialog box. The first option you can set is Start Time. Use this control to set when the first event occurs. The format for the time is hh:mm:ss.mss. The minimum value is 00:00.000, and the maximum value is 59:59.999. The default value is zero (0). If you are defining a discrete event, you don't need to set any other properties.

If you are defining a looping event, increase the value of the Loop field. This property sets the number of times this event occurs within the duration of the event. The default value is zero (0), and the maximum is 32767. You'll notice that as you change the Loop value, the Duration changes. Duration displays the entire length of time that this event fires. Duration is calculated by multiplying Interval times Loop (Duration = Interval * (Loop–1)).

You also have the option of defining a Continuous event. To do this, place a check in the Continuous check box. A continuous event occurs as long as the timeline is active. The timeline is active for as long as the page is loaded or until it is changed through a script. When you place a check in the Continuous check box, the Loop check box is disabled. You can see that as you define events and set their properties, the settings are reflected in the time scale of the event.

> **Tip**
> To change the increments shown on the scale, use the Up and Down arrows on the end of the scale.

If you plan to have multiple events fire at the same time, set the precedence for each event by setting the Tie Break property. The number you assign through the Tie Break property determines which event fires first. The event with the lowest Tie Break value fires first.

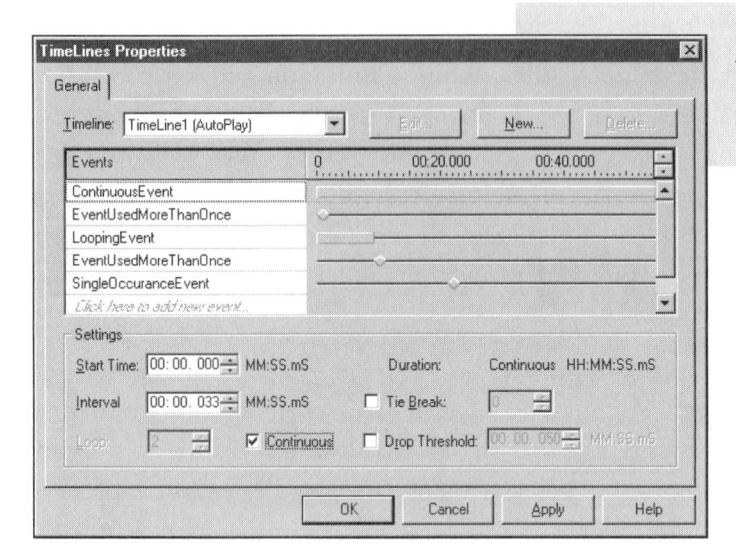

Figure C.3
This timeline contains discrete, continuous, and looping events

You can cause the same event to occur multiple times in your timeline by using the same event name multiple times in your event list. This way you can have the same event occur before and after another event. Figure C.3 illustrates a timeline with a variety of events defined.

You can rename an event by double-clicking on it and typing a new name. To delete an event, select it and press the Delete key.

After you create timelines, you need to use the Source view to add a function for each event specified in the timelines. When defining the function, use the format of *timelinename_eventname*. For example, if you have a timeline named tlBegin that contains an event named bouncinglogo, you need to create a function named tlBegin_bouncinglogo.

> **Caution**
>
> Your page will generate errors if you don't have a function defined for each event named in the timeline.

Appendix D

What's On the CD-ROM

The CD that accompanies this book contains example projects from the book, as well as a large collection of Web tools and utilities to assist you in your Visual InterDev development efforts.

Running the CD

To make the CD more user friendly and take up less of your disk space, no installation is required. This means that the only files transferred to your hard disk are the ones you choose to copy or install.

> **Caution**
>
> This CD has been designed to run under Windows 95/98 and Windows NT 4. Please be advised that, while it will run under Windows 3.1, you may encounter unexpected problems. In addition, many of the software programs contained on the CD are 32bit programs, and as such, will not run in Windows 3.1.

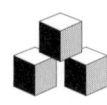

Windows 95/98/NT4

Since there is no install routine, running the CD in Windows 95/98/NT4 is a breeze, especially if you have autorun enabled. Simply insert the CD in the CD-ROM Drive, close the tray, and wait for the CD to load.

If you have disabled autorun, place the CD in the CD-ROM drive and follow these steps:

1. From the Start menu, select Run.
2. Type **D:\prima.exe** (where D:\ is the CD-ROM drive).
3. Select OK.

The Prima User Interface

Prima's user interface is designed to make viewing and using the CD contents quick and easy. The opening screen contains five category buttons and a command bar with three navigational buttons. Click on a category button to jump to the associated page containing the available software titles or book examples. Once you reach a category page, click on a title button to display a pop-up menu with options for installing and viewing the software and examples.

Category and Title Buttons

Book Examples. Example files from *Hands On Visual InterDev 6*.

Developer Tools. An assortment of handy tools and utilities to aid in your development efforts.

Multimedia. This collection of image, sound, and animation tools will enable you to create, view, and enhance multimedia elements for all of your Web projects.

Utilities. File compression, FTP, and assorted file management utilities.

Web Tools. A variety of Web management tools that will enable you to monitor and maintain your Web site with ease.

Command Bar Buttons

Exit. When you're finished using the CD, shut it down with this button.

Explore. Use this button to view the contents of the CD using the Windows Explorer.

Navigate. Click on this button to display a pop-up menu containing links to the various category pages.

Next and Previous. The arrows located at either end of the command bar are Previous (left side) and Next(right side) buttons that will move you to the page before or after the current page.

Pop-Up Menu Options

Install. If the selected title contains an install routine, choosing this option begins the installation process.

Explore. Selecting this option allows you to view the folder containing the program files using Windows Explorer.

Information. Use this menu item to open the Readme file associated with the selected title. If no Readme file is present, the help file will be opened.

Visit Web Site. If you're running Windows 95/98/NT4 and a recent version of Internet Explorer or Netscape Navigator and have established an Internet connection, selecting this option will launch your browser and take you to the associated Web site.

The Software

This section gives you a brief description of some of the shareware and evaluation software you'll find on the CD. This is just a sampling. As you browse the CD, you will find much more.

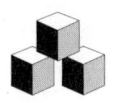

> **Note:** Any shareware distributed on this disk is for evaluation purposes only, and should be registered with the shareware vendor if used beyond the trial period.

1st Java Navigator. 1st Java Navigator works just like a customizable "File Manager" and "Filofax" for a Web site or Intranet—all in one single product.

Artemis for Visual Studio. Artemis is an enhanced data control for Visual Basic and Visual C++. It supports files used by CA-Clipper (.dbf/.dbt/.ntx) and FoxPro (.dbf/.fpt/.idx/.cdx).

Browse And Zip. This handy plugin for Netscape and Internet Explorer will supercharge your Web browser's handling of Zip files.

HTML Validator. A highly user-configurable HTML development tool that assists in the creation of syntactically correct HTML documents.

Mabry Software Internet Pack. This package contains an assortment of VBXes and 32-bit OLE controls (OCXes) for giving your applications access to the Internet.

QUERYer. QUERYer is a database query and report tool designed for application developers, IT professionals, and end-users.

TeeChart Pro. TeeChart Pro ActiveX version is a comprehensive charting tool for developers across programming language boundaries. It includes extended TeeChart functionality and additional features.

WinZip. One of the most popular file compression utilities for Windows 95/98 and Windows NT.

Glossary

A

Active Data Objects
Active Data Objects (ADO) supply an open, application-level data access object model that allows corporate programmers to write database applications to access OLE DB data using any language.

Active Server Pages (ASP)
HTML files that include embedded scripts executed on the Web server. The output of the scripts is included as part of the HTML that is downloaded to the browser.

ADO
See Active Data Objects.

Alias
An alternative name for a table or column in database query expressions.

ANSI
American National Standards Institute.

ASP
See Active Server Pages.

B

Breakpoint
Pauses your script's execution at a designated point. When you pause a procedure, its source is displayed and you can test it.

Broken link
When a reference to an item cannot be found, it is said to have a broken link. This can occur because the URL is not valid, the item the link points to does not exist, or there are other technical problems.

Broken links report
This report gives you detailed information about link usage and issues in a text format

Browser
An application that interprets HTML files and other files posted on the Internet and displays them for the user. Microsoft Internet Explorer is an example of a browser.

C

Cascading Style Sheets (CSS)
These display definitions of HTML elements that are used to enforce a standard look and feel throughout your Web site. You can also manipulate CSS attributes with client-side scripting to create dynamic HTML.

Check box
Check Box controls have two uses. One is as a toggle selection. If a check box has a check mark, then the user has set the item to true. Otherwise, the user has set it to false. The Check Box control is also used to present a user with multiple choices.

Child page
A page with a parent page in a site diagram.

Client
See Browser.

Collapsed item
An item whose in and out links do not appear in the link diagram.

Column
Database tables are typically represented using two dimensions, rows and columns. Columns correspond to a table's fields.

Combo box
A Combo Box control is functionally a cross between a list box and a text box. It allows a user to either type in a value or select from a list.

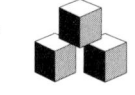

Glossary

Command button
Used to prompt a user to select an action. For example, you may have a form with the following command buttons on it: Yes, No, and Cancel. A user clicks on the desired button, and the associated action is initiated. A command button ordinarily appears as a gray rectangle with rounded corners.

Comparison operator
A character such as ">" (greater than) or a combination of characters such as "<=" (less than or equal to) that defines the relationship between two values or expressions.

Conditional logic
Controls the flow of program code.

Constant
A placeholder for static data.

Control
An item, such as a button or a text box, that is added to an HTML page so that it may perform an action. In terms of code, a control is an object on a form or report that displays data, performs an action, or acts as a decorative element.

Cookie
Information sent to a browser that is stored there and automatically returned to the Web server upon subsequent requests. Cookies are useful for saving application state information on behalf of the user.

Criteria
Criteria are restrictions you place on a query or an advanced filter to identify the specific records you want to work with.

Crosstab query
A crosstab query displays values from one field summarized by an aggregate function (such as a sum, average, or count) and groups them by another field or group of fields listed down the left side of the datasheet as row headings. It also uses another field or group of fields listed across the top as column headings.

CSS
See Cascading Style Sheets.

D

Data connection
A collection of information required to access a specific database. The information includes a data source name (DSN) and login information.

Data validation
Data validation involves verifying the data entered by a user to make sure that it meets the information needs of the system.

Database
A set of related data tables and other elements such as forms and reports.

Database designer
When you work with a SQL Server or Oracle database, you can use this tool to display your database as a database diagram. When your database is displayed in this manner, you can create indexes, add or change table and column definitions, define relationships between tables, and add constraints.

Database project
In Visual InterDev terms, a project with a connection to a database. In a database project, you can manipulate database objects such as tables, columns, records, and queries.

Databound Design-Time Controls (DTCs)
Controls used to create pages that display from and write data to a database. Examples of databound DTCs include labels and text boxes.

Data source
An entity that provides data.

Data Source Name
See DSN.

Debugging
The process of finding and correcting errors in code.

DE command
A Data Environment command such as a saved query.

Deployment
Deployment is the process of moving a Web application from the development server to the production server.

GLOSSARY

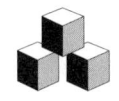

DHTML (Dynamic HTML)
A set of additions to HTML that allows page authors and developers to dynamically change the style and attributes of elements on an HTML page, as well as insert, delete, or modify elements and text after a page has been loaded.

Document
In Visual InterDev terms, a document is a file associated with an application, such as Microsoft Word.

DSN (Data Source Name)
The collection of information used to connect an application to an ODBC database.

DTCs
See Databound Design-Time Controls.

Dynamic Web Application
A project that is not built on static text. To be dynamic, it relies on a way to have the contents of the application change without changing the application itself.

E

Exclusive checkout
Exclusive checkout allows only one user to check out a file at a time when using Visual SourceSafe for source control.

Expanded item
An item whose in and out links appear in the link diagram.

Extranet
A specialized Web site that is exposed only to trusted users—for example, a site where only trusted sales personnel can access product cost and stock level values. *See also* Intranet.

F

Field
A field, also referred to as a column, contains one part of a record's information.

Filters
Used to display rows that meet certain criteria that you select or enter.

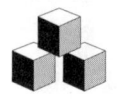

Font
The typeface and size applied to text. The font changes the appearance of the text. Examples of fonts include Courier 14, Times New Roman 12, and Arial 24.

Foreign key
A foreign key is a field that is used to relate one table to another.

FrontPage
FrontPage is a Microsoft product providing Web-authoring tools designed to be used by nonprogrammers.

G

Global navigation bar
A global navigation bar has links to the most-used or useful links for your site.

H

Home page
A home page is the main page of a Web site. A home page is generated by a Web author and typically has links to other pages.

HTML
Hypertext Markup Language (HTML) is a standard language that uses various tags to mark up the text, such that the information can be viewed by users with browsers.

Hyperlink
An address to a location, such as a folder on your computer or a Web page. When you click on a hyperlink, you jump to the location defined in the hyperlink.

I

Independent Page
A page without parent pages or child pages in a site diagram.

Index
A specified order for retrieving the records of a table. Indexes usually speed up data access.

Inner join
A join in which the records from two tables are combined and added to a query's results, only if the values of the joined fields match and meet any specified conditions.

In links
Resources that point at the current item.

Integrity
Integrity means that data must be accurate and consistent. To say that data is accurate means that it adheres to your business policies. An example of this is the requirement that no one makes less than the federal minimum wage. Data consistency means that separate but related parts of a database agree with each other. If you have a customer table in which you have defined the customer ID to be a four-digit code, all customer ID fields in all other tables should be four-digit codes matching values found in the customer table.

IntelliSense
When you start typing the name of an object, IntelliSense displays a list of methods and properties available for that object. Once a method or property is selected, it displays parameters needed by that method or property.

Intranet
An internal network patterned after and often connected to the Internet. *See also* Extranet.

Item
A resource that is part of a Web site.

J

Jet engine
Visual Basic's native database engine, used to store, retrieve, and update data. The Jet engine provides the programmer with the DAO programming interface.

Join
When two or more tables are linked by a similar field or fields (typically a key field), the tables are said to be joined. *See also* Inner Join.

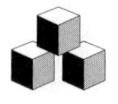

Just-in-time debugging
Refers to debugging a client script in response to an error or debugger statement.

L

Label
A static area of text on your forms. This text may be helpful information, a graphic's caption, a description for a control, or the like.

Layout
A template for the way that information, navigation bars, and graphics are positioned on a page.

Link
A link is the relationship between items in a Web site.

Link diagram
A link diagram is a graphical representation of the structure of a Web site.

Local mode
When you work in Local mode, changes are made to a working copy of the Web application without affecting the master Web application. This is because you are working with a local copy of the Web project, which resides on your workstation. *See also* Master mode.

Locking
Locking is the process of restricting access to records in a multiuser environment to maintain integrity and avoid concurrent access problems.

Logic error
Logic errors are the result of programming errors and typically have to do with your approach to a situation.

M

Many-to-many relationship
In this type of relationship, a record in the first table can have many matching records in the second table, and a record in the second table can have many matching records in the first table. To support this type of relationship, you must define a third table, called a junction table, whose primary key consists of two fields that are the foreign keys from the first and second tables.

Master file
The primary copy of a project file.

Master mode
When you work in Master mode, changes to the project and its files are saved to both the local workstation and to the master files on the Web server, making your changes active immediately. *See also* Local mode.

Method
Methods tell an object to do something and can be thought of as object-specific functions.

Multiple checkouts
This option allows more than one person to check out the same file at a time when using Visual SourceSafe for source control.

N

Navigation bar
A page element that provides navigation links to other pages that are part of the Web site.

Normalization
The process of simplifying the design of a database to achieve the most efficient and optimized structure.

O

ODBC
See Open Database Connectivity.

ODBC Direct
Allows you to access ODBC databases without the Jet engine.

Object browser
Displays classes, properties, methods, events, and constants available from object libraries and the procedures in your project.

OLE DB
OLE DB specifies a set of Microsoft Component Object Model (COM) interfaces that encapsulate, or hide, various database management system services.

One-to-many relationship
The most common type of relationship, in which a record in the first table can have many matching records in the second table, but a record in the second table has only one matching record in the first table.

One-to-one relationship
The least common type of relationship, in which each record in the first table can only have one matching record in the second table, and each record in the second table can only have one matching record in the first table.

Open Database Connectivity (ODBC)
A method of communicating with client/server databases such as Microsoft SQL Server. ODBC allows programmers to write applications that are independent of the underlying database.

Operator
A sequence of one or more characters in a formula that defines the action to be performed, such as addition or multiplication.

Option button
Use Option Button controls to display multiple choices for an item. Option buttons allow a user to select only one of the available options. *See also* Check Boxes.

Outer join
An outer join is used to select all the records from one table or query, whether or not it has matching records in the other table or query.

Out links
Resources that the current item points to.

P

PageNavBar control
A design-time control that automatically generates navigation bar links based on the information stored in the site structure file for the Web project.

Parameter query
A query designed to prompt a user for criteria.

Parent page
A page with one or more child pages.

Personal files
Local files that have not been copied to the master directory.

Primary key
A single field that will identify the record. It is unique by nature.

Project
A project organizes the files used for a Web application. These files include documents, graphics, and HTML pages.

Property
Properties control the appearance and behavior of objects. They can be set with code, which is referred to as setting properties at run time, or through the Property window or Property pages, which is called setting properties at design time.

Proxy server
A special server that provides Web caching and security between the Internet and your local area network.

Q

Query
A query is the process of asking questions about the database.

Query designer
This designer lets you visually create SQL statements using click, drag, and drop techniques to query or modify a database.

R

RDBMS
See Relational Database Management System.

Record
A collection of information about one subject.

Recordset
The set of records returned from a table or query.

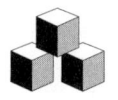

Referential integrity
A set of rules developed to protect the integrity of data. It prevents a user from altering table relationships by adding data to one table in a relationship without adding matching information to the related table. It also prevents the user from deleting data involved in a relationship.

Relational database management system
An application such as Microsoft Access that is used for the creation, storage, manipulation, querying, and editing of relational databases.

Relationship
A relationship is a connection between two tables accomplished through common fields. *See also* one-to-many relationship, one-to-one relationship, and many-to-many relationship.

Replication
The ability to make a copy of a database and then later synchronize the copy with the original database. This allows for independent accessing of the database with the benefits of a single data source.

Row
Database tables are typically represented using two dimensions, rows and columns. Rows correspond to a table's records.

Rule
A database object that is bound to a column or to a user-defined data type. Rules specify what data can be entered in that column.

Run-time error
A run-time error is any error that causes a program to stop running.

S

Scope
The parameters and means of declaring variables and constants, which determines where you can use them.

Script Editor
This window is similar to the Source view. The Script Editor is used for creating SQL scripts.

Script Outline
Lists objects and their events. You can use the Script Outline window to

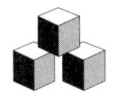

create event handlers. In the Script Outline window, expand the node for the object you are working with, and then double-click on the name of the event you want to write a handler for.

Scripting Object Model (SOM)
The Scripting Object Model (SOM) simplifies Web development by introducing a familiar object-oriented programming model to HTML and script programming.

Security
A system for a database to establish user access requirements to restrict undesirable actions.

Select
The Select SQL statement retrieves data from tables.

Server script
A script run by the server after the page is requested but before it is passed to the browser.

Sibling page
A page that shares a parent page with another page.

Site diagram
A site diagram provides you with a graphical representation of the navigational structure of a Web site.

Solution
A collection of Web projects and dependent projects that organizes a Web application.

SQL
See Structured Query Language.

Stored procedure
A set of SQL statements (SQL Server also supports flow control statements in stored procedures) that are stored under a procedure name so that the statements can be executed as a group by the database server.

Stored procedure editor
Certain databases such as SQL Server use stored procedures, which are SQL procedures that can accept arguments. You can use this editor to create stored procedures.

Structured Query Language (SQL)
A widely adopted standard for getting answers to particular questions about your data.

Synchronization
The process of updating either the local or master copies of your files.

Syntax error
A syntax error is the result of using the script language incorrectly.

T

Table
An organized collection of fields (columns) and records (rows) that holds data.

Task
A task is an item of work. It is a "to-do" item that relates to the project.

Theme
In Visual InterDev, themes are used to create a consistent look and feel to an entire Web site. *See also* Cascading Style Sheets.

Toolbox
The set of tools that you use in the Design window to place controls on a form or report. The toolbox is a small window that appears when you open the Design window for a form or report.

Transaction
The ability to group more than one database action and treat it as a single unit. If any action fails to perform correctly, the entire group fails and the database can be rolled back (returned to the state before the transaction was executed).

Transaction logs
Areas reserved by SQL Server to record changes to the database. Each change made to a database is automatically recorded in the transaction log for that database. SQL Server uses transaction logs during automatic recovery.

Transact-SQL
A superset of the SQL language used by Microsoft SQL Server and Sybase SQL Server.

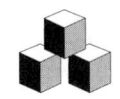

Tree
A tree is a group of related pages in a site diagram.

Trigger
A special form of a stored procedure that executes automatically when data in a specified table is modified.

Typeface
The character style of text. Typefaces change the appearance of the text. Examples of typefaces include Courier, Times New Roman, and Arial.

U

Uniform Resource Locator
See URL.

Universal Data Access
Universal Data Access enables all Visual Studio tools to access any data source on any platform. Universal Data Access consists of three core technologies. OLE DB, ActiveX_Data Objects (ADO), and Open Database Connectivity (ODBC).

Update query
This type of action query makes changes to a group of records.

URL (Uniform Resource Locator)
The address used to identify a resource on the World Wide Web. It is also used by some local area networks and intranets.

V

Validation
Data validation is the process of controlling how data is entered into your database.

Variable
A temporary holding place for data.

View
A view is a subset of columns from one or more tables that presents data to a user.

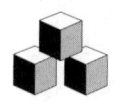

View Designer
The View Designer lets you visually create the SQL Statement that defines a view.

Visual Component Manager
Allows you to organize, locate, and add components into your Visual InterDev project.

Visual SourceSafe
A sophisticated source control tool.

W

Watch expression
A watch expression is a variable or expression whose value you wish to monitor as your application progresses.

Web application
A Web application contains the files that hold your Web content and functionality for your Web site. These files include .htm, .asp, and image files.

Web project
A Web project is not part of the Web application file set, but is a file used by Visual InterDev to point to the files associated with your Web application. You use the Web project to identify and manipulate your Web application files. The project file is the road map that the Web application consults to traverse the files the application uses.

Web server
A computer that acts as a host for Web sites and Web-based applications.

Wildcard
Wildcards are pattern-matching characters used with the Like operator. The two most widely used wildcard characters are the question mark (?) and the asterisk (*).

WYSIWYG (What You See Is What You Get)
This means that the document you see on the screen looks exactly the same when printed.

Index

<%@ LANGUAGE= %> tag, 255

A

Add, Add Item command, 69
Add Data command, 154, 171, 281
Add Data Connection command, 169
Add Item dialog box, 63–64, 88, 187, 304
    ASP Page option, 254
    Existing tab, 69
    HTML Page icon, 89
addRecord method, 285
ADO (ActiveX Data Objects), 129–130
aligning
    buttons on forms, 191–193
    elements, 321
    text objects, 33
alphabetizing properties, 33
application files, 80
applications
    drag-and-drop design, 2
    implementing with database connections, 120
    setting breakpoints, 204–206
Apply Theme and Layout dialog box, 74–75, 77
    Layout tab, 76–77
    Theme tab, 77, 90
Arcs theme, 19, 62
.asp files, 81–82
ASPs (Active Server Pages), 12, 187, 223, 252
    creation of, 253–254
    debugging, 213–214
    server scripts, 252
.AVI files, 69

B

background images, 314–317
background sound, 250
<B>...</B> tag, 101
<BGSOUND> tag, 250
bold text, 68
    HTML (Hypertext Markup Language), 101
Bookstore project
    adding another page to, 169
    adding source control, 239–240
    setting breakpoints, 204–206
Breakpoint (F9) function key, 204–205
breakpoints, 10, 201, 203–207
    removing, 205
broken links, 109–110
    repairing, 115–116
Broken Links Report, 114–115
browsers
    capabilities of supported, 39
    opening Web pages, 176
    viewing Web pages, 74
bulleted lists, 324–325
Button control, 5, 191
    ID property, 271
    Name property, 271
    property settings, 282
Button Properties dialog box, 191–193

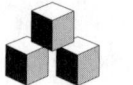

buttons, 5
    adding to and removing from toolbars, 28–30
    .cmd or .btn prefix, 261
    new toolbars, 30–31
    returning default to toolbars, 30

C

Cannot access server information for the file *name* **message,** 124
categorizing properties, 33
centering text, 68
Checkbox control, 4, 162, 186, 260
checkboxes, 4, 260
    .chk prefix, 260
Choose File dialog box, 4
classes, 310
    displaying, 34
client scripts, 251
    versus server scripts, 223, 255–256
Code window margin indicator bar, 204
color
    Source view, 214–216
    text, 68
Color Picker dialog box, 68
color0.css file, 310
Command1 Properties dialog box, 281
comments <!- -> tag, 105
commonly used tags, 101
comparison operators, 155–156, 274–275
components, managing, 34
conditional logic, 273–286
    conditional operators, 274–276
conditional operators, 274–276
Connection Properties dialog box, 170
Connection1 Properties dialog box, 154
Const keyword, 267
constants, 267–268
    displaying, 34
    scope, 268
Construc folder, 310
container tags, 101
Context-Sensitive Help (F1) function key, 36

context-sensitive menus, 25
controls
    Button, 5, 191
    Checkbox, 4, 162, 186
    data-bound, 139, 161–163
    Display mode actions, 196
    drop-down list, 4
    Edit mode actions, 196–197
    form actions, 195–197
    FormManager, 194
    Grid, 181–185
    labels, 5
    list boxes, 4
    listing properties available, 33
    multiline text input, 4
    as objects, 259–261
    PageNavBar, 93
    radio buttons, 4
    Recordset, 159–161, 172–173, 181, 189, 281
    Recordset1, 178
    RecordsetNavBar, 163–165, 173, 190
    resetting form's, 5
    Textbox, 162, 189
Copy Project dialog box, 121
Corporate Web site
    building, 249–286
    gathering information, 225–230
    multimedia, 222–223, 250–251
    requirements, 221–222
    security, 223, 229–230
    testing, 287–298
    Visual SourceSafe, 222, 232–239
Create a New Data Source Wizard, 11
Create New Data Source dialog box, 169–170
Create URL dialog box, 70
CSS (cascading style sheets), 45, 307–329
    aligning elements, 321
    background images, 314–317
    borders, 317–320
    bulleted lists, 324–325
    changes for themes, 303
    cursor style, 322

INDEX

editing, 309–329
fonts, 311–314
lists, 324
margins, 318
padding, 319
positioning elements on page, 325–328
previewing, 323
resizing text, 312
scaling elements, 322
subscripts and superscripts, 322
transparent background, 316
viewing source code, 328–328
CSS Editor, 7, 309
Advanced tab, 325–328
Background tab, 314–317
Borders tab, 317–320
Font tab, 311–314
Layout tab, 320–322
Lists tab, 324–325
Preview tab, 323
property options, 309
Selector tree, 309
Size group box, 312
Source tab, 328–329
.css file, 309
CUA (Common User Access), 259
cursor style, 322
Customize command, 28–29
Customize dialog box, 28–30
customizing
themes, 302
toolbars, 28–31
windows in development environment, 22–24

D

data, viewing through scripts, 176–179
data access, testing, 118
Data Connection Wizard, 8, 11
data connections, 11, 138
data environment, 136–140
Data Script project
adding page, 280

data validation, 142
Data view, 139
Northwind.mdb file, 171
Tables folder, 156
Data View window, 9, 132, 148–151
viewing table contents, 152
database connections, 146–148
database design tools, 132–133
Database Designer, 139
database tools, 8–11
Data Connection Wizard, 8
Data View window, 9
Data-bound DTCs (Design-Time Controls), 9
Query Designer, 9
Database Web project
building, 167–200
connecting to database, 132
database project creation, 131
designing, 145–165
design-time controls, 180–186
FormManager, 186–200
gathering information, 135–144
requirements, 130–131
scripts, 174–179
database-level security, 295
databases
amount of data stored, 140–141
connecting to, 8, 132
connecting to Microsoft Access, 168–172
data validation, 142
displaying data in grid, 181–185
DSN (data source name), 138
forms, 186–200
implementing applications with database connections, 120
joined tables, 155
live view of data, 9, 148–151
managing, 138–139
number of users accessing, 142–143
object properties, 151
ODBC drivers, 138
ODBC or OLE DB data sources, 13

databases *(continued)*
   ODBC-compliant, 136
   pages that read from and write to, 9
   project creation, 131
   querying, 153–159
   querying and displaying information, 133
   referential integrity, 142
   relationships, 155
   replication, 142
   security, 142
   selecting for Web site, 140–144
   viewing and modifying data, 186–200
   viewing records from home page, 159–165
   viewing table contents, 152
   views, 150
   which one you have, 144
data-bound controls, 139, 161–163
data-bound DTCs (Design-Time Controls), 9
<%#DataConnection#%> delimiter, 305
DE (Data Environment) commands, 160
Debug, Add Watch command, 209
Debug, End command, 206, 208, 212
Debug, Insert Breakpoint menu, 204
Debug, Remove Breakpoint command, 205
Debug, Restart command, 206
Debug, Start command, 205
Debug, Step Into command, 212
Debug dialog box, 162
debugging, 133–134
   ASPs (Active Server Pages), 213–214
   breakpoints, 203–207
   code, 118
   errors, 203
   Immediate window, 224
   just-in-time, 207–208
   logic errors, 203
   process, 202
   run-time errors, 203
   scripts, 288
   server script, 213–214
   Source view, 204
   stepping through lines, 211–212
   stepping through procedures, 202
   syntax errors, 203
   tools, 10
   watch expressions, 36, 209–211
   watches, 201
   Web sites, 40
Default.asp file, 64
Default.htm file, 64
delete method, 228
deleting
   themes, 75
   toolbars, 31
deploying solutions, 118–123
   actual deployment to Web server, 120–122
   FrontPage Server Extensions, 121–122
   manually, 122
   Posting Acceptor, 122
   preparation stage, 119
   verification of production server content, 122–123
   Web Publishing Wizard (Wpwiz.exe), 122
   without FrontPage Server Extensions, 122
deploying Web site, 40
Design mode, 26
Design toolbar, 26
Design view, 5–7
   editors, 98
   home pages, 65
   HTML (Hypertext Markup Language), 102
Design window
   Design tab, 66
   PageNavBar control, 95
   Quick View tab, 66
design-time controls, 180–186
development environment, 20–21, 63
   customizing windows, 22–24
DHTML (Dynamic HTML), 13, 261
Diagram, Add to Global Navigation Bar command, 91
Diagram, Reorder Global Navigation Bar command, 91
Dim statement, 266

INDEX

Display mode
    control actions, 196
    forms, 194
dockable items, 22
Dockable option, 22, 24
docking
    changing options, 22–24
    Properties window, 33
    toolboxes, toolbars, or windows, 22
documents, viewing containing server elements, 99
drop-down list control, 4
drop-down lists, 4
DSN (data source name), 138
dynamic Web applications, 136

E

ECMAScript, 12
Edit, Apply Theme and Layout command, 77, 90
Edit, Undo command, 264
Edit menu, 25
Edit mode
    control actions, 196–197
    forms, 194
editing CSS (Cascading Style Sheets), 310–329
editors, 47
    Design view, 98
    Quick view, 98–99
    Source view, 99–100
elements
    changing appearance, 27–28
    Z-order, 328
empty tags, 101
Enable Source Control dialog box, 239
End Debugging (Shift+F5) key combination, 207
Err object, 291
error handling, 224, 291
error messages, 123–124
error types, 203
event procedures, 178, 257
events, 257
    displaying, 34

exiting
    Visual InterDev, 78

F

fields collection, 257
File, Exit command, 78
File, New Project command, 11, 60, 147
File, Print command, 260
File, Save As command, 304
File, Save CheapBooks command, 159
File, Save command, 71, 90, 273
File, Save Data Script.htm command, 282
File, Save Form Example, 197
File, Save Page1.htm command, 95
File, Save Page2.htm command, 111, 115
File, Save Products command, 186
File, Save _Themes/construc/color0.css command, 312, 314, 318, 320–321
File, Save Turtle.wdm command, 64
File field tool, 4
file formats, 60
File menu, 25
<%#FilenameWithExtension#%> delimiter, 305
files
    adding to projects, 88–90
    read-enabled copies, 82
    uploading, 4
    write-enabled copies, 82
First project, 17–21
fonts
    CSS (cascading style sheets), 311–314
    new, 67
    sizing, 33
    Source view, 215–216
    weight, 313–314
.FontSize property, 33
Form Example.asp file, 242
formatting text, 67–69
FormManager control, 133, 186–200
FormManager Properties dialog box, 194
    Actions tab, 197–198
    Form Mode tab, 194–196

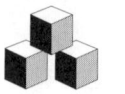

forms, 186–200
    actions for controls, 195–197
    adding controls, 189–190
    aligning buttons, 191–193
    Cancel command button, 190
    Display command button, 190
    Display mode, 194
    Edit command button, 190
    Edit mode, 194
    mode transitions, 196–197
    Recordset control, 189
    RecordsetNavBar control, 190
    resetting controls, 5
    Save command button, 190
    submitting, 5
    Textbox control, 189
FrontPage Server Extensions, 120–122
functions, 262–263

G

Gallery sample application, 11
Get Working Copy command, 310
getValue method, 176, 258, 262–263
.GIF files, 69
global navigation bar, 91–97
Global Navigation Bar dialog box, 91–92
Global.asa file, 84
    processing for security, 296
graphics
    for home page, 54
    home pages, 69–71
    HTML documents, 106–107
    obtaining, 54
Grid control
    changing appearance, 183–185
    changing number of rows displayed, 185
    unbound column, 182–183
Grid Properties dialog box
    Data tab, 181–182, 183
    Format tab, 183–184
    General tab, 183
    Navigation tab, 185

H

<head>...</head> tag, 105
help, 36
    accessing, 34
Help menu, 25
home pages, 45–48
    adding graphics, 69–71
    adding text, 65–66
    changing look and feel, 73–77
    Checkbox controls, 162
    creation, 60–63, 63–72
    data-bound controls, 161–163
    Design view, 65
    formatting text, 67–69
    graphics, 54
    layout, 52
    multimedia, 69
    navigation, 46
    new, 63–65
    previewing, 66
    record navigation, 163–165
    Recordset controls, 159–161
    RecordsetNavBar control, 163–165
    saving, 71
    selecting format, 52
    text, 53
    Textbox controls, 162
    themes, 45, 52, 73–76
    viewing records, 159–165
Horizontal rule control, 5
horizontal rules, 5
.htm files, 81–82
HTML, Image command, 69, 110
HTML documents, 105–107
HTML (Hypertext Markup Language), 100–108
    bold text, 101
    code example, 104–105
    Design view, 102
    Quick view, 102
    Source view, 102
    tags, 100
    text components color, 103

Index

HTML toolbar, 27–28
    Paragraph Format box, 311
HTML Toolbox, 271
<html>...</html> tag, 105

I

IDE (integrated development environment)
    CSS (cascading style sheets) Editor, 7
    features, 2–8
    Site Designer, 7
    Toolbox, 2–5
    WYSIWYG Page Editor, 5–7
If statement, 276–280
    nested, 278–279
If...Then statement, 276
If...Then...Else statement, 277
<IMG DYNSRC=> tag, 251
Immediate window, 224, 289–290
in links, 109
IncludeHome property, 94–97
index.htm file, 64
input boxes, 268–273
Insert Image dialog box, 69, 110–111
Insert Table dialog box, 191
IntelliSense, 11, 272
interface features, 2–8
italic text, 68
items
    dockable, 22
    viewing links for, 110–112

J

JavaScript case-sensitivity, 262
joined tables, 155
JScript
    case-sensitivity, 262
    debugging process, 202
just-in-time debugging, 207–208

L

Label tool, 5
labels, 5
    Data-bound DTCs (Design-Time Controls), 9
layouts, 46, 52, 61–62
    removing, 76
link diagrams, 109–110
    horizontal layout, 112
    radial layout, 112
    viewing links for items, 110–112
<link> tag, 105
Link view, 109–110
    changing layout of diagram, 112–114
    refreshing, 116
    retrieving link information, 110
Link View toolbar, 112, 114
links, 109–116
    broken, 109–110
    Broken Links Report, 114–115
    repairing broken, 115–116
    retrieving information on, 110
    verifying, 118
    viewing for items, 110–112
List box control, 4
list boxes, 4
    .lst prefix, 261
local files, 85
    discarding changes to, 86
    synchronizing with master files, 84–86
    working offline, 87
Local mode, 9–10, 47, 61, 77, 80–81
    making copies of master and related files, 82–83
    multideveloper environment, 77, 81
    setting projects to, 83
    working in, 81–82
logic errors, 203
logical operators, 275–276

M

master files, 80, 85
    copying, 82–83
    getting copy of, 242
    reviewing differences, 85
    synchronizing with local files, 84–85
    updating, 85
    working independently of, 9–10, 80
Master mode, 10, 47, 78, 80–81, 84
master Web application folder, 84
memory requirements, 18
menu bar, 25
menus, 25
Merge dialog box, 85
message boxes, 268–273
<meta> tag, 105
methods, 175, 257, 262–263
    displaying, 34
    Recordset object, 280
Microsoft Access, 130, 141
    connecting to database, 168–172
    displaying query results, 172–174
    file size limitation, 141
    multiple concurrent users, 142
    Visual InterDev and, 168–174
Microsoft FoxPro, 130
Microsoft Internet Explorer
    Active Desktop mode, 202
    viewing Web pages in, 74
Microsoft Internet Information Server, 64
Microsoft Management Console, 236–239
Microsoft Personal Web Server, 64
Microsoft SQL Server, 129
    file size limitation, 141
    multiple concurrent users, 142
    SQL Server Login dialog box, 147–148
    starting, 147
    transaction logs, 142
move method, 228, 280
moveAbsolute method, 228, 280
moveFirst method, 228, 280

moveLast method, 228, 280
moveNext method, 228, 280
movePrevious method, 280, 282
MsgBox function, 272
    argument values, 269–270
    buttons argument, 270
    helpfile argument, 270
    return values, 271
    title argument, 270
multideveloper environment, 226–227
multiline text input tool, 4
multimedia, 69
    background sound, 250
    Corporate Web site, 222–223, 250–251
    video files, 251

N

naming
    projects, 19, 61
    toolbars, 30
navigating
    between project files, 34
    Travel Web site, 76–77
    Web sites, 46
navigation bars
    defining, 76
    including home page in, 94–95
    placing, 61
nested if statements, 278–279
New dialog box, 30
New Page Editor, 5–7
New Project dialog box, 17, 60–61, 147
Nonbreaking space control, 5
nonbreaking spaces, 5
Northwind database, connecting to, 168–172
Northwind.mdb file, 171

O

Object Browser, 34
object-oriented programming, 12

INDEX

objects
    controls as, 259–261
    events, 257
    finding available, 34
    having focus, 71
    methods, 257
    names, 33
    properties, 33, 176, 257, 262
    VBScript, 175
    Visual InterDev, 258–262
ODBC drivers, 138
ODBC Microsoft Access 97 Setup dialog box, 170
ODBC or OLE DB data sources, 13
ODBC-compliant databases, 136
On Error Resume Next statement, 291
On Error statement, 291
onclick event procedure, 272, 282–284
online and offline work, 46–47
online Help, 36
    accessing, 34
onrowenter event, 257
option buttons, 260
    .opt prefix, 260
OptionButton control, 260
Options dialog box, 103
    Debugger option, 207
    Text Editor, 215
out links, 109
overlined text, 313

P

<p> tag, 105
padding, 319
page properties, 33
Page1.htm file, 90
Page2.htm file, 90
Page3.htm file, 90
page-level themes, 90
PageNavBar control, 93
    IncludeHome property, 94–95
    properties, 94
    Type property, 96–97
Paragraph break control, 5
paragraph breaks, 5
paragraph formats, 69
Password tool, 4
passwords, 4
personal files, 85
Personal Web Server connecting with Windows 95, 18
pop-up menus, 25
Posting Acceptor, 122
Private reserved word, 266
programmer's tools, 24–25
programming features, 251
Programs, Microsoft Visual Studio 6.0, Microsoft Visual SoftSafe, Visual SoftSave 6.0 Admin command, 235
Project, Add Data Connection command, 147
Project, Add Item command, 63, 88, 189, 254, 304
Project, Source Control, Add to Source Control command, 239
Project, Source Control, Disconnect Web Project command, 246
Project, Web Files, Discard Changes command, 86
Project, Web Files, Get Latest Version command, 82–83
Project, Web Files, Get Working Copy command, 82
Project, Web Files, Release Working Copy command, 85
Project, Web Project, Copy Web Application command, 121
Project, Web Project, Refresh Project View command, 83, 86
Project, Web Project, Synchronize Files command, 86
Project, Web Project, Working Mode, Local command, 83
Project, Web Project, Working Mode, Master command, 84
Project, Web Project, Working Mode, Work Offline command, 78, 87–88

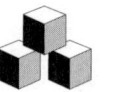

project development process, 36–40
   browser capabilities, 39
   building Web site, 40
   deploying Web site, 40
   identifying content, 38–39
   links to other Web sites, 39
   mission statement, 38
   page design, 39
   purpose of Web site, 37
   testing and debugging Web site, 40
   themes or moods, 39
   Web site point of view, 37–38
Project Explorer
   Bookstore project, 246
   Check In command, 245
   Check In Item(s) dialog box, 243
   Check In Page1.htm command, 243
   Check Out Item(s) dialog box, 241
   debugging server script, 213–214
   Default page, 159
   file list, 85
   Get Latest Version dialog box, 242
   Get Latest Version of Form Example.asp command, 242
   images folder, 69
   Merge dialog box, 245
   NorthDC, 171
   Project, Source Control, Add to Source Control command, 239
   refreshing, 86
   Source tab, 102
   Themes folder, 310
   Undo Checkout dialog box, 244
   Undo Checkout of Page1.htm command, 244
Project Explorer window, 34
project files, 80
Project menu, Source Control, Add to Source Control command, 242
Project Properties dialog box, 74–76
projects
   adding files, 88–90
   adding files to, 63
   changing themes, 74
   creation, 11
   data connections, 11, 138
   database connections, 146–148
   defining, 16
   displaying elements of, 34
   expanding, 88–109
   file formats, 60
   layout, 61–62
   live view of data, 148–151
   managing components, 34
   Master mode, 84
   naming, 19, 61
   navigating between files, 34
   new, 17, 45, 60–63
   page-level themes, 90
   placing navigation bars, 19, 61
   previewing appearance, 61
   prototyping new versions, 77
   removing themes, 74–75
   Sample Tracking Worksheet, 56
   selecting theme, 19
   setting to Local mode, 83
   setting working mode, 83
   Site Tracking Worksheet, 56
   themes, 62
   views, 32
   working offline, 77
   working online, 77
Projects, Web Project, Web Permissions command, 297–298
properties, 33, 94–97
   alphabetizing, 33
   categorizing, 33
   description of, 33
   displaying, 34
   listing available, 33
   objects, 257, 262
   options, 95
   PageNavBar control, 94
   Source view, 100
   VBScript, 176

Index   377

Properties command, 74–76, 159, 164, 172–173, 181–183, 185, 188, 189–194, 258, 263
Properties dialog box, 164, 172, 188, 190
   General tab, 258, 263
Properties window, 33, 100, 151, 171
   docking and undocking, 33
   listing available properties, 33
   object name, 33
   text box, 177
Property Pages dialog box, 213
   breakpoints, 201
   Launch tab, 213–214
Property pages dialog box, 257
Property window, 257
prototyping projects, 77
Public reserved word, 266

Q

queries
   adding criteria to, 155
   comparison operators, 155–156
   displaying Microsoft Access results, 172–174
   displaying results, 156
   Query Designer, 154–158
   relationships between tables, 155
   saving, 159
   select, 153
   table listings, 155
Query Designer, 9, 139, 154–158, 186
   Diagram pane, 155
   Grid pane, 155
   joins, 171
   Result pane, 156
   SQL pane, 156
Query toolbar, 158, 172
Quick View, 66
   editors, 98–99
   HTML (Hypertext Markup Language), 102

R

RAD (rapid application development), 16
Radio button control, 4
radio buttons, 4
read-enabled copies of files, 82
record navigation, 163–165, 280–286
Recordset control, 159–161, 172–173, 181, 189, 281
Recordset object methods, 280
Recordset Properties dialog box, 159–161, 172, 189, 281
Recordset1 control, 178
Recordset1 object, 257
RecordsetNavBar control, 163–165, 173, 190
referential integrity, 142
Refresh (Ctrl+R) keyboard shortcut, 116
refreshing project view, 86
related files, copying, 82–83
relationships, 155
removing layouts, 76
replication, 142
resizing
   text, 68
   windows, 22
Response.Write method, 253
Restart Debugging (Ctrl+Shift+F5) key combination, 206
run-time errors, 203

S

Sample Application Wizard, 11
Sample Tracking Worksheet, 56
saving
   queries, 159
   Web pages, 71
scaling elements, 322
Script Editor, 139
Script Outline window, 264–265, 282
   btnTalkToMe, 271

scripting languages
    setting, 263
    support, 12
scripts, 174–179
    clients, 223, 251
    debugging, 288
    debugging process, 202
    finding available objects, 34
    just-in-time debugging, 207–208
    logic errors, 203
    run-time errors, 203
    Script Outline window, 264–265
    servers, 223, 251
    stepping through lines, 211–212
    syntax errors, 203
    viewing data, 176–179
<SCRIPT>...</SCRIPT> tag, 252, 265
Search.htm file, 84
security, 142, 292–298
    Corporate Web site, 223, 229–230
    database-level, 295
    Global.asa file processing, 296
    locations, 293–294
    source control, 295
    system-level, 294
    Web application permissions, 297–298
    Web application-level, 295–296
    Web pages, 296–297
    Web server-level, 294–295
Select Data Source dialog box, 147, 169–170
Select Database dialog box, 170
select queries, 153
server scripts, 251
    <% %> delimiter, 252, 254
    ASPs (Active Server Pages), 252–254
    versus client scripts, 255–256
    debugging, 213–214
    <SCRIPT>...</SCRIPT> tag, 252
    Source view, 252
Set as Start Page command, 204
Site Designer, 7

Site Diagram toolbar, 91
site diagrams, 63, 88
    adding another page to Bookstore project, 169
    Diagram menu, 91
    new home page, 63–65
Site Tracking Worksheet, 56
.sln (solution definition files), 81
solutions, 45, 60
    deploying, 118–123
SOM (scripting object model), 12, 187, 256–265
    enabling, 258
    objects, 256–262
source code, viewing, 328–328
source control
    adding files to Web applications, 242
    adding to projects, 239–240
    checking files out, 240–241
    disabling, 245–246
    reenabling, 246
    security, 295
    usage, 240–245
Source view, 5–7, 178
    changing text component colors, 103
    colors, 214–216
    debugger, 204
    editors, 99–100
    fonts, 215–216
    HTML (Hypertext Markup Language), 102
    Immediate window, 206
    Properties window, 100
    redefining colors, 215–216
    server scripts, 252
    setting properties, 100
SourceSafe Options dialog box, 244
SQL Server Login dialog box, 147–148
SQL (Structured Query Language), 9, 131, 153
Standard toolbar, 26
Start, Programs, Microsoft Visual Studio 6.0, Microsoft Visual SourceSafe, Visual SourceSafe 6.0 Admin command, 238, 244

Index 379

Start, Programs, Windows NT 4.0 Option pack, Microsoft Personal Web Server, Internet Service Manager command, 236
Start Debugging (F5) function key, 205, 208, 210–211
Start (F5) function key, 250–251, 254
static text, 5
Step Into (F11) function key, 212
stepping through procedures, 10
Stop (Shift+F5) key combination, 250–251
Stored Procedure Editor, 139
stored procedures, 151
strikethrough text, 313
style sheets, 7
styles, 69
submitting forms, 5
subscripts and superscripts, 322
synchronization, 84–85
syntax errors, 203
system-level security, 294

T

Table, Insert Table command, 191
tables
    joined, 155
    viewing contents, 152
<table>...</table> tag, 106
tags, 100–101
Task List window, 35
task lists, 35
    listing and prioritizing tasks, 35
    task created by Broken Links Report, 114–115
<td> tag, 105
templates
    <%# #%> delimiters, 305
    designing, 303–305
    prompts, 305
    usage, 304–305
testing
    Corporate Web site, 287–298
    data access, 118
    debugging code, 118
    list for, 292
    verifying links, 118
    Web pages, 117–118
    Web sites, 40, 48
text
    adding to home pages, 65–66
    bold, 68, 101
    boldness, 313–314
    capitalization, 314
    centering, 68
    color, 68
    displaying in Web page, 100
    formatting, 67–69
    home pages, 53
    italic, 68
    multiline input tool, 4
    new fonts, 67
    nonbreaking spaces, 5
    overlined, 313
    paragraph breaks, 5
    paragraph formats, 69
    resizing, 68, 312
    static, 5
    strikethrough, 313
    styles, 69
    underlined, 313
    user-entered, 4
Text area control, 4
text boxes, 4
    Data-bound DTCs (Design-Time Controls), 9
    .txt prefix, 260
text objects, 33
.textAlign property, 33
Textbox control, 4, 162, 189, 259
Textbox Properties dialog box, 281
<%#ThemeName#%> delimiter, 305
themes, 39, 52, 62, 73–76, 302–303
    applying to single page, 73
    changing, 74
    CSS (Cascading Style Sheet) changes, 303

themes *(continued)*
  customized, 302
  deleting, 75
  home pages, 45
  page-level, 90
  removing, 74–75
  selecting, 19
Themes directory, 302
Themes folder, 310
thisPage object, 258
<title>...</title> tag, 105
toolbar shortcut menu, 28
toolbars, 26–31
  adding and removing buttons, 28–30
  Bold button, 68
  Center button, 68
  customizing, 28–31
  deleting, 31
  docking, 22
  Font Name drop-down list, 67
  Font Size drop-down list, 68
  Foreground Color button, 68
  Italic button, 68
  moving, 22
  naming, 30
  new, 30–31
  Paragraph Format drop-down list, 69
  Reset button, 5
  returning default buttons, 30
  Submit button, 5
Toolbox, 2–5, 31
  Browse button, 4
  Button control, 191
  customizable, 2
  Design-Time Controls, 159, 172, 181, 189, 281
  displaying, 32
  docking, 22
  FormManager control, 194
  HTML group, 177
  moving, 22
  Recordset control, 159, 172, 181, 189
  RecordsetNavBar control, 164, 173
  Restore button, 24
  tabs, 2
  title bar, 22
Tools, Options command, 103, 108, 204, 207, 215, 244
<tr> tag, 105
TRABANNA.GIF file, 69–70, 82
transaction logs, 142
transparent background, 316
Travel Web site
  activities, 53
  adding graphics to home page, 69–71
  adding navigation, 76–77
  adding text to home page, 65–66
  additional elements, 55
  changing fonts, 67
  changing look and feel of home page, 73–77
  design objectives, 43–44
  designing, 59–78
  formatting text, 67–69
  gathering content, 51–58
  graphics for home page, 54
  home page, 45–48
  home page creation, 60–63, 63–72
  home page format, 52
  hotels and restaurants, 53
  introduction, 53
  new project, 60–63
  outdoor recreation, 53
  paragraph formats, 69
  previewing pages, 66
  saving pages, 71
  testing, 117–124
  text for home page, 53
  themes, 73–76
  viewing pages in browser, 72
Trigger Editor, 140
triggers, 140
Turtle.wdm file, 88–90
txtDiscountedPrice object, 257
txtDiscountedPrice property, 178
Type property, 96–97

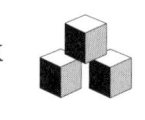

Index

U

Unable to Connect Remotely to Windows 95 or Windows 98 Web Server message, 123
underlined text, 313
undocking
    Properties window, 33
    windows, 22
unique IDs, 310
updateRecord method, 285
updating master Web application, 85
uploading files, 4
user-entered text, 4

V

value property, 258
variables, 265–266
    assigning value, 267
    declaring, 266–267
    scope, 268
VBScript, 12, 174–179, 265–268
    adding immediately, 228
    adding records to record set, 228
    conditional logic, 273–286
    Const keyword, 267
    constants, 267–268
    controls added to form, 229
    debugging process, 202
    Dim statement, 266
    event procedures, 178
    If statement, 276–280
    message boxes and input boxes, 268–273
    methods, 175
    navigating records, 227–228
    objects, 175
    Option Explicit statement, 266
    Private reserved word, 266
    properties, 176
    Public reserved word, 266
    scope, 268
    variables, 265–267
    Variants, 266–267
    writing code, 227–229
VDE (visual development environment), 15
.vic (Visual InterDev Cache files), 81
video files, 251
View, Broken Links Report command, 114
View, Debug Windows, Watch command, 36, 210
View, Open command, 65
View, Other Windows, Object Browser command, 34
View, Other Windows, Script Outline command, 264, 282
View, Other Windows, Task List command, 35, 115
View, Other Windows, Visual Component Manager command, 34
View, Refresh command, 116, 243, 312, 314, 318, 320–321
View, Toolbox menu, 32
View, View in Browser command, 92, 94–95, 99, 163–164, 173, 179, 182–183, 185–186, 197
View, View Links command, 111
View Designer, 139
View menu, 26
View Window, 32
views, 150
    changing default, 108
    projects, 32
.vip (Visual InterDev project files), 81
Visual Basic, 12
Visual Basic Application Edition, 175
Visual Component Manager, 34
Visual FoxPro file size limitation, 141
Visual InterDev
    capabilities, 12–13
    database tools, 8–11
    debugging tools, 10
    definition of, 2
    development environment, 20–21
    exiting, 78
    familiar look and feel, 16
    features, 2–8
    IntelliSense support, 11
    Local mode, 9–10

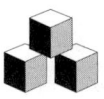

Visual InterDev *(continued)*
　Master mode, 10
　Microsoft Access and, 168–174
　modes, 79–88
　objects, 258–262
　programmer's tools, 24–25
　programming features, 251
　starting, 16–21
　as VDE (visual development environment), 15
　Windows 95 and, 18
　Windows NT and, 18
　wizards, 11
Visual InterDev Web sites, 36
Visual InterDev window
　menus, 25
　Object Browser, 34
　Project Explorer window, 34
　Properties window, 33
　Task List window, 35
　toolbars, 26–31
　Toolbox, 31
　View Window, 32
　Visual Component Manager, 34
　Watch window, 36
Visual SourceSafe, 222, 226–227
　Add User dialog box, 236
　adding source control to projects, 239–240
　Admin user password, 235
　Administrator, 235–236, 238–239
　checking files in and out, 226–227, 240–241, 243
　discarding changes to file, 244
　enabling source control for applications, 226
　exclusive checkout, 240, 241
　getting copy of master file, 242
　granting permissions to users, 226
　installing on master Web server, 232–239
　installing on Web servers, 222
　merging changes, 245
　multiple checkouts, 241, 244–245
　setting up, 232
　user permissions, 235–236
　Users, Add User command, 236
　Users, Change Password command, 235
　Windows NT, 236–239
Visual Studio
　Enterprise Edition, 165
　Installation Wizard, 233–234
　Professional Edition, 165
　Setup program, 233

W

watch expressions, 36, 209–211
Watch (Shift+F9) key combination, 210
Watch window, 36, 209–211
watches, 10, 201
.WAV files, 69
Web application-level security, 295–296
Web applications, 80
　adding files to, 242
　advantages, 119
　copying, 83
　dynamic, 136
　ease of maintenance, 119
　file formats, 60
　files and objects, 81–82
　permissions, 297–298
Web pages
　background images, 314–317
　changing default view, 108
　changing element appearance, 27–28
　design, 39
　displaying text in, 100
　horizontal rules, 5
　links, 109–116
　opening in browser, 176
　placing navigation bars, 19
　positioning elements, 325–328
　querying and displaying database information, 133
　reading from and writing to databases, 9
　record navigation, 173–174
　Recordset controls, 172–173

saving, 71
for security, 296–297
setting language, 255
testing, 117–118
viewing in browser, 74
Web Permissions dialog box, 297–298
Web Project Wizard, 11
connecting to server, 18–19
layout, 61–62
Local mode, 61
naming project, 19
placing navigation bars, 19, 61
previewing project appearance, 61
project name, 61
selecting server, 17–18, 61
themes, 19, 62
Web projects, 80
definition files, 81
live view of data, 9
Web Publishing Wizard (Wpwiz.exe), 122
Web server-level security, 294–295
Web servers
actual deployment of application, 120–122
connecting to before starting Visual InterDev, 17
contacting, 18–19
installing Visual SourceSafe, 222, 232–239
selecting, 17–18, 61
working directly with files, 10
Web sites
building, 40
constructing, 7
debugging, 40
deploying, 40
formatting text, 67–69
global navigation bar, 91–97
home page, 63

identifying content, 38–39
links to, 39
mission statement, 38
multimedia, 222–223
navigation, 46
point of view, 37–38
previewing pages, 66
purpose of, 37
quick development, 16
selecting database for, 140–144
testing, 40, 48
themes or moods, 39
Visual InterDev, 36
visually consistent appearance, 90
Window, Link View command, 116
Window, Page 2 command, 115
Window, Turtle.wdm command, 91
windows, customizing in development environment, 22–24
Windows 95, 18
Windows NT
anonymous user account, 236–239
Visual InterDev and, 18
Visual SourceSafe, 236–239
wizards, 11
working offline, 87–88
working online, 77–78
write-enabled copies of files, 82
WYSIWYG Page Editor, 5–7

Y

Yahoo! Web site, 54

Z

Z-order, 328

Build Databased Web Solutions with Microsoft Technology

ACCESS-OFFICE-VB ADVISOR is the only independent technical magazine devoted to Microsoft database, Visual Basic, and web technology. Written by the leading experts, each monthly issue brings you the designs, tools, techniques, add-ons, RAD methods and management practices you need to implement the best custom enterprise solutions.

ACCESS-OFFICE-VB ADVISOR is packed with professional techniques using these Microsoft tools:

- Access
- Visual Basic
- SQL Server
- Visual InterDev
- Office
- Outlook
- Internet Information Server
- Exchange Server
- Excel
- Transaction Server
- Site Server
- ActiveX

"Thanks for all the great tips and techniques...they have saved me many, many times!"

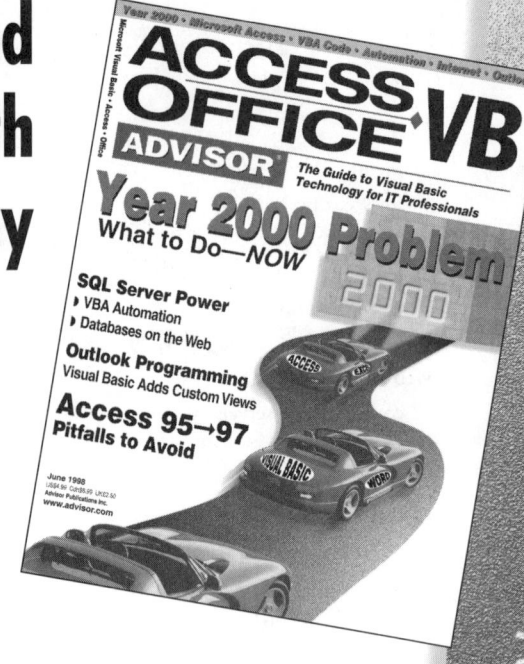

ABOUT THE TECHNICAL EDITORS:

With over 20 years experience with computer systems, Richard Campbell is a former MIS manager turned independent technical consultant who works with a variety of clients and organizations.

A senior consultant with MCW Technologies, and a teacher for Application Developers Training Company, Ken Getz specializes in tools and applications written in Microsoft Access, Visual Basic, and the rest of the Office suite.

An ADVISOR DEVCON planner, and a frequent speaker at other database conferences and workshops, Michael Groh is an independent consultant and author of several books on Microsoft technology.

MAGAZINE ONLY
12 Issues: US $39, Canada $59, Other Countries $79

MAGAZINE + PROFESSIONAL RESOURCE CD
12 Issues + 12 CDs: US $129, Canada $169, Other Countries $199

To Subscribe, Call Toll Free
800-336-6060

Outside U.S. call (619)278-5600 • Fax (619)279-4728
subscribe@advisor.com • www.advisor.com

Mountains of Wisdom... in compact, portable form!

The 1998 Edition is Coming Soon!

Using the very latest Windows-based technology, these CDs hold 6 full years of magazines, along with the PROFESSIONAL RESOURCE CD files from each issue.

Full-text search allows you to locate articles from all issues within seconds. See diagrams, figures, photos, and code as originally published—in full color. Copy and paste published routines right into your applications!

NEW!
The Complete ACCESS-OFFICE-VB ADVISOR 1998 CD-ROM

Also Available:
THE COMPLETE ACCESS-OFFICE-VB ADVISOR 1997 CD-ROM
THE COMPLETE ACCESS/VISUAL BASIC ADVISOR 1996 CD-ROM
THE COMPLETE ACCESS/VISUAL BASIC ADVISOR 1995 CD-ROM
THE COMPLETE ACCESS ADVISOR 93-94 CD-ROM

EACH ANNUAL EDITION: U.S. $49, Other Countries $59

CALL TOLL FREE 800-336-6060
Outside U.S. (619)278-5600 · Fax (619)279-4728
order@advisor.com · www.advisor.com

System Requirements: 386 or 486 PC, 4MB RAM, VGA, 4MB disk space, CD-ROM drive, Microsoft Windows 3.1 or later

License Agreement/Notice of Limited Warranty

By opening the sealed disk container in this book, you agree to the following terms and conditions. If, upon reading the following license agreement and notice of limited warranty, you cannot agree to the terms and conditions set forth, return the unused book with unopened disk to the place where you purchased it for a refund.

License:
The enclosed software is copyrighted by the copyright holder(s) indicated on the software disk. You are licensed to copy the software onto a single computer for use by a single concurrent user and to a backup disk. You may not reproduce, make copies, or distribute copies or rent or lease the software in whole or in part, except with written permission of the copyright holder(s). You may transfer the enclosed disk only together with this license, and only if you destroy all other copies of the software and the transferee agrees to the terms of the license. You may not decompile, reverse assemble, or reverse engineer the software.

Notice of Limited Warranty:
The enclosed disk is warranted by Prima Publishing to be free of physical defects in materials and workmanship for a period of sixty (60) days from end user's purchase of the book/disk combination. During the sixty-day term of the limited warranty, Prima will provide a replacement disk upon the return of a defective disk.

Limited Liability:
THE SOLE REMEDY FOR BREACH OF THIS LIMITED WARRANTY SHALL CONSIST ENTIRELY OF REPLACEMENT OF THE DEFECTIVE DISK. IN NO EVENT SHALL PRIMA OR THE AUTHORS BE LIABLE FOR ANY OTHER DAMAGES, INCLUDING LOSS OR CORRUPTION OF DATA, CHANGES IN THE FUNCTIONAL CHARACTERISTICS OF THE HARDWARE OR OPERATING SYSTEM, DELETERIOUS INTERACTION WITH OTHER SOFTWARE, OR ANY OTHER SPECIAL, INCIDENTAL, OR CONSEQUENTIAL DAMAGES THAT MAY ARISE, EVEN IF PRIMA AND/OR THE AUTHOR HAVE PREVIOUSLY BEEN NOTIFIED THAT THE POSSIBILITY OF SUCH DAMAGES EXISTS.

Disclaimer of Warranties:
PRIMA AND THE AUTHORS SPECIFICALLY DISCLAIM ANY AND ALL OTHER WARRANTIES, EITHER EXPRESS OR IMPLIED, INCLUDING WARRANTIES OF MERCHANTABILITY, SUITABILITY TO A PARTICULAR TASK OR PURPOSE, OR FREEDOM FROM ERRORS. SOME STATES DO NOT ALLOW FOR EXCLUSION OF IMPLIED WARRANTIES OR LIMITATION OF INCIDENTAL OR CONSEQUENTIAL DAMAGES, SO THESE LIMITATIONS MAY NOT APPLY TO YOU.

Other:
This Agreement is governed by the laws of the State of California without regard to choice of law principles. The United Convention of Contracts for the International Sale of Goods is specifically disclaimed. This Agreement constitutes the entire agreement between you and Prima Publishing regarding use of the software.